The Civil War Trust's

OFFICIAL GUIDE TO THE CIVIL WAR DISCOVERY TRAIL®

EDITED BY THE CIVIL WAR TRUST

Susan Collier Braselton, Editor

MACMILLAN • USA

Acknowledgments

HE CIVIL WAR TRUST ACKNOWLEDGES with deep gratitude the assistance and support provided by its partners in the Civil War Discovery Trail: The U.S. Department of the Interior, in particular the American Battlefield Protection Program staff and the staff of the National Park Service; the National Trust for Historic Preservation; State Partners and State Coordinators in all participating Civil War Discovery Trail states; staff at all Civil War Discovery Trail sites; and all others who provided material for this guide. The editor thanks Jim Reed, and Melissa Meisner for research and editorial assistance; Julie Fix and Elliot Gruber for continued support of the trail; and Margot Weiss, our editor at Macmillan Travel.

The Civil War Trust is not responsible for changes that occur after publication and regrets any errors and omissions in this book. We advise your calling prior to visiting a site, to confirm the information in this guide. We encourage your comments and suggestions by mail to: The Civil War Trust, 2101 Wilson Blvd., Suite 1120, Arlington, VA 22201, or by e-mail to: civilwartrust@CivilWar.org. Visit us on the World Wide Web: www.CivilWar.org.

Contents

THE CIVIL WAR TRUST™

Enriching Our Future By Preserving Our Past.

*T*HE MISSION OF THE CIVIL WAR TRUST is to promote appreciation and stewardship of our nation's historical, cultural, and environmental heritage through preservation of significant Civil War sites and through supporting preservation and education programs.

The Civil War Trust is a private, nonprofit organization with more than 24,000 members across the country that works to preserve our nation's most important Civil War sites. Since its formation in 1991, The Civil War Trust has

- secured Congressional passage of the Civil War Battlefield Commemorative Coin Act to generate private funds for battlefield preservation

- protected land at Antietam and South Mountain, MD; Byram's Ford, MO; Mill Springs, KY; Harpers Ferry, WV; Cross Keys, VA; Port Hudson, LA; Franklin, TN; and New Bern, NC

- launched the Civil War Discovery Trail

- created the Civil War Explorer, an educational introduction to the Civil War that uses interactive multimedia technology that is available now for visitors to use at Gettysburg National Military Park, Antietam National Battlefield, Prairie Grove State Park, and other Civil War Discovery Trail sites

- created a Commemorative Coin Grant Program and made grants to assist in the purchase and preservation of significant battlefield land at Third Winchester, VA; Cedar Creek, VA; Perryville, KY; Mill Springs, KY; Corinth, MS; Brices Crossroads, MS; Spring Hill, TN; Malvern Hill, VA; Resaca, GA; Rich Mountain, WV; Prairie Grove, AR; Glorieta, NM; Gettysburg, PA; Stones River, TN; and Fredericksburg, VA

Battlefields memorialize the ideals, courage, character, and sacrifice of the men and women who struggled for freedom to make "these United States" into the United States. These living landscapes add to the quality of our lives with their beauty and invite our visits to rest and reflect. Fewer than 15 percent of our nation's Civil War battlefields are now protected.

The Trust's national campaign unites concerned citizens, businesses, landowners, historians, public officials, and others to foster strong, community-based preservation activities.

The Civil War Trust encourages partnerships and welcomes your membership, support, and participation in its efforts. Your membership in The Civil War Trust will help to preserve the tangible reminders of our nation's history for the understanding and appreciation of future generations. For more information about membership or programs, call ☎ 1-800-CWTRUST or visit our Web site at www.CivilWar.org.

Foreword

THE CIVIL WAR DEFINED AMERICA as a nation and left deep impressions on the character of the many communities it touched. There still remain lessons to be learned from the experiences of this turbulent era. How better to learn these lessons than by walking the streets and fields where the events unfolded?

The historic sites selected for the Civil War Discovery Trail must meet high standards to ensure historical authenticity, informative interpretive programs, and relevance to events today.

This expanded third edition of *The Civil War Trust's Official Guide to the Civil War Discovery Trail* ® provides an itinerary for visiting many of the places that influenced the course of the struggle. It is a tool equally valuable to the recreational traveler and to the serious student of history.

Proceeds from the sale of the *Official Guide* support the work of The Civil War Trust, a nonprofit, national membership organization that works to preserve and protect endangered Civil War battlefields.

The Trust is grateful to its national, state, and Trail site partners for their enthusiastic support for the development of the Civil War Discovery Trail®.

Edgar M. Andrews III
President
The Civil War Trust

Preserving Civil War Battlefields

HE NATION'S CIVIL WAR HERITAGE is in grave danger! It is disappearing under buildings, parking lots, and highways. Of the 384 principal Civil War battlefields, 71 (19 percent) have already been lost. Half of the rest are now threatened by development. If we do not act swiftly to protect the remaining battlefields, within 10 years we may lose fully two-thirds of the nation's principal battlefields.

Some have asked: Why do anything more to protect the battlefields? Are not the principal battlefields already preserved in national and state parks? Can we not understand the important political and social changes that resulted from the war without studying the battles? Does not this preoccupation with "hallowed ground" romanticize violence and glorify war? These questions deserve answers.

First, an understanding of military campaigns and battles is crucial to comprehending all other aspects of the Civil War. Individual battles swayed elections, shaped political decisions, determined economic mobilization, brought women into the war effort, and influenced decisions to abolish slavery as well as to recruit former slaves as soldiers.

The Seven Days battles produced an early Union victory and changed the conflict from a limited to a total war; Antietam forestalled European recognition of the Confederacy and prompted the Emancipation Proclamation; Vicksburg, Gettysburg, and Chattanooga reversed a tide of Confederate victories that had threatened the Northern will to keep fighting; Sherman's capture of Atlanta and Sheridan's victories in the Shenandoah secured Abraham Lincoln's reelection, confirmed emancipation as a Northern war aim, and ensured continuation of the war to unconditional victory. Any different outcome might have changed the course of the war—and perhaps the world's history.

The battles were important, but why do we need to preserve the battlefields to learn from them? In part, understanding is simply a matter of being able to visualize how geography and topography shaped a battle—the pattern of fields and woods, roads and rock outcroppings, and rivers and streams. Learning cannot take place if the historical landscape has been paved over, cluttered with buildings, or carved into a different shape.

Being present on a battlefield, we can experience an emotional tie to those who fought there. With a little imagination, we can hear the first Rebel yell at Manassas, imagine the horror as brushfires overtook the wounded at Wilderness, experience the terror of raw recruits at Perryville, or hear the hoarse shouts of exhausted survivors of the Twentieth Maine as they launched a bayonet charge at Gettysburg's Little Round Top.

These experiences help us understand what the Civil War was all about. Understanding is not a matter of glorifying or romanticizing war. Quite the contrary, it is a matter of comprehending the grim reality of war. The battlefields are monuments to the gritty courage of the men and women who fought and died there. None condemned the war more than those who suffered the horror and trauma of battle. In 1862, a Confederate veteran of Shiloh wrote home: "O it was too shocking too horrible. God grant that I may never be the partaker in such scenes again. . . . When released from this I shall ever be an advocate of peace." Civil War veterans took the lead in creating the first national battlefield parks— not to glorify the war, but to commemorate the sacrifice of friends they had lost.

(Adapted from *Civil War Sites Advisory Commission Report on the Nation's Civil War Battlefields* [National Park Service, 1993].)

Explore the Civil War Discovery Trail

The Civil War Discovery Trail links more than 500 sites in 28 states to inspire and to teach the story of the Civil War and its haunting impact on America.

Along the Trail, visitors may explore destinations such as Ford's Theatre where President Lincoln was shot; Antietam National Battlefield, the site of the bloodiest one-day battle in American history; antebellum plantations in Mississippi and Tennessee; and Port Hudson, Louisiana, where hundreds of African American soldiers fought and died. The Trail includes battlefields, historic homes, railroad stations, cemeteries, and parks.

Civil War Discovery Trail sites are especially selected for their historic significance and educational opportunities. Each year, new sites and states will be added to the Trail. The Civil War Discovery Trail is an initiative of The Civil War Trust, with support from the National Trust for Historic Preservation, the National Park Service, state agencies, and local communities.

Internet Access to the Trail: www.CivilWar.org

Visit the Civil War Discovery Trail on the World Wide Web for up-to-the-minute Trail information, virtual and real tours of Trail sites, and links to individual Trail sites. The Civil War Trust's Web site, www.CivilWar.org, is also your source for information about battlefield preservation, Civil War history, special events and reenactments, Civil War travel, and more.

Using This Book

For ease of use, this guide is organized alphabetically by state, then city, then site. Each state chapter begins with a brief overview of the role of each state in the Civil War and with an orientation map giving the general location of sites in that state. Directions in each listing lead visitors from the closest major interstate highway to the site. We suggest also using a state highway map with the maps and directions in this guide. Sites are listed under the closest town. The address listed under the site name may be only the mailing address. Whenever possible, each site listing includes a phone number to call for further information. The availability of handicapped access refers to access for persons with wheelchairs, walkers, and so forth, without having to climb stairs.

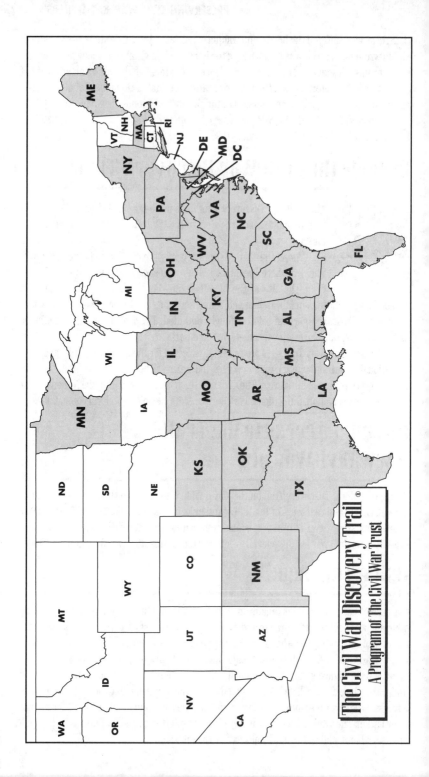

The Civil War Discovery Trail ®
A Program of The Civil War Trust

The American Civil War

by Dr. James M. McPherson

HE CIVIL WAR IS THE CENTRAL EVENT in America's historical consciousness. While the Revolution of 1776–83 created the United States, the Civil War of 1861–65 determined what kind of nation it would be. The war resolved two fundamental questions left unresolved by the revolution: whether the United States was to be a dissolvable confederation of sovereign states or an indivisible nation with a sovereign national government; and whether this nation, born of a declaration that all men were created with an equal right to liberty, would continue to exist as the largest slave-holding country in the world.

Northern victory in the war preserved the United States as one nation and ended the institution of slavery that had divided the country from its beginning. But these achievements came at the cost of 625,000 lives—nearly as many American soldiers as died in all the other wars in which this country has fought combined. The American Civil War was the largest and most destructive conflict in the Western world between the end of the Napoleonic Wars in 1815 and the onset of World War I in 1914.

The Civil War started because of uncompromising differences between the free and slave states over the power of the national government to prohibit slavery in the territories that had not yet become states. When Abraham Lincoln won election in 1860 as the first Republican president on a platform pledging to keep slavery out of the territories, seven slave states in the deep South seceded and formed a new nation, the Confederate States of America. The incoming Lincoln administration and most of the Northern people refused to recognize the legitimacy of secession. They feared that it would discredit democracy and create a fatal precedent that would eventually fragment the no-longer United States into several small, squabbling countries.

The event that triggered war came at Fort Sumter in Charleston Bay on April 12, 1861. Claiming this United States fort as its own, the Confederate army on that day opened fire on the Federal garrison and forced it to lower the American flag in surrender. Lincoln called out the militia to suppress this "insurrection." Four more slave states seceded and joined the Confederacy. By the end of 1861 nearly a million armed men confronted one another along a line stretching 1,200 miles from Virginia to Missouri. Several battles had already taken place—near Manassas Junction in Virginia, in the mountains of western Virginia where Union victories paved the way for creation of the new state of West Virginia, at Wilson's Creek in Missouri, at Cape Hatteras in North Carolina, and at Port Royal in South Carolina where the Union navy established a base for a blockade to shut off the Confederacy's access to the outside world.

But the real fighting began in 1862. Huge battles like Shiloh in Tennessee, Gaines Mill, Second Manassas, and Fredericksburg in Virginia and Antietam in Maryland foreshadowed even bigger campaigns and battles in later years, from Gettysburg in Pennsylvania to Vicksburg on the Mississippi to Chickamauga and Atlanta in Georgia. By 1864 the original Northern goal of a limited war to restore the Union had given way to a new strategy of "total war" to destroy the Old South and its basic institution of slavery and to give the restored Union a "new birth of freedom," as President Lincoln put it in his address at Gettysburg to dedicate a cemetery for Union soldiers killed in the battle there.

For three long years, from 1862 to 1865, Robert E. Lee's Army of Northern Virginia staved off invasions and attacks by the Union Army of the Potomac commanded by a series of ineffective generals until Ulysses S. Grant came to Virginia from the Western Theater to become general in chief of all Union armies in 1864. After bloody battles at places with names like The Wilderness, Spotsylvania, Cold Harbor, and Petersburg, Grant finally brought Lee to bay at Appomattox in April 1865. In the meantime Union armies and river fleets in the theater of war comprising the slave states west of the Appalachians won a long series of victories over Confederate armies commanded by hapless, unlucky Confederate generals. In 1864–65 Gen. William Tecumseh Sherman led his army deep into the Confederate heartland of Georgia and South Carolina, destroying their economic infrastructure while Gen. George Thomas virtually destroyed the Confederacy's Army of the Tennessee at the battle of Nashville.

By the spring of 1865 all the principal Confederate armies surrendered, and when Union cavalry captured the fleeing Confederate president Jefferson Davis in Georgia on May 10, 1865, resistance collapsed and the war ended. The long, painful process of rebuilding a united nation free of slavery began.

ALABAMA

ON JANUARY 11, 1861, ALABAMA BECAME the fourth state to secede from the Union. Within a short time, state troops seized the Federal arsenal at Mt. Vernon and the forts in Mobile. On February 4, 1861, delegates from six of the seven seceded states convened in Montgomery, and on February 8 they officially adopted the constitution of the Confederate States of America. Montgomery served as the provisional capital. On February 18, 1861, Jefferson Davis was inaugurated as president of the provisional government; and the first national flag of the Confederacy was raised above the capitol on March 4, 1861. On April 12, 1861, acting on instructions that had been telegraphed from Montgomery, Gen. P. G. T. Beauregard ordered the bombardment of Fort Sumter in Charleston, South Carolina.

During the war, 194 military land events and eight naval engagements occurred within the boundaries of the state. Significant among these were Streight's Raid (April 26–May 3, 1863), Wilson Raid (March 22–April 16, 1865), and the Battle of Mobile Bay (August 5, 1864). The campaign for Mobile culminated in the assault on Spanish Fort (April 8, 1865), Blakeley (April 9, 1865), and the final capitulation of the city on April 12, 1865. On May 4, 1865, at Citronelle, Alabama, Gen. Richard Taylor finally surrendered the Confederate forces in the Department of Alabama, Mississippi, and East Louisiana.

by Robert Bradley, Alabama Department of Archives and History

Dauphin Island

| 1 | **Site:** FORT GAINES, 51 Bienville Blvd. Mailing address: P.O. Box 97, Dauphin Island, AL 36528, ☎ 334/861-6992 |

Description: Fort Gaines is a pre–Civil War brick fort set within a few feet of the gulf. The fort was a key element in the "Battle of Mobile Bay" and after its capture was used in planning and staging the attack on Mobile. Many of the Civil War structures and courtyard buildings remain.

Open to Public: *Winter:* Daily 9am–5pm. *Summer:* Daily 9am–6pm.

Admission Fees: Adults $3, children 7–12 $1. Groups: Two for one (call in advance).

Visitor Services: Museum, gift shop, information, rest rooms, handicapped access.

Regularly Scheduled Events: *Jan:* Confederate encampments; Annual Battle of Mobile Bay; *Aug:* Annual Damn the Torpedoes; *Nov:* Women's encampment; *Second week in Dec:* Christmas at the Fort.

Directions: Exit I-10 to Hwy. 193 south to Dauphin Island. Once on the island, turn left at the water tower and proceed 3 miles to Fort Gaines.

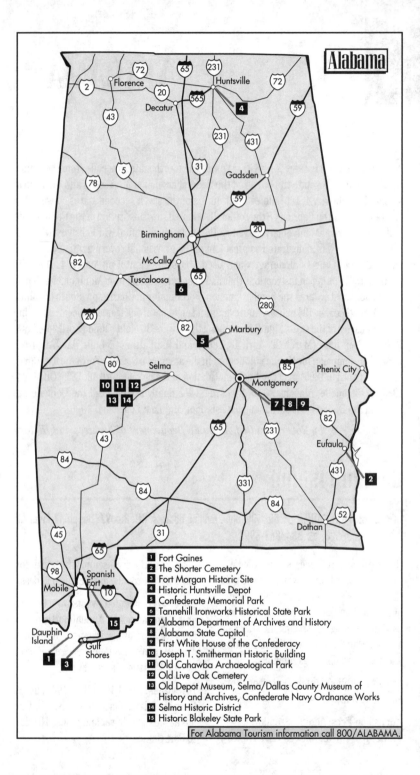

Alabama

1 Fort Gaines
2 The Shorter Cemetery
3 Fort Morgan Historic Site
4 Historic Huntsville Depot
5 Confederate Memorial Park
6 Tannehill Ironworks Historical State Park
7 Alabama Department of Archives and History
8 Alabama State Capitol
9 First White House of the Confederacy
10 Joseph T. Smitherman Historic Building
11 Old Cahawba Archaeological Park
12 Old Live Oak Cemetery
13 Old Depot Museum, Selma/Dallas County Museum of History and Archives, Confederate Navy Ordnance Works
14 Selma Historic District
15 Historic Blakeley State Park

For Alabama Tourism information call 800/ALABAMA.

Eufaula

2 **Site:** THE SHORTER CEMETERY, 510 St. Francis Rd., Eufaula, AL 36027,
☎ 334/687-3793

Description: This cemetery, which belongs to the Shorter family, includes the grave of John Gill Shorter, a Civil War governor. The cemetery also houses slave plots.

Open to Public: Daily from dawn to dusk.

Admission Fees: Free.

Visitor Services: Information.

Directions: Go to the east end of Hwy. 82 and turn south in front of the Holiday Inn. Go approximately 4 blocks and follow signs to cemetery.

Gulf Shores

3 **Site:** FORT MORGAN HISTORIC SITE, 51 Hwy. 180 West, Gulf Shores, AL 36542,
☎ 334/540-7125

Description: This fort was the primary defensive work at the entrance to Mobile Bay. Alabama state troops seized the fort in January 1861. Following the Battle of Mobile Bay, the fort underwent a 2-week siege resulting in surrender on August 23, 1864.

Open to Public: *Winter:* Daily 9am–5pm. *Summer:* Daily 9am–6pm.

Admission Fees: Adults $3, children 6–12 $1. Group rates available for 15 or more.

Visitor Services: Museum, gift shop, information, rest rooms, handicapped access.

Regularly Scheduled Events: *First weekend in Aug:* Living History Encampment commemorating the Battle of Mobile Bay and Siege of Fort Morgan in 1864.

Directions: South from I-10: take Hwy. 59 to Gulf Shores, AL. At Gulf Shores, take AL Hwy. 180 west for 22 miles to Fort Morgan.

Huntsville

 Site: HISTORIC HUNTSVILLE DEPOT, 320 Church St., Huntsville, AL 35801,
☎ 800/678-1819 or 205/539-1860

Description: This depot was built in 1860 as the eastern division headquarters of the Memphis & Charleston Railroad. As a vital east-west Confederate rail line, it was captured by the Federals in 1862 and used as a prison. There is legible graffiti on the third floor left by Civil War soldiers.

Open to Public: Mon–Sat 9am–5pm.

Admission Fees: Adults $6, students $3.50, seniors $5, groups 50¢ off. Ask about special history pass.

Visitor Services: Museum, gift shop, information, rest rooms, handicapped access.

Directions: From I-565 east or west: take exit 19C (Washington/Jefferson St.); you will see the Roundhouse on the right as you exit I-565. Proceed right and enter the free parking lot.

Marbury

5   Site: CONFEDERATE MEMORIAL PARK, 437 County Rd. 63, Marbury, AL 36051, ☎ 205/755-1990

Description: Confederate Memorial Park is dedicated to preserving the memory of Alabama's heroic struggle during the War Between the States and to interpreting the site of Alabama's only Old Soldiers Home for Confederate Veterans (1902–1939). The museum houses documents, uniforms, weapons, and war equipment emphasizing Alabama's participation. It also displays relics from the Soldiers Home, including photographs, books, and veterans' medals.

Admission Fees: Free.

Open to Public: *Park:* Daily 6am–sunset. *Museum:* Daily 9am–5pm.

Visitor Services: Trail, museum, gift shop, information, rest rooms, handicapped access.

Regularly Scheduled Events: *Mar:* Confederate Flag Day ceremony; *Apr:* Confederate Memorial Day ceremony; *Dec:* Christmas in the South.

Directions: From I-65 south: take exit 205; go south onto U.S. 31 for 9 miles and follow signs. From I-65 north: take exit 186; go north on U.S. 31 for 13 miles and follow signs.

McCalla

6   Site: TANNEHILL IRONWORKS HISTORICAL STATE PARK, 12632 Confederate Pkwy., McCalla, AL 35111, ☎ 205/477-5711

Description: This 1,500-acre park was created around the Civil War–era iron-making furnaces. Furnaces were a major producer of iron for the Selma arsenal and were destroyed by Union cavalry raiders in 1865. The park includes a museum; more than 40 restored log cabins; and other period buildings, including a working gristmill, church, and school.

Open to Public: *Museum:* Mon–Fri 9am–5pm, Sat–Sun 10am–5pm. *Park:* Daily 7am–dusk.

Admission Fees: Adults $2, children $1, seniors $1.

Visitor Services: Lodging, camping, trails, food, museum, gift shop, information, rest rooms, handicapped access.

Regularly Scheduled Events: *Third weekend, Mar–Nov:* Tannehill Trade Days.

Directions: From I-59: take exit 100 and follow signs (2 miles). From I-459: take exit 1 and follow signs (7 miles).

Montgomery

7 **Site:** ALABAMA DEPARTMENT OF ARCHIVES AND HISTORY, 624 Washington Ave., Montgomery, AL 36130-0100, ☎ 334/242-4363 (ext. 1)

Description: Located across the street from the State Capitol, which served as the provisional capital of the Confederate States of America, the museum and archives contain the largest collection of Civil War materials in the state. Significant among these is the department's collection of Civil War flags, which are displayed on a rotational basis.

Open to Public: Mon–Fri 8am–5pm, Sat 9am–5pm.

Admission Fees: Free.

Visitor Services: Museum, information, rest rooms, handicapped access.

Regularly Scheduled Events: *Every third Thurs:* Architreats, a lunchtime lecture series.

Directions: From I-85 south: exit right on Union St. Turn left at the third traffic light (Washington Ave.). From Birmingham or Mobile on I-65: take interstate to I-85 north; exit right onto Court St. Stay on service road. At the seventh traffic light, turn left (Union St.). Turn left at the fourth traffic light (Washington Ave.).

8 **Site:** ALABAMA STATE CAPITOL, 600 Dexter St., Montgomery, AL 36104, ☎ 334/242-3900

Description: In 1861, Southern delegates met in the House Chamber to form the Confederate States of America. Earlier, the House of Representatives of the state of Alabama had voted for secession in the same Chamber. Jefferson Davis was sworn in on the Capitol steps as the first and only president of the Confederate States of America.

Admission Fees: Free.

Open to Public: Mon–Sat 9am–4pm.

Visitor Services: Museum, museum shop, information, rest rooms, handicapped access.

Directions: From I-85: take Union St. exit; travel 4 blocks to Washington Ave. On-street parking is available.

9 **Site:** FIRST WHITE HOUSE OF THE CONFEDERACY, 644 Washington Ave., Montgomery, AL 36130, ☎ 334/242-1861

Description: This house was used by the provisional government of Confederate President Jefferson Davis and his family from February until May 1861. In June, the government was moved to Virginia. The

First White House of the Confederacy was built in 1835.

Open to Public: Mon–Fri 8am–4:30pm.

Admission Fees: Free.

6 ALABAMA

Visitor Services: Museum, information, handicapped access, rest rooms.

Regularly Scheduled Events: *Jan:* Robert E. Lee's Birthday; *Apr:* Confederate Memorial Day; *June:* Jefferson Davis's Birthday.

Directions: From I-85: take Union St. exit; go 4 blocks to Washington St. and turn left. Look for first house on the left.

First White House of the Confederacy, Montgomery, AL. (Photograph courtesy of The Civil War Trust.)

Selma

10 **Site:** JOSEPH T. SMITHERMAN HISTORIC BUILDING, 109 Union St., Selma, AL 36701, ☎ 334/874-2174

Description: Built in 1847 by the Selma Masonic Order to serve as a university, this building served as a hospital for Confederate soldiers during the Civil War and later as the county courthouse and as a military school.

Open to Public: Tues–Fri 9am–4pm, Sat 8am–4pm. Other times by appointment.

Admission Fees: $3 (age 14 and over). Group rates available.

Visitor Services: Museum, information, rest rooms, handicapped access.

Regularly Scheduled Events: *Mar:* Pilgrimage headquarters.

Directions: From Montgomery: take Hwy. 80 west to Selma. From I-65 in Birmingham: take exit 22 at Clanton; follow Hwy. 22 to Selma. Take Alabama Ave. to Smitherman Bldg.

11 **Site:** OLD CAHAWBA ARCHAEOLOGICAL PARK, 9518 Cahaba Rd., Orville, AL, 36767, ☎ 334/872-8058

Description: Alabama's first State Capital and Civil War boomtown is now an archaeological park. Home to the Cahawba Rifles, 5th Alabama Regiment, this ghost town was the center of activity during the antebellum and Civil War years. It is also the site of Castle Morgan, a prison for captured Union soldiers.

Open to Public: Daily 9am–5pm.

Admission Fees: Free.

Visitor Services: Trails, museum, gift shop, information, rest rooms, handicapped access, picnic area.

Regularly Scheduled Events: *Second Sat in May:* Cahawba Festival, including reenactments, arts and crafts, music, and so forth.

Directions: Take Hwy. 80 from Montgomery to Selma. From Selma, take Hwy. 22 south for 8 miles; turn left at sign for park; follow signs for 5 miles.

---

12 **Site:** OLD LIVE OAK CEMETERY, 110 Dallas Ave., Selma, AL 36701, ☎ 334/874-3161

Description: This cemetery contains the graves of Confederate soldiers and prominent Selma residents. It features a statue of Elodie B. Todd, half-sister of Mary Todd Lincoln; mausoleum of Vice President William Rufus King; and grave of Benjamin Sterling Turner, the former slave who went on to become the first black U.S. Congressman from Alabama.

Open to Public: Daily from dawn to dusk.

Admission Fees: Free.

Visitor Services: None.

Regularly Scheduled Events: *Mar:* Cemetery Tours and Living History during Pilgrimage; *Apr:* Memorial service during Battle of Selma reenactment.

Directions: From Montgomery: take Hwy. 80 west to Selma. From I-65 in Birmingham: take exit 22 at Clanton; follow Hwy. 22 to Selma. In Selma, follow Hwy. 22 (Dallas Ave.) to cemetery.

---

13 **Site:** OLD DEPOT MUSEUM, Selma/Dallas County Museum of History and Archives, Confederate Navy Ordnance Works, Water Ave. & Martin Luther King St., Selma, AL 36702, ☎ 334/874-2197

Description: Artifacts from the Civil War era are found in abundance at this museum. Other artifacts date from 7000 B.C. through the Gulf War.

Admission Fees: Adults $4, seniors $3, children $1.

Open to Public: Mon–Sat 10am–4pm, Sun 2–5pm.

Visitor Services: Museum, information, handicapped access.

Regularly Scheduled Events: *Mar:* Pilgrimage; *Apr:* Battle of Selma; *second Sat in Oct:* Open House Riverfront Market.

Directions: From I-65: take Selma exit; take Hwy. 80; go over Alabama River, over Pettus Bridge; turn right on Water Ave. Street dead-ends at museum. Located at the corner of Water Ave. and Martin Luther King St.

---

14 **Site:** SELMA HISTORIC DISTRICT, Chamber of Commerce, 513 Lauderdale St., Selma, AL 36701, ☎ 800/45-SELMA or 334/875-7241

Description: The war was almost over when Union troops under the leadership of Gen. James H. Wilson and 13,500 cavalry and mounted infantry (the Raiders) invaded Alabama. Anticipating the invasion, Selma prepared as best it could. But Lt. Gen. Nathan Bedford Forrest's highly outnumbered 2,000 men, mostly old men and boys, could not hold Wilson's Raiders. The people of Selma were doomed even before the battle on April 2, 1865. Selma has the largest historic district in the state of Alabama, and it is the second oldest surviving city in the state. The "Windshield Tour," a self-guided driving tour of Selma, features Civil War–era homes and buildings and their history. The map is available from the Chamber of Commerce or the Selma Visitor Information Center.

Open to Public: *Chamber of Commerce (513 Lauderdale St.):* Mon–Fri 8:30am–5pm. *Visitor Information Center (2207 Broad St.):* Daily 8am–8pm.

Regularly Scheduled Events: *Fourth weekend in April:* Battle of Selma reenactment.

Directions: From Montgomery: take Hwy. 80 west to Selma. From I-65 in Birmingham: exit at Clanton; take Hwy. 22 to Selma.

Spanish Fort

15 Site: HISTORIC BLAKELEY STATE PARK, 33707 State Hwy. 225, Spanish Fort, AL 36527, ☎ 334-626-0798

Description: The last major battle of the Civil War was fought at Blakeley; it ended on the same day, but after the surrender of Gen. Robert E. Lee miles away in Virginia. The Battle of Blakeley was a major news event in the coverage of the Civil War.

Open to Public: Daily 9am–dusk.

Admission Fees: Adults $2, children $1. Groups (25 or more): Adults $1.50, children 75¢.

Visitor Services: Lodging, 15 miles of nature trails, camping, information, rest rooms.

Regularly Scheduled Events: Civil War Demonstrations and Living History Demonstrations. Call for dates

Directions: Located 5 miles north of I-10 on Hwy. 225; 16 miles south of I-65; north of Spanish Fort, AL, in Baldwin County; 20 minutes east of Mobile; and 45 minutes west of Pensacola, FL.

CIVIL WAR TECHNOLOGY

"In the arts of life, man invents nothing; but in the arts of death he outdoes nature herself, and produces by chemistry and machinery all the slaughter of plague, pestilence and famine."

—*George Bernard Shaw*

The Civil War in the United States has often been called "the first modern war." There were so many technological advances during this period that the war truly did bring in a new era of warfare.

In naval warfare, the first submarine was used, and the first ironclad ships were engaged in ship-to-ship combat. During this time, naval mines, called "torpedoes," (though they were a bit different from what we currently refer to as torpedoes) were used as well.

The railroad also led to new war developments. For the first time, artillery was mounted on rail cars, and the railroads became a major means of transporting both troops and supplies. The railroad was also used for moving the wounded on "hospital trains."

Some other "firsts" include the use of portable telegraph units on the battlefield; hot air balloons for military reconnaissance; and machine guns, repeating rifles, and carbines in battle. Large numbers of photographs were taken on battlefields, and the first Medals of Honor were received by American soldiers and naval personnel.

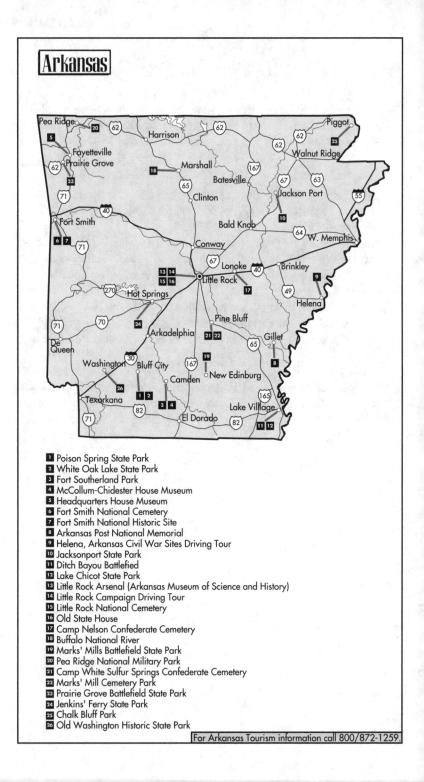

Arkansas

1 Poison Spring State Park
2 White Oak Lake State Park
3 Fort Southerland Park
4 McCollum-Chidester House Museum
5 Headquarters House Museum
6 Fort Smith National Cemetery
7 Fort Smith National Historic Site
8 Arkansas Post National Memorial
9 Helena, Arkansas Civil War Sites Driving Tour
10 Jacksonport State Park
11 Ditch Bayou Battlefied
12 Lake Chicot State Park
13 Little Rock Arsenal (Arkansas Museum of Science and History)
14 Little Rock Campaign Driving Tour
15 Little Rock National Cemetery
16 Old State House
17 Camp Nelson Confederate Cemetery
18 Buffalo National River
19 Marks' Mills Battlefield State Park
20 Pea Ridge National Military Park
21 Camp White Sulfur Springs Confederate Cemetery
22 Marks' Mill Cemetery Park
23 Prairie Grove Battlefield State Park
24 Jenkins' Ferry State Park
25 Chalk Bluff Park
26 Old Washington Historic State Park

*A*RKANSAS PLAYED A MAJOR STRATEGIC ROLE during the Civil War, serving as an avenue and staging area for many of the important operations involving bordering states.

In 1862, the northwest corner of the state was the major battleground. Fighting at Pea Ridge and Prairie Grove kept Missouri in the Union and helped close that section of the state as a Confederate invasion route into Missouri. Fighting in 1863 at Helena reflected that city's importance to the Vicksburg campaign. Rebel troops sought to seize the strategic river town and vital supply post in order to relieve pressure on the besieged Mississippi fortress. Ironically for the southern troops, the battle was fought and lost on the day Vicksburg fell. The defeat at Helena led to the fall of Little Rock and restricted Confederate control to a small area of southwest Arkansas. In 1864, Union troops were on the move in a two-pronged operation with Louisiana-based Yankees. They sought to conquer the cotton-rich Red River area. This time, however, it was the Northern forces who tasted defeat, barely escaping to Little Rock at the conclusion of the abortive Camden Expedition.

The state witnessed the Civil War at its worst. Partisans, jayhawkers, and gangs of armed thieves terrorized rural areas of Arkansas, leaving both Union and Confederate troops with the challenge of containing the lawlessness. The war left economic devastation and a psychological bitterness in Arkansas that persisted for decades.

by Mark K. Christ, Arkansas Historic Preservation Program

Bluff City

1 **Site:** POISON SPRING STATE PARK, Hwy. 76, Bluff City, AR 71722, ☎ 870/685-2748

Description: The Battle of Poison Spring took place on April 18, 1864, during the Camden Expedition of the Red River campaign. Confederate troops attacked a Union column taking supplies to the Federal occupiers of Camden.

Open to Public: Daily 6am–10pm.

Admission Fees: Free.

Visitor Services: Trails, information.

Regularly Scheduled Events: *Mar:* Demonstrations of the Battle of Poison Spring.

Directions: From I-30: take exit 44 for Prescott and proceed east on State Hwy. 24 through Prescott for 33 miles. After passing through Bragg City, look for Arkansas State Park sign for Poison Spring State Park. Turn right on State Hwy. 76 and go about 5 miles. Park is located on the right.

2 **Site:** WHITE OAK LAKE STATE PARK, Rte. 2, Box 28, Bluff City, AR 71222,
☎ 870/685-2748

Description: The evening before the Battle of Poison Spring, the Union forces camped on White Oak Creek near where the state park is located today. The park, which is the "gateway" to Poison Spring and the nearest campground to the southern arm of the Red River Campaign National Historic Landmark, provides a convenient and comfortable site from which to tour the area from Old Washington State Park to Camden. The visitors center includes a display of battle artifacts, images, and information on the Red River Campaign.

Open to Public: *Visitor Center:* Daily 8am–5pm. *Park:* Daily 24 hours.

Admission Fees: Free; fee for camping.

Visitor Services: Camping, trails, food, gift shop, information, rest rooms, handicapped access.

Regularly Scheduled Events: Poison Spring encampment; Arkansas Heritage Day; Wildflower Weekend; Star Party. Contact park for schedule.

Directions: From I-30 at Prescott: turn east on State Hwy. 24. From Prescott, travel 19 miles to Bluff City; then take State Hwy. 387 to the park.

Camden

3 **Site:** FORT SOUTHERLAND PARK, Bradley Ferry Rd., Camden, AR 71701,
☎ 870/836-6436

Description: Fort Southerland represents an excellently preserved example of urban Civil War defensive earthworks erected along the periphery of Camden. They were erected in 1864 in anticipation of a Federal attack from Little Rock.

Open to Public: Daily from dawn to dusk.

Admission Fees: Free.

Visitor Services: None.

Directions: From I-30 at Prescott: take State Hwy. 24 east to Camden; turn from Hwy. 24 onto State Hwy. 4 Spur and follow 4 Spur and U.S. Hwy. 79 to Bradley Ferry Rd. Site is located 2 blocks down on the left.

4 **Site:** MCCOLLUM-CHIDESTER HOUSE MUSEUM, 926 Washington St., Camden, AR
71701, ☎ 870/836-9243

Description: This house, built in 1847, retains its furnishings brought here by steamboat in 1863 by the Chidester family. The city of Camden was occupied by Northern Gen. Frederick Steele in 1864, during the Battle of Poison Spring.

Open to Public: Wed–Sat 9am–4pm.

Admission Fees: Adults $3, children $1.

Visitor Services: Tours, rest rooms.

Directions: From I-30 at Prescott: take State Hwy. 24 east to Camden, turn from Hwy. 24 onto State Hwy. 4 Spur, and follow Washington St. to museum at 926 Washington St.

Fayetteville

5 **Site:** HEADQUARTERS HOUSE MUSEUM, 118 East Dickson St., Fayetteville, AR 72701, ☎ 501/521-2970

Description: Headquarters House was built in 1853 by Judge Jonas Tebbetts, a Northern sympathizer who was jailed by Gen. Ben McCulloch and then finally released to St. Louis for the duration of the war. The house was used at various times as headquarters for both the Federal and the Confederate armies. The Battle of Fayetteville was fought on the house grounds and across the street on April 18, 1863. One of the doors still carries a hole made by a minié ball.

Open to Public: Mon 10am–12pm, Thurs 10am–4pm, Sat 10am–12pm.

Admission Fees: Adults $3, children $1.

Visitor Services: Living history tours by appointment, bookstore.

Regularly Scheduled Events: *Apr:* Battle of Fayetteville reenactment; *Third Sat in Aug:* Ice Cream Social.

Directions: From I-40: travel north on Rte. 71 to Fayetteville. Rte. 71 turns into College Ave. House is at the corner of College Ave. and Dickson.

Fort Smith

6 **Site:** FORT SMITH NATIONAL CEMETERY, 522 Garland Ave., Fort Smith, AR 72901, ☎ 501/783-5345

Description: This burial place for Union and Confederate soldiers includes three generals and 1,500 unknown soldiers. The site offers a brochure, a minimuseum of local military history, and tours if arranged ahead.

Open to Public: *Gates:* Daily 24 hours. *Office:* Mon–Fri 8am–4:30pm.

Admission Fees: Free.

Visitor Services: Information, rest rooms, handicapped access.

Regularly Scheduled Events: *Sun closest to Memorial Day:* Memorial Day ceremony; *Nov:* Veterans Day ceremony; *Dec 7:* Pearl Harbor Day of Remembrance.

Directions: From I-540: take exit 8A (Rogers) and proceed toward the downtown area. At the "Y," go to the right and take Garrison Rd. to Sixth St. Turn left on Sixth St. Cemetery is at the end of Sixth St., where it intersects Garland.

7 **Site:** FORT SMITH NATIONAL HISTORIC SITE, corner of Third and Rogers. Mailing address: P.O. Box 1406, Fort Smith, AR 72902, ☎ 501/783-3961

Description: Fort Smith National Historic Site preserves the site of two military posts

and the historic Federal Court for the Western District of Arkansas. The second Fort

Smith (1838–1871) served as a military supply and command center for both the Confederate and Union forces on the western frontier.

Open to Public: Daily 9am–5pm.

Admission Fees: Fee waived during rehabilitation through the year 2000.

Visitor Services: Museum, gift shop, information, rest rooms, handicapped access.

Regularly Scheduled Events: Tours and demonstrations throughout the summer.

Directions: From I-40 west: take Rogers Ave and go west to the end of the road downtown. From I-40 east: take exit 64B, go 6 miles east, make the first right after crossing the bridge over the Arkansas River.

Gillett

8 Site: ARKANSAS POST NATIONAL MEMORIAL, 1741 Old Post Rd., Gillett, AR 72055, ☎ 870/548-2207

Description: By mid-1862, Union gunboats commanded most of the Mississippi River. When the gunboats went up the White River into the heart of Arkansas, the Confederates began to prepare defenses on the Arkansas River, an important water route to the capital at Little Rock. Before the end of 1862, Confederate Gen. Thomas J. Churchill completed an earthen fortification at Arkansas Post, called Fort Hindman or Post of Arkansas. A battle took place on January 10, 1863, when Union forces captured the fort.

Open to Public: *Park:* Daily from dawn to dusk. *Visitor Center:* Daily 8am–5pm.

Admission Fees: Free.

Visitor Services: Trails, museum, gift shop, information, rest rooms, handicapped access.

Directions: From Little Rock: take 65 south to Gould and then 212 east at Gould to Hwy. 165; take 165 north to 169 and follow to park. From Brinkley: take 49 south to Marvell, Hwy. 1 to 165, and 165 to 169. From Forrest City: take Hwy. 1 to DeWitt and then take 165 to 169.

Helena

9 Site: HELENA, ARKANSAS CIVIL WAR SITES DRIVING TOUR, c/o 226 Perry St., Helena, AR 72342, ☎ 501/338-9831

Description: Confederate forces suffered heavy casualties in the July 4, 1863 attack on Helena, an attack intended to relieve pressure on besieged Vicksburg. The outnumbered Union defenders used a system of hilltop fortifications and artillery from the gunboat Tyler to decimate the attacking Rebel force. This driving tour features Batteries A, B, C, and D and the Helena Confederate Cemetery.

Open to Public: Daily from dawn to dusk. *Tourist Information Center:* Daily 8:30am–5pm.

Admission Fees: Free.

Visitor Services: None.

Regularly Scheduled Events: *Columbus Day weekend in Oct:* King Biscuit Blues Festival.

Directions: From 1-40 east: take U.S. 49 southeast to Helena. From I-40 at Memphis: take U.S. 61 south to U.S. 49. Take U.S. 49 west to Helena. Pick up driving tour brochure at the Tourist Information Center on Hwy. 49.

Jacksonport

10 **Site:** JACKSONPORT STATE PARK, P.O. Box 8, Jacksonport, AR 72075, ☎ 870/523-2143

Description: During the Civil War, Jacksonport was occupied by both Confederate and Union armies because of its strategic position accessible to the Mississippi and Arkansas rivers. Five generals used the town as their headquarters. On June 5, 1865, Confederate Gen. Jeff Thompson, "Swampfox of the Confederacy," surrendered 6,000 troops to Lt. Col. C. W. Davis at the Jacksonport Landing. Tour the Jacksonport Courthouse Museum; its War Memorial Room; and the Mary Woods No. 2 steamboat, restored to the 1890s period.

Open to Public: *Park:* Daily all year. *Note:* Museum and Riverboat are closed for repairs of tornado damage; call for reopening dates in 1999. *Museum:* Open all year: Wed–Sat 9am–5pm, Sun 1–5pm; closed Mon and Tues. *Riverboat:* Open

Apr 30–Sept 2: Sun 1–5pm, Tues–Thurs 10am–8pm, Fri–Sat 9am–5pm; closed Mon.

Admission Fees: *Park:* Free. *Museum:* Adults $2, children $1. *Riverboat:* Adults $2, children $1. *Combination ticket to museum and riverboat:* Adults $3.50, children $1.50.

Visitor Services: Camping, trails, museum, gift shop, information, rest rooms, handicapped access.

Regularly Scheduled Events: *Sat before Easter:* Easter egg hunt; *Autumn:* Radio-Control Fun Fly (exhibition of model airplanes); *Dec:* Christmas open house.

Directions: From Hwy. 67 at Newport: take exit 83 and follow the Jacksonport State Park signs.

Lake Village

11 **Site:** DITCH BAYOU BATTLEFIELD, Lake Chicot State Park, 2542 Hwy. 257, Lake Village, AR 71653, ☎ 870/265-5480

Description: Roadside exhibits interpret the 1864 Battle of Ditch Bayou, in which a small Confederate force under Col. Colton Greene inflicted heavy casualties on a much larger

Union formation commanded by Gen. A. J. Smith. This was the largest battle in Chicot County and the last significant battle on Arkansas soil. It is part of a driving tour of Civil

War sites along Lake Chicot. Brochures are available at Lake Chicot State Park.

Open to Public: Daily 24 hours.

Admission Fees: Free.

Visitor Services: Wayside exhibits.

Directions: From I-20 at Tallulah, LA: take Hwy. 65 north 85 miles to the intersection with Hwy. 82 in Chicot Co., AR. Turn right and proceed east for 2 miles. Exhibits are on the left.

---

12 **Site:** LAKE CHICOT STATE PARK, 2542 Hwy. 257, Lake Village, AR 71653, ☎ 870/265-5480

Description: Lake Chicot State Park houses exhibits and research material on local Civil War history. The park interpreter presents living history programs and conducts an annual reenactment. A driving tour brochure of local Civil War sites is available from the park office.

Open to Public: *Visitor Center:* Daily 8am–5pm. *Park:* Daily 24 hours.

Admission Fees: Free.

Visitor Services: Museum, lodging, gas, camping, trails, food, gift shop, information, rest rooms, handicapped access.

Regularly Scheduled Events: *Oct:* Civil War Weekend.

Directions: From I-20 at Tallulah, LA: take Hwy. 65 north 85 miles to the intersection with Hwy. 82. Turn left and proceed north to Lake Village, AR. Take Hwy. 144 for 8 miles to park.

Little Rock

13 **Site:** LITTLE ROCK ARSENAL (ARKANSAS MUSEUM OF SCIENCE AND HISTORY), MacArthur Park, Little Rock, AR 72202, ☎ 501/396-7050

Description: In February 1861, Arkansas citizens marched on Little Rock and took the arsenal, even though Arkansas had not yet seceded from the Union. For the next 2 years, the arsenal was under the control of the Confederacy. It was reclaimed when Federal troops took Little Rock in 1863.

Open to Public: Mon–Sat 9am–4:30pm, Sun 1–4:30pm.

Admission Fees: Adults $2, children and seniors $1.50, groups (up to 49) $10, groups (50–100) $20.

Visitor Services: Museum, gift shop, information, rest rooms, handicapped access.

Directions: From I-30: take the East Ninth St. exit. MacArthur Park lies west of the interstate, only 1 block from the exit.

---

14 **Site:** LITTLE ROCK CAMPAIGN DRIVING TOUR, Central Arkansas Civil War Heritage Trail Committee, P.O. Box 2125, Little Rock, AR 72203, ☎ 501/376-3800

Description: The Little Rock Campaign of 1863 began with the Union advance from Helena, culminating 40 days later in seizure of the state capitol from Confederate forces after numerous actions and skirmishes. The driving tour includes detailed exhibit panels at Brownsville, near Lonoke; Reed's Bridge at Jacksonville; Ashley's Mills and Willow Beach Lake near Scott; and Fourche Bayou and Riverfront Park in Little Rock.

Open to Public: Daily 24 hours.

Admission Fees: Free.

Visitor Services: Roadside pull-offs with wayside exhibits.

Directions: All sites are accessible from I-40 between Lonoke and Little Rock. Contact Central Arkansas Civil War Heritage Trail for driving tour brochure with detailed directions.

---

15 **Site:** LITTLE ROCK NATIONAL CEMETERY, 2523 Confederate Blvd., Little Rock, AR 72206, ☎ 501/324-6401

Description: The grounds were used as a Union campground by U.S. troops. When the troops left, the Confederates buried their dead on the west side. It was then bought by the U.S. government for a military burial ground of occupation troops. A wall was erected between the Union and Confederate sections but was taken down in 1913.

Open to Public: *Cemetery:* Mon–Fri dawn to dusk. *Office:* Mon–Fri 7:30am–4:30pm.

Admission Fees: Free.

Visitor Services: Information, rest rooms.

Regularly Scheduled Events: *Apr:* Confederate Memorial Day; *May:* Memorial Day; *Nov:* Veterans Day.

Directions: From I-30: take the Roosevelt Rd. exit; go east 3 blocks to Confederate Blvd. From I-440: take the Confederate Blvd. exit; go north about 1 mile.

---

16 **Site:** OLD STATE HOUSE, 300 West Markham St., Little Rock, AR 72201, ☎ 501/324-9685

Description: Constructed from 1836 to 1842, the Old State House was the state's original capitol and is now a museum of Arkansas history. It was the site of many significant events, including the 1861 secession convention. In 1863, the Confederate government fled the area, and the town fell to Union troops. Gen. Frederick Steele quartered his army in the State House during his occupation.

Open to Public: Closed until spring of 1999 for major restoration.

Directions: From I-30: take the Markham St./Cantrell Rd. exit and follow the signs.

Lonoke

17 **Site:** CAMP NELSON CONFEDERATE CEMETERY, P.O. Box 431, Lonoke, AR 72086, ☎ 501/676-6403

Description: While camped near Old Austin, Arkansas, a large group of Texas Confederate soldiers were overcome by a measles epidemic, causing the deaths of several hundred. The soldiers were buried near the encampment. In 1907, the General Assembly appropriated funds to remove the remains to the area that became the cemetery. The remains were not identified on the stone markers; a monument at the cemetery tells this story.

Open to Public: Daily from dawn to dusk.

Admission Fees: Free.

Visitor Services: Handicapped access.

Regularly Scheduled Events: *June:* Flag Day Celebration.

Directions: From I-40: take Remington exit (7 miles west of Lonoke). Take Hwy. 15 north for 2.5 miles to where it crosses and becomes Hwy. 89. Continue on Hwy. 89 to the junction of Hwy. 321. Turn right on Hwy. 321 and continue approximately 2 miles to Cherry Rd. Turn left on Cherry Rd. Site is approximately .5 mile on the right.

Marshall

18 **Site:** BUFFALO NATIONAL RIVER. Mailing address: P.O. Box 1173, Harrison, AR 72602, ☎ 870/741-5443; Tyler Bend Visitor Center (near Marshall, AR), ☎ 870/439-2505

Description: Buffalo National River is a 95,000-acre National Park that preserves unique natural and cultural features of the Arkansas Ozarks. During the Civil War, the rugged terrain became a battleground between aggressive independent Confederate units and the Union forces holding northwest Arkansas. The residents caught in the middle of the constant skirmishing lost farms, possessions, and lives. Skirmish sites, saltpeter caves, and Civil War–era farms are interpreted. For Civil War orientation, the Park staff recommends visiting the Tyler Bend Visitor Center near Marshall, Arkansas.

Open to Public: Daily. *Tyler Bend Visitor Center:* Daily 8am–4:30pm.

Admission Fees: Free.

Visitor Services: Lodging, camping, trails (some are rugged), museum, gift shop, information, rest rooms.

Regularly Scheduled Events: Summer tours and interpretive talks. Call for a schedule.

Directions: From I-40 at Conway: exit onto Hwy. 65 and proceed north. The Tyler Bend Visitor Center is about 10 miles north of Marshall; follow the signs. Tyler Bend Visitor Center is about 100 miles from Little Rock and about 100 miles from Springfield, MO.

New Edinburg

19 **Site:** MARKS' MILLS BATTLEFIELD STATE PARK. Mailing address: c/o Arkansas State Parks, One Capitol Mall, Little Rock, AR 72201, ☎ 501/682-1191

NORTHWEST ARKANSAS CIVIL WAR HERITAGE TRAIL

The Union armies of Samuel Curtis and James Blunt and the Confederate armies of Earl Van Dorn, Sterling Price, and Stand Watie, along with hordes of jayhawkers and bushwhackers roamed and fought throughout this frontier region. The Northwest Arkansas Civil War Heritage Trail includes national, state, and local historic sites associated with Union and Confederate activities in northwest Arkansas, northeast Oklahoma, southwest Missouri, and southeast Kansas.

Primary sites in Arkansas include: Pea Ridge National Military Park, Prairie Grove Battlefield State Park, Fort Smith National Historic Site, Buffalo National River, Headquarters House Museum, Old Fort Museum, Fayetteville National Cemetery; Fayette Confederate Cemetery, Fort Smith National Cemetery, and Fort Smith Oak Cemetery.

For more information: Call Pea Ridge National Military Park (☎ 501/451-8122), Fort Smith National Historic Site (☎ 501/783-3961), Prairie Grove Battlefield State Park (☎ 501/846-2990), or Buffalo National River (☎ 501/741-5443) to order the "Northwest Arkansas Civil War Heritage Trail" brochure, a general guide to Civil War sites in this much-fought-over region of the Trans-Mississippi theater of operations. Copies are also available at most Arkansas Tourist Information Centers. The trail also includes sites in Missouri, Oklahoma, and Kansas.

This is one of four battles that defined the limits of Union Gen. Frederick Steele's foray into south Arkansas during the Red River Campaign of 1864. Following the crushing Federal defeat at Marks' Mills, Steele abandoned Camden and retreated to Little Rock.

Open to Public: Daily 24 hours.

Admission Fees: Free.

Visitor Services: Wayside exhibit panels.

Directions: From I-30 at Malvern: turn south on U.S. Hwy. 270. In Malvern, take State Hwy. 9 south; 2 miles south of Princeton, take Hwy. 8 and continue through Fordyce to the site, near New Edinburg. This route traces a significant portion of Steele's retreat from Camden, going through Tulip and Princeton and passing just 13 miles southwest of the final battle of the campaign at Jenkins' Ferry.

Pea Ridge

20 **Site:** PEA RIDGE NATIONAL MILITARY PARK, P.O. Box 700, Pea Ridge, AR 72751-0700, ☎ 501/451-8122

Description: On March 7 and 8, 1862, the 10,500-man Union Army of the Southwest and the 16,200-man Confederate Army of the West met in combat at two separate battlefields, Leetown and Elkhorn Tavern, on the gently rolling plain called Pea Ridge. The battle at Leetown ended after the death of two Confederate generals on March 7, while the battle at Elkhorn Tavern continued until the Confederates ran out of ammunition on March 8. The decisive Union victory ensured that Missouri would remain in Federal control and paved the way for Grant's Vicksburg campaign.

Open to Public: Daily 8am–5pm.

Admission Fees: Adults $2, children under 16 free, cars $4.

Visitor Services: Trails, museum, information, rest rooms, handicapped access, bookstore.

Regularly Scheduled Events: *Weekend nearest the anniversary of the battle:* Living history exhibit; *Memorial and Veterans Days:* Commemorative ceremonies; *Summer and early autumn:* Living history demonstrations.

Directions: From I-40: exit to Hwy. 71 north; drive 60 miles to Hwy. 72 east; take 72 to Hwy. 62 east. Located on Hwy. 62, approximately 10 miles north of Rogers, AR.

Pine Bluff

21 **Site:** CAMP WHITE SULFUR SPRINGS CONFEDERATE CEMETERY, 2620 W. 28th St., Pine Bluff, AR 71603, ☎ 870/534-1909

Description: Sulphur Springs was used as a campground by a number of Arkansas, Texas, and Louisiana units between late 1861 and early 1863. Many of them died of disease and were buried in this cemetery. Units known to have camped at the site include the 19th, 24th, 33rd, and 38th Arkansas Infantry and Hart's Arkansas Battery; Nutt's and Denson's Louisiana Cavalry Companies; the 6th and 17th Texas Infantry; and the 24th and 25th Texas Cavalry, dismounted. The site is currently maintained as a cemetery and features interpretation.

Open to Public: Daily 24 hours.

Admission Fees: Free.

Visitor Services: Trails.

Regularly Scheduled Events: *October:* Memorial service.

Directions: From I-30 in Little Rock: take U.S. Hwy. 65 south to Pine Bluff; travel south on U.S. Hwy. 79 to State Hwy. 54 and then to Sulphur Springs.

22 **Site:** MARKS' MILLS CEMETERY PARK, 8501 Woodhaven Dr., Pine Bluff, AR 71603, ☎ 870/879-3712

Description: Marks' Mills Cemetery Park features an intact section of the Camden-Pine Bluff Road, where one of Union Gen. Frederick Steele's foraging parties was ambushed and decimated by Confederates under James Fagan on April 25, 1864. The Federal forces suffered some 1,500 casualties, mostly captured. The Marks' Mills Cemetery Park features wayside exhibits interpreting the battle.

Open to Public: Daily 24 hours.

Admission Fees: Free.

Visitor Services: Wayside exhibits.

Regularly Scheduled Events: *Apr:* Reenactment; *Third Sun in July:* Marks' Family Reunion.

Directions: From U.S. 65 at Pine Bluff: take U.S. 79 south to Kingsland; take State Hwy. 97 south for 5 miles. The road entrance is approximately .25 mile north of the intersection of State Hwys. 8 and 97 on the east side of the road.

Prairie Grove

23 **Site:** PRAIRIE GROVE BATTLEFIELD STATE PARK, P.O. Box 306, Prairie Grove, AR 72753, ☎ 501/846-2990

Description: The Battle of Prairie Grove was fought on December 7, 1862, between the Confederate Army of the Trans-Mississippi and the Federal Army of the Frontier. It was the last major Civil War battle in northwest Arkansas and paved the way for control of the region by the Federal army.

Open to Public: *Park:* Daily 8am–10pm. *Museum:* Daily 8am–5pm.

Admission Fees: *Park:* Free. *Museum:* Adults $2, children 6–12 $1.

Prairie Grove Battlefield State Park, Prairie Grove, AR. (Photograph courtesy of Prairie Grove Battlefield State Park.)

Visitor Services: Civil War Explorer, trails, museum, gift shop, information, rest rooms, handicapped access.

Regularly Scheduled Events: *May:* Memorial Day Tribute; *Labor Day weekend:* Clothesline Fair; *First weekend in Dec in even-numbered years:* Battle reenactment.

Directions: From I-40 at Alma, AR: turn north on U.S. 71 for 40 miles to Fayetteville; then turn west on U.S. 62 for 10 miles to Prairie Grove Battlefield.

Prattsville

24 **Site:** JENKINS' FERRY STATE PARK, 1200 Catherine Park Rd., Hot Springs, AR 71913, ☎ 501/844-4176

Description: This site is connected with the Battle of Jenkins' Ferry, the last major

Arkansas battle in the Camden Expedition of the Red River Campaign. The April 30,

1864, battle was fought in flooded, foggy conditions as Gen. Frederick Steele's Union army desperately and successfully withheld Confederate attacks and crossed the Saline River to escape to Little Rock.

Open to Public: Daily from dawn to 10pm.

Admission Fees: Free.

Visitor Services: Rest rooms, picnic area.

Directions: From I-30: take exit 98, Hwy. 270, to Prattsville; turn right on Rte. 291 and go to Rte. 46; turn right on 46 and proceed to the ferryboat site.

St. Francis

25 | **Site:** CHALK BLUFF PARK, P.O. Box 385, Piggott, AR 72454, ☎ 870/598-2667

Description: Chalk Bluff was a strategic crossing into Missouri used by both sides during the Civil War. General Marmaduke's 1863 Raid into Mississippi ended here as he fought off pursuing Union troops.

Open to Public: Daily 8am–5pm.

Admission Fees: Free.

Visitor Services: Camping, trails, rest rooms, handicapped access.

Regularly Scheduled Events: *April:* Civil War encampment.

Directions: Take U.S. 62 to St. Francis; turn west from town for 1.5 miles; then turn north for 1.25 miles to Chalk Bluff site. There are signs from St. Francis.

THE RED RIVER CAMPAIGN TRAIL

The trail includes nationally significant sites associated with the Arkansas leg of the Union Red River Campaign of 1864, in which a Union army under Maj. Gen. Frederick Steele sought to link up with an army under Nathaniel Banks in Louisiana and capture a cotton-rich section of Texas. Both Banks and Steele suffered a series of defeats; Steele's starving army managed to escape pursuing Confederates and returned to Little Rock a little more than a month after advancing into southern Arkansas. It was the last major Union military campaign in Arkansas.

Primary sites include: Poison Spring Battlefield State Park; Marks' Mill Battlefield State Park; Marks' Mill Cemetery Park; White Oak Lake State Park; Prescott Depot Museum; Fort Southerland, Camden; McCollum-Chidester House, Camden; Jenkins' Ferry Battlefield State Park; and Old Washington Historic State Park.

For more information: The Arkansas Department of Parks and Tourism offers a brochure on "The Red River Campaign" that guides visitors to many of the sites included in the Arkansas portion of the campaign. To receive a copy, write Arkansas State Parks, One Capitol Mall, Little Rock, AR 72201, or call ☎ 502/682-1191. The brochure is also available at many of the Tourist Information Centers in Arkansas.

Washington

26 **Site:** OLD WASHINGTON HISTORIC STATE PARK, P.O. Box 98, Washington, AR 71862,
☎ 870/983-2684

Description: Old Washington Historic State Park offers insight into a 19th-century community and builds understanding of the people, times, and events of the Territorial, Antebellum, Civil War, and Reconstruction eras in Arkansas history. This was the state capital from 1863 to 1865 and a cultural, economic, and political center, especially after Little Rock was taken by the Union army in 1863. The site is on the Southwest Trail. Two home tours are available, the Old Town tour and the Living in Town tour, as well as the Old Washington Museum Experience, which includes the gun, blacksmith, and print museums.

Open to Public: Daily 8am–5pm.

Admission Fees: *Old Town Tour or Living in Town Tour:* Adults $6.50, children $3.25. *Old Washington Museum Experience:* Adults $4.25, children $2.25. Day pass for both tours and all museums:

Adults $12, children $6. Family pass for both tours and all museums: Parents and dependent children ages 6–16 $27.50. All prices include tax. Groups of 20 or more with advance reservations: $1 off prices listed.

Regularly Scheduled Events: *Feb:* Valentine's Day dinner in tavern; *Mar:* Jonquil Festival with tours, special events, arts and crafts; *Nov:* Civil War Reenactments Weekend (Old Territorial Days, primitive camp, and demonstrations); *Oct:* Frontier Days (19th-century crafts); *Nov:* Christmas Decorations; *Dec:* Christmas and Candlelight Tour.

Directions: From I-30: take exit 30. Go north on Rte. 4 for 9 miles. Old Washington State Park is located east and west of Hwy. 4; the information desk is located in the 1874 Courthouse on Southwest Trail, which intersects Hwy. 4.

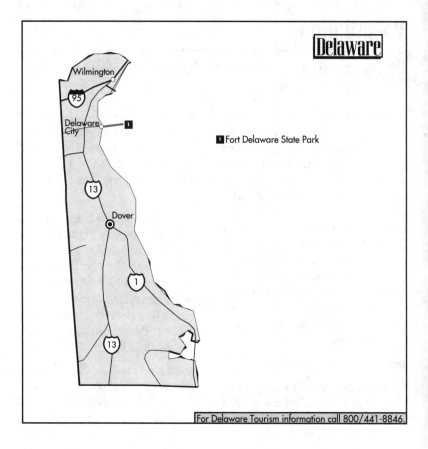

Delaware

Wilmington

95

Delaware City ■ 1

1 Fort Delaware State Park

13

Dover

1

13

For Delaware Tourism information call 800/441-8846.

DELAWARE

*D*ELAWARE WAS A SLAVE-HOLDING STATE with sympathies for the south. These sympathies caused loud discussion in the Delaware legislature, but the mood of the general populace was "go in peace." If Maryland had joined the secessionist movement, Delaware probably would have joined as well. The war did not visit Delaware except at tiny Pea Patch Island where 33,000 Confederate prisoners were kept at Fort Delaware during the war. It was a frightening, disease-ridden place where 2,740 died. The fort was known as the "Andersonville of the North."

Delaware contributed many of its sons, black and white, as soldiers to the Union and Confederate armies. Among them were members of the DuPont family—the leading family of the state. Admiral Samuel DuPont was a naval hero; Lamar DuPont, an officer of the 5th Delaware infantry, served some of his time at Fort Delaware. The state of Delaware also contributed the products of its heavy industrial base, including locomotive engines and ironclad ships, built in Wilmington's shipyards. The DuPont company turned out tons of high-quality gunpowder from its mills on the Brandywine. In spite of sympathies for secession, Delaware contributed greatly to the victory for the Union and the rebirth of the nation.

by Lee Jennings, Nature Center Manager for Fort Delaware,
Fort DuPont, and Fort Penn

Delaware City

1 **Site:** FORT DELAWARE STATE PARK, 45 Clinton St., P.O. Box 170, Delaware City, DE 19706, ☎ 302/834-7941

Description: Fort Delaware was originally constructed as a mid-19th-century coastal defense site. In 1861, the War Department determined that it would be an ideal site for Confederate prisoners. During the course of the war, 33,000 Confederates were imprisoned at the fort. Over 2,700 died while in prison. It was reputed to be the "Andersonville of the North." The fort is located on Pea Patch Island in the Delaware River; visitors travel to the island aboard the *Delafort*, a 90-passenger ferryboat.

Open to Public: 10am–6pm. Last Sun in Apr–last Sun in Sept: Open weekends and holidays. Mid-June–Labor Day: open Wed–Sun, closed Mon–Tues, except Mon holidays.

Admission Fees: *Ferry fare to Fort Delaware:* Adults $6, children 2–12 $4, children under 2 free, seniors $6.

Visitor Services: Nature preserve, educational programs for groups (call in advance), trails, food, museum, gift shop, information, rest rooms, disability access.

Regularly Scheduled Events: *Second Sun in June:* Polish Day; *Third weekend in Aug:* Garrison Weekend; Living history every day; Other special activities each weekend. Call ☎ 302/834-7941 for information.

Directions: From I-95: take State Rte. 1 exit near Christiana Mall; travel south on Rte. 1 to exit 152 (Rte. 72). Turn left onto Rte. 72 east; proceed past Star Refinery and follow signs on Rte. 9 to Delaware City. Turn left at the traffic light on Clinton St.; travel about 6 blocks; look for State Park office and boat dock on the right.

Fort Delaware on Pea Patch Island near Delaware City, DE. (Photograph courtesy of the Fort Delaware Society.)

FLORIDA

*I*N JANUARY 1861, FLORIDA BECAME the third state to secede from the Union. Governor Madison Perry and his successor, John Milton, were ardent secessionists, although the state had a sizable unionist minority. From an 1860 population of about 140,000, nearly half of whom were slaves, Florida provided 15,000 soldiers for Confederate service. Several thousand white and black Floridians joined the Federal military. The state proved most important, however, for the cattle, salt, and other supplies that it provided to the Confederacy.

Florida was the scene of one major battle and numerous small engagements. Additionally, the Union navy maintained a blockade around the peninsula throughout the war. From the outbreak of the war, Federal forces controlled Fort Jefferson in the Dry Tortugas, Fort Zachary Taylor at Key West, and Fort Pickens near Pensacola. The first fighting of the conflict nearly occurred in early 1861 at Pensacola, as Confederate troops gathered there in an attempt to force the Federals from nearby Fort Pickens. In early 1862, Confederate officials ordered the evacuation of northeast Florida and Pensacola and sent the defending troops to more active theaters of the war. Subsequently, Fernandina and St. Augustine were occupied by Federal forces, and Jacksonville suffered the first of four separate occupations.

The major battle in Florida took place on February 20, 1864, at Olustee. Political concerns played a major role in the background to the battle, as did the desire to cut off Florida supplies to the rest of the Confederacy. The fight ended in a stinging defeat for the Federals, who retreated back to their Jacksonville stronghold. Military activity in the state increased from 1864 to 1865, with engagements at Gainesville, Marianna, Station Number 4, Fort Myers, and Natural Bridge. This last battle occurred south of Tallahassee in March 1865 and ensured that the capital would remain in Confederate hands until the war's end. Confederate forces in the state capitulated in May and early June 1865, ending the fighting in Florida. During the southern collapse, a number of government officials escaped southward through Florida in an attempt to reach Cuba or the Bahamas.

by David Coles, Bureau of Archives and Records Management,
Florida Department of State

Ellenton

1 | **Site:** GAMBLE PLANTATION STATE HISTORIC SITE; THE JUDAH P. BENJAMIN CONFEDERATE MEMORIAL, 3708 Patten Ave., Ellenton, FL 34222, ☎ 941/723-4536

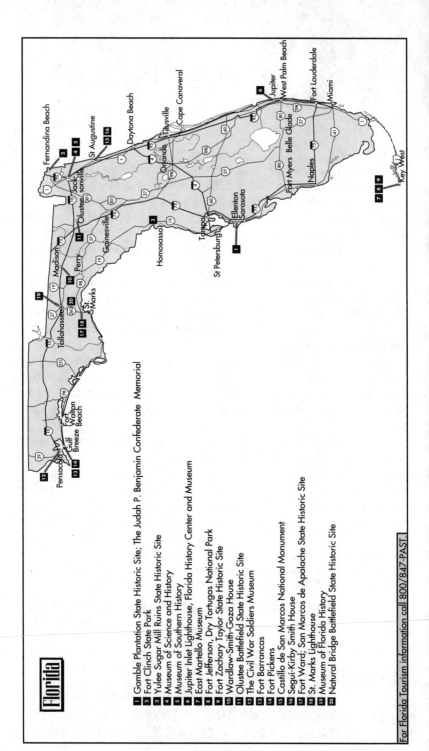

Florida

1 Gamble Plantation State Historic Site; The Judah P. Benjamin Confederate Memorial
2 Fort Clinch State Park
3 Yulee Sugar Mill Ruins State Historic Site
4 Museum of Science and History
5 Museum of Southern History
6 Jupiter Inlet Lighthouse, Florida History Center and Museum
7 East Martello Museum
8 Fort Jefferson, Dry Tortugas National Park
9 Fort Zachary Taylor State Historic Site
10 Wardlaw-Smith-Goza House
11 Olustee Battlefield State Historic Site
12 The Civil War Soldiers Museum
13 Fort Barrancas
14 Fort Pickens
15 Castillo de San Marcos National Monument
16 Segui-Kirby Smith House
17 Fort Ward; San Marcos de Apalache State Historic Site
18 St. Marks Lighthouse
19 Museum of Florida History
20 Natural Bridge Battlefield State Historic Site

For Florida Tourism information call 800/847-PAST.

Description: The mansion was the home of Maj. Robert Gamble and served as the center of a large sugar plantation in the antebellum period. Confederate Secretary of State Judah P. Benjamin took refuge in the house as he fled the country during the fall of the Confederacy.

Open to Public: *By tour only:* Thurs–Mon 9:30am, 10:30am, 1pm, 2pm, 3pm, and 4pm. *Park:* 8am–dusk.

Admission Fees: Adults $3, children 6–12 $1.50.

Visitor Services: Visitors center, tours, picnic facilities, handicapped access.

Directions: From I-75: take exit 43; go 1 mile west on Hwy. 301.

Fernandina Beach

2 **Site:** FORT CLINCH STATE PARK, 2601 Atlantic Ave., Fernandina Beach, FL 32034, ☎ 904/277-7274

Description: The construction of Fort Clinch was begun in 1847 but was never fully completed. It was occupied by Confederate troops from early 1861 until it was evacuated under threat of a large Union naval expedition in March 1862. Union troops occupied the fort for the rest of the war.

Open to Public: *Fort:* Daily 9am–5pm. *Park:* Daily 8am–dusk.

Admission Fees: *Park:* Cars $3.25. *Fort:* Adults $1, children under 6 free.

Visitor Services: Visitors center, guided tours.

Regularly Scheduled Events: *First weekend of each month:* Reenactors join park rangers in performing sentry duty and drills; *Fri and Sat, Apr–Oct:* Candlelight tours; *First weekend in May:* Special Union garrison reenactment; *Last week in Oct:* Confederate garrison is reenacted.

Directions: From I-95: take A1A to Amelia Island and then to Fernandina; turn right onto Atlantic; go 2 miles.

Homosassa

3 **Site:** YULEE SUGAR MILL RUINS STATE HISTORIC SITE. Mailing address: c/o Crystal River State Archaeological Site, 3400 N. Museum Point, Crystal River, FL 34428 ☎ 352/795-3817

Description: The Yulee Sugar Mill Ruins were originally part of the sugar plantation of Confederate Senator David Levy Yulee of Florida. The mill operated for 13 years and supplied sugar products for the Confederate war effort. Yulee's plantation was burned by Union forces during the war, but the mill was spared. Today, the mill has been partially restored. Interpretive signs guide visitors through the complex.

Open to Public: Daily 8am–sunset.

Admission Fees: Free.

Directions: Located on State Rd. 490, west of U.S. 19 in Homosassa. From I-75: take Wildwood exit; go west on State Rd. 44 to U.S. 19; then travel south about 10 miles on U.S. 19 to Homosassa Springs. Turn right on State Rd. 490 and proceed about 2.5 miles to the site.

Jacksonville

4 **Site:** MUSEUM OF SCIENCE AND HISTORY, 1025 Museum Circle, Jacksonville, FL 32201, ☎ 904/396-7061

Description: This general museum includes an exhibit on the Union transport ship Maple Leaf, which struck a Confederate mine in St. Johns River and sank in 1864. Recently discovered and partially excavated, the shipwreck has yielded well-preserved examples of military and civilian equipment.

Open to Public: Mon–Fri 10am–5pm, Sat 10am–6pm, Sun and holidays 1–6pm.

Admission Fees: Adults $6, seniors and active military $4.50, children 3–12 $4.

Visitor Services: Museum.

Directions: From I-95 north: take San Marco Blvd. exit; go left onto Gary St. At the stoplight, take a left onto Prudential Dr.; take a left into museum circle. From I-95 south: take Prudential Dr. exit to Main St.; go 3 lights and take River Place to museum circle.

5 **Site:** MUSEUM OF SOUTHERN HISTORY, 4304 Herschel St., Jacksonville, FL 32210, ☎ 904/388-3574

Description: This museum displays artifacts and memorabilia from the antebellum and Civil War periods. Topics presented include camp life, military equipment, and civilian personal items. The museum has an adjoining historical research library, with genealogical research assistance available.

Open to Public: Tues–Sat 10am–5pm.

Admission Fees: Adults $1, children under 16 free with an adult.

Visitor Services: Museum, information.

Directions: From I-95: go west on I-10; then take U.S. 17 south to San Juan Ave.; turn left; go to the first light (Herschel St.) and turn left; proceed 1 block.

Jupiter

6 **Site:** JUPITER INLET LIGHTHOUSE, FLORIDA HISTORY CENTER AND MUSEUM, 805 North U.S. Hwy. 1, Jupiter, FL 33477, ☎ 561/747-6639

Description: The lighthouse was designed by then Lt. George G. Meade, later Federal commander at Gettysburg. Construction was completed in 1860. Early in the Civil War, Confederate sympathizers removed the illuminating apparatus and buried it in Jupiter Creek. At the end of the war, the newly appointed lighthouse keeper recovered the lighting mechanism, and it was relighted in 1866.

Open to Public: *Lighthouse:* Sun–Wed 10am–4pm. *Museum:* Tues–Fri 10am–5pm, Sat–Sun noon–5pm.

Admission Fees: $5.

Visitor Services: Museum, visitors center, information, guided tours.

Directions: From I-95: take Jupiter exit. Travel east on Indiantown Rd. to U.S. Hwy. 1. Take U.S. Hwy. 1 north approximately 2 miles to the intersection of State Rd. 707, to Florida History Center on right in Burt Reynolds Park. Lighthouse is one-half mile north on U.S. 1 from History Center.

Key West

7 **Site:** EAST MARTELLO MUSEUM, 3501 South Roosevelt Blvd., Key West, FL 33040, ☎ 305/296-3913

Description: The East Martello Museum in Key West, Florida, once a military battery for the U.S. Army, is now home to Civil War artifacts, Stanley Papio sculptures, and Mario Sanchez art. The museum sponsors a variety of temporary art and history exhibitions, educational programs, and art classes, as well as permanent displays of Florida Keys history. The battery was built in 1862 to defend Fort Taylor from possible threat from land attack during the Civil War, but the East and West Martello Towers were never finished. No attack ever occurred, and today the East Martello Tower houses a general art gallery and Key West museum.

Open to Public: Daily 9:30am–5pm. Last admission is at 4pm.

Admission Fees: Adults $6, children 7–12 $2.

Visitor Services: Gift shop, rest rooms.

Directions: From A1A: turn left on South Roosevelt Blvd. Located next to the Key West Airport.

8 **Site:** FORT JEFFERSON, Dry Tortugas National Park. Mailing address: 40001 State Rd. 9336, Homestead, FL 33034, ☎ 305/242-7700

Description: This is the largest all-masonry fort in the Western Hemisphere and is called the "Key to the Gulf of Mexico." It was garrisoned by Union troops throughout the Civil War and also served as a military prison. Located in the Gulf off Key West.

Open to Public: Daily from dawn to dusk.

Admission Fees: Free.

Visitor Services: Visitor center with video and exhibits, self-guided tours, bookstore, camping, snorkeling, fishing, swimming, bird watching.

Directions: Garden Key, Dry Tortugas, 70 miles west of Key West. Accessible only by boat or seaplane.

---

9 **Site:** FORT ZACHARY TAYLOR STATE HISTORIC SITE, Southard St. Mailing address: P.O. Box 6560, Key West, FL 33041, ☎ 305/292-6713

Description: When Florida seceded from the Union, Federal troops in Key West quickly moved to secure Fort Taylor and prevented it from falling into Confederate hands. The cannons that have been found buried inside the fort constitute one of the largest groups of Civil War heavy artillery in existence.

Open to Public: Daily 8am–sunset.

Admission Fees: *Cars:* $4 plus 50¢ per person. *Individuals:* Adults $1.50, children 6 and under free.

Visitor Services: Tours: Daily noon and 2pm.

Regularly Scheduled Events: *Feb:* Civil War Days reenactment and living history weekend.

Directions: Located at the southwest end of Key West, FL, at Southard St. on Truman Annex.

Fort Zachary Taylor in the Florida Keys. (Photograph courtesy of Phillip M. Pollock, the Museum of Florida History.)

Madison

10 **Site:** WARDLAW-SMITH-GOZA HOUSE. Mailing address: North Florida Community College, 1000 Turner Davis Dr., Madison, FL 32340. Physical address: 103 N. Washington St., ☎ 850/973-2288, ext. 132/107

Description: This antebellum mansion, built around 1860, was briefly used as a hospital for casualties following the Battle of Olustee in 1864. The next year, Confederate Secretary of War John C. Breckinridge reportedly spent the night here, while making his escape during the fall of the Confederate government.

Open to Public: Tues–Thurs 10am–2pm.

Admission Fees: $2.

Visitor Services: Tours, conference center.

Directions: From I-10: take the Madison-Perry exit and take State Rd. 14 north to Madison; turn left on U.S. 90 at the Courthouse; proceed 2 blocks; house is on the right.

Olustee

11 Site: OLUSTEE BATTLEFIELD STATE HISTORIC SITE, P.O. Box 40, Olustee, FL 32072, ☎ 904/758-0400

Description: The Olustee Battlefield is the site of the only major Civil War battle fought in Florida. On February 20, 1864, a Union force of approximately 5,000 troops clashed with a Confederate force of similar size. After bloody fighting, the Union force was defeated and forced to retreat to Jacksonville.

Open to Public: *State Park:* Daily 8am–5pm. *Interpretive Center:* Thurs–Mon 9am–5pm.

Admission Fees: Free.

Visitor Services: Interpretive center, trails, information.

Regularly Scheduled Events: *Feb:* Reenactment of the Battle of Olustee; *Sept:* Civil War Expo.

Directions: About 15 miles east of Lake City; 2 miles east of Olustee on U.S. 90.

Pensacola

12 Site: THE CIVIL WAR SOLDIERS MUSEUM, 108 South Palafox Pl., Pensacola, FL 32501, ☎ 850/469-1900

Description: The museum exhibits include the arms, equipment, and personal effects of Civil War soldiers, both northern and southern. Special areas of interest include artifacts dealing with Civil War medicine and documents related to Pensacola during the Civil War.

Open to Public: Mon–Sat 10am–4:30pm.

Admission Fees: Adults $5, Active Military $4, children 6–12 $2, children under 6 free.

Visitor Services: Bookstore, gift shop, museum.

Directions: From I-110: take Cervantes exit; go west; then turn left onto Palafox St., which becomes Palafox Pl. Located across from the Pensacola Post Office.

13 Site: FORT BARRANCAS, Gulf Islands National Seashore. Mailing address: 1801 Gulf Breeze Pkwy., Gulf Breeze, FL 32561, ☎ 850/934-2600

Description: Confederate forces occupied this fort from early 1861 until they withdrew in May 1862. Artillery fire was exchanged in late 1861 and early 1862 with Union-held Fort Pickens in the harbor.

Open to Public: Apr–Oct: Daily 9:30am–5pm. Nov–Mar: Wed–Sun 10:30am–4pm.

Admission Fees: Free.

Visitor Services: Self-guided tours, guided tours on weekends.

Directions: Take Rte. 292 to U.S. Naval Air Station. Located on the base of Pensacola U.S. Naval Air Station at the south end of Navy Blvd.

---

14 Site: FORT PICKENS, Gulf Islands National Seashore. Mailing address: 1801 Gulf Breeze Pkwy., Gulf Breeze, FL 32561, ☎ 850/934-2600

Description: Originally built in 1829–1834, Fort Pickens was held by Union troops throughout the Civil War. The Fort's commander refused demands that the fort surrender to state forces at the beginning of the war.

Open to Public: Apr–Oct: Daily 9:30am–5pm. Nov–Mar: daily 8:30am–4pm.

Admission Fees: Cars $6 for 7 days; persons over age 62 free; pedestrians, bicycles, and motorcycles $3.

Visitor Services: Visitors center, guided tours.

Directions: Take U.S. 98 east across Pensacola Bay to Gulf Breeze. Take Hwy. 399 to Pensacola Beach; then travel 9 miles west on Fort Pickens Rd.

St. Augustine

15 Site: CASTILLO DE SAN MARCOS NATIONAL MONUMENT, 1 S. Castillo Dr., St. Augustine, FL 32084, ☎ 904/829-6506

Description: Built in 1672–1695 as a colonial Spanish fortress, it was renamed Fort Marion in 1821; its original Spanish name was restored in 1942. Confederate forces occupied this fort from early 1861 until they withdrew the next year, on arrival of a Union naval force.

Open to Public: Daily 8:45am–4:45pm.

Admission Fees: Adults $4, under 17 free.

Visitor Services: Self-guided tours, exhibits, unscheduled ranger talks.

Directions: From I-95: exit at Rte. 16 east into St. Augustine; turn right for 2 miles on San Marcos St.

---

16 Site: SEGUÍ-KIRBY SMITH HOUSE. Mailing address: 271 Charlotte St., St. Augustine, FL 32084. Physical address: 6 Artillery Lane, ☎ 904/824-2872

Description: This house was the birthplace of Gen. Edmund Kirby Smith, the last Confederate general to surrender. His mother, Frances Kirby Smith lived in this house during the early part of the Union occupation of St. Augustine until she was exiled from the city for spying. The house is now the St. Augustine Historical Society research library. The collection is open to the public for research and contains files and books on Florida history, including the Civil War period and the Kirby Smith family. There is a plaque inside the building commemorating its famous former resident.

Open to Public: Tues–Fri 9am–4:30pm.

Admission Fees: Free.

Visitor Services: Research library.

Directions: From I-95: exit at State Rd. 16; travel east 6 miles; turn right on U.S. 1; turn left at King St.(the third traffic light); proceed east for .25 miles; turn right on Aviles St.; proceed south 1 block; house is at the corner of Aviles St. and Artillery Lane.

St. Marks

17 **Site:** FORT WARD, SAN MARCOS DE APALACHE STATE HISTORIC SITE. Mailing address: 1022 Desoto Park Dr., Tallahassee, FL 32301, ☎ 850/925-6216 or 850/922-6007

Description: These ruins are located at the confluence of the St. Marks and Wakulla rivers. The site has been occupied by Spanish, British, American, and Confederate troops. During the Civil War, Confederate soldiers built earthworks and placed artillery at the fort, which was threatened but not attacked in March 1865.

Open to Public: Thurs–Mon 9am–5pm.

Admission Fees: Adults $1, children under 7 free.

Visitor Services: Museum, visitors center, information.

Directions: Off State Rd. 363: turn right to Old Fort Rd. and turn left to site (located south of Tallahassee).

18 **Site:** ST. MARKS LIGHTHOUSE, St. Marks National Wildlife Refuge, P.O. Box 68, St. Marks, FL 32355, ☎ 850/925-6121

Description: The lighthouse was the site of several military operations during the Civil War. In June 1862, the Union navy shelled the area, destroying a small Confederate fortification nearby. A year later, the navy returned and burned the lighthouse's interior steps, trying to prevent its use as a Confederate lookout tower.

Open to Public: *Refuge:* Daily from dawn to dusk. *Lighthouse:* Armed Forces Day 9am–10pm.

Admission Fees: Cars $4, adults $1.

Visitor Services: Trails.

Directions: Located in the St. Marks National Wildlife Refuge, south of Tallahassee off County Rd. 59, south of Newport.

Tallahassee

19 **Site:** MUSEUM OF FLORIDA HISTORY, 500 South Bronough St., Tallahassee, FL 32399-0250, ☎ 850/488-1484

Description: The state history museum includes a Civil War exhibit that displays selected military arms, soldiers' personal effects, and battle flags carried by Florida's Confederate units. The museum also administers the state's Old Capitol, which houses exhibits on the antebellum, Civil War, and Reconstruction periods in Florida's history.

Open to Public: Mon–Fri 9am–4:30pm, Sat 10am–4:30pm, Sun and holidays noon–4:30pm.

Admission Fees: Free.

Visitor Services: Museum, gift shop.

Directions: From I-10: take Havana/Tallahassee exit; proceed south on Monroe St. for 7 miles; turn right on Jefferson St.; travel past 3 stoplights to museum. Located on the ground floor of the R. A. Gray Building, 500 South Bronough St., 1 block west of the Capitol Building.

20 **Site:** NATURAL BRIDGE BATTLEFIELD STATE HISTORIC SITE, 1022 Desoto Park Dr., Tallahassee, FL 32301, ☎ 850/922-6007

Description: On March 6, 1865, a small battle was fought south of Tallahassee at Natural Bridge, where the St. Marks River goes underground. Confederate troops, supported by cadets and home guards, defeated a Union attempt to cross the river and forced the Union troops to retreat to the coast.

Open to Public: Daily 8am–sunset.

Admission Fees: Free.

Visitor Services: Picnic area, information.

Regularly Scheduled Events: *Early Mar:* Reenactment of the Battle of Natural Bridge.

Directions: Travel south from Tallahassee on State Rd. 363 to Woodville; then proceed 6 miles east of Woodville on Natural Bridge Rd.

GEORGIA

$\mathcal{G}$EORGIA'S GEOGRAPHIC POSITION in the heart of the Confederacy made the state almost immune from invasion during the first 2 years of the Civil War. Its coastline was an exception. But Georgians fought in almost every battle and supplied approximately 112,000 soldiers to the Confederate cause. Former slaves, many native Georgians, served in the Forty-fourth United States Colored Infantry.

From the early months of the war, the coast of Georgia saw much activity, with the Union navy blockading the coastline in an attempt to cut off supplies to the Confederacy. Union forces invaded Georgia in September 1863 and fought the Battle of Chickamauga. Two days of hard fighting between the Confederate forces of Gen. Braxton Bragg and the Federal army of Gen. William S. Rosecrans ended with Rosecrans retreating to Chattanooga. Chickamauga was among the 10 bloodiest battles of the war. The cost to the Confederacy for the victory was one from which they never recovered.

The next spring, Gen. William T. Sherman invaded Georgia, and his 100,000 men repeatedly outmaneuvered Gen. Joseph E. Johnston's 70,000 troops. The war came to the heart of Georgia with engagements at Rocky Face Ridge, Resaca, New Hope Church, Pickett's Mill, Cassville, and Kennesaw Mountain. After being outflanked at numerous positions, including his Chattahoochee River Line, Johnston was replaced by Gen. John B. Hood.

Atlanta was a strategic supply and communications center for the Confederacy. With no troop reinforcements available, Atlanta's fortifications were hurriedly strengthened by thousands of impressed slaves. Twelve miles of heavy fortifications surrounded the city from which General Hood launched attacks on the Union forces during three major battles in July 1864. At the conclusion of these battles and after a 40-day siege, General Hood was forced to retreat from Atlanta to avoid entrapment by Union flanking movements. On September 2, the mayor of Atlanta formally surrendered the city to the Union army. In early October, Hood turned north, hoping to cut Sherman's supply lines and lure him away from the city. Sherman then detached part of his army to follow Hood northward, and by the middle of November, Hood was well on his way to Tennessee. After Hood's departure, Sherman ordered the evacuation of the city and set much of what was left on fire. Atlanta was in flames as Sherman departed southward November 15, 1864, on his March to the Sea. After many skirmishes with Confederate cavalry and poorly organized bands of militia during this march, he arrived in Savannah on December 22.

The end of the war came with a series of surrenders. President Jefferson Davis hoped to continue the war from the Trans-Mississippi region. He was pursued across Georgia and was captured near Irwinville in southern Georgia on May 10, 1865.

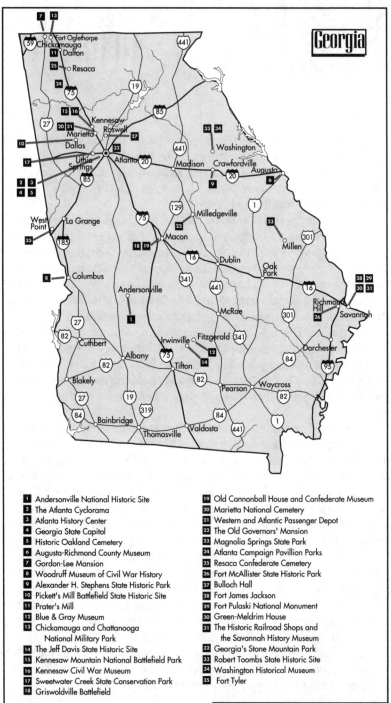

Georgia

1. Andersonville National Historic Site
2. The Atlanta Cyclorama
3. Atlanta History Center
4. Georgia State Capitol
5. Historic Oakland Cemetery
6. Augusta-Richmond County Museum
7. Gordon-Lee Mansion
8. Woodruff Museum of Civil War History
9. Alexander H. Stephens State Historic Park
10. Pickett's Mill Battlefield State Historic Site
11. Prater's Mill
12. Blue & Gray Museum
13. Chickamauga and Chattanooga National Military Park
14. The Jeff Davis State Historic Site
15. Kennesaw Mountain National Battlefield Park
16. Kennesaw Civil War Museum
17. Sweetwater Creek State Conservation Park
18. Griswoldville Battlefield
19. Old Cannonball House and Confederate Museum
20. Marietta National Cemetery
21. Western and Atlantic Passenger Depot
22. The Old Governors' Mansion
23. Magnolia Springs State Park
24. Atlanta Campaign Pavillion Parks
25. Resaca Confederate Cemetery
26. Fort McAllister State Historic Park
27. Bulloch Hall
28. Fort James Jackson
29. Fort Pulaski National Monument
30. Green-Meldrim House
31. The Historic Railroad Shops and the Savannah History Museum
32. Georgia's Stone Mountain Park
33. Robert Toombs State Historic Site
34. Washington Historical Museum
35. Fort Tyler

For More Information

*L*ook for "THE PRESENCE OF THE PAST—TRACKING GEORGIA'S CIVIL WAR HERITAGE." This brochure identifies 41 selected sites, including museums, buildings, and battlefields, that represent Georgia's Civil War history. "The Presence of the Past" is available at Georgia's Welcome Centers or by calling ☎ **404/657-7294.**

Andersonville

1 **Site:** ANDERSONVILLE NATIONAL HISTORIC SITE, Rte. 1, Box 800, Andersonville, GA 31711, ☎ 912/924-0343

Description: Andersonville, Georgia, was the location of Camp Sumter, a Confederate prisoner of war camp. During its 14 months of operation, 45,000 Union prisoners were held here; 12,920 of them died and are buried in the National Cemetery. Andersonville is also the memorial to all prisoners of war in American history. The National Prisoner of War Museum opens in the spring of 1998 and tells of POW experiences from the American Revolution to the present.

Open to Public: Mon–Sun 8am–5pm.

Admission Fees: Free.

Visitor Services: Museum, gift shop, rest rooms, handicapped access.

Regularly Scheduled Events: *Last weekend in Feb:* Living history commemorating the opening of the prison; *First weekend in Oct:* Living history commemorating the dedication of the National Cemetery. Call for more events.

Directions: From I-75: take exit 42 (Perry); travel on GA 224 to Montezuma. Turn right on GA 26; go through the outskirts of Montezuma and Oglethorpe until the intersection with GA 49. Turn left and go approximately 6 miles. Andersonville is on the left on GA 49. Also accessible from exit 46 (Hwy. 49 south) off I-75 (Byron).

Andersonville National Historic Site, National Cemetery at Andersonville, GA. (Photograph courtesy of Eastern National.)

ANDERSONVILLE

During the Civil War, both Union and Confederate armies had to deal with thousands of prisoners and to find ways to care for them. Neither side expected a long conflict or the eventual need that arose to care for large numbers of prisoners. As the numbers of prisoners increased, special prison camps were built, many similar to the one at Andersonville, in Georgia.

Of the more than 211,400 Union soldiers captured by Confederate forces, 30,208 died in prison camps. Union forces captured 462,000 Confederates, including those surrendered at the war's close. Of these, 25,976 died in prison camps.

The most common problems confronting prisoners in both the North and South were overcrowding, poor sanitation, and an improper diet. The confined soldiers suffered terribly. Mismanagement by prison officials as well as by the prisoners themselves brought on additional hardships.

Andersonville, or Camp Sumter as it was known officially, was the largest of many Confederate military prisons established during the Civil War. It was built in early 1864 after Confederate officials decided to move the large number of Federal prisoners in and around Richmond to a place of greater security and more abundant food. During the 14 months it existed, more than 45,000 Union soldiers were confined here. Of these, almost 13,000 died of disease, poor sanitation, malnutrition, overcrowding, or exposure to the elements.

Andersonville prison ceased to exist in April and May 1865. During July and August 1865, Clara Barton, together with a detachment of laborers and soldiers and a former prisoner named Dorence Atwater, went to Andersonville to identify and mark the graves of the Union dead. Atwater, a member of the second New York Cavalry, was 19 years old when he was sent to Andersonville and became keeper of the books in which prisoners' deaths were recorded. His lists proved invaluable to Clara Barton.

Clara Barton's efforts to get medical supplies, aid, and care for the troops led President Lincoln to ask her to try to ascertain the whereabouts of missing soldiers so that relatives could be informed. This mission was what brought her to Andersonville.

Today, Andersonville National Historic Site is unique in the National Park System as the only park to serve as a memorial to all Americans ever held as prisoners of any war.

Credit: National Park Service

Atlanta

2 **Site:** THE ATLANTA CYCLORAMA, 800-C Cherokee Ave., SE, Atlanta, GA 30315, ☎ 404/658-7625 or 404/624-1071

Description: This site is a painting in the round that depicts "The Battle of Atlanta." The painting is 42 feet in height and 358 feet in circumference, weighs more than 9,000 pounds, and covers a canvas area more than 16,000 square feet. A three-dimensional panorama with music and narration awaits the visitor. There is also a film narrated by James Earl Jones on the Atlanta Campaign.

Open to Public: *Fall and winter:* Daily 9:30am–4:30pm. *Spring and summer:* Daily 9:30am–5:30pm.

Admission Fees: Adults $5, seniors $4, children 6–12 $3, groups of adults $4, groups of children $2.

Visitor Services: Museum, gift shop, information, handicapped access, rest rooms.

Directions: From downtown take I-20 east: take exit 26. Follow the signs.

---

3 **Site:** ATLANTA HISTORY CENTER, 130 West Paces Ferry Rd., NW, Atlanta, GA 30305, ☎ 404/814-4000

Description: Learn how Atlanta grew into the South's leading city and about African American history, the Civil War, *Gone With the Wind*, and a whole lot more. The Atlanta History Center's all-new exhibition, "Turning Point: The American Civil War," interprets the key turning points in the Civil War, including the Atlanta Campaign of 1864. The museum has the largest collection of Civil War artifacts in Georgia and one of the five largest Civil War collections in the country, housing approximately 7,500 objects of all types: guns, uniforms, military equipment, and memorabilia. Also visit the 1840s Tullie Smith Farm and the Swan House, an elegant 1928 mansion. McElreath Hall contains the Center's research library and archives.

Open to Public: Mon–Sat 10am–5:30pm, Sun noon–5:30pm.

Admission Fees: Adults $7, seniors 65 and over $5, students 18 and over with ID $5, youths 6–17 $4, children 5 and under free. Group rates available with a reservation. Additional small charge for the historic homes.

Visitor Services: Wooded trails, museum, library/archives, historic houses, Coca-Cola cafe, Swan Coach House restaurant, picnic area, gift shop, rest rooms, handicapped access.

Regularly Scheduled Events: *Apr:* Sheep to Shawl; *July:* Civil War encampment; *Sept:* Folklife festival; *Nov or Dec:* Candlelight tours.

Directions: From I-75: take the West Paces Ferry Rd. exit. Go east 2.6 miles on West Paces Ferry Rd., and the Atlanta History Center is on the right. By MARTA: from the Lenox station, take Bus #23 to the intersection of Peachtree and West Paces Ferry roads; walk west on West Paces Ferry Rd. past the second traffic light (Slaton Dr.) to pedestrian entrance.

---

4 **Site:** GEORGIA STATE CAPITOL, 431 State Capitol, Atlanta, GA 30334, ☎ 404/651-6996

Description: In 1864, Federal troops encamped on the grounds of Atlanta City Hall. Today, Georgia's capitol stands on this site. The dome of the classical Renaissance building is topped with native gold. Statues of Civil War governors and other historic figures as well as UDC historic markers are on the grounds. Capitol museum collections include Confederate-era flags, portraits, and statuary.

Open to Public: Mon–Fri 8am–5:30pm. Tours 10am, 11am, 1pm, and 2pm.

Admission Fees: Free.

Visitor Services: Museum, information, rest rooms, handicapped access.

Directions: From the south: take I-75/I-85 north; take exit 90 (Capitol Ave.). Continue through stop sign. At the first light, turn left onto Capitol Ave. Capitol is 1 mile on the left. From the north: take I-75/I-85 south; take exit 93 (Martin Luther King, Jr. Dr.). Capitol is on the left.

---

5 **Site:** HISTORIC OAKLAND CEMETERY, 248 Oakland Ave., SE, Atlanta, GA 30312, ☎ 404/658-6019

Description: Oakland Cemetery is the repository for approximately 6,800 soldiers, both known and unknown. It has been the site of Memorial Day services since 1866 and boasts two beautiful monuments to the Confederate dead. It is also the final resting place for five generals.

Open to Public: Daily 8am–6pm. Open until 7pm during daylight savings time. *Business office:* Mon–Fri 9am–5pm.

Admission Fees: Free. Guided tours: Adults $3, seniors $2, children and students $1.

Visitor Services: Rest rooms, handicapped access.

Regularly Scheduled Events: *Fall:* Sunday in the Park (Victorian afternoon at the cemetery).

Directions: From I-75 south: take Memorial Dr. exit 1 mile east. From I-75 north: take exit 93 onto Butler St.; make first right onto Decatur St. Go 3 lights to Grant St. and turn right; at stop sign, turn left. The gate will be in front of you.

Augusta

6 **Site:** AUGUSTA-RICHMOND COUNTY MUSEUM, 560 Reynolds St., Augusta, GA 30901, ☎ 706/772-8454

Description: Augusta was a major manufacturing center for the Confederacy with the Augusta Arsenal and the Confederate Powder Works Factory. Artifacts from both Confederate munitions centers are exhibited in the museum. In addition, the museum features Confederate uniforms, accouterments, flags, firearms, and swords.

Open to Public: Tues–Sat 10am–5pm, Sun 2–5pm.

Admission Fees: Adults $4, children 6–18 $2, children 5 and under free, seniors $3.

Visitor Services: Museum, museum shop, information, rest rooms, handicapped access, Augusta Riverwalk.

Directions: From I-20: take exit 66, Riverwatch Pkwy. Follow signs to Augusta, staying on Riverwatch as it enters Augusta and becomes Jones St. Continue on Jones St. until it ends at a T intersection. Turn left on 10th St.; turn right on Reynolds St. Follow Reynolds St. to 6th St. Museum is on 6th St. between Reynolds and Broad sts. Parking is available off either street.

Chickamauga (see also Fort Oglethorpe, GA)

7 **Site:** GORDON-LEE MANSION, 217 Cove Rd., Chickamauga, GA 30707,
☎ 706/375-4728

Description: This antebellum mansion was completed in 1847 and is now a bed-and-breakfast. Located in the Chickamauga Battlefield area, the home served the Union army first as General Rosecrans's headquarters and then as its main hospital during the bloodiest 2 days in American history, when 37,000 Civil War soldiers became casualties. The Gordon-Lee mansion is open for tours by appointment only.

Open to Public: Call for appointment.

Admission Fees: Group tours by appointment only: $5/person.

Visitor Services: Tours, museum, information, rest rooms, lodging, catering for parties and receptions.

Directions: From I-75: take exit 141. Turn left on Hwy. 2 toward the Chickamauga Battlefield. Follow Hwy. 2 for 6 miles. Turn left on Hwy. 27 south. Go through the battlefield and turn right at the first traffic signal after leaving the park. Go to the next traffic signal and turn left. Travel to the traffic signal in downtown Chickamauga and turn left. The mansion is the fourth building on the right.

Columbus

8 **Site:** WOODRUFF MUSEUM OF CIVIL WAR HISTORY, P.O. Box 1022, Columbus, GA
31902, ☎ 706/327-9798

Description: The Confederate Naval Museum displays the recovered remains of the ironclad ram *Jackson* and sail/steam gunboat *Chattahoochee*. Museum exhibits interpret the Confederate Navy's innovative efforts to counter the established U.S. Navy and display artifacts recovered from the ships.

Open to Public: Tues–Fri 10am–5pm, Sat–Sun 1–5pm.

Admission Fees: Free.

Visitor Services: Museum, gift shop, information, rest rooms.

Directions: Located at the intersection of U.S. 280 and U.S. 27 in the South Commons parking lot.

Crawfordville

9 | Site: ALEXANDER H. STEPHENS STATE HISTORIC PARK, P.O. Box 283, Crawfordville, GA 30631, ☎ 706/456-2602

Description: This historic park consists of the 1875 house and outbuildings of Alexander Stephens, vice president of the Confederacy. Located beside Stephens's home is a Confederate museum that houses one of Georgia's finest collections of Civil War artifacts.

Open to Public: Tues–Sat 9am–5pm, Sun 2–5pm. Last tour at 4pm.

Admission Fees: Adults $2.50, children 5–18 $1.50. Call for group rates.

Visitor Services: Camping, trails, museum, gift shop, information, rest rooms.

Directions: From I-20: take exit 55 and follow signs to the park (approximately 2 miles).

Dallas

10 | Site: PICKETT'S MILL BATTLEFIELD STATE HISTORIC SITE, 2640 Mt. Tabor Rd., Dallas, GA 30132, ☎ 770/443-7850

Description: The Battle of Pickett's Mill involved 24,000 troops and resulted in a Confederate victory. The Union forces under Gen. Oliver O. Howard suffered 1,600 casualties, while the Confederates, under Gen. Patrick R. Cleburne, suffered only 500. The battlefield is in an excellent state of preservation.

Open to Public: Tues–Sat 9am–5pm, Sun noon–5pm. Closed Mon (except federal holidays).

Admission Fees: Adults $2, children $1, groups of adults $1.50 each, groups of children 75¢ each. For groups of 15 or more, call for rates.

Visitor Services: Trails, museum, gift shop, information, rest rooms.

Regularly Scheduled Events: *First weekend in June:* Annual living history encampment; *Autumn:* Reenactment of the Confederate night attack; *All year:* Weekend interpretive programs.

Directions: From I-75: take exit 120 and follow Hwy. 92 south to Dallas-Acworth Rd. Take Dallas-Acworth Rd. to Mt. Tabor Rd. and turn left; after 1 mile, you will see the entrance on the left.

Dalton

11 | Site: PRATER'S MILL. Mailing address: P.O. Drawer H, Varnell, GA 30756, ☎ 706/275-MILL (6455)

Description: Built in 1855, Prater's Mill is a water-powered gristmill that still grinds corn and wheat the old-fashioned way. During the Civil War, both Union and Confederate troops camped at the mill.

Open to Public: Grounds open daily. Buildings open twice annually during the fair.

Admission Fees: None.

Visitor Services: Interpretive markers.

Regularly Scheduled Events: *Mother's Day weekend in May and Columbus Day weekend in Oct:* Prater's Mill Country Fair.

Directions: Located on GA 2, 10 miles northeast of Dalton. From I-75: take exit 138; travel north on Hwy. 210 for 4.5 miles; turn right on GA 2 and continue 2.6 miles to the site.

Fitzgerald

12 **Site:** BLUE & GRAY MUSEUM, Municipal Building (Old Depot), P.O. Box 1285, Fitzgerald, GA 31750, ☎ 912/423-5375

Description: Fitzgerald's Blue & Gray Museum tells a story unique in the nation: how a colony of Union veterans cleared a forest and built this town in Georgia among former enemies, replaced hatred and division with understanding and brotherhood, and organized Battalion 1, Blue and Gray. A true reuniting of America here!

Open to Public: Mar–Oct: Mon–Fri 2–5pm.

Admission Fees: Adults $1, children 50¢.

Visitor Services: Museum, rest rooms.

Regularly Scheduled Events: *Daily:* Museum conducts a Roll Call of the States. Visitors have their picture taken with the flag of their state.

Directions: From I-75: take exit 28 in Ashburn. Go east under overpass for 5 miles. Turn right on 107; travel 20 miles straight until dead end on Merrimac Dr.; turn right on Merrimac. Go to traffic light and take a left onto Central Ave. Watch for museum signs.

Fort Oglethorpe

13 **Site:** CHICKAMAUGA AND CHATTANOOGA NATIONAL MILITARY PARK, P.O. Box 2128, Fort Oglethorpe, GA 30742, ☎ 706/866-9241

Description: This National Military Park commemorates the Battle of Chickamauga and the Battle for Chattanooga. The objective was the Chattanooga, Tennessee, region—the gateway to the Deep South. Without a fight, the Union army maneuvered the Confederates out of Chattanooga; and, despite being defeated at Chickamauga on September 19–20, 1863, they were able to hold onto the city. The Confederates, failing to properly exploit their Chickamauga victory, only lay siege to the town and two months later were defeated in the battles for Chattanooga on November 23–25, 1865. Fighting on Lookout Mountain and Missionary Ridge was most decisive.

Open to Public: *Visitors Center:* Daily 8am–4:45pm, summer 8am–5:45pm. *Battlefield grounds:* 8am–dusk.

Admission Fees: Free. *Orientation film:* Adults $3, children 6–16 $1.50, children under 6 free, seniors $1.50.

Visitor Services: Trails, museum, bookstore, information, rest rooms, handicapped access, tours.

Regularly Scheduled Events: *Sept and Nov on weekend closest to battle dates:* Anniversary commemorations.

Directions: From I-75 in GA: take exit 141; go west on GA 2 for 6 miles to U.S. 27; turn left onto U.S. 27 to battlefield. From I-24 in TN: take exit 180B; go south on U.S. 27 to battlefield.

Irwinville

 Site: THE JEFF DAVIS STATE HISTORIC SITE. Mailing address: 338 Jeff Davis Park Rd., Fitzgerald, GA 31750, ☎ 912/831-2335

Description: On May 10, 1865, after a flight that lasted nearly a month and saw the breakdown of the remnant Confederate government, President Jefferson Davis was captured here by forces of the 1st Wisconsin and the 4th Michigan cavalries. In the rush to apprehend Davis and collect a piece of the $100,000 reward for his capture, two Michigan soldiers, John Rupert and John Hines, were mistakenly shot and killed by friendly Wisconsin troopers. It was also here that the falsehood of Davis's trying to escape in his wife's clothing was started. Most important, it was here that the Confederacy breathed its last breath and, with the fall of the executive branch, ceased to exist.

Open to Public: Tues–Sat 9am–5pm, Sun 2–5:30pm. Closed Mon (except legal holidays).

Admission Fees: Adults $2, children 6–18 $1. Group rates available on request.

Visitor Services: Museum, gift shop, information, rest rooms, handicapped access.

Regularly Scheduled Events: *Commemoration Day (Jefferson Davis's Birthday):* Call for schedule.

Directions: From I-75: take exit 26; go east 14 miles to Irwinville on GA 32; follow the signs once you are in town. The park is 1 mile north of Irwinville.

Kennesaw

15 Site: KENNESAW MOUNTAIN NATIONAL BATTLEFIELD PARK, 905 Kennesaw Mountain Dr., Kennesaw, GA 30152, ☎ 770/427-4686

Description: In June 1864, Gen. William T. Sherman's advance toward Atlanta was delayed for 2 weeks at Kennesaw Mountain by Confederate Gen. Joseph E. Johnston.

The 2,884-acre National Park preserves the battleground where Johnston's army temporarily stopped the Union advance southward.

Open to Public: *Visitors Center:* 8:30am–5pm. *Park:* Daylight hours.

Admission Fees: Free.

Visitor Services: Trails, museum, gift shop, information, rest rooms, handicapped access.

Regularly Scheduled Events: *June:* Anniversary commemoration.

Directions: From I-75: take exit 116 and follow signs. The park is approximately 4 miles from the interstate.

---

16 **Site:** KENNESAW CIVIL WAR MUSEUM, 2829 Cherokee St., Kennesaw, GA 30144, ☎ 770/427-2117

Description: This museum houses "The General," the train that was stolen by a group of Union soldiers known as Andrews' Raiders. The Andrews's Railroad Raid is an interesting chapter in Civil War history and has been the subject of numerous books and even a Walt Disney movie. Besides housing "The General," the museum also contains an extensive collection of Civil War artifacts.

Open to Public: Mon–Sat 9:30am–5:30pm, Sun noon–5:30pm.

Admission Fees: Adults $3, children 7–15 $1.50, seniors $2. Group rate available.

Visitor Services: Museum, gift shop, handicapped access.

Regularly Scheduled Events: *Apr:* Big Shanty Day.

Directions: From I-75: take exit 118 (Wade Green Rd.). Turn left, and it is 2.5 miles to Kennesaw site. The museum is approximately 30 miles north of Atlanta.

Lithia Springs

17 **Site:** SWEETWATER CREEK STATE CONSERVATION PARK, P.O. Box 816, Lithia Springs, GA 30122, ☎ 770/732-5871

Description: The park features a variety of natural and cultural resources, including the ruins of the New Manchester Manufacturing Company, a Civil War–era textile mill. Gen. William T. Sherman's forces burned the mill and the surrounding town during their campaign for Atlanta in 1864, and the factory's female factory workers were deported to the North.

Open to Public: *Park:* Daily 7am–9:45pm. *Trails:* Close at dusk.

Admission Fees: Parking $2. Free guided tours are available to groups with a reservation.

Visitor Services: Trails, snacks, gift shop, information, rest rooms, handicapped access, boat rentals.

Regularly Scheduled Events: *Sept (date varies):* New Manchester Day—a living history demonstration; *June:* Native American Day.

Directions: From I-20 west: take exit 12 (Thornton Rd. exit) and turn left onto Camp Creek Pkwy.; go .25 mile and across bridge to Blairs Bridge Rd.; go about 2 miles to a 4-way stop. Turn left on Mt. Vernon Rd., which leads into the park. The park office is the first left after you cross the bridge.

Macon

18 Site: GRISWOLDVILLE BATTLEFIELD. Mailing address: c/o Georgia State Parks, 205 Butler St., Ste. 1352, Atlanta, GA 30334, ☎ 404/656-2770

Description: The town of Griswoldville was based on a mill and armament factory that produced Griswold pistols and other equipment. On November 20, 1864, Maj. Gen. William T. Sherman's columns on their March to the Sea engaged and all but destroyed the Georgia Militia and the town of Griswoldville. A 17-acre tract that was the site of the battle has been purchased and preserved; it is managed by Georgia State Parks as an unmanned site.

Open to Public: Daily during daylight hours.

Admission Fees: Free.

Visitor Services: Interpretive sign, parking.

Directions: From Macon: take U.S. 80 east to GA 57; take GA 57 toward Gordon to Henderson Rd.; turn left and proceed approximately 1.25 miles; turn right on Griswoldville Rd. and proceed approximately 1.5 miles to Baker Cemetery Rd. The battle site and parking are on the left.

19 Site: OLD CANNONBALL HOUSE AND CONFEDERATE MUSEUM, 856 Mulberry St., Macon, GA 31201, ☎ 912/745-5982

Description: The house was struck during the Battle of Dunlap's Hill on July 30, 1864, by a cannonball fired from General Stoneman's battery, positioned on a bluff overlooking the river at what is now Ocmulgee National Monument. The Union forces were firing on the Johnston-Hay house on the next corner, which was known to store the Confederate Treasury.

Open to Public: Mon–Sat 10am–4pm.

Admission Fees: Adults $4, students $1, children 50¢, seniors $3.50.

Visitor Services: Museum, gift shop, garden, located on walking tour with other points of interest.

Regularly Scheduled Events: *Sept:* Cherry Blossom Tours; *Dec:* Victorian Tea Parties under the tree.

Directions: Take I-75 to I-16; exit at Spring St.; turn right, cross bridge, and proceed through 2 traffic lights; turn left on Mulberry St. Museum is fourth house on the right.

Marietta

20 **Site:** MARIETTA NATIONAL CEMETERY, 500 Washington Ave., Marietta, GA 30060,
☎ 770/428-5631

Description: The National Cemetery is the burial site of more than 13,000 Union soldiers who were casualties from battles in the area, such as New Hope Church, Pickett's Mill, and Kennesaw Mountain.

Open to Public: *Cemetery:* Daily from dawn to dusk. *Office:* Mon–Fri 8am–4:30pm.

Admission Fees: Free.

Visitor Services: Rest rooms.

Regularly Scheduled Events: Services held on Memorial Day and Veterans Day; *First week in Feb:* Four Chaplains Day; *Second week in Sept:* Special POW/MIA Day; *Anniversary week of Dec 7:* Pearl Harbor Day.

Directions: From I-75 north: take exit 113; turn left onto N. Marietta Pkwy. (120 Loop). Turn left onto Cole St. The cemetery is straight ahead. There is access to the cemetery from Cole St. or Washington St.

21 **Site:** WESTERN AND ATLANTIC PASSENGER DEPOT, Marietta Welcome Center & Visitors
Bureau, No. 4 Depot St., Marietta, GA 30060, ☎ 770/429-1115

Description: This Victorian brick structure was built in 1898 on the site of the original passenger depot (1840s) that was burned by Gen. William T. Sherman's troops in 1864. The depot in Marietta is where, in 1862, Andrews' Raiders boarded "The General" and began their fateful journey toward "the great locomotive chase" (Andrews' Raid). The depot is also the site from which women workers from the Roswell mills were deported to the North as prisoners of war.

Open to Public: Mon–Fri 9am–5pm, Sat 11am–4pm, Sun 1–4pm.

Admission Fees: Free.

Visitor Services: Gift shop, information, rest rooms, handicapped access.

Regularly Scheduled Events: *Last Sun in Apr:* Taste of Marietta—a food festival; *First weekend in Dec:* Marietta pilgrimage Christmas home tour.

Directions: From I-75: take exit 113. Heading west toward Marietta, proceed 2.5 miles to Mill St.; turn left onto Mill St. A parking lot is immediately on the right. The Welcome Center is across railroad tracks from the parking lot.

Milledgeville

22 **Site:** THE OLD GOVERNORS' MANSION, 120 South Clarke St., Milledgeville, GA 31061,
☎ 912/445-4545

Description: This was the executive residence of Georgia's governors from its completion in 1839 until 1868. Governor Joseph E. Brown and his family lived in the mansion during the Civil War. Gen. William T. Sherman spent a night at the mansion during his March to the Sea.

Open to Public: Tues–Sat 10am–4pm, Sun 2–4pm. Closed Christmas Eve–New Year's Day.

Admission Fees: Adults $5, children $2. Groups: 9 or more adults with reservation $3, children $1.

Visitor Services: Museum, gift shop, handicapped access, rest rooms.

Regularly Scheduled Events: *Thanksgiving–Christmas:* Victorian Christmas at the mansion.

Directions: From I-20: take 441 South to Milledgeville. From I-16: take the Spring St. exit to Hwy. 49 to Milledgeville. The mansion is on the corner of Hancock (Hwy. 49) and Clarke sts., directly across from Georgia College and State University.

Millen

23 Site: MAGNOLIA SPRINGS STATE PARK, Rte. 5 Box 488, Millen, GA 30442, ☎ 912/982-1660

Description: Because of the overflow from Andersonville Prison, three sites were chosen to relieve the overcrowding. During the Civil War, this site was called Camp Lawton and was used as a prison camp because of its natural springs, plentiful timber for building stockades, and proximity to the railroad. Fort Lawton was the largest prison in the world during its time.

Open to Public: *Park:* Daily 7am–10pm. *Park office:* Daily 8am–5pm.

Admission Fees: Parking $2; free parking on Wed.

Visitor Services: Aquarium, lodging, camping, snacks, gift shop, information, rest rooms.

Regularly Scheduled Events: *Last weekend of Mar:* Arts & Crafts Festival with Civil War living history encampment; *End of Nov:* A square dance and clogging weekend.

Directions: From I-16 at Metter, GA: take Hwy. 121 to Millen; take a left onto 121/25. The park is 5 miles north of Millen on Hwy. 25. From I-20: exit onto Bobby Jones Expressway (Hwy. 520); go approximately 7 miles; exit on Peach Orchard Hwy. and Windsor Spring Rd. (Hwy. 25); go through first light to dead end. Turn right; go through Waynesboro (30 miles) and proceed 17 miles south to park.

Northwest Georgia

24 Site: ATLANTA CAMPAIGN PAVILION PARKS

Description: These five roadside parks were constructed in the 1930s by the WPA to graphically describe the Atlanta Campaign, which occurred from May 7 to September 2, 1864. The parks are located along the Hwy. 41 corridor in Ringgold, Dalton, Resaca, Cassville, and Dallas.

Open to Public: Daily during daylight hours.

Admission Fees: Free.

Visitor Services: Memorial plaques.

Directions: Located along Hwy. 41, which parallels I-75 in northwest GA. The Blue and Gray Trail brochure includes a map and directions. The brochure and map are available free from Northeast Georgia Travel Association, P.O. Box 184, Calhoun, GA 30703-0184, ☎ **706/624-1488,** or on the Internet at http:/www.ngeorgia.com/travel/bgtrail.html.

THE BLUE AND GRAY TRAIL

Northwest Georgia was the setting for some of the Civil War's most dramatic events. The trail features 61 sites that are accessible to visitors, including battlefields, museums, cemeteries, forts, and railroad depots.

For more information: The Blue and Gray Trail brochure includes a map and directions and is available free from: Northeast Georgia Travel Association, P.O. Box 184, Calhoun, GA 30703-0184, ☎ **706/624-1488,** or on the Internet at http:/www.ngeorgia.com/travel/bgtrail.html.

Resaca

25 Site: RESACA CONFEDERATE CEMETERY, c/o Calhoun-Gordon Co. Chamber of Commerce, 300 S. Wall St., Calhoun, GA, ☎ 800/887-3811

Description: The Resaca Confederate Cemetery is the final resting place for approximately 400 Confederate soldiers who fell in the bloody 2-day Battle of Resaca on May 14–15, 1864, between the forces of Generals Johnston and Sherman. The daughters of Maj. John Green, the Superintendent of the Georgia Railroad, collected and reinterred the bodies from shallow graves to this plot known as the Confederate Cemetery, the first of its kind in Georgia.

Open to Public: Daily during daylight hours.

Admission Fees: Free.

Visitor Services: Brochure available.

Regularly Scheduled Events: *Third weekend in May:* Memorial service during the reenactment of the Battle of Resaca.

Directions: From I-75: take exit 133 and travel east on Hwy. 136. Turn left (north) on Hwy. 41 and proceed 1.7 mile. Turn right into the cemetery.

Richmond Hill

26 **Site:** FORT MCALLISTER STATE HISTORIC PARK, 3894 Ft. McAllister Rd., Richmond Hill, GA 31324, ☎ 912/727-2339

Description: Located on the south bank of the Great Ogeechee River, this park is the home of the best-preserved earthwork fortification of the Confederacy. The earthworks and bombproofs withstood bombardments by the heaviest naval guns and have been restored to their 1863–1864 appearance. This beautiful coastal park offers a museum containing Civil War artifacts as well as camping and picnic facilities.

Open to Public: Tues–Sat 9am–5pm, Sun 2–5:30pm.

Admission Fees: Adults $2, children $1. Group prices vary.

Visitor Services: Camping, museum, gift shop, information, rest rooms, handicapped access.

Regularly Scheduled Events: *Sat before Memorial Day:* Memorial Day celebration; *First weekend in Dec:* Winter Civil War Muster.

Directions: From I-95: take exit 15; proceed 9 miles southeast on Hwy. 144. Turn left on Spur 144 to park.

Roswell

27 **Site:** BULLOCH HALL, 180 Bulloch Ave., P.O. Box 1309, Roswell, GA 30077, ☎ 770/992-1731

Description: This 1840 home was built by Major James Bulloch and was the site of the December 1853 marriage between Martha Bulloch and Theodore Roosevelt of New York (later becoming parents of President Theodore Roosevelt and grandparents of Eleanor Roosevelt, wife of President Franklin D. Roosevelt). The house is now a museum, featuring period rooms, a research library, and a Civil War–artifact room. The surrounding historic district features many structures of the Civil War period. The Roswell Presbyterian Church was a Union hospital in 1864. The former locations of several mills that were burned by General Sherman are marked.

Open to Public: Mon–Sat 10am–3pm (last tour at 2pm), Sun 1–4pm (last tour at 3pm).

Admission Fees: Adults $5, children $3.

Visitor Services: Tours, museum, information, gift shop, rest rooms, handicapped access to main floor and rest room.

Regularly Scheduled Events: *Mid-Mar:* Great American Coverup quilt show; *Two days in early Dec:* Reenactment of 1853 wedding; *Dec:* Christmas at Bulloch Hall.

Directions: From I-85 or I-285: travel north on GA 400. Take Northridge exit and turn right. Take the next right onto Dunwoody Place. Stay on Dunwoody Place until you reach Roswell Rd. Turn right onto Roswell Rd., go to Historic Roswell Sq., and turn left at the light onto Hwy. 120. The parking lot is 200 yards ahead on the right.

Savannah

28 Site: FORT JAMES JACKSON, 1 Old Fort Jackson Rd., Savannah, GA 31404, ☎ 912/232-3945

Description: The fort saw its greatest use as the headquarters for the Confederate defenses of the Savannah River during the Civil War and is the oldest standing fort in Georgia, dating from the 1740s.

Open to Public: Daily 9am–5pm.

Admission Fees: Adults $2.50; students, military, and seniors $2; children under 5 free.

Visitor Services: Museum, gift shop, information, rest rooms, handicapped access.

Directions: From I-16: take Montgomery St. exit; turn right on Bay St., which merges with President St. Follow President St. for approximately 1.5 miles. Look for Old Fort Jackson sign.

29 Site: FORT PULASKI NATIONAL MONUMENT, P.O. Box 30757, Savannah, GA 31410-0757, ☎ 912/786-5787

Description: On April 11, 1862, Union forces overtook the fort in only 30 hours. The fall of Fort Pulaski secured Union control over Southern ports and kept Savannah from exporting cotton and importing vital military and civilian goods. This remarkably intact example of 19th-century military architecture is preserved for future generations.

Open to Public: Daily 8:30am–5:15pm. Call for extended summer hours.

Admission Fees: Adults $2, seniors free with Golden Age Passport, children under 16 free. Maximum charge of $4 per car.

Visitor Services: Trails, museum, gift shop, information, rest rooms, handicapped access.

Regularly Scheduled Events: *Apr:* Siege and Reduction Weekend; *Memorial Day and Labor Day:* Troop encampment; *Dec:* Confederate nog party and candle lantern tours.

Directions: From I-95: follow I-16 or U.S. 80 to Savannah, GA. Head east on U.S. 80 toward Tybee Island. Fort Pulaski is approximately 15 miles east of Savannah.

30 Site: GREEN-MELDRIM HOUSE, St. John's Church, 1 West Macon St., Savannah, GA 31401, ☎ 912/232-1251

Description: This restored and furnished mid-19th-century Gothic Revival–style home of Charles Green served as the headquarters for Union General Sherman during the winter of 1864–1865. The house is owned and operated by St. John's Episcopal Church.

Open to Public: Tues, Thurs, Fri, and Sat 10am–4pm; closed Mon, Wed, and Sun.

Closed also 2 weeks before Easter, Dec 15–Jan 15, and the week of Nov 10–11.

Admission Fees: Adults $4, children $2. Call for special group rates.

Visitor Services: Guided tours.

Directions: At the end of I-16 east is Montgomery St. At the first traffic signal, turn right on Liberty St. Go 5 blocks and turn right on Bull St. Go 1 block to Madison Sq. The house fronts Madison Sq. between Charlton and Harris sts.

---

31 **Site:** THE HISTORIC RAILROAD SHOPS AND THE SAVANNAH HISTORY MUSEUM, 303 Martin Luther King, Jr. Blvd., Savannah, GA 31401, ☎ 912/238-1779

Description: Both sites are National Historic Landmarks. A restored 19th-century railroad terminal houses this museum and a theater that tells the history of Savannah. The Historic Railroad Shops are a railroad repair and manufacturing facility, the oldest surviving and best example of a mid-19th-century integrated railroad shop in the United States. The railroad complex was used in the filming of the movie *Glory*, about the Fifty-fourth Massachusetts Colored Infantry.

Open to Public: *Museum:* Daily 8:30am–5pm. *Railroad Shops:* Daily 10am–4pm.

Admission Fees: *Museum:* Adults $3, seniors $2.50, children 6–12 $1.75. *Railroad Shops:* Adults $2.50; students, military, and seniors $2; children under 5 free.

Visitor Services: Food, museum, gift shop, information, rest rooms, handicapped access.

Directions: Take I-16 east until it merges into Montgomery St.; turn left onto Liberty St.; go 1 block and turn right on Martin Luther King, Jr. Blvd. Go a half block and turn left under a brick archway into the parking lot.

Stone Mountain

32 **Site:** GEORGIA'S STONE MOUNTAIN PARK, P.O. Box 778, Stone Mountain, GA 30086, ☎ 770/498-5690

Description: Located 16 miles east of Atlanta, Stone Mountain Park is a 3,200-acre world of recreation and family fun. The centerpiece of the Park is Stone Mountain itself, the world's largest exposed mass of granite. The memorial carving on the face of the mountain is about the size of a football field. The carving commemorates the Confederate states with the figures of Jefferson Davis, Robert E. Lee, and Stonewall Jackson. The Park also features a restored antebellum plantation and the Discovering Stone Mountain Museum, containing a large Civil War collection.

Open to Public: *Attractions:* Daily 10am–5:30pm. Memorial Day–Labor Day: Daily 10am–8pm. *Park:* Daily all year, 6am–midnight.

Admission Fees: *Park entry:* Free. Vehicle parking permit: Cars $6/day or $25 annual pass. Separate attractions (Skylift, train, riverboat, antebellum plantation, Antique Car and Treasure Museum, Discovering Stone Mountain Museum, Road to Tara Museum): Adults $3.50–$4, children 3–11) $2.50–$3. Call for group rates.

Visitor Services: Lodging (2 hotels), conference center, golf, tennis, camping, trails, food, museum, gift shops, information, rest rooms, handicapped access.

Regularly Scheduled Events: *Last weekend of each month:* Civil War living history demonstrations; *Mid-Apr:* Civil War encampment; *Late Mar:* Taste of the South; *First weekend after Labor Day:* Yellow Daisy Festival; *Mid-Oct:* Highland Games; *Late Oct:* Tour of Southern Ghosts; *First weekend in Dec:* Deck the Halls at the Antebellum Plantation.

Directions: From I-285: take exit 30B (U.S. 78); go 7 miles east to Stone Mountain Park exit.

Washington

33 **Site:** ROBERT TOOMBS STATE HISTORIC SITE, 216 E. Robert Toombs Ave., Washington, GA 30673, ☎ 706/678-2226

Description: This site was the home of Gen. Robert Augustus Toombs, a successful planter, lawyer, and outspoken Georgia politician, who used his influence to persuade the state to secede from the Union. As Secretary of State to the Confederacy, general, and seasoned battle leader, he never took the Oath of Allegiance to the United States and died as an unreconstructed Rebel.

Open to Public: Tues–Sat 9am–5pm, Sun 2–5:30pm; closed Mon (except federal holidays).

Admission Fees: Adults $2.50, youth 6–18 $1.50, children under 6 free. Groups of adults $2, groups of youths $1.50, groups of children 25¢.

Visitor Services: Information, rest rooms, handicapped access to first floor.

Regularly Scheduled Events: *First Sat in Apr:* Spring home tour; *Last Sun in June:* Toombs family reunion; *Second Sun in Dec:* Christmas tea at the Toombs House.

Directions: Washington is 45 miles east of Athens, GA, on Hwy. 78 and 50 miles west of Augusta, GA. From I-20: take exit 59 (Thomson/Washington). Follow Hwy. 78 east into downtown Washington. Turn left on Robert Toombs Ave.

34 **Site:** WASHINGTON HISTORICAL MUSEUM, 308 E. Robert Toombs Ave., Washington, GA 30673, ☎ 706/678-2105

Description: Exhibits in this Federal-style house (ca. 1835) highlight the Confederacy and Reconstruction as well as domestic art and local history. A guided tour is available to interpret memorabilia from the last Confederate cabinet meeting as Jefferson Davis fled south. The display includes Jefferson Davis's camp chest, original photos, signed documents, and Gen. Robert Toombs' uniform.

Admission Fees: Adults (age 13 and over) $2, children 5–12 $1, children under 5 free. Call for special rates for groups of 15 or more.

Visitor Services: Tour, museum, information, gift shop, rest rooms.

Directions: From I-20: take exit 59 (U.S. 78). Follow U.S. 78 west for 20 miles to downtown Washington. The museum is located on E. Robert Toombs Ave.

West Point

35 **Site:** FORT TYLER, West 6th Ave., P.O. Box 715, West Point, GA 31833-0715, ☎ 706/645-8162

Description: The earthen fort was built to defend strategic Chattahoochee River bridges and the military depot in West Point. The fort was also the site of one of the last engagements of the Civil War, fought on April 16, 1865, between Union cavalry under command of Col. Oscar LaGrange and Confederates under Gen. Robert Tyler. The Confederates, numbering fewer than 300 men, managed to withstand advances by 3,500 Union soldiers for 8 hours before the fort was finally captured.

Open to Public: Daily during daylight hours.

Admission Fees: Free.

Visitor Services: Trails, handicapped access.

Regularly Scheduled Events: *Weekend in mid-Apr:* Battle anniversary reenactment of Confederate Guard.

Directions: From I-85: take exit 1 to West Point. Cross over the Chattahoochee River and turn right on Third Ave. in downtown. Turn left on 10th St. Turn right at the historical marker on West Sixth Ave. Monument marks trail to fort.

ILLINOIS

*B*Y 1860, THE REPUBLICAN AND DEMOCRATIC CONVENTIONS nominated as their standard-bearers two political giants from Illinois: Abraham Lincoln and Stephen A. Douglas. If Lincoln's election accelerated events leading to the outbreak of war, his leadership guided a nation through war toward reconciliation in 1865.

While no major battle was fought within Illinois, it became an important supply area for much of the Western campaign. In spite of a large population with family ties to the South, Southern Illinois remained loyal to the Union cause.

More than 250,000 men from Illinois served in the Union forces. Illinois was one of a few states to exceed its quota for troops throughout the war. Through the political leadership of Abraham Lincoln and the military leadership of Ulysses S. Grant, Illinois provided extraordinary individuals to confront the nation's most serious crisis.

by Thomas Schwartz, State Historian, Illinois Historic Preservation Agency

THE LINCOLN HERITAGE TRAIL

The Lincoln Heritage Trail allows travelers to gain a greater understanding of one of the nation's most revered presidents by tracing his life from his modest birthplace in Kentucky, to his frontier youth in Indiana, to his early successes as a country lawyer in Illinois. The Lincoln Heritage Trail guides visitors to National Park properties and state historic sites that mark the places where Lincoln lived, studied, played, and worked.

Primary sites in Illinois include: Lincoln's New Salem State Historic Site, New Salem; and Lincoln Home National Historic Site, Springfield. Other Illinois attractions include the Lincoln Trail Memorial, Vandalia Statehouse State Historic Site, Lincoln Log Cabin State Historic Site, Mt. Pulaski Courthouse State Historic Site, Postville Courthouse State Historic Site, David Davis Mansion State Historic Site, Metamora Courthouse State Historic Site, and Lincoln Tomb State Historic Site.

For more information: A free brochure that covers the entire Lincoln Heritage Trail in Kentucky, Indiana, and Illinois can be ordered from the Illinois Bureau of Tourism: ☎ 800/223-0121. The brochure is also available at places along the Trail.

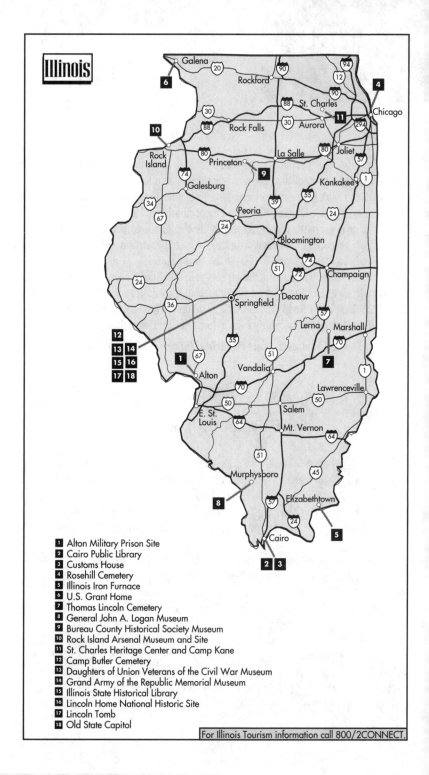

Illinois

Galena
20
Rockford
94
12
6
90
88   St. Charles
90
30
10
88   Rock Falls   Aurora   294   Chicago
30
4
Rock   80   La Salle   80   Joliet
Island   Princeton   57
74   9   1
Galesburg   39   55   Kankakee
34
55
67   Peoria   24
24
Bloomington
51
74
24   72   Champaign
36   Springfield   Decatur
12   55   Lerna   57   Marshall
13   14   70
15   16   67   51   7
17   18   1   Vandalia
Alton
1
70
50   Lawrenceville
E. St.   50
Louis   64   Salem
Mt. Vernon   64
51
45
Murphysboro   57   Elizabethtown
8   24   5
Cairo
2   3

1 Alton Military Prison Site
2 Cairo Public Library
3 Customs House
4 Rosehill Cemetery
5 Illinois Iron Furnace
6 U.S. Grant Home
7 Thomas Lincoln Cemetery
8 General John A. Logan Museum
9 Bureau County Historical Society Museum
10 Rock Island Arsenal Museum and Site
11 St. Charles Heritage Center and Camp Kane
12 Camp Butler Cemetery
13 Daughters of Union Veterans of the Civil War Museum
14 Grand Army of the Republic Memorial Museum
15 Illinois State Historical Library
16 Lincoln Home National Historic Site
17 Lincoln Tomb
18 Old State Capitol

For Illinois Tourism information call 800/2CONNECT.

Alton

1 **Site:** ALTON MILITARY PRISON SITE. Mailing address: 100A E. Broadway, Alton, IL 62002. Physical address: 212 William St., ☎ 618/465-6676

Description: Erected as the first Illinois State Penitentiary, it served as the Alton Federal Military Prison from February 1862 to July 1865, housing more than 15,000 prisoners during the Civil War. Confederate POWs, Federal soldiers, guerrillas, and civilians were held as prisoners. More than 2,000 died of disease. A monument to the 1,543 Confederate soldiers who died at the prison is located 2 miles north of the site.

Open to Public: Daily from dawn to dusk.

Admission Fees: Free.

Visitor Services: Interpretive panels.

Directions: From I-270: take Rte. 367 north. Cross Clark Bridge and turn left at the Alton end of the bridge. Follow 67 to Broadway and turn left. Proceed 2 blocks to Williams St. and turn right. Proceed one-half block; the prison site is on the left.

Cairo

2 **Site:** CAIRO PUBLIC LIBRARY, 1609 Washington Ave., P.O. Box 151, Cairo, IL 62914-0151, ☎ 618/734-1840

Description: Cairo played a critical role in the Civil War. Cairo was a bastion for Union Gen. Ulysses S. Grant, enabling him to penetrate deeply into the South, controlling major waterways and railroads. The Federal Army of the Tennessee, the Siege of Vicksburg, and the Naval Battle for the Mississippi were all launched from Cairo's riverbanks. The Cairo Public Library contains an extensive collection of primary and secondary research documents relating to the city's role in the Union army's control of the Western Theater in the Civil War.

Open to Public: Mon–Fri 10am–5pm, Sat 9am–noon.

Admission Fees: Free.

Visitor Services: Information.

Directions: From I-57: take exit 1 and proceed south on U.S. 51 to downtown Cairo. The library is located on the west side of Washington St. in the downtown business district.

3 **Site:** CUSTOMS HOUSE, 14th and Washington, Cairo, IL 62914-0724, ☎ 618/734-3637

Description: This local history museum with exhibits on Cairo's pivotal role in the Civil War includes artifacts from the USS *Cairo*, a gunboat built in the local shipyards, sunk by a Confederate torpedo in 1862, and raised in 1964.

Open to Public: Mon–Fri 10am–noon and 1–3pm.

Admission Fees: Free; donations accepted.

Visitor Services: Museum, information.

Directions: From I-57: take exit 1 and proceed south on U.S. 51 to downtown Cairo. The Customs House is located on the east side of Washington St. in the downtown business district.

Chicago

4 **Site:** ROSEHILL CEMETERY, 5800 N. Ravenswood Ave., Chicago, IL 60660, ☎ 773/561-5940

Description: Rosehill Cemetery contains the graves of 14 Union generals, six drummer boys, and hundreds of Civil War soldiers. Members of the Eighth Illinois Cavalry, the unit that fired the first shots at Gettysburg, are buried here. Also buried here is a Chicago mayor who was charged with, and later acquitted of, assisting Confederate prisoners in escaping from Camp Douglas.

Open to Public: Mon–Sat 8am–5pm, Sun 10am–4pm.

Admission Fees: Free.

Visitor Services: Self-guided tours, information, rest rooms, handicapped access.

Directions: From I-94 (Edens Expwy.): travel east on Foster Ave. and then north on Ravenswood. From Lakeshore Dr.: travel north on Lakeshore (U.S. 41) and then west on Foster to Ravenswood.

Elizabethtown

5 **Site:** ILLINOIS IRON FURNACE, U.S. Forest Service, Elizabethtown, IL 62931, ☎ 618/287-2201

Description: During the Civil War, this structure was a principal furnace used for smelting iron ore. The restored structure features interpretive information. Fishing, hiking, and picnicking facilities are available.

Open to Public: Daily 6am–10pm.

Admission Fees: Free.

Visitor Services: Information.

Directions: Located about 5 miles from Rosiclare near the intersection of State Rtes. 146 and 34. Follow signs.

Galena

6 **Site:** U.S. GRANT HOME, 510 Bouthillier St., Galena, IL 61036, ☎ 815/777-0248

Description: On August 18, 1865, citizens of Galena celebrated the return of its Civil War hero Gen. Ulysses S. Grant by presenting him with this handsome furnished home. The house is typical of the Italianate style and is furnished with many original items from the Grant family.

Open to Public: Daily 9am–5pm. Closed most state and federal holidays.

Admission Fees: Suggested donations: Adults $2, children 18 and under $1.

Visitor Services: Tours, museum, information, rest rooms.

Directions: Galena is located on U.S. 20 and State Rte. 84; follow signs to the Grant home. Galena is 160 miles from Chicago, 85 miles from Moline, and 95 miles from Madison, WI.

U.S. Grant Home, Galena, IL. (Photograph by Jim Quick.)

Lerna

7 **Site:** THOMAS LINCOLN CEMETERY, 12988 Lincoln Hwy., Lerna, IL 62440, ☎ 217/345-4088

Description: This cemetery is the final resting place for many Civil War veterans and for Thomas and Sarah Lincoln, Abraham Lincoln's father and stepmother.

Open to Public: Daily from dawn to dusk.

Admission Fees: Free.

Visitor Services: None.

Directions: From I-59: exit at State Rte. 16 east and proceed toward Charleston; at the first traffic light, turn south; follow markers to Lincoln Memorial Hwy. to Thomas Lincoln Cemetery (approximately 10 miles).

Murphysboro

8 **Site:** GEN. JOHN A. LOGAN MUSEUM, 1613 Edith St., Murphysboro, IL 62966, ☎ 618/684-3455

Description: The Gen. John A. Logan Museum chronicles the life of this Civil War general from the time his parents arrived in Illinois until the death of his widow. The site includes a log cabin and the 1887 home of Samuel H. Dalton, former slave and Civil

War veteran. The site also tells the story of volunteer soldiers, black and white, who served throughout the war.

Open to Public: Apr–May and Sept–Oct: Sat–Sun 1–4pm. June–Aug: Mon, Wed, Fri, Sat, and Sun 1–4pm.

Admission Fees: Adults $1, children 50¢.

Visitor Services: Tours, museum, information, gift shop, rest rooms, handicapped access.

Directions: From I-57: take State Rte. 13 west to Murphysboro; the museum is located 2 blocks off Rte. 149 (Walnut St.).

Princeton

9 | **Site:** BUREAU COUNTY HISTORICAL SOCIETY MUSEUM, 109 Park Ave. West, Princeton, IL 61356-1927, ☎ 815/875-2184

Description: The 93rd Illinois Infantry was mustered from Bureau County for service in the Union army. The County Historical Museum contains an outstanding and extensive collection of artifacts and documents associated with the regiment. The collection is well researched and documented.

Open to Public: Mon and Wed–Sun 1–5pm. Closed Tues and Dec 24–Jan 31.

Admission Fees: Adults $2, children 50¢.

Visitor Services: Tours, museum, genealogy, gift shop.

Directions: From I-80: take Princeton exit and proceed into Princeton. (The road becomes Main St.) Continue on Main through two business districts to the 4-way stop, just before the courthouse. Turn right onto Park Ave., which curves. The museum is located at the end of the curve, across from the courthouse.

Rock Island

10 | **Site:** ROCK ISLAND ARSENAL MUSEUM AND SITE, Attn.: SIORI-CFM, Rock Island Arsenal, Rock Island, IL 61299-5000, ☎ 309/782-5021

Description: This was the site of a Confederate prison camp. The cemetery contains graves of nearly 2,000 Confederate prisoners. The adjoining national cemetery is the burial place of Union prison guards and subsequent veterans. The museum displays the history of Rock Island Arsenal and features an extensive collection of small arms. Rock Island Arsenal is an active U.S. Army installation.

Open to Public: Daily 10am–4pm. Closed Thanksgiving Day, Christmas Eve, Christmas Day, New Year's Eve, and New Year's Day.

Admission Fees: Free.

Visitor Services: Museum, information, gift shop, rest rooms, handicapped access; food available Mon–Fri.

Directions: From I-74 in Moline, IL: take 7th Ave. exit west to 14th St. Turn right and follow to the Island. Follow signs to museum.

St. Charles

11 **Site:** ST. CHARLES HERITAGE CENTER AND CAMP KANE, MAIN MUSEUM, 2 E. Main St., St. Charles, IL 60174, ☎ 630/584-6967

Description: During the Civil War, St. Charles played an important role as a training ground for the 8th and 17th Illinois Cavalry, as a recruiting center, and as the home of Gen. John Farnsworth. The Main Museum exhibits artifacts, pictures, and written information about St. Charles' association with the Underground Railroad and the Civil War. Camp Kane trained more than 1,000 men for the Union army, including the 8th and 17th Illinois Cavalry units. General Farnsworth donated the land for Camp Kane, which today is a community park. The museum interprets the Civil War history of St. Charles and Camp Kane.

Open to Public: Mar–Dec: Sun–Fri noon–4pm. Langum Park (former site of Camp Kane) is open daily from dawn to dusk.

Admission Fees: Free; donations welcome.

Visitor Services: Tours, gift shop, rest rooms, handicapped access.

Regularly Scheduled Events: *Sept:* Heritage Walk.

Directions: From I-88: exit at N. Farnsworth; follow north to Rte. 64 (Main St.); turn left (west) on Main St. and proceed into downtown. Museum is at the northeast corner of Fox River and Main St.

Springfield

12 **Site:** CAMP BUTLER CEMETERY, 5063 Camp Butler Rd., Springfield, IL 62702, ☎ 217/522-5764

Description: This was once the site of a Union Civil War training camp and Confederate prison. It is now a cemetery for veterans and their dependents.

Open to Public: Mon–Fri 8am–4:30pm.

Admission Fees: Free.

Visitor Services: Information, rest rooms.

Directions: From I-72: exit at Camp Butler Rd.; continue north on Camp Butler Rd. to the cemetery entrance.

13 **Site:** DAUGHTERS OF UNION VETERANS OF THE CIVIL WAR MUSEUM, 503 South Walnut St., Springfield, IL 62704-1932, ☎ 217/544-0616

Description: Collections of this museum include Civil War medals, photographs, currency, drums, uniforms, and a complete set of the official records.

Open to Public: Mon–Fri 9am–noon and 1–4pm.

Admission Fees: Free; donations welcome.

Visitor Services: Museum, gift shop.

Directions: From I-55: take the South Grand Ave. west exit to Walnut.

---

14 **Site:** GRAND ARMY OF THE REPUBLIC MEMORIAL MUSEUM, 629 South Seventh, Springfield, IL 62701, ☎ 217/522-4373

Description: This museum includes a large assortment of Civil War memorabilia, including tintypes by Civil War photographer Matthew Brady.

Open to Public: Tues–Sat 10am–4pm.

Admission Fees: Free; donations welcome.

Visitor Services: Museum.

Directions: From I-55: take the South Grand Ave. west exit to Ninth St.; turn north on Ninth St. to Cook St.; turn west on Cook St. to Seventh.

---

15 **Site:** ILLINOIS STATE HISTORICAL LIBRARY, 1 Old State Capitol Plaza, Springfield, IL 62701, ☎ 217/524-6358

Description: The Illinois State Historical Library collects the political, social, business, and military history of the State of Illinois. The collections include many Civil War letters, manuscripts, photographs, maps, Illinois regimental histories, and other memorabilia. The collections also include the largest single collection devoted to the prepresidential career of Abraham Lincoln.

Open to Public: Mon–Fri 8:30am–5pm. Closed on state and national holidays.

Admission Fees: Free.

Visitor Services: Displays, information, rest rooms.

Directions: From I-55: take the Clear Lake exit to Ninth St.; turn south on Ninth to Adams St.; turn west on Adams St. to the Old State Capitol Plaza. The Library is located in the underground facility below the Old State Capitol.

---

16 **Site:** LINCOLN HOME NATIONAL HISTORIC SITE, 413 South Eighth St., Springfield, IL 62701, ☎ 217/492-4241

Description: The Lincoln Home National Historic Site preserves 4 city blocks

surrounding the only home Abraham Lincoln ever owned. Erected in 1839, the house was purchased by Lincoln in 1844 and served as the Lincolns' home for 17 years until their departure for Washington, D.C., in 1861.

Open to Public: Daily 9am–5pm.

Admission Fees: Free.

Visitor Services: Tours, museum, gift shop, visitors center, rest rooms.

Directions: From I-55: take the South Grand Ave. west exit to Ninth St.; turn north on Ninth St. and proceed to Capitol Ave.; turn west on Capitol Ave. to Eighth St.; turn south to the Lincoln Home Visitors Center.

---

17 Site: LINCOLN TOMB, Oak Ridge Cemetery, Springfield, IL 62702, ☎ 217/782-2717

Description: The 117-foot-tall tomb is constructed of granite and is the final resting place of President Abraham Lincoln, his wife Mary, and three of their four children. Near the entrance is a bronze bust of Lincoln. The tomb designer, Larkin Mead, created the monumental bronze military statues and the statue of Lincoln on the terrace. Mead's design has been popularly interpreted as symbolizing Lincoln's role in the preservation of the Union.

Open to Public: Daily 9am–5pm. *Note:* Site closes at 4pm Nov–Feb. Closed

New Year's Day, Martin Luther King Day, Presidents Day, General Election Day, Veterans Day, Thanksgiving Day, and Christmas Day.

Admission Fees: Free.

Visitor Services: Tours, museum, information, rest rooms, and handicapped access.

Directions: From I-55: take Sangamon Ave. exit to Peoria Rd; turn south on Peoria Rd. to North Grand Ave. Go west on North Grand Ave. to Monument Ave.; then go north on Monument to the cemetery.

---

18 Site: OLD STATE CAPITOL, 1 Old State Capitol Plaza, Springfield, IL 62701,
☎ 217/785-7961

Description: The Old State Capitol is a magnificently restored Greek Revival building that served as the center of the Illinois government from 1839 to 1876. U.S. Senator Stephen Douglas and a young legislator, Abraham Lincoln, were powerful figures of the time who frequented the halls of the Capitol. Abraham Lincoln delivered his famous "House Divided" speech in the Representatives Hall and lay in state there before his interment in the Oak Ridge Cemetery.

Open to Public: Daily 9am–4:30pm. Closed state and national holidays.

Admission Fees: Free.

Visitor Services: Tours, museum, gift shop, visitors center, rest rooms, handicapped access from elevator in kiosk south of the main entrance, Braille guide available.

Directions: From I-55: take Clear Lake exit to Ninth St., turn south on Ninth St. to Adams St., and turn west on Adams St. to the Old State Capitol.

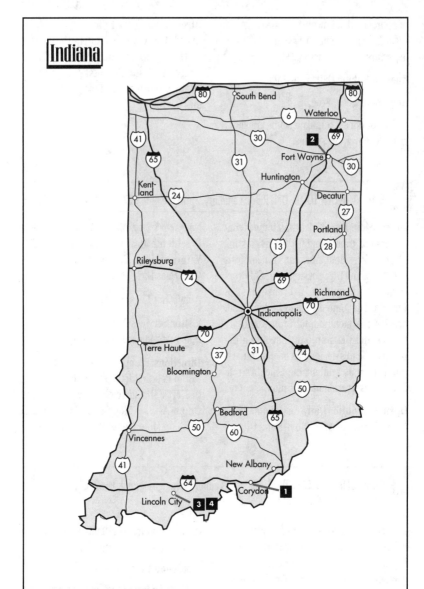

Indiana

1 Corydon Battlefield
2 The Lincoln Museum
3 Lincoln Boyhood National Memorial
4 Lincoln Amphitheater and Lincoln State Park

INDIANA

*I*NDIANA SUPPLIED MORE than men, money, and munitions in the Civil War. Led by autocratic Gov. Oliver P. Morton—the "War Governor"—Indiana anchored the resolve of the western states to help save the Union.

When men and materials were most needed to shore up Northern armies, President Lincoln called on Morton, and his ally responded. Boldly playing his cards in politics and war, Morton defied his opponents in the Indiana legislature, over and over coming up with the troops Lincoln required to fight the war. Morton operated outside his state as well, marshaling support throughout the Midwest. When he could not raise funds from his own lawmakers, Morton borrowed from men of wealth. Railroad financier James Lanier of Madison, Indiana, first lent Morton $400,000 to finance the war effort, then later an additional $600,000—a million dollars!—much of which Morton kept in his own safe, and all of which was eventually repaid.

The Civil War raged only miles away from Indiana, below the Ohio River. The flames of fighting, in fact, lapped onto the Hoosier State in July 1863, when a large Confederate force, led by Gen. John Hunt Morgan, crossed the Ohio just downriver from Louisville, and proceeded northward, primarily in search of fresh horses for Confederate cavalry.

Just south of the little town of Corydon, the original state capital of Indiana, a hastily gathered "home guard" of about 600 threw up a line of defense in a deep woods, pitting themselves against Morgan's 4,000 regular troops. The home guard, made up mostly of men too young or too old to be off to war, laid down intense fire, but eventually "skedaddled" when Morgan wheeled up his artillery. Later that day, July 9, 1863, Morgan was informed that Lee had been defeated at Gettysburg. Confederate wounded were taken to the Presbyterian Church and were cared for by women from the town. Lest anyone try to harm the fallen Southerners, one of the women stood with a gun ready at the church door to protect the wounded enemy men.

Morgan was soon on his way, but the delay at the Battle of Corydon allowed Union pursuers to be hard on his heels, and probably diminished the success of Morgan's Raid. As the Union soldiers passed through town the next day, those same Corydon women braved the dust and heat to fetch water for the fast-marching Northern soldiers. The efforts of one of those women, Miss Abbie Slemmons, proved too exhausting, and she died of fatigue and fever some days later—another casualty of a cruel war.

In all, Indiana sent 196,363 men to the Civil War, and more than one-eighth never returned: 7,243 died in battle, and another 17,785 succumbed to the diseases of war. As they have in every war, Hoosiers demonstrated in the Civil War their bravery and determination—and on more than one occasion, their compassion.

by William Doolittle, Creative Projects, Louisville, Ky.;
research assistance by William B. Doolittle Sr.

THE LINCOLN HERITAGE TRAIL

See THE LINCOLN HERITAGE TRAIL box on page 57 for more information.

Primary sites in Indiana include: The Lincoln Boyhood National Memorial, Lincoln City; and The Lincoln Museum, Fort Wayne. Other Indiana attractions include: Colonel William Jones State Historic Site, Lincoln State Park, Young Abe Lincoln Outdoor Drama, and the John Hay Center and Birthplace.

For more information: A free brochure that covers the entire Lincoln Heritage Trail in Kentucky, Indiana, and Illinois can be ordered from Indiana Tourism Development: ☎ 800/289-6646. The brochure is also available at places along the Trail.

Corydon

1 **Site:** CORYDON BATTLEFIELD, c/o 310 N. Elm St., Corydon, IN 47112,
☎ 888/738-2137

Description: The Battle of Corydon was the only official Civil War battle in Indiana and the only battle site north of the Ohio River. The site commemorates the effort of Confederate Gen. John Hunt Morgan to spread the war to the north. The Corydon Battlefield is a 5-acre park located on the east side of State Rte. 135, just south of Corydon. The park is a heavily wooded area covered with hardwood trees, some of which date from 1863. Although the park area looks much as it did in 1863, a drive to a parking lot on the property, several historic markers, and a log cabin moved to the site in the 1930s represent changes to the historic landscape.

Open to Public: Daily 24 hours.

Admission Fees: Free.

Visitor Services: Information.

Directions: From I-64: take State Rte. 135 south through Corydon. The battle site is approximately 1 mile south of the city.

Fort Wayne

2 **Site:** THE LINCOLN MUSEUM, 200 E. Berry St., Fort Wayne, IN 46802,
☎ 219/455-3864

Description: The Lincoln Museum is the world's largest museum featuring the life of Abraham Lincoln. The permanent exhibit, "Abraham Lincoln and the American Experiment," includes two galleries that tell the story of all the men who led the nation through this "fiery trial."

Open to Public: Tues–Sat 10am–5pm, Sun 1–5pm. Closed on major holidays.

Admission Fees: Adults $2.99; children, seniors, and groups of 12 or more $1.99.

Visitor services: Free parking, closed-captioned audiovisuals, handicapped access.

Regularly Scheduled Events: *Oct:* Civil War Ball.

Directions: From I-69 north: take exit 112A to Coldwater Rd. south; proceed into downtown. Coldwater becomes Clinton St. The museum is at the southeast corner of Clinton and Berry sts. (4 blocks after passing under train overpass). From I-69 south: take exit 102 and travel east on Jefferson St. into downtown. Turn left on Lafayette St. (Holiday Inn is on corner). Proceed 3 blocks, turn left on Berry St., and go 2 blocks to museum at corner of Clinton and Berry sts.

Lincoln City

3 **Site:** LINCOLN BOYHOOD NATIONAL MEMORIAL, P.O. Box 1816, Lincoln City, IN 47552, ☎ 812/937-4541

Description: This was the boyhood home of Abraham Lincoln, where he lived from age 7 to 21. The park includes the Memorial Visitor Center; the grave site of Nancy Hanks Lincoln, Abraham Lincoln's mother; and the Lincoln Living Historical Farm, a typical 19th-century farm on the Indiana frontier.

Open to Public: Daily 8am–5pm. Closed Thanksgiving Day, Christmas Day, and New Year's Day.

Admission Fees: Adults $2, maximum of $4/family.

Visitor Services: Trails, tours, museum, visitors center, rest rooms, handicapped access to Memorial Visitor Center.

Regularly Scheduled Events: *Feb, Sun closest to Lincoln's birthday:* Lincoln Day.

Directions: From I-64: exit at U.S. Hwy. 231 and travel south for 8 miles. Travel east on State Hwy. 162 at Gentryville. Proceed 2 miles to site.

Memorial Building at the Lincoln Boyhood National Memorial in Indiana. (Photograph courtesy of the National Park Service.)

4 **Site:** LINCOLN AMPHITHEATER AND LINCOLN STATE PARK, Box 7-21, Lincoln City, IN 47552-0126, ☎ 800/264-4ABE or 812/937-4710 (park)

Description: Within walking distance of the Lincoln homestead, the Lincoln Amphitheater, America's most beautiful outdoor covered stage, presents a musical drama for all ages. *Young Abe Lincoln* re-creates the pioneer upbringing of our 16th president from age 7 to 21. The Lincoln story reveals how his greatness developed from a humble origin, made rich by his mother's love and his own passion for learning. The amphitheater is located in the 1,747-acre state park.

Open to Public: *Drama performances:* Mid-June–mid-Aug: Tues–Sun at 8pm. *Box office:* Mid-June–mid-Aug: Mon 9am–5pm, Tues–Sun 9am–8pm. *Off-season hours:* Mid-Aug.–mid-June: Mon–Fri 9am–4:30pm. *Park (all year):* Daily 7am–11pm.

Admission Fees: *Drama:* Adults $12, children $7, seniors 60 and over $10, groups $8/person. *Park:* $2/in-state vehicle, $5/out-of-state vehicle. *Note:* additional charges for camping and boat rental.

Visitor Services: Drama: information, gift shop, food, rest rooms, handicapped access. Park: Camping, picnicking, hiking, swimming, boating, fishing.

Regularly Scheduled Events: *June (call for date):* Opening night celebration.

Directions: From I-64: take exit 57; take U.S. 162 to Lincoln State Park. Amphitheater is located in the state park.

KANSAS

*I*N KANSAS, THE CIVIL WAR BEGAN in 1854 as North and South fought to impose their cultural systems on the new territory. Westerners, the great majority of settlers in the Kansas Territory, often tried to ignore the conflict as they pursued their peaceful day-to-day activities, but when forced to choose sides, most went with the antislavery cause. When the national Civil War erupted in 1861, Kansans overwhelmingly supported the Union and rushed to enlist in disproportionate numbers.

Although thousands of Kansans served in the Eastern theaters of battle, the major focus of the new state was on the Missouri-Kansas border. Old hatreds from the territorial period were pursued in the continuing border war. Time and again, Kansas Jayhawkers swept into western Missouri to rob, pillage, and burn. Guerrillas from Missouri struck back with a vengeance. Quantrell's destruction of Lawrence in 1863 is the best-known incident, but many other Kansas localities suffered the wrath of Quantrell and his kind.

Certain Native Americans saw the war as an opportunity to stop the western spread of settlement in Kansas. As Federal troops and the militia watched for invasion from the east, the natives of the Plains struck from the west. Raids throughout north-central Kansas drew away soldiers who had hoped to fight rebels, not Native Americans.

Regular battles in the state centered primarily on Price's Raid in October 1864. Gen. Sterling Price's Confederate troops had marched across Missouri in search of recruits and supplies. They were turned back at the Battle of Westport, Missouri, on October 23 and retreated southward through Kansas. Union cavalry struck them at the Marais des Cygnes River, at Mine Creek, and at the Little Osage River. The greatest havoc came at Mine Creek, where two Confederate generals were captured and Price's rear guard was overwhelmed. He escaped destruction but at the cost of thousands of men and most of his wagon train.

by Dale E. Watts, Kansas State Historical Society

Baxter Springs

1   **Site:** FORT BLAIR, c/o Baxter Springs Historical Society, P.O. Box 514, Baxter Springs, KS 66713, ☎ 316/856-2385

Description: Baxter Springs was a stopping place on the old Military Rd. between Ft. Scott and Ft. Gibson. In the summer of 1863, Ft. Blair was built. On October 6, 1863, the fort was attacked by William Quantrill and more than 300 guerrilla troops. Though greatly outnumbered, two companies of the 3rd Wisconsin Cavalry and a company of 2nd Kansas Colored Infantry at the fort repulsed the attack.

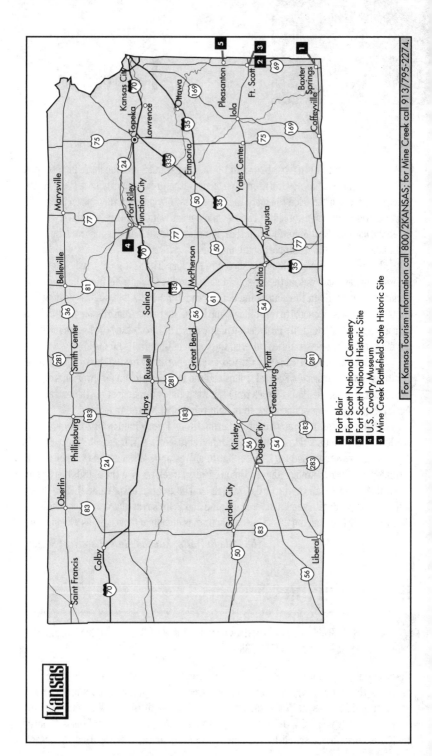

Kansas

1 Fort Blair
2 Fort Scott National Cemetery
3 Fort Scott National Historic Site
4 U.S. Cavalry Museum
5 Mine Creek Battlefield State Historic Site

For Kansas Tourism information call 800/2KANSAS; for Mine Creek call 913/795-2274.

Subsequently, Quantrill turned north and attacked a military supply train under Gen. James Blunt. Unaware of the earlier attack at the fort, Blunt was unprepared for the surprise attack. Overwhelmed by the superior numbers of the enemy, nearly all of the more than 100 men under Blunt were killed, many while trying to surrender. The victims are buried in the national cemetery plot west of the present town of Baxter Springs. A portion of the site of the Battle of Fort Blair has been developed for visitors. An interpretive center is located in the Baxter Springs Historical Museum 1 block south of the fort site. A self-guided auto tour traces the attack on the fort and the battle outside Baxter Springs.

Open to Public: *Fort site:* Daily from dawn to dusk. *Museum:* Tues–Sat 10:30am–4:30pm, Sun 1–4pm.

Admission Fees: Free.

Visitor Services: Museum, audiovisual presentation, gift shop, rest rooms.

Directions: Take Hwy. 69 south of Ft. Scott and Hwy. 69A into Baxter Springs. Or from I-44: take U.S. 400 exit to Baxter Springs. Fort site is located at 6th and East Ave. Museum is at 8th and East Ave.

Fort Scott

2 **Site:** FORT SCOTT NATIONAL CEMETERY, 900 E. National Ave., Fort Scott, KS 66701, ☎ 316/223-2840

Description: Established in 1862 as one of the 12 original National Cemeteries, this cemetery is the final resting place of Union, American Indian, African American, and Confederate soldiers who died during the Civil War.

Open to Public: Daily 24 hours. *Office:* Mon–Fri 8am–4pm.

Admission Fees: Free.

Visitor Services: Brochure available, rest rooms.

Regularly Scheduled Events: *May:* Memorial Day ceremony; *Nov 11:* Veterans Day ceremony.

Directions: From U.S. 54 at Fort Scott: turn south on National Ave. and go 20 blocks to E. National Ave.; proceed 5 blocks to cemetery.

3 **Site:** FORT SCOTT NATIONAL HISTORIC SITE, Old Fort Blvd., Fort Scott, KS 66701, ☎ 316/223-0310

Description: Fort Scott mirrored the course of western settlement along the middle border. From 1842 to 1853, troops helped keep peace on this Indian frontier. Between 1854 and 1861, the years of "Bleeding Kansas," the town was caught up in the violent struggle between "free-soilers" and slaveholders. During the Civil War, the fort served as the headquarters of the Army of the Frontier, a supply depot, a refugee center for displaced Indians, and a base for one of the first black regiments raised during the war—the First Kansas Colored Infantry.

Open to Public: Daily 8am–5pm. Closed Thanksgiving Day, Christmas Day, and New Year's Day. Call for extended summer hours.

Admission Fees: $2 (age 17 and over).

Visitor Services: Tours, information, visitors center, museum, gift shop, rest rooms, limited handicapped access.

Regularly Scheduled Events: *Spring:* Civil War encampment; *Summer:* Evening programs; *Sept:* Mexican War encampment; *Fall:* American Indian heritage weekend; *First weekend in Dec:* Frontier Candlelight tour.

Directions: Located about 90 miles south of Kansas City and 60 miles north of Joplin, MO. Go to where U.S. 69 and U.S. 54 intersect at Fort Scott; the fort is in the center of town.

Fort Riley

4 **Site:** U.S. CAVALRY MUSEUM, P.O. Box 2160, Bldg. 205, Ft. Riley, KS 66442-0160, ☎ 913/239-2737

Description: Fort Riley was established in 1852 near where the Smoky Hill and Republican join to form the Kansas River. During the 1850s, infantry and cavalry troops patrolled the plains, protecting the overland trails to Santa Fe and the Colorado gold fields. Officers such as Philip St. George Cooke, "Jeb" Stuart, and John Buford were stationed here and participated in events that came to be known as "Bleeding Kansas." The first territorial legislature met at the fort in the summer of 1855. During the Civil War, as regular troops returned East, the fort was garrisoned by state militia units who continued to protect the frontier.

Open to Public: Mon–Sat 9am–4:30pm, Sun noon–4:30pm. Closed New Year's Day, Easter, Thanksgiving Day, and Christmas Day.

Admission Fees: Free.

Visitor Services: Museum, gift shop, rest rooms, handicapped access.

Directions: Located approximately 120 miles west of Kansas City on I-70. From I-70: take exit 301 (Marshal Army Airfield); follow signs after crossing the Kansas River bridge.

Pleasanton

5 **Site:** MINE CREEK BATTLEFIELD STATE HISTORIC SITE, c/o Kansas State Historical Society, 6425 SW Sixth, Topeka, KS 66615-1099, ☎ 913/795-4365

Description: On October 25, 1864, some 10,000 Union and Confederate troops clashed at Mine Creek. They had been fighting off and on for several days as Gen. Sterling Price's Confederates marched through Missouri and then were turned back at the Battle of Westport. The Union cavalry caught up with the rear guard of Price's wagon train at Mine Creek and crushed them in one of the greatest cavalry charges of the Civil War. A portion of the battlefield is preserved by the state of Kansas. Interpretive trail loops on both sides of Mine Creek are now in place. A major interpretation center with attendant programs opens in the fall of 1998.

Open to Public: Daily during daylight hours.

Admission Fees: Free.

Visitor Services: Trails. *Note:* Museum, gift shops, visitors center, and rest rooms are scheduled to open in the fall of 1998.

Regularly Scheduled Events: *Late Oct:* Encampment or festival.

Directions: From I-70 or I-435: take U.S. 69 south; take KS 52 west 2 miles south of Pleasanton; proceed 1 mile and turn left (south) on a county road for .5 mile to the site parking lot.

Bridge over Mine Creek at Mine Creek Battlefield in Kansas. (Photograph courtesy of the Kansas State Historical Society.)

KENTUCKY

$\mathcal{T}$HE SMOKE AND FIRE OF THE CIVIL WAR HAVE long since faded from Kentucky's landscape, but its legacy remains a vital part of the Commonwealth's history. Kentuckians figured prominently at the highest levels of the conflict. Both the U.S. president, Abraham Lincoln, and the Confederate President, Jefferson Davis, were born in Kentucky—less than a year and 100 miles apart.

The irony of the opposing leaders' origins highlights Kentucky's deep divisions. While the state never officially left the Union—retaining Frankfort as the state capital—a Confederate capital was established at Bowling Green. There was a star for Kentucky on the Southern flag. More than 45,000 men left their Kentucky homes to fight for the South, while twice that number fought for the Union—including 20,000 African Americans, the second-highest number among all the states.

Trying to avoid the conflict, Kentucky declared itself neutral. This neutrality quickly vanished, as both Union and Confederate forces, recognizing the strategic importance of the state, sought to gain control—leading to a number of significant battles. Resentful of Union treatment during the war, Kentucky later became so southern-sympathetic that it was said "Kentucky seceded after the war."

by Daniel Kidd, Kentucky Department of Travel Development

$\mathcal{F}$or More Information

To receive a free Kentucky Civil War guide, call ☎ **800/225-TRIP** (8747), or write: Kentucky Department of Travel Development, Ste. 2200, 500 Mero St. Frankfort, KY 40601-1968.

THE LINCOLN HERITAGE TRAIL

See THE LINCOLN HERITAGE TRAIL box on page 57 for more information.

Primary sites in Kentucky include: Abraham Lincoln Birthplace National Historic Site, Hodgenville; and the Lincoln Boyhood Home at Knob Creek, Hodgenville. Other Kentucky attractions include: Lincoln Museum, Mordecai Lincoln House, Washington Co. Courthouse, Old Fort Harrod State Park, Mary Todd Lincoln House, Farmington, and Lincoln Homestead State Park.

continues

For more information: A free brochure covering the entire Lincoln Heritage Trail in Kentucky, Indiana, and Illinois can be ordered from the Kentucky Dept. of Travel: ☎ 800/225-TRIP. The brochure is also available at places along the Trail.

Bardstown

1 **Site:** OLD BARDSTOWN VILLAGE CIVIL WAR MUSEUM, 310 East Broadway, Bardstown KY 40004, ☎ 502/349-0291 (museum), 502/638-4877 (local tourism office)

Description: This museum focuses on "the War in the West," which witnessed the military beginnings of such famous Union generals as Grant, Sherman, and Sheridan. Many historians agree that the outcome of the Civil War was largely based on what took place in its western theater.

Open to Public: Tues–Sat 10am–5pm, Sun noon–5pm.

Admission Fees: Adults $5, seniors $4, children 6–12 $2.50. Group rates available.

Visitor Services: Museum, rest rooms, gift shop.

Directions: From the Blue Grass Parkway: take exit 25; travel west on U.S. 150. Proceed through 2 traffic lights and turn right on Old Bloomfield Road after the second light. Turn left at stop sign and follow signs to the museum.

2 **Site:** SPALDING HALL, 114 North Fifth St., Bardstown, KY 40004, ☎ 502/348-2999

Description: Spalding Hall is a large, five-story, Federal-style brick building erected in 1826 as part of the former St. Joseph's College. It was used as a hospital during the Civil War. Now a museum, Spalding Hall includes a room featuring Civil War artifacts and memorabilia. The museum guide can provide information on Bardstown's role in the Civil War.

Open to Public: May–Oct: Mon–Sat 9am–5pm, Sun 1–5pm. Nov–Apr: Tues–Sat 10am–4pm, Sun 1–4pm.

Admission Fees: Free.

Visitor Services: Museum, rest rooms.

Directions: From Southbound Bluegrass Pkwy.: take exit 25; turn right onto U.S. 150, which becomes Stephen Foster Ave. Turn right at the fourth traffic light (circle halfway around the county courthouse in the center of town) onto North Fifth St. From Northbound Bluegrass Pkwy.: take exit 21 and travel north (turn left) on U.S. 31E. Turn right on West Stephen Foster Ave., proceed to first traffic light, and turn left onto North Fifth St.

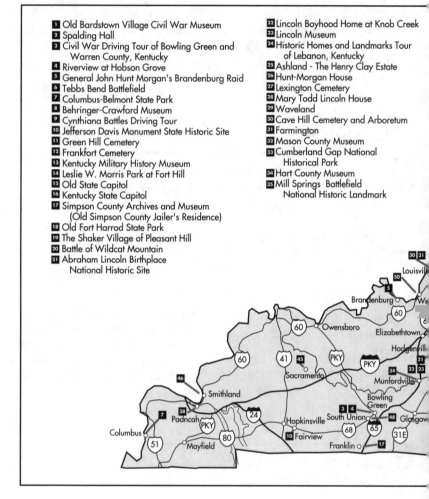

1. Old Bardstown Village Civil War Museum
2. Spalding Hall
3. Civil War Driving Tour of Bowling Green and Warren County, Kentucky
4. Riverview at Hobson Grove
5. General John Hunt Morgan's Brandenburg Raid
6. Tebbs Bend Battlefield
7. Columbus-Belmont State Park
8. Behringer-Crawford Museum
9. Cynthiana Battles Driving Tour
10. Jefferson Davis Monument State Historic Site
11. Green Hill Cemetery
12. Frankfort Cemetery
13. Kentucky Military History Museum
14. Leslie W. Morris Park at Fort Hill
15. Old State Capitol
16. Kentucky State Capitol
17. Simpson County Archives and Museum (Old Simpson County Jailer's Residence)
18. Old Fort Harrod State Park
19. The Shaker Village of Pleasant Hill
20. Battle of Wildcat Mountain
21. Abraham Lincoln Birthplace National Historic Site
22. Lincoln Boyhood Home at Knob Creek
23. Lincoln Museum
24. Historic Homes and Landmarks Tour of Lebanon, Kentucky
25. Ashland - The Henry Clay Estate
26. Hunt-Morgan House
27. Lexington Cemetery
28. Mary Todd Lincoln House
29. Waveland
30. Cave Hill Cemetery and Arboretum
31. Farmington
32. Mason County Museum
33. Cumberland Gap National Historical Park
34. Hart County Museum
35. Mill Springs Battlefield National Historic Landmark

Bowling Green

3 **Site:** CIVIL WAR DRIVING TOUR OF BOWLING GREEN AND WARREN COUNTY, KENTUCKY. Mailing address: Bowling Green / Warren County Tourist and Convention Commission, 352 Three Springs Rd., Bowling Green, KY 42104, ☎ 502/782-0800

Description: Eleven sites compose this driving tour of historic Bowling Green and Warren County, which both the Union and Confederacy wanted to control. Notably, Bowling Green served as the capital of Confederate Kentucky.

Open to Public: *Bowling Green/Warren County Visitors Center:* All year: Mon–Fri 8am–5pm. Memorial Day–Labor Day: Sat–Sun 9am–5pm. *National Corvette Museum branch:* Daily 9am–5pm.

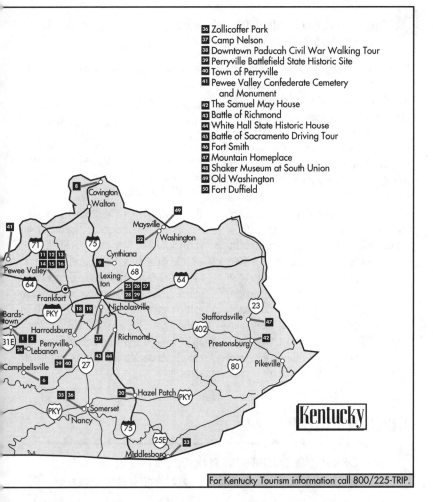

36 Zollicoffer Park
37 Camp Nelson
38 Downtown Paducah Civil War Walking Tour
39 Perryville Battlefield State Historic Site
40 Town of Perryville
41 Pewee Valley Confederate Cemetery
   and Monument
42 The Samuel May House
43 Battle of Richmond
44 White Hall State Historic House
45 Battle of Sacramento Driving Tour
46 Fort Smith
47 Mountain Homeplace
48 Shaker Museum at South Union
49 Old Washington
50 Fort Duffield

For Kentucky Tourism information call 800/225-TRIP.

Admission Fees: A free driving tour brochure is available at the Visitors Center of the Bowling Green/Warren County Tourist and Convention Commission, located at 352 Three Springs Rd. in Bowling Green. A branch visitors center is located in the lobby of the National Corvette Museum, 350 Corvette Dr., in Bowling Green. Tour sites are scattered. Of the 11 sites, admission is charged at Kentucky Museum (☎ 502/745-2592), Riverview—The Hobson House (☎ 502/843-5565), and Lost River Cave Valley (☎ 502/793-1023).

Visitor Services: See brochure for individual site services.

Directions: From I-65 south: take exit 28, follow the ramp to the first light, and turn left on Corvette Drive. The branch visitors center is in the lobby of the National Corvette Museum. From I-65 north: take exit 22, turn left on U.S. 231 (Scottsville Road) for a short distance, and then left again on KY 884 (Three Springs Road). The visitors center is on the left at 352 Three Springs Rd.

4 | Site: RIVERVIEW AT HOBSON GROVE, 1100 West Main St., Bowling Green, KY 42102, ☎ 502/843-5565

Description: The Hobson House, an Italianate mansion, was partially constructed before the Civil War. Col. William Hobson, son of builder Atwood Hobson and the youngest Union colonel on record, requested that Brig. Gen. Simon Bolivar Buckner, commanding Southern officer during the Confederate occupation of Bowling Green, spare the property. Buckner filled the basement of the unfinished mansion with Confederate ammunition. Atwood Hobson, one of the most ardent Union supporters in southern Kentucky, brought a French military professor to his home for the purpose of instructing William and his contemporaries in French military tactics ("Zouaves"). Atwood, president of a local bank, borrowed $30,000 to advance the Union cause. He also purchased 300 rifles to arm local citizens against the Confederates.

Open to Public: Mon–Sat 10am–4pm, Sun 1–4pm.

Admission Fees: Adults $3.50, children $1.50. Call in advance to arrange for groups.

Visitor Services: Tours, museum, gift shop, rest rooms. No handicapped access, but a video will be available to those unable to take the guided tour.

Directions: From southbound I-65: take exit 28 and follow signs to Bowling Green via U.S. 68/80. Turn right on Sixth Ave., which becomes Veterans Memorial Lane and leads to Hobson Grove Park; follow signs. From northbound I-65: take exit 20 onto the Green River Pkwy. Take Morgan-town Rd. exit onto U.S. 231. Turn right toward Bowling Green. Turn left onto Veterans Memorial Lane and follow signs.

Brandenburg

5 | Site: GENERAL JOHN HUNT MORGAN'S BRANDENBURG RAID, P.O. Box 483, Brandenburg, KY 40108, ☎ 502/422-3626 (Chamber of Commerce)

Description: Follow the 4-day action of Gen. John Hunt Morgan's raid on this scenic Ohio River community—a well-known shipping and trading place throughout much of the 19th century. A free brochure chronicles the Confederate leader's July 6–9, 1863, time here, which included a skirmish on the river and the burning of a steamer named the *Alice Dean.* Pick up the brochure from the local Chamber of Commerce office or the public library.

Open to Public: *Chamber of Commerce office:* Mon–Fri noon–4pm. *Meade Co.*

Public Library: Mon, Tues, Wed, Fri 9:30am–5:30pm; Thurs 9:30am–8pm; Sat 10am–4pm; Sun 2–5pm. Closed on Sunday during summer.

Admission Fees: Free.

Visitor Services: Chamber of Commerce office: Rest rooms, handicapped access. Meade Co. Public Library: Rest rooms.

Directions: From I-64 at Corydon, IN: take exit 62, travel on State Hwy. 135 south (approximately 20 miles), cross Ohio River, and take Hwy. 1051. At 4-way stop, turn left on High St./Hwy. 79 and proceed 2 miles. Chamber office is inside City Hall at 735 High St. The library is located at 400 Library Pl. (off Broadway/Hwy. 448).

Campbellsville

6   **Site:** TEBBS BEND BATTLEFIELD, Taylor County Tourist Commission, Courthouse, Broadway and Court, P.O. Box 4021, Campbellsville, KY 42719, ☎ 800/738-4719 or 502/465-3786

Description: The 1863 Battle of Tebbs Bend/Green River Bridge took place on a bend in the Green River 8 miles from Campbellsville and was an early omen of the disaster to befall Gen. John Hunt Morgan on his Great Indiana and Ohio Raid. A self-guided driving tour brochure of the battlefield is available at the tourist commission or at Green River Lake Corps of Engineers Visitor Center.

Open to Public: Daily from dawn to dusk. *Tourist Commission:* Mon–Fri 8:30am–4:30pm.

Admission Fees: Free.

Visitor Services: Rest rooms; picnic area; Atkinson-Griffin House/Confederate Hospital museum at Green River Lake Corps of Engineers Visitor Center, adjacent to battlefield.

Directions: From Campbellsville: obtain driving tour brochure at the Tourist Commission located on the courthouse square that is on Hwy. 55. Take Hwy. 55 south for 8 miles and turn right on Morgan-Moore Trail to begin tour. From the south: take exit 49 off Cumberland Pkwy. to Columbia and follow Hwy. 55 north for 12 miles to Green River Lake Corps of Engineers Visitor Center. Obtain brochure at the Interpretive Center. Return to park entrance, turn right on Hwy. 55, and travel 2 miles. Turn left on the Morgan-Moore Trail to begin tour.

Columbus

7   **Site:** COLUMBUS-BELMONT STATE PARK, KY 58 and KY 123/80, P.O. Box 8, Columbus, KY 42032, ☎ 502/677-2327

Description: This is the site of a massive chain and anchor used to block the passage of Union gunboats during the Civil War. There is also a Confederate cannon, a network of earthen trenches, and a museum that was a Civil War hospital.

Open to Public: May–Sept: Daily 9am–5pm. Open weekends only in Apr and Oct.

Admission Fees: *Museum:* 50¢; *Group members:* 35¢ each person.

Visitor Services: Camping, trails, museum, gift shop, rest rooms, snack bar, picnic area.

Regularly Scheduled Events: *Early Oct:* Civil War Days.

Directions: From Purchase Pkwy.: take exit 1, U.S. 51, north to Clinton; go north-west on KY 58 to Columbus and the park.

Covington

8 | **Site:** BEHRINGER-CRAWFORD MUSEUM, 1600 Montague Rd., P.O. Box 67, Covington, KY 41012, ☎ 606/491-4003

Description: Covington's Behringer-Crawford Museum preserves the area's natural and cultural heritage. It is located in the 1848–1880 Devou family home in the 700-acre Devou Park. The permanent collections span 450 years, including a fine display of Civil War artifacts. Also, a battery in the park offers interpretive Civil War signage.

Open to Public: Tues–Fri 10am–5pm, Sat–Sun 1–5pm.

Admission Fees: Adults $3, children $2, seniors $2.

Visitor Services: Gift shop, museum, rest rooms, handicapped access, private library.

Regularly Scheduled Events: *June:* Periodic Civil War reenactments; *Sept:* FreshArt Auction; *Nov–Dec:* Holiday trains and Victorian house decorations.

Directions: From I-71/75: take exit 192, go west on Fourth St., and follow signs to Devou Park.

Cynthiana

9 | **Site:** CYNTHIANA BATTLES DRIVING TOUR, 117 Court St., Cynthiana, KY 41031, ☎ 606/234-5236

Description: Confederate Gen. John Hunt Morgan fought two battles here: the first in 1862 and the second in 1864. A self-guided tour brochure of the battles is available at the Cynthiana/Harrison County Chamber of Commerce.

Open to Public: *Chamber office:* Mon–Fri 9am–4pm.

Admission Fees: Free.

Visitor Services: None.

Directions: From I-75: take exit 126 at Georgetown; go northeast on U.S. 62 through Oxford and Leesburg to U.S. 27 and into Cynthiana. The chamber office is behind the Harrison County Courthouse on Main St.

Fairview

10 | **Site:** JEFFERSON DAVIS MONUMENT STATE HISTORIC SITE, U.S. 68, P.O. Box 10, Fairview, KY 42221-0010, ☎ 502/886-1765

Description: The monument is a 351-foot-high stone obelisk that marks the site where, on June 3, 1808, Jefferson Davis, the only president of the Confederacy, was born. There is an elevator to an observation room high atop the structure for a panoramic view of the western Kentucky countryside.

Open to Public: May–Oct: Daily 9am–5pm. Closed Nov 1–Apr 31.

Admission Fees: Adults and children $2, school groups $1.

Visitor Services: Gift shop, rest rooms, handicapped access.

Regularly Scheduled Events: *First weekend in June:* Jefferson Davis birthday celebration; Miss Confederacy pageant; Living history camps; Artillery and infantry demonstrations.

Directions: Take Pennyrile Pkwy. south to Hopkinsville where it ends; go approximately 10 miles east on U.S. 68 to Fairview.

Frankfort

11 **Site:** GREEN HILL CEMETERY, located on Atwood Avenue, off East Main Street in Frankfort, ☎ 502/564-3265

Description: The ladies of the George M. Monroe Chapter #8, Kentucky "Colored" Corps—a division of the Women's Relief Corps of the Grand Army of the Republic—erected a simple yet noble monument in 1924. It honors the 141 black men from Central Kentucky who fought for the Union—all of whom were mustered into Federal service at Camp Nelson, Kentucky.

Open to Public: Daily from dawn to dusk.

Admission Fees: Free.

Visitor Services: None.

Directions: From I-64: take exit 58 (Frankfort/Versailles), travel on U.S. 60 west, which turns left at its intersection with U.S. 460 and becomes East Main St. Turn left between a Chevron station (859 East Main St.) and the sign for "East Side Shopping Center" (863 East Main) onto a paved way. This way becomes Atwood Ave.; follow it around a curve to Green Hill Cemetery on the left. Turn into the cemetery's circular lane and go one-third around the circle; the monument is approximately 75 feet away to the right.

12 **Site:** FRANKFORT CEMETERY, 215 East Main St. Frankfort, KY 40601, ☎ 502/227-2403

Description: Frankfort Cemetery is a highly scenic cemetery whose southern edge overlooks the Kentucky River, the State Capitol, and the town of Frankfort. The cemetery has been described as "Kentucky's Westminster" because so many famous people are buried here. A brochure gives the location of the graves of many Civil War notables, the Confederate monument and surrounding unknown graves, and the state military monument that describes Kentucky's role in the Civil War.

Open to Public: Brochures available at the Frankfort Cemetery office Mon–Fri 8am–4pm or at the Frankfort Tourist Information Center (100 Capitol Ave.) on weekends. *Cemetery:* Mon–Sat 7:30am–dusk, Sun 8am–dusk. *Note:* Buses and motor coaches are not allowed in the Frankfort Cemetery.

Admission Fees: Free.

Visitor Services: Information.

Directions: From I-64: take exit 58 (Frankfort/Versailles). Travel on U.S. 60 toward Frankfort and follow signs for downtown Frankfort and East Main St.; U.S. 60 turns left at the intersection with U.S. 460 and becomes East Main St. Turn left onto East Main St. To proceed to Frankfort Cemetery: turn left at traffic light onto Glenn's Creek Rd.; immediately turn right into cemetery. To reach the Tourist Center: continue on East Main past the turn to Frankfort Cemetery. Turn left onto Capitol Ave. Tourist Center is at 100 Capitol Ave. on the right.

---

13 **Site:** KENTUCKY MILITARY HISTORY MUSEUM, East Main St. at Capitol Ave., P.O. Box 1792, Frankfort, KY 40602, ☎ 502/564-3265

Description: The Kentucky Military History Museum is housed in the 1850 State Arsenal and has a large collection of Kentucky Union and Confederate memorabilia, including identified uniforms, flags, guns, and other equipment. During the war, the arsenal was a cartridge factory for the Union army, as well as a regional supply center for Northern troops from Midwestern states.

Open to Public: Mon–Sat 9am–4pm, Sun and holidays noon–4pm.

Admission Fees: Free.

Visitor Services: Museum, handicapped access, rest rooms.

Directions: From I-64: take exit 58; go 5 miles west on U.S. 60 (U.S. 60 turns into East Main St.); museum is located on the left before Capitol Ave. Bridge.

---

14 **Site:** LESLIE W. MORRIS PARK AT FORT HILL. Mailing address: c/o Kentucky Historical Society, P.O. Box 1792, Frankfort, KY 40602-1792, ☎ 502/564-3265 (Kentucky Military History Museum), 502/564-3016 (Old State Capitol), 800/960-7200 (Frankfort Tourist Commission)

Description: Within the park is Fort Boone, an 1863 earthen fort attacked by a detachment of Morgan's cavalry. Adjacent is the New Redoubt, a second and larger fortification built to protect Kentucky's pro-Union government.

Open to Public: Daily during daylight hours. A self-guided tour brochure for the forts may be picked up at the Old State Capitol (see separate listing in this *Guide* for hours).

Admission Fee: Free.

Visitor Services: *Morris Park:* Trails. *Old State Capitol:* Brochure, rest rooms, gift shop.

Directions: To Old State Capitol, from I-64: take exit 58, travel 5 miles west on

U.S. 60 (U.S. 60 turns into East Main St.) to downtown, and follow signs. Entrance to the park is at the Capital Plaza Tower on Mero St. in Frankfort.

---

15 Site: OLD STATE CAPITOL, Broadway & Lewis St., c/o Kentucky Historical Society, Box 1792, Frankfort, KY 40602, ☎ 502/564-3016

Description: This 1829 Greek Revival masterpiece was the only Union capitol captured by Southern troops. Here Kentucky's legislature voted first to maintain official neutrality, although the state later became bitterly divided. Resentful of wrongful Union treatment, Kentucky—following the war's end—became so southern-sympathetic that it was observed, "Kentucky seceded after the war."

Open to Public: *Old Capitol:* Mon–Fri 9am–4pm, Sat noon–5pm, Sun 1–5pm. *Library:* Mon–Fri 8am–4pm, Sat 9am–4pm.

Admission Fees: Free.

Visitor Services: Handicapped access, rest rooms, gift shop.

Directions: From I-64: take exit 58, go 5 miles west on U.S. 60 (U.S. 60 becomes East Main St.) to downtown, and follow signs.

---

16 Site: KENTUCKY STATE CAPITOL, c/o Information Desk, 700 Capitol Ave., Frankfort, KY 40601, ☎ 502/564-3449

Description: The rotunda of Kentucky's handsome 1910 State Capitol features statues of prominent Kentuckians, including Abraham Lincoln, sculpted by A. Weinman; and Jefferson Davis, sculpted by Frederick C. Hibbard. Both leaders were born in Kentucky—less than 1 year and 100 miles apart. In 1904, the Kentucky legislature appropriated $1 million, a debt collected from the U.S. War Department as reparations for damages inflicted by Federal soldiers during the Civil War, to build the new capitol.

Open to Public: Mon–Fri 8am–4:30pm, Sat 8:30am–4:30pm, Sun 1–4:30pm.

Admission Fees: Free.

Visitor Services: Handicapped access, information, food.

Directions: From I-64 west: take exit 58, go 5 miles west on U.S. 60 (East Main St.) to bridge, and follow U.S. 60 up Capitol Ave. to building. From I-64 east: take exit 52, go north on U.S. 127 and then east on U.S. 60, and follow signs.

Franklin

---

17 Site: SIMPSON COUNTY ARCHIVES AND MUSEUM (OLD SIMPSON COUNTY JAILER'S RESIDENCE), 206 North College St., Franklin, KY, 42134, ☎ 502/586-4228

Description: Confederate prisoners or Union officers, or maybe both, executed drawings (thought to be in charcoal) on plaster walls in a second-story room of this brick house (built ca. 1835). The drawings portray soldiers on both sides, one bearing a striking resemblance to the "Thunderbolt of the Confederacy," Brig. Gen. John Hunt Morgan. One of the displays tells of Franklin native Marcellus Jerome Clarke, the best known of Kentucky's Civil War guerrillas, who went by the nom de guerre "Sue Mundy."

Open to Public: Mon–Fri 9am–4pm. Closed Sat and Sun.

Admission Fees: Free.

Visitor Services: Museum, rest rooms, handicapped access to first floor only.

Regularly Scheduled Events: *Aug:* Heritage Day; *Sept:* Civil War encampment and skirmish.

Directions: From I-65 southbound: take exit 6 and travel west on KY 100 to Franklin. Turn right on 31W (Main St.); turn left on Kentucky Ave. Go 1 block and turn right on North College to stone jail and brick house. From I-65 northbound: take exit 2, turn left onto 31W north, and travel into Franklin (31W becomes Main St.). Turn left onto Kentucky Ave., go 1 block to North College St., and turn right.

Harrodsburg

18 Site: OLD FORT HARROD STATE PARK, Lexington and College streets (U.S. 68 and U.S. 127), P.O. Box 156, Harrodsburg, KY 40330-0156, ☎ 606/734-3314

Description: Located on the grounds of this state park is the Lincoln Marriage Temple, a brick pavilion enshrining the cabin in which the parents of President Abraham Lincoln were wed on June 12, 1806. Also, the "Mansion Museum" features Confederate and Union rooms. Exhibits include paintings, photographs, newspapers, documents, and firearms.

Open to Public: *Museum:* Mar 16–Nov 30: Daily 8:30am–5pm. *Fort (all year):* Daily 8:30am–5pm. Extended hours for fort: Mid-June–Aug: 8:30am–8pm.

Admission Fees: Adults $3.50, children $2. Groups (20 or more): Adults $3, children $1.50.

Visitor Services: Museum, gift shop, rest rooms, handicapped access.

Regularly Scheduled Events: *May 1:* May Day celebration; *Mid-June:* Old Fort Harrod Heritage Festival; *Mid-Nov:* Holiday gala tour.

Directions: From Bluegrass Pkwy.: take exit 59, travel 15 miles south on U.S. 127 to intersection of U.S. 127 and U.S. 68.

19 Site: THE SHAKER VILLAGE OF PLEASANT HILL, 3501 Lexington Rd. (on U.S. 68, 7 miles northeast of Harrodsburg), Harrodsburg, KY 40330, ☎ 606/734-5411

Description: The Shaker Village of Pleasant Hill is a restored indoor and outdoor living history museum that interprets the lives of the Shakers. This unique American religious community is located on a turnpike that was a strategic conduit for both Union and Confederate soldiers throughout the Civil War, but especially during the 1862 Kentucky campaign. The Shakers were both Unionists and emancipationists, but their dedication to pacifism prevented their participation in the conflict. The Shakers extended generous hospitality to both armies as they marched through the village. The only non-Shaker buried in the cemetery is a Confederate soldier who died there shortly after the nearby battle of Perryville. Also, the Shaker Landing on the Kentucky River was critical to the Union effort throughout the war.

Open to Public: Daily 9:30am–5pm.

Admission Fees: Adults $9, children 6–11 $4.50. Groups: Call in advance for special prices for more than 20 people.

Visitor Services: Trails, tours, museum, gift shop, rest rooms, food, lodging, conference facilities, limited access for disabled.

Regularly Scheduled Events: *Even numbered years:* Civil War living history weekend.

Directions: From I-64/75 near Lexington: access New Circle Rd. (KY 4) from exit 115 (Newtown Pike), exit 113 (Paris Pike/N. Broadway), or exit 110 (Winchester Rd.) and go east or south to U.S. 68. Travel south on U.S. 68, a Kentucky Scenic Byway, for 21 miles to the Shaker Village of Pleasant Hill.

Hazel Patch

20 Site: BATTLE OF WILDCAT MOUNTAIN, c/o Camp Wildcat Preservation Foundation, P.O. Box 1510, London, KY 40743-1510, ☎ 800/348-0095 (London-Laurel County Tourist Commission)

Description: The October 1861 Battle of Wildcat Mountain was the earliest major Civil War battle as well as the first Union victory in Kentucky. This action was part of CSA Gen. Felix Zollicoffer's Mill Springs campaign. The battlefield is undeveloped but accessible over a single-lane, graveled county road. Monuments and interpretive signs are located on U.S. 25 near Hazel Patch, Kentucky, and at the battlefield site on Wildcat Mountain. Original locations of the Wilderness Road are visible at the site.

Open to Public: Daily from dawn to dusk.

Admission Fee: Free.

Visitor Services: Interpretive signs. This site has recently been acquired and preserved and is being developed for visitors.

Directions: From I-75: take exit 49; proceed north on KY 909 to U.S. 25. Turn right (south) on U.S. 25 and proceed approximately 1 mile. Turn left on Hazel Patch Rd. Travel approximately 1 mile to a graveled county road and turn left. This road is marked with a directional sign to the battlefield. Proceed approximately 2 miles to the battlefield site.

Hodgenville

 Site: ABRAHAM LINCOLN BIRTHPLACE NATIONAL HISTORIC SITE, 2995 Lincoln Farm Rd., Hodgenville, KY 42748, ☎ 502/358-3137

Description: The 116-acre park features the enshrined cabin traditionally thought to be Lincoln's birthplace and the spring where the Lincoln family drew water.

Open to Public: Memorial Day–Labor Day: Daily 8am–6:45pm (EDT). Rest of the year: 8am–4:45pm (EST).

Admission Fees: Free.

Visitor Services: Visitors center, exhibits, orientation film, bookstore, picnic area, nature trails, rest rooms, handicapped access.

Regularly Scheduled Events: *Sun before the Mon holiday in Jan:* Martin Luther King Jr's. Birthday; *Feb 12:* Lincoln's Birthday; *Weekend closest to July 16–17:* Founder's Day; *Second week in Oct:* Lincoln Days festival; *Second Thurs in Dec:* Christmas in the Park.

Directions: From the south on I-65: take exit 81 and go east on KY 84 (Sonora) approximately 9 miles. From the north on I-65: take exit 91 (Elizabethtown) and go south on KY 61 for approximately 12 miles.

22 Site: LINCOLN BOYHOOD HOME AT KNOB CREEK, 7120 Bardstown Rd., Hodgenville, KY 42748, ☎ 502/549-3741

Description: Lincoln's Boyhood Home is a replicated log cabin made of material from another cabin erected in 1800. The Lincoln family resided on the site from 1811 to 1816 before leaving for Indiana because of a faulty land title and ensuing disputes.

Open to Public: Apr 1–Oct 31: Daily. Call for hours.

Admission Fees: Adults $1, children 50¢, children under 5 free.

Visitor Services: Gift shop, museum, handicapped access, rest rooms.

Directions: From I-65: take exit 81, go northeast on KY 84 into Hodgenville, and proceed 6 miles northeast on U.S. 31E. Property is on the left.

23 Site: LINCOLN MUSEUM, 66 Lincoln Sq., Hodgenville, KY 42748, ☎ 502/358-3163

Description: On the square in downtown Hodgenville, birthplace of Abraham Lincoln, is the Lincoln Museum, which features with realistic wax models 12 scenes from Lincoln's life. There is also an art collection, a film, and Civil War memorabilia.

Open to Public: Mon–Sat 8:30am–5pm, Sun 12:30–5pm.

Admission Fees: Adults $3, children $1.50, seniors and military $2.50. Groups (12 or more): Adults $2, children $1.

Visitor Services: Gift shop, rest rooms, museum.

Regularly Scheduled Events: *Feb:* Lincoln's Birthday; *Second weekend in Oct:* Lincoln Days festival.

Directions: From I-65: take exit 81 and go east on KY 84 approximately 10 miles into Hodgenville.

Lebanon

24 **Site:** HISTORIC HOMES AND LANDMARKS TOUR OF LEBANON, KENTUCKY, c/o Lebanon-Marion County Chamber of Commerce, 21 Court Sq., Lebanon, KY 40033, ☎ 502/692-9594

Description: This self-guided tour offers a significant glimpse at a town where the Civil War came as a severe blow. Lebanon was the site of three battles—1861, 1862, and 1863. Its railway location made it susceptible to attack. A free tour brochure may be obtained at the Lebanon-Marion County Chamber of Commerce.

Open to Public: *Chamber of Commerce office:* Mon–Fri 9am–5pm. The brochure may also be obtained at the library, 201 East Main; the Hatfield Inn, 720 West Main; Super America, 601 West Main; and at some local restaurants.

Admission Fees: Free.

Visitor Services: Chamber of Commerce office: Rest rooms, information.

Directions: From the Blue Grass Parkway: take exit 42 and travel south on KY 555, bypassing Springfield and crossing U.S. 150. The road turns into KY 55. Proceed 8 miles into Lebanon and to U.S. 68, which becomes Main St.; turn right at the second traffic light. Chamber office is on the left, next door to the courthouse. From I-65 south: take exit 112 (16 miles south of Louisville) and proceed southeasterly on KY 245—bypassing Bardstown—to U.S. 150. Proceed on U.S. 150 to Springfield and KY 55; then follow directions as above.

Lexington

25 **Site:** ASHLAND—THE HENRY CLAY ESTATE, 120 Sycamore Rd., Lexington, KY 40502, ☎ 606/266-8581

Description: Ashland, a National Historic Landmark, was the home of "the Great Compromiser," Henry Clay, from 1811 until his death in 1852. Clay was a U.S. Senator, Speaker of the House, Secretary of State, and a presidential candidate three times. He is especially noted for his devo-

tion to the Union, and during his lifetime, he tried valiantly to prevent the ensuing Civil War. Ashland was rebuilt in the 1850s by Clay's son. A Civil War skirmish took place near Ashland, and the house was used as a hospital afterward. The estate includes 20 acres; several ante bellum dependencies; and a large, formal garden.

Open to Public: Mon–Sat 10am–4:30pm, Sun 1–4:30pm; closed Mondays in Feb, Mar, Nov, and Dec. Closed the month of Jan and on holidays. *Note:* Tours on the hour; last tour at 4pm. No tours during Jan.

Admission Fees: Adults $6, students 13–college $3, children 6–12 $2, children under 6 free.

Visitor Services: Tours, museum, gift shop, food, rest rooms.

Regularly Scheduled Events: *Summer:* Reenactments; Abraham and Mary Todd Lincoln living history: call for special events; *Dec:* Christmas events.

Directions: Accessible from I-75 and I-64. Located at the corner of Richmond Rd. (also E. Main St.) and Sycamore Rd.

---

26 **Site:** HUNT-MORGAN HOUSE, 201 North Mill St., Lexington, KY 40507,
☎ 606/253-0362

Description: Built in 1814 for John Wesley Hunt, possibly the first millionaire west of the Alleghenies, this outstanding example of regional Federal architecture is interpreted as an urban antebellum (1814–1840) dwelling set in historic Gratz Park where Civil War divisions among neighbors are dramatically pointed out. It was the family home of Gen. John Hunt Morgan, "Thunderbolt of the Confederacy," and the birthplace of Nobel laureate Dr. Thomas Hunt Morgan, pioneer geneticist. See family and period furnishings throughout and a delightful city garden. The Alexander T. Hunt Civil War Museum occupies several rooms.

Open to Public: Mar–Nov: Tues–Sat 10am–4pm, Sun 2–5pm. *Note:* Tours begin at 15 minutes past the hour. Last tour 45 minutes before closing.

Admission Fees: Adults $5, students $3, groups (15 or more) $4. Call for school rates.

Visitor Services: Gift and book shop, museum, rest rooms, limited handicapped access.

Directions: From I-64/75: take exit 113; go south on N. Broadway; turn left on W. Third St. and almost immediately right on Mill St. The house is at the corner of Mill and Second sts., with parking off Second St.

---

27 **Site:** LEXINGTON CEMETERY, 833 West Main St., Lexington, KY 40508,
☎ 606/255-5522

Description: A self-guided tour leads visitors to graves of historical interest, including Civil War Confederate generals. The tour points out grave sites of Civil War luminaries such as Confederate General John Hunt Morgan and John C. Breckinridge. Also, relatives of Mary Todd Lincoln are interred here, as are both Union and Confederate soldiers, the latter being honored by two notable monuments.

Open to Public: Daily 8am–5pm.

Admission Fees: Free.

Visitor Services: Information.

Directions: From I-64/I-75: take exit 115 and proceed south on Newtown Pike (Hwy. 922) to West Main St. (Hwy. 421). Go right on West Main and turn into large stone cemetery gatehouse on the right. Information is available at offices in gatehouse or at the Lexington Convention and Visitors Bureau on Vine St.

---

28 **Site:** MARY TODD LINCOLN HOUSE, 578 West Main St., P.O. Box 132, Lexington, KY 40501, ☎ 606/233-9999

Description: First Lady Mary Todd Lincoln resided in this fashionable brick home between the ages of 14 and 21, and Abraham Lincoln was a guest here following their marriage. Personal articles from the Lincoln and Todd families are on display. Restored garden to the rear.

Open to Public: Tues–Sat 10am–4pm; last tour at 3:15pm.

Admission Fees: Adults $5, children 6–12 $2, groups (20 or more) $3.50.

Visitor Services: Museum, handicapped access, gift shop.

Directions: From I-64/75: take exit 115, go south on Newtown Pike (Hwy. 922), cross New Circle Rd. (Hwy. 4), and go to West Main St. (Hwy. 421). Go left on West Main, and house is on the right on the corner of West Main and Tucker, just before Rupp Arena.

---

29 **Site:** WAVELAND, 225 Waveland Museum Rd., Lexington, KY 40514-1601, ☎ 606/272-3611

Description: Both Confederate and Union armies prized the Standardbred horses raised on this plantation, which primarily grew tobacco and hemp. Everyday antebellum life of the Bryan family—including their slaves—is interpreted here. The 1847 brick residence is of classic Greek Revival design; three original outbuildings, including slave quarters, remain.

Open to Public: Mar–Dec: Mon–Sat 10am–5pm, Sun 1–5pm. Last tour at 4pm.

Admission Fees: Adults $5, students K–college $2, seniors $4.

Visitor Services: Tours, rest rooms, picnic area. First floor has handicapped access, and a notebook with photos of second floor is available.

Regularly Scheduled Events: *Feb:* "Tours and Teas"; *Dec:* Christmas Candlelight Tours.

Directions: From New Circle Road (KY 4): travel south on Nicholasville Road (U.S. 27) for 2 miles; turn right on Waveland Museum Lane; parking is on the right.

Louisville

---

30 | **Site:** CAVE HILL CEMETERY AND ARBORETUM, 701 Baxter Ave., Louisville, KY 40204, ☎ 502/451-5630

Description: The National Cemetery here contains the remains of many Union soldiers, including three Union generals. Local Southern sympathizers provided a separate section for Confederate dead, including three of their generals.

Open to Public: *Office and cemetery:* Daily 8am–4:45pm. Gates are locked promptly at 5pm.

Admission Fees: Free.

Visitor Services: Information, rest rooms (no handicapped access).

Directions: From I-64: take exit 8 and follow Grinstead Dr. west approximately .5 mile to the Grinstead Dr. entrance to Cave Hill Cemetery.

---

31 | **Site:** FARMINGTON, 3033 Bardstown Rd., Louisville, KY 40205, ☎ 502/452-9920

Description: Farmington is an 1810 house that was built to plans designed by Thomas Jefferson. The site interprets life on the plantation from 1812 through the Civil War, including the roles of African Americans who lived at Farmington. Joshua Fry Speed, son of the original owners of Farmington, went to Springfield, Illinois, in 1835 and later shared living quarters in Springfield with future president Abraham Lincoln. Speed became Lincoln's most trusted friend and confidant, and Lincoln spent 6 weeks as a guest at Farmington in 1841. Joshua Fry Speed served as Lincoln's advisor on western affairs during the Civil War but declined the president's offer to appoint him secretary of state. However, his brother, James Speed, did serve as attorney general during Lincoln's second term.

Open to Public: Mon–Sat 10am–4:30pm, Sun 1:30–4:30pm. Closed Jan. 1, Easter, Derby (first Sat in May), Thanksgiving Day, Christmas Eve, and Christmas Day.

Admission Fees: Adults $4, children 6–17 $2, children under 6 free, seniors $3. Call for group rates.

Visitor Services: Tours, museum, information, gift shop, visitors center, rest rooms, wheelchair lift to first floor.

Regularly Scheduled Events: *Apr:* Plant sale; *First Sat in May:* Kentucky Derby breakfast; *Dec:* Lunchtime theater; Candlelight tours; Call for additional events.

Directions: From I-264 (Watterson Expressway): take exit 15, go north on Bardstown Rd., and follow signs to Farmington (less than .5 mile).

Maysville

---

32 | **Site:** MASON COUNTY MUSEUM, 215 Sutton St., Maysville, KY 41056-1109, ☎ 606/564-5865 (museum), 606/564-9411 (Maysville Tourism)

Description: A permanent exhibit, book collection, and part of a video shown here offer a significant glimpse into the region's Civil War heritage. Maysville was a divided community throughout the conflict: it had economic ties to the free and neighboring North—as well as cultural ties to the slave-holding South. Take time also to see the impressive 1887 Union monument in the Maysville Cemetery (on KY 10, near the city limits).

Open to Public: Jan–Mar: Tues–Sat 10am–4pm. Apr–Dec: Mon–Sat 10am–4pm.

Admission Fee: Adults $2, children 50¢.

Visitor Services: Museum tours, research assistance, information, gift shop, art gallery.

Directions: From the Alexandria-Ashland ("AA") Highway (KY 9): exit at U.S. 68, follow U.S. 68 north to Bridge St., turn right on Bridge St., and take the next left onto Second St.. Proceed to Sutton St. (third traffic light). The museum is the second building on the right.

Middlesboro

33 **Site:** CUMBERLAND GAP NATIONAL HISTORICAL PARK. Mailing address: P.O. Box 1848, Middlesboro, KY 40965, located on U.S. 25E South, ☎ 606/248-2817

Description: Cumberland Gap is the historic mountain pass on the Wilderness Road that opened the pathway for westward migration. During the Civil War, Cumberland Gap was first held by the South and then captured by Union troops. Each side held the gap twice.

Open to Public: Mid-June–Labor Day: Daily 8am–6pm. Labor Day–mid-June: Daily 8am–5pm. Visitors Center closed Christmas and New Year's Days.

Admission Fees: Free.

Visitor Services: Bookstore, rest rooms, trails, museum, information, camping, handicapped access.

Directions: From I-75: take exit 29 at Corbin and follow signs on U.S. 25E (Cumberland Gap Pkwy.) through Middlesboro. The park is .25 mile south of Middlesboro, KY. From I-81 in Tennessee: access U.S. 25E going north at Morristown. Park is approximately 50 miles north of Morristown.

Munfordville

34 **Site:** HART COUNTY MUSEUM, 109 Main St., P.O. Box 606, Munfordville, KY 42765, ☎ 502/524-0101

Description: Hart County's seat of government is Munfordville, site of a Civil War battle in 1862. The museum includes Civil War memorabilia related to the battle of Munfordville and to two Munfordville natives, CSA Brig. Gen. Simon Bolivar Buckner (later governor of Kentucky) and USA Maj. Gen. Thomas Wood. Buckner and Wood were childhood friends and classmates at West Point, an association that amply illustrates Kentucky's deep divisions during the Civil War. Museum staff can direct you to sites of the Battle of Munfordville.

Open to Public: Mon–Fri 10am–2pm.

Admission Fees: Free.

Visitor Services: Museum, rest rooms.

Regularly Scheduled Events: *Sept:* Battle of Munfordville reenactment.

Directions: From I-65: take exit 65 (U.S. 31W) 1 mile south into Munfordville. U.S. 31W becomes Main St. Museum is in a two-story brick building next to city hall.

Nancy

35 Site: MILL SPRINGS BATTLEFIELD NATIONAL HISTORIC LANDMARK. Mailing address: P.O. Box 814, Somerset, KY 42502, ☎ 606/679-1859

Description: The Battle of Mill Springs was the first major Union victory of the Civil War. This victory turned the Confederate flank in Kentucky and opened up an invasion route to east Tennessee and even Nashville. Confederate Gen. Felix K. Zollicoffer was killed in this battle; he was the first general killed in the west. The Union forces were commanded by Gen. George H. Thomas, who would later gain fame as "the Rock of Chickamauga."

Open to Public: Daily from dawn to dusk.

Admission Fees: Free.

Visitor Services: Driving tour, information, handicapped access, guided tours for six persons or more with 1 week advance notice.

Regularly Scheduled Events: *Weekend closest to Jan 19 and Memorial Day:* Battle of Mill Springs Commemoration Ceremony.

Directions: From I-75: take the London/U.S. 80 exit and follow U.S. 80 west to Somerset. At Somerset, take the Cumberland Pkwy. west. (U.S. 80 and the Parkway are the same route briefly in Somerset.) From the Cumberland Pkwy., take the second left and then the first right. You will then be headed west on KY 80. Proceed approximately 9 miles to Nancy. At Nancy, turn left (south) on KY 235. Proceed approximately 1 mile to Zollicoffer Park on the left. Watch for the brown signs for Mill Springs Battlefield NHL.

36 Site: ZOLLICOFFER PARK. Mailing address: P.O. Box 814, Somerset, KY 42502. Physical address: Hwy. 235, 1 mile south of Nancy, ☎ 606/679-1859

Description: Zollicoffer Park marks the site of the fiercest fighting in the Battle of Mill Springs, an important early–Civil War conflict. The park is named for Confederate Gen. Felix K. Zollicoffer,

mortally wounded in the battle. The park contains a one-half-mile walking trail, interpretive signs, the Confederate mass grave, and the Zollicoffer Confederate Memorial Cemetery.

Open to Public: Daily from dawn to dusk.

Admission Fees: Free.

Visitor Services: Driving tour, information, guided tours for six persons or more with 1-week advance notice.

Regularly Scheduled Events: *Weekend closest to Jan 19 and Memorial Day:* Battle of Mill Springs commemoration ceremony.

Directions: See Mill Springs Battlefield listing.

Nicholasville

37 | **Site:** CAMP NELSON, off U.S. 27 South, 8 miles south of Nicholasville; Camp Nelson Preservation Office, 105 Court Row, Nicholasville, KY 40356, ☎ 606/881-9126

Description: Camp Nelson was a major Union supply depot for the armies of the Ohio and Cumberland. It supplied the Union invasion of Knoxville and the Battles of Saltville in southwest Virginia. It was also the third-largest recruiting base for African American soldiers in the United States, with more than 10,000 black soldiers recruited here. On request, the visitors center at Camp Nelson National Cemetery shows a video highlighting the history of Camp Nelson (call ☎ 606/885-5727 to arrange). Approximately 200 acres of the 4,000-acre depot site have been purchased and are being preserved. A 10-stop driving tour highlights the county's Civil War history. A brochure is available from the Camp Nelson Preservation office at the address above or at the Camp Nelson National Cemetery visitors center.

Open to Public: *Site:* Daily from dawn to dusk. *Camp Nelson Preservation office:* Hours vary; tour brochure available from box outside office.

Admission Fees: Free.

Visitor Services: Information, driving tour.

Regularly Scheduled Events: *May:* Living history weekend.

Directions: From I-75: take exit 110 (U.S. 60) west to New Circle Rd. (KY 4) in Lexington. Follow KY 4 east to the Nicholasville Rd. exit; take Nicho-lasville Rd. (U.S. 27) south approximately 10 miles to Nicholasville and proceed to Camp Nelson Preservation office at 105 Court Row, next to the County Courthouse. Camp Nelson is 8 miles farther south on U.S. 27.

Paducah

38 | **Site:** DOWNTOWN PADUCAH CIVIL WAR WALKING TOUR. Mailing address: 128 Broadway, Paducah, KY 42002, ☎ 800/PADUCAH or 502/443-8783

Description: The tour map is based on one drawn in 1861 by a Federal captain who was among the troops occupying Paducah

by order of Gen. Ulysses S. Grant. In addition, one of the magnificent murals adorning the flood wall concerns the Civil War in

Paducah. The eight sites are scattered throughout downtown Paducah, based around U.S. 45 and U.S. 60.

Open to Public: *Paducah Visitors Center:* Mon–Fri 9am–5pm. On weekends, the brochure may be obtained at the White-haven Welcome Center, I-24, exit 7; the Museum of the American Quilter's Society, 215 Jefferson; the Market House Museum, 200 Broadway; or in various local antique shops.

Admission Fees: Free.

Visitor Services: *Paducah Visitors Center:* Information, rest rooms.

Directions: From I-24: take exit 4 (this route is called the Downtown Loop of I-24), follow signs for Quilter's Museum—with street numbers descending—into downtown area, and turn left on Broadway to visitors center.

Perryville

39 **Site:** PERRYVILLE BATTLEFIELD STATE HISTORIC SITE, P.O. Box 296, Hwy. 1920, Perryville, KY 40468-9999, ☎ 606/332-8631

Description: Kentucky's greatest Civil War battle took place outside Perryville on October 8, 1862. It was the South's last serious attempt to gain possession of the state, and a museum on the grounds interprets the battle and its aftermath.

Open to Public: Daily 9am–5pm. Closed Nov 1–Mar 31.

Admission Fees: *Museum:* Adults $2, children $1. Groups (10 or more): Adults $1.50, children 50¢.

Visitor Services: Gift shop, rest rooms, museum, handicapped access, trails.

Regularly Scheduled Events: *Weekend closest to Oct 8:* Battle reenactment.

Directions: From Bluegrass Pkwy.: take exit 59, go 24 miles south on U.S. 127 through Harrodsburg to Danville, take 127/150 bypass, go west (turn right) on U.S. 150, go 9 miles to Perryville, and then go north (turn right) on KY 1920.

The Dug Road at Perryville Battlefield, Perryville, KY. (Photograph courtesy of The Civil War Trust.)

40 **Site:** TOWN OF PERRYVILLE, U.S. 68 and U.S. 150, P.O. Box 65, Perryville, KY 40468, ☎ 606/332-1862

Description: The town of Perryville has been a National Register district since 1976. Looking much as it did during the 1862 Battle of Perryville, this site is one of the most intact 19th-century communities in the state. The 1840s commercial district, "Merchants' Row," still stands. Numerous homes and churches served as field hospitals, and remnants of the battle's aftermath remain to a large extent.

Open to Public: Daily from dawn to dusk.

Admission Fees: Free.

Visitor Services: Food, gas, gift shop, rest rooms, lodging.

Regularly Scheduled Events: *Weekend closest to Oct 8:* Battle of Perryville reenactment.

Directions: From Bluegrass Pkwy.: take exit 59, go 24 miles south on U.S. 127 through Harrodsburg to Danville, take 127/150 bypass, and go west (turn right) on U.S. 150 for 9 miles to Perryville.

Pewee Valley

41 **Site:** PEWEE VALLEY CONFEDERATE CEMETERY AND MONUMENT. Mailing address: c/o Oldham County Planning Commission, 110 West Jefferson, LaGrange, KY 40031.

Description: The Pewee Valley Confederate Cemetery and Monument are all that remain from the Kentucky Confederate Home, established in 1904. Interred here are 313 Confederate veterans—most of whom had been residents of the former institution.

Open to Public: Daily from dawn to dusk.

Admission Fees: Free.

Visitor Services: None.

Regularly Scheduled Events: *First Sat in June:* Confederate Memorial Day service.

Includes Confederate reenactors and the firing of period artillery.

Directions: From I-265 (Gene Snyder Fwy.): take exit 30 (Pewee Valley-Anchorage Exit), turn right on LaGrange Rd. (Hwy. 146), proceed 1.9 miles, and turn right on Maple Ave. At this intersection is a historical marker about the cemetery. The cemetery and monument are located on Maple Ave. .8 miles beyond the intersection.

Prestonsburg

42 **Site:** THE SAMUEL MAY HOUSE. Mailing address: Friends of the Samuel May House, P.O. Box 1460, Prestonsburg, KY 41653. Physical address: 1135 North Lake Dr., Prestonsburg, ☎ 606/889-9608 or 606/886-1341

Description: This recently restored, Federal-style house was the boyhood home of Col. Andrew Jackson May, the leading

Confederate organizer in Eastern Kentucky. In the meadow below the house, Colonel May and Col. Hiram Hawkins organized the 5th Kentucky Infantry Regiment. From time to time during the Civil War, the house served as a Confederate recruiting station.

Open to Public: Wed–Fri 10am–5pm, Sat–Sun 10am–6pm.

Admission Fees: Adults $5, children 12–18 $3.50, children under 12 free.

Visitor Services: Tours, gift shop, rest rooms, handicapped access.

Directions: From the Mountain Pkwy.: continue on KY 114 20 miles past the termination of the Mountain Pkwy. (in Salyersville) to Prestonsburg. After crossing the bridge over the Big Sandy River, turn left (north) on U.S. 23/460 and drive 1 mile past a Wendy's Restaurant on the right. The May House is on the left. Turn left down a hill; the parking lot is below the house.

Richmond

43 **Site:** BATTLE OF RICHMOND, c/o Tourism Commission, Visitor Center, 345 Lancaster Ave., Richmond, KY 40475, ☎ 800/866-3705

Description: The Battle of Richmond was part of the important 1862 Perryville campaign. Richmond was the site of one of the Confederacy's greatest victories. A self-guided tour brochure and taped narrative are available at the Richmond Visitor Center. The eight "stations" of the driving tour begin at the top of Big Hill southeast of Berea and end at the Madison County Courthouse in Richmond.

Open to Public: *Tourism office:* Mon–Fri 8am–5pm.

Admission Fees: Refundable deposit for tape: $5.

Visitor Services: Rest rooms, information.

Directions: From I-75: take exit 87 and follow signs to Richmond Visitor Center (near Eastern Kentucky University campus) on Lancaster Ave.

44 **Site:** WHITE HALL STATE HISTORIC SITE, 500 White Hall Shrine Rd., Richmond, KY 40475-9159, ☎ 606/623-9178

Description: Cassius Marcellus Clay, "the Lion of White Hall," was an outspoken emancipationist, newspaper publisher, and minister to Russia under his friend Abraham Lincoln. This Italianate mansion, furnished in period pieces, was built for Clay and has many noteworthy features.

Open to Public: Apr–Labor Day: Daily 9am–5pm. Labor Day–Oct: Wed–Sun 9am–5pm. Closed from end of Oct to Apr 1.

Admission Fees: Adults $4, children $2.50. Groups (10 or more): Adults $3, children $2.

Visitor Services: Handicapped access, gift shop.

Regularly Scheduled Events: *Sept:* Living history weekend; *Oct:* Ghost Walk; *Dec:* A Victorian Christmas.

Directions: From I-75: take exit 95, travel on Hwy. 627, and cross U.S. 25. The house is located at the end of Hwy. 627.

Sacramento

45 **Site:** BATTLE OF SACRAMENTO DRIVING TOUR. Mailing address:
c/o City Clerk, P.O. Box 245, Sacramento, KY 42372,
☎ 502/736-5114

Description: The Battle of Sacramento took place early in the Civil War, and the 10-stop driving tour re-creates its daring action and introduces the combat's participants. CSA Lt. Col. Nathan Bedford Forrest emerged the victor. A free driving-tour brochure is available at the Sacramento City Hall, located at 292 East Main St. in Sacramento.

Open to Public: The free brochure is available at the Sacramento City Hall, which is open Mon–Fri 8am–4pm. During other hours and on weekends, the brochure may be picked up at Sam's Y Market, near the junction of KY 85 and KY 81.

Admission Fees: Free.

Visitor Services: City Hall: Rest rooms, information.

Regularly Scheduled Events: *Third weekend in May:* Annual reenactment.

Directions: From Western Kentucky Pkwy.: take exit 58 and travel north on U.S. 431 5 miles to unincorporated community of South Carrollton. Turn left on KY 81 and proceed to Sacramento. City Hall is located at 292 Main St.

Smithland

46 **Site:** FORT SMITH, c/o Smithland Area Chamber of Commerce, P.O. Box 196,
Smithland, KY 42081, ☎ 502/928-2446

Description: The star-shaped, earthen Fort Smith was constructed by Union forces after Gen. Ulysses S. Grant seized Paducah in 1861. The fort was part of a larger complex designed to protect the mouth of the Cumberland River at the Ohio River. From this location, soldiers were sent down the Cumberland River to participate in the expedition against Forts Henry and Donelson near the Tennessee-Kentucky border. As many as 2,000 Union troops were stationed in Smithland during the Civil War. By 1864, the fort was manned by a contingent of the 13th U.S. Colored Heavy Artillery. Several of these men are buried in the cemetery adjacent to the fort.

Open to Public: Daily from dawn to dusk. Obtain brochure at the Chamber of Commerce Mon–Fri 9am–4:30pm.

Admission Fees: Free.

Visitor Services: Trails, information (at chamber office).

Regularly Scheduled Events: *First weekend in May:* Civil War living history, artillery demonstration, Grand Ball, and sutlers.

Directions: From I-24: take exit 31 onto Rte. 453. Travel approximately 15 miles to Smithland. To Chamber office: at caution light in Smithland, turn left; proceed 3 blocks; turn right onto Wilson Ave.; the

Chamber office is located at 310 Wilson Ave. (Smithland City Hall). To Fort Smith: at the caution light in Smithland, turn left; proceed 1 block and turn left; cross intersection of Wilson Ave. and proceed up steep hill into Smithland Cemetery. Follow the road to the water tower. Travel on foot on the trail to the right (west) of the tower approximately 50 feet; the fort is on the right of the trail.

Staffordsville

47 **Site:** MOUNTAIN HOMEPLACE, Rte. 2275, P.O. Box 1850, Staffordsville, KY 41256, ☎ 606/297-1850

Description: This Mountain Homeplace recreates life in Johnson County from 1850 to 1875. The historic buildings that have been assembled here include a one-room schoolhouse, a blacksmith shop, and other buildings and implements used to operate a farm. Interpreters provide oral information about the Civil War in this area of Kentucky. An award-winning video shown at the visitors center features actor Richard Thomas who spent summers with his family in Johnson County during his youth. The video includes a segment about Johnson County's tenuous situation during the Civil War. Both sides had ardent sympathizers here, and neither the Union nor the Confederate flag was allowed to fly above the county courthouse.

Open to Public: Wed–Sat 10am–6pm, Sun 1–6pm.

Admission Fees: Adults $5, children $3, seniors $4. Groups: Call in advance for special rates.

Visitor Services: Trails, tours, museum, information, gift shop, visitors center, rest rooms.

Directions: From the west on I-64: take exit 98 (several miles east of Winchester) and travel south on Mountain Pkwy. for approximately 70 miles to Salyersville. Turn left on U.S. 460 and proceed 15 miles to KY 40. Turn left onto KY 40 and proceed approximately 3.5 miles. Turn right on Paintsville Lake Rd. (Rte. 2275) past intersection with Hwy. 172 and follow signs. From the east on I-64: take exit 191 (south of Catlettsburg) and proceed south on U.S. 23 for 59 miles to the intersection with U.S. 460. Turn right on U.S. 460 and travel approximately 3.5 miles. Turn right on Paintsville Lake Rd. (Rte. 2275) past the intersection with Hwy. 172 and follow signs.

South Union

48 **Site:** SHAKER MUSEUM AT SOUTH UNION. Mailing address: South Union, KY 42283, ☎ 502/542-4167

Description: Scores of encampments occurred within this pacifist village. Afterward, it was estimated that over 100,000 meals had been provided to soldiers on both sides.

Open to Public: Mar–Dec 15: Mon–Sat 10am–5pm, Sun 1–5pm. Open off-season by appointment.

Admission Fees: $4.

Visitor Services: Museum, tours, gift shop, lodging at nearby Shaker Tavern (located on KY 73 1.5 miles from the museum).

Regularly Scheduled Events: *Summer:* Shaker Festival; *Fall:* Candlelight Tour; Civil War Shaker Breakfast; *Dec:* Christmas at Shakertown Celebration.

Directions: Located on U.S. 68, 10 miles west of Bowling Green. From I-65: take exit 20 (Natcher Pkwy.) to exit 5 (U.S. 68/80). Turn left and follow signs, approximately 10 miles to South Union.

Washington

49 **Site:** OLD WASHINGTON, 2215 Old Main St., P.O. Box 227, Washington, KY 41096, ☎ 606/759-7411

Description: Civil War–associated sites within this 1785 outpost for pioneers traveling the Buffalo Trace include the birthplace and childhood home of Confederate Gen. Albert Sidney Johnston; the Methodist Episcopal Church South, significant in African American history; Paxton Inn, a documented Underground Railroad station; and the site of the slave auction that inspired Harriet Beecher Stowe to write *Uncle Tom's Cabin.*

Open to Public: Apr–Dec: Mon–Sat 10am–4:30pm, Sun 1–4:30pm. Closed Jan–Mar.

Admission Fees: Adults $3, children $1.

Visitor Services: Tours, museum, information, gift shop, visitors center, rest rooms, food.

Directions: From Ashland-Alexandria Hwy. ("AA" Hwy./KY 9): exit at U.S. 68 and travel 2 miles south. Old Washington borders old U.S. 68 to the east of new U.S. 68.

West Point

50 **Site:** FORT DUFFIELD, 509 Elm St., West Point, KY 40177, ☎ 502/922-4260

Description: This 1861 Union fortification protected the supply route from Louisville over the Old L & N Turnpike. One of the best preserved and largest forts in Kentucky, it was designed to be manned by 1,000 troops.

Open to Public: Daily from dawn to dusk.

Admission Fees: Donations welcome.

Visitor Services: Trails, information, handicapped access.

Regularly Scheduled Events: *Memorial Day:* Reenactment.

Directions: From I-65: take exit 125 west on I-265 (Gene Snyder Fwy.) to U.S. 31 W/60, cross bridge into Hardin County, and watch for entrance sign on left; or turn right into town of West Point and go to visitors center, in a red caboose at Fourth and Main St., for information.

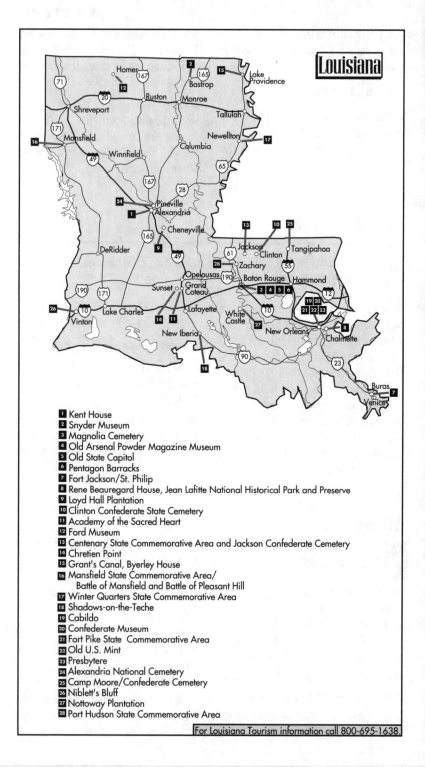

Louisiana

1 Kent House
2 Snyder Museum
3 Magnolia Cemetery
4 Old Arsenal Powder Magazine Museum
5 Old State Capitol
6 Pentagon Barracks
7 Fort Jackson/St. Philip
8 Rene Beauregard House, Jean Lafitte National Historical Park and Preserve
9 Loyd Hall Plantation
10 Clinton Confederate State Cemetery
11 Academy of the Sacred Heart
12 Ford Museum
13 Centenary State Commemorative Area and Jackson Confederate Cemetery
14 Chretien Point
15 Grant's Canal, Byerley House
16 Mansfield State Commemorative Area/
   Battle of Mansfield and Battle of Pleasant Hill
17 Winter Quarters State Commemorative Area
18 Shadows-on-the-Teche
19 Cabildo
20 Confederate Museum
21 Fort Pike State Commemorative Area
22 Old U.S. Mint
23 Presbytere
24 Alexandria National Cemetery
25 Camp Moore/Confederate Cemetery
26 Niblett's Bluff
27 Nottoway Plantation
28 Port Hudson State Commemorative Area

LOUISIANA

*L*OUISIANA WAS NOT A MAJOR BATTLEGROUND because it was essentially taken out of the war by mid-1863. But several important battles and campaigns were fought in the state—more than 500 engagements in all.

New Orleans was naturally a primary target for Union attack. Possession of New Orleans, the South's largest city and major port, was necessary for control of the Mississippi. Additionally, New Orleans was the site of large commercial, financial, and industrial firms. In April 1862, a Union fleet under Flag Officer David G. Farragut began operations against the Crescent City. Farragut's vessels steamed past Forts Jackson and St. Philip early on April 24 and destroyed the small Confederate fleet that supported them. Confederate troops evacuated New Orleans rather than submit to a bombardment. The city surrendered to Farragut, and Union troops began occupying New Orleans on May 1.

In the spring of 1863, Gen. Nathaniel P. Banks's Union army moved against the Confederate stronghold at Port Hudson, acting in conjunction with Gen. Ulysses S. Grant's attack on Vicksburg, Mississippi. The siege of Port Hudson lasted from May 23 to July 9, the longest genuine siege in American military history. Confederate Gen. Franklin Gardner surrendered to Banks after hearing of the fall of Vicksburg. The last Confederate stronghold on the Mississippi fell into Union hands, placing the river under Federal control and splitting the Confederacy in two.

In mid-March 1864, General Banks launched the Red River campaign. His objective was to drive Gen. Richard Taylor's Confederate army from Louisiana and to plant the Union flag in the interior of Texas. After an initial retreat, Taylor attacked the Union army near Mansfield on April 8, and the Confederates inflicted a severe defeat on the Federals. Banks retreated to Pleasant Hill during the night, and Taylor attacked again the next day. The Battle of Pleasant Hill was a draw. Taylor's success in the Red River campaign delayed Union victory in the war by several months. Only small skirmishes occurred in the state after the Red River campaign. In mid-May 1865, Confederate Gen. Edmund Kirby Smith contacted Union Gen. Edward R. S. Canby about a surrender of the Trans-Mississippi Department. Terms were worked out and signed on May 26. The war was finally over for Louisiana.

by Dr. Arthur W. Bergeron, Jr.

For More Information

"The Louisiana Civil War Heritage Guide," available through the Louisiana Office of Tourism, outlines significant military actions in Louisiana during the Civil War (such as the role it played in the capture of the Mississippi River). The guide also highlights some of the economic and social issues in the state at the time and lists cultural attractions of the era that are of interest to visitors.

A copy of the guide can be obtained through the state's 10 Welcome Centers or by calling ☎ **800/ 695-1638** or **504/342-8119.**

Alexandria

1 **Site:** KENT HOUSE, 3601 Bayou Rapides Rd., P.O. Box 12248, Alexandria, LA 71315-2248, ☎ 318/487-5998

Description: Kent House, a raised French-Creole cottage built in 1796, is the oldest remaining structure in Central Louisiana. The courageous owner, Robert Hynson, refused to leave his home, thus preventing Union troops retreating from the battle of Mansfield from setting the house on fire.

Unfortunately, Hynson could not save his stock or outbuildings from the ravaging army. Many of Kent House's destroyed structures are replicated with antebellum dependencies from other plantations. The complex includes a kitchen, slave cabins, carriage house, milk house, blacksmith shop, and sugar mill. The site features living history events throughout the year.

Open to Public: Mon–Sat 9am–5pm, Sun 1–5pm.

Admission Fees: Adults $5, children 6–12 $2, children under 6 free, seniors $4.

Visitor Services: Tours, museum, information, gift shop, rest rooms.

Directions: From I-49: exit onto MacArthur Blvd. Remain on MacArthur until it intersects Bayou Rapides Rd. Turn left on Bayou Rapides Rd., continue .5 mile, and turn left to Kent House.

Bastrop

2 **Site:** SNYDER MUSEUM, 1620 East Madison St. (U.S. 165N), Bastrop, LA 71220, ☎ 318/281-8760

Description: This museum highlights local history, including a special display dedicated to the Civil War. It also houses a genealogical section.

Open to Public: Mon 9am–1pm, Tues–Fri 9am–4pm.
Admission Fees: Free.
Visitor Services: Rest rooms.

Directions: From I-20: take Rte. 165 through Monroe to Bastrop. Rte. 165 becomes East Madison St. Museum is located on U.S. 165 North.

Baton Rouge

3 **Site:** MAGNOLIA CEMETERY, located at North Dufrocq and Main streets, c/o Foundation for Historical Louisiana, 900 N. Blvd., Baton Rouge, LA 70802, ☎ 504/387-2464

Description: Much of the heaviest fighting of the Battle of Baton Rouge took place in this cemetery on August 5, 1862. The battle pitted Union forces under the overall command of Brig. Gen. Thomas Williams against Confederate forces of Maj. Gen. John C. Breckinridge. Though Union forces were pushed back to the river, guns from the Federal fleet forced Confederate withdrawal after expected support from the Rebel ironclad gunboat *Arkansas* did not materialize. The ferocity of the attack, however, convinced the Federal command to withdraw their forces to protect New Orleans, allowing General Breckinridge to fortify Port Hudson. This delayed Federal domination of the Mississippi River until July 1863. Confederate soldiers who died at Magnolia Cemetery are buried in a mass grave. A brochure is available from the address listed above and at the site.

Open to Public: Daily from dawn to dusk.

Admission Fees: Donations welcome.

Visitor Services: Interpretive center under construction.

Regularly Scheduled Events: *Sat closest to Aug 5:* Battle of Baton Rouge commemoration.

Directions: From I-10: exit onto Florida St. Circle around. The cemetery is bounded by Florida and Laurel sts. and 19th and 22d sts., near downtown Baton Rouge.

4 **Site:** OLD ARSENAL POWDER MAGAZINE MUSEUM, P.O. Box 94125, Baton Rouge, LA 70804-9125, ☎ 504/342-0401

Description: Before Louisiana seceded from the Union on January 26, 1861, the governor ordered the state militia to seize the arsenal. Shortly thereafter, Louisiana joined the Confederate States of America, and the weapons, ammunition, and powder in the Baton Rouge compound were rushed to the embattled Southern armies. In May 1862, Union forces captured Louisiana's capital city. Federal troops occupied the arsenal and the fortifications.

Open to Public: Mon–Sat 9am–4pm, Sun 1–4pm.

Admission Fees: Adults $1; students 6–17 50¢; children under 6, seniors and chaperones of organized children's groups free.

Visitor Services: Self-guided tours, museum, interpretive center.

Directions: From I-10: take Capital Access/Governor's Mansion exit. Keep straight toward the State Capitol. Arsenal is located on the State Capitol grounds, between the Capitol and the governor's mansion.

---

5 **Site: OLD STATE CAPITOL, 100 North Blvd., Baton Rouge, LA 70804,
☎ 504/342-0500**

Description: This building served as the State House of Louisiana until the state capital was moved to Opelousas to avoid capture by Federal troops. The Gothic structure was burned in 1862 when it was a Federal prison. On the grounds is the grave of Henry Watkins Allen, Confederate governor of Louisiana and brigadier general.

Open to Public: Tues–Sat 10am–4pm, Sun noon–4pm.

Admission Fees: Adults $4; children, seniors, and veterans $2.

Visitor Services: Tours, museum.

Directions: From I-10: take Government St. exit and turn left at light. Keep straight on Government St. until it changes to River Rd. Keep straight until you pass the Centroplex Complex (on right); turn right at North Blvd. The Old State Capitol can be seen on the right.

---

6 **Site: PENTAGON BARRACKS, 959 North Third St., Baton Rouge, LA, ☎ 504/342-1866**

Description: The Pentagon Barracks were constructed from 1819 to 1929 to house United States troops and were used as a garrison until 1877. From 1861 to 1862, the site was held by the Confederates. The barracks served as quarters for many famous soldiers, including Generals Wade Hampton, Robert E. Lee, and Stonewall Jackson.

Open to Public: Tues–Sat 10am–4pm, Sun 1–4pm.

Admission Fees: Free.

Visitor Services: Museum, interpretive center, rest rooms, tours.

Directions: From I-10: take Capital Access/Governor's Mansion exit. Keep straight around the Capitol until you see a flashing light; turn left. The Pentagon Barracks is the two-story brick building on the right. Parking lot in front.

Buras

7 **Site: FORT JACKSON/ST. PHILIP, P.O. Box 7043, Buras, LA 70041, ☎ 504/657-7083**

Description: This restored fort (1822–1832) was built to defend New Orleans and the mouth of the Mississippi River.

Open to Public: Daily 7am–5pm. *Museum:* Daily 9am–4:30pm.

Admission Fees: Free.

Visitor Services: Museum, walking tours.

Directions: From I-10 through New Orleans: cross the New Orleans Bridge, going west to Gretna. Get onto Westbank Expressway and proceed 1.5 miles to LA Hwy. 23. The fort is 60 miles south.

Chalmette

8 **Site:** RENE BEAUREGARD HOUSE, JEAN LAFITTE NATIONAL HISTORICAL PARK AND PRESERVE, 8686 West St. Bernard Hwy., Chalmette, LA 70043, ☎ 504/589-4430

Description: Located on the Battle of New Orleans (War of 1812) site, this two-story, cement-covered house was the home of Judge Rene Beauregard, son of Confederate Gen. P. G. T. Beauregard.

Open to Public: Daily 8:30am–5pm.

Admission Fees: Free.

Visitor Services: Interpretive center, information, tours, rest rooms.

Directions: From I-10 through the city of New Orleans: take I-610 east. Take Chalmette/Littlewood exit south to I-510 and then to State Rd. 47; turn right onto St. Bernard Hwy. After 2 miles, the Chalmette National Park sign will be visible.

Cheneyville

9 **Site:** LOYD HALL PLANTATION, 292 Loyd Bridge Rd., Cheneyville, LA 71325, ☎ 800/240-8135 or 318/776-5641

Description: This beautifully restored Greek Revival–Italianate mansion was used by the Union and Confederate troops during the Civil War. Tales of ghosts dating to that era are included in the tour.

Open to Public: Mon–Sat 10am–4pm, Sun 1–4pm.

Admission Fees: Adults $5, children 6–12 $3, children under 6 free.

Visitor Services: Tours, lodging.

Directions: From I-49 north: take exit 61 on Hwy. 167 north (Turkey Creek), go 1.8 miles, turn right, and go 1 mile to plantation.

Clinton

10 **Site:** CLINTON CONFEDERATE STATE CEMETERY, East Feliciana Parish, Marston St. Mailing address: P.O. Box 245, Clinton, LA 70722, ☎ 504/683-8324

Description: This 4-acre cemetery contains remains of hundreds of Civil War troops from both sides. Because Clinton was connected to the Mississippi River by railroad, the town received many sick and wounded soldiers from nearby Port Hudson.

Open to Public: Daily from dawn to dusk.

Admission Fees: Free.

Visitor Services: Tours by appointment.

Directions: Located north of Baton Rouge on LA 67 in Clinton. Go straight to the caution light, turn left on St. Helen St., turn left on Bank St., go 2 blocks, turn right, and continue 1½ blocks. Cemetery is on the right.

Grand Coteau

11 **Site:** ACADEMY OF THE SACRED HEART, P.O. Box 310, Grand Coteau, LA 70541, ☎ 318/662-5275

Description: This Catholic girls' school, established in 1821, was known for its beautiful formal gardens and oak alley. The Academy has remained in continuous operation through fire, epidemics, and the Civil War. In 1863, General Banks headed Federal troops pouring into the Teche country, and he made his headquarters at Grand Coteau for a brief time. His daughter attended a Sacred Heart school in New York, and the superior of the convent there requested that the general look after the nuns at Grand Coteau. The general protected the students and the nuns and even provided food and supplies to the convent, allowing the school to remain open during the war.

Open to Public: Mon–Fri 10am–2pm; weekends by appointment.

Admission Fees: Adults $5, children $3, seniors $3.

Visitor Services: Tours, museum, information, gift shop, rest rooms.

Directions: Take I-10 to Opelousas and exit to I-49. Follow I-49 toward Opelousas to the Grand Coteau/Sunset exit. Exit on Hwy. 93 toward Grand Coteau. Hwy. 93 becomes Main St. Turn left at the traffic light onto Church St. and follow Church St. to the Academy.

Homer

12 **Site:** FORD MUSEUM, 519 South Main St., Homer, LA 71040, ☎ 318/927-9190

Description: Homer was a departure point for Confederate soldiers during the Civil War and also served as a regional refugee center for persons fleeing Union-occupied territory. The museum houses a fascinating collection of memorabilia and artifacts from the north Louisiana hill country, including Civil War items.

Open to Public: Mon, Wed, and Fri 9:30am–12pm and 1:30–4pm; Sun 2–4pm.

Admission Fees: $1.

Visitor Services: Tours.

Directions: From I-20 west: take exit at Minden and follow U.S. 79 for 20 miles. It's on the right at the first light in Homer.

Jackson

13 **Site:** CENTENARY STATE COMMEMORATIVE AREA AND JACKSON CONFEDERATE CEMETERY.
Centenary address: P.O. Box 574, Jackson, LA 70748, ☎ 504/634-7925.
Cemetery address: P.O. Box 546, St. Francisville, LA 70775, ☎ 504/635-3739

Description: The Centenary State Commemorative Area is a former college that interprets the history of education in Louisiana. The college buildings were used as hospitals for Confederate soldiers from 1862 to 1863. A small skirmish was fought on the grounds on August 3, 1863. The Jackson Confederate Cemetery across the street from this site contains more than 100 unmarked graves of soldiers who died during the war.

Open to Public: *Centenary State Commemorative Area:* Daily 9am–5pm. *Jackson Confederate Cemetery:* Daily from dawn to dusk.

Admission Fees: *Centenary State Commemorative Area:* Adults $2, children under 12 free, adults 62 and over free, buses $60. *Jackson Confederate Cemetery:* Free.

Visitor Services: *Centenary State Commemorative Area:* Tours, museum, information, visitors center, rest rooms, handicapped access. *Jackson Confederate Cemetery:* None.

Directions: Take I-10 north through Baton Rouge. Exit at U.S. 61 and turn right. Turn right again at LA 10 and follow signs to Centenary State Commemorative Area, which is located at East College and Pine sts. in the town of Jackson in East Feliciana Parish. Jackson Confederate Cemetery is located adjacent to Centenary State Commemorative Area; information on the cemetery can be obtained at Centenary State Commemorative Area.

Lafayette

14 **Site:** CHRETIEN POINT, Rte. 1, P.O. Box 162, Sunset, LA 70584, ☎ 318/662-5876

Description: The front lawn of this plantation was the site of the Battle of Buzzard's Prairie during the Red River Campaign. Another battle, the Battle of Bayou Bourbeau, was fought on the rear acreage of the plantation. A bullet hole can be found in one of the front doors of the mansion.

Open to Public: Daily 10am–5pm; last tour at 4pm.

Admission Fees: Adults $6.50, children $3.

Visitor Services: Bed-and-breakfast, tours.

Directions: From Lafayette via I-10: take I-10 west to exit 97. From exit 97, drive north through Ossun, Vatican, and Cankton (approximately 8 miles). Go 2.2 miles north of Cankton and turn left on Parish Rd. 356 toward Bristol. Proceed 1 block, turn right onto Chretien Point Rd., and travel 1 mile. Plantation is on the left. From Lafayette and Opelousas via I-49: take I-49 to exit 11 at Sunset/Grand Coteau. Travel through Sunset on LA Hwy. 93 south.

Stay on LA 93 for another 3.8 miles. Turn right on Bristol/Bosco Rd., go 1 block, turn right, and proceed 1 mile. Plantation is on the left.

Lake Providence

15 **Site:** GRANT'S CANAL, Byerley House, 600 Lake St., Lake Providence, LA 71254, ☎ 318/559-5125

Description: Grant's Canal, Park, and Lake Overlook are located on U.S. Hwy. 65. The canal is all that remains of Grant's attempt in 1863 to circumvent the fortifications at Vicksburg through the back water of Louisiana. The canal is approximately 1,000 feet long. The western end of the canal can be viewed from the 600-foot pier and nature walk, which also offers a view of Lake Providence. Byerley House, adjacent to the park, serves as a visitor information center.

Open to Public: *Park:* Daily from dawn to dusk. *Byerley House:* Daily 9am–5pm.

Admission Fees: Free.

Visitor Services: Information at visitors center.

Directions: From Vicksburg: take I-20 west to Tallulah. In Tallulah, take the U.S. 65 north exit to Lake Providence. Grant's Canal and Byerley House are located on U.S. 65 at the eastern end of Lake Providence.

Mansfield

16 **Site:** MANSFIELD STATE COMMEMORATIVE AREA/BATTLE OF MANSFIELD AND BATTLE OF PLEASANT HILL, 15149 Hwy. 175, Mansfield, LA 71052, ☎ 318/872-1474

Description: The Battle of Mansfield took place on April 8, 1864. Under the leadership of Gen. Richard Taylor, an army of fewer than 9,000 Confederate soldiers from Texas and Louisiana defeated 13,000 Union troops of Gen. Nathaniel Banks. The day after the Battle of Mansfield, on April 9, the fierce Battle of Pleasant Hill was fought with both sides taking heavy losses and withdrawing from the field after dark. Local historians have been constructing a series of marble road markers denoting and interpreting the Battle of Pleasant Hill. The marker trail leads the visitor on the road from Mansfield, with a chronology of events. Markers are located on U.S.

Hwy. 175 between Mansfield State Commemorative Area and Pleasant Hill.

Open to Public: Daily 9am–5pm.

Admission Fees: Adults $2, seniors and children under 12 free.

Visitor Services: Museum, maps and interpretive programs of the battle, rest rooms.

Regularly Scheduled Events: Reenactments and living history program.

Directions: From I-20: go through Shreveport to Hwy. 171 south, go approximately 35 miles to Mansfield, and turn onto U.S. 84 west. From I-49: exit at U.S. 84 west.

Newellton

17 **Site:** WINTER QUARTERS STATE COMMEMORATIVE AREA, Rte. 1, Box 91, Newellton, LA 71357, ☎ 888/677-9468 or 318/467-5439

Description: Winter Quarters, a home listed on the National Register of Historic Places, stands today as a rare survivor of the ravages of the Civil War and as a tribute to the courage of one woman. Julia Nutt not only saved her home but also preserved the architectural work of her talented planter and inventor husband, Dr. Haller Nutt. The home was taken over by Grant's troops during the Civil War.

Open to Public: Daily 9am–5pm.

Admission Fees: Adults $2, children 12 and under free, adults 62 and over free.

Visitor Services: Tours, plantation home, information, rest rooms.

Directions: From 1-20: take the Tallulah (U.S. 65) exit south. Travel on U.S. 65 south to Newellton. Turn left on Hwy. 4, go to Hwy. 605, and turn right. Take Parish Rd. 605 to 608 and turn left. Winter Quarters is located on 608, on Lake St. Joseph.

New Iberia

18 **Site:** SHADOWS-ON-THE-TECHE, 317 East Main St., New Iberia, LA 70560, ☎ 318/369-6446

Shadows-on-the-Teche, a National Trust for Historic Preservation property, New Iberia, LA. (Photograph courtesy of The Civil War Trust.)

Description: This 1834 plantation home and gardens on the banks of Bayou Teche were home to the Weeks family for four generations before becoming a National Trust site in 1958. Letters found in trunks in the attic provide documentation for tours that give an authentic picture of life on a Louisiana sugar plantation, particularly during the Civil War years, including the 1863 occupation of the site.

Open to Public: Daily 9am–4:30pm.

Admission Fees: Adults $6, children 6–11 $3, groups (12 or more with reservations) $4.50.

Visitor Services: Museum, information, gift shop, rest rooms, handicapped access.

Regularly Scheduled Events: *Every other year* (call for more information): Civil War encampment.

Directions: From I-10: take exit 103A. Take Evangeline Thruway (Hwy. 90), take LA 14 exit off Hwy. 90, go left off ramp on Center St., and proceed to end. In New Iberia, turn left at E. Main St. Located at 317 E. Main St.

New Orleans

19 **Site:** CABILDO, on Jackson Square, 701 Chartres, New Orleans, LA 70116, ☎ 800/568-6968

Description: Built in 1795 to house the municipal government of the Spanish colony, the Cabildo was also the setting for transfer of the Louisiana Purchase. Part of the State Museum, the landmark houses exhibits that chronicle Louisiana's past from European settlement through Reconstruction. Of particular interest are sections on the antebellum era and the Civil War. Artifacts of slavery, weaponry, uniforms, documents, and photographs are included. A rare prototype of the Confederate Battle flag and the quill used to sign documents emancipating Louisiana slaves are included.

Open to Public: Tues–Sun 9am–5pm.

Admission Fees: Adults $4; students, seniors, and active military $3; children 12 and under free.

Visitor Services: Information, rest rooms, handicapped access.

Directions: From I-10: take French Quarter exit (Orleans). Follow Basin to signs for French Quarter via Toulouse. Take Toulouse several blocks to Chartres and turn right on Chartres to St. Peter. The Cabildo is at the corner of St. Peter and Chartres.

"DIXIE"

Although many people refer to the deep South as "Dixie," few know the source of the term. Just before the Civil War, New Orleans was a booming port city. Steamships lined up for miles to unload their cargo, and money flowed like water. But there was one small problem—the city was still divided between the Americans and the Creoles, with Canal Street serving as the dividing line. The boatmen who wished to spend their money were forced to use American money on the up-river side of Canal Street and French money on the down-river side. Citizens Bank on Toulouse Street finally solved the boatmen's problem by printing the most common bill in use—the $10.00 bill—in both English and French. The French word for *ten* is *DIX*, so the bill read both *ten* and *dix* on each side. Eventually, the boatmen began to call the bills *Dixies,* and ever since, the deep South has been known as "Dixie."

20 **Site:** CONFEDERATE MUSEUM, 929 Camp St., New Orleans, LA 70130,
☎ 504/523-4522

Description: This is the oldest museum in Louisiana. Civil War memorabilia include flags, uniforms, weapons, medical instruments, currency, and personal effects of President Jefferson Davis, Gen. Robert E. Lee, and other Southern leaders.

Open to Public: Mon–Sat 10am–4pm.

Admission Fees: Adults $5, students and seniors $4, children $2.

Visitor Services: Tours.

Directions: From Baton Rouge: take I-10 to New Orleans. Take Business District/ Tchoupitoulas St. exit and turn left at Calliope St. Continue to Camp St. and turn right. Get in left lane. The Confederate Museum is located on the corner of Camp and Howard sts.

21 **Site:** FORT PIKE STATE COMMEMORATIVE AREA, Rte. 6, Box 194, New Orleans, LA
70129, ☎ 888/662-5703 or 504/662-5703

Description: Before the actual start of the Civil War, the Louisiana militia captured Fort Pike. Confederates held it until Union forces took New Orleans in 1862, whereupon the Southerners evacuated the fort. In spite of much activity, not a single cannonball was ever fired in battle from Fort Pike.

Open to Public: Daily 9am–5pm.

Admission Fees: Adults $2, children free, seniors 62 and over free.

Visitor Services: Museum, picnic area, rest rooms, tours.

Directions: Fort Pike is located on U.S. 90, 23 miles east of downtown New Orleans. It is also accessible from I-10 via LA 11 south, which connects to U.S. 90.

22 **Site:** OLD U.S. MINT, 400 Block of Esplanade Ave., New Orleans, LA 70116,
☎ 800/568-6968 or 504/568-6968

Description: Operational from 1838 to 1909, the Old U.S. Mint produced $5 million in coins monthly at its peak. For a short time during the Civil War, it was the only mint of the Confederate states. Now part of the Louisiana State Museum, the building has been restored and houses popular exhibits on jazz and Mardi Gras, plus a collection of historical documents.

Open to Public: Tues–Sun 9am–5pm.

Admission Fees: Adults $4, students and seniors $3, children 12 and under free.

Visitor Services: Tours.

Directions: Take I-10 to Elysian Fields; go south toward the river and turn right to Esplanade Ave.

23 **Site:** PRESBYTERE, on Jackson Square, 751 Chartres St., New Orleans, LA 70116,
☎ 800/568-6968

Description: Built in 1795, the Presbytere, intended as a residence for the priests of neighboring St. Louis Cathedral, has served a variety of purposes over the decades. Part of the State Museum since 1912, it houses various exhibitions on Louisiana's cultural heritage. Of particular interest is a Civil War submarine, exhibited in its open air arcade. Believed by some to be the *Pioneer,* the "mystery vessel" was recovered from area waters soon after the war.

Open to Public: Tues–Sun 9am–5pm.

Admission Fees: Adults $4; students, seniors, and active military $3; children 12 and under free.

Visitor Services: Information, rest rooms, handicapped access.

Directions: From I-10: take French Quarter exit (Orleans). Follow Basin to signs for French Quarter via Toulouse. Take Toulouse 1 block to Burgundy and turn left. At St. Ann, turn right. The Presbytere is at the corner of St. Ann and Chartres.

Pineville

24 Site: ALEXANDRIA NATIONAL CEMETERY, 209 East Shamrock St., Pineville, LA, ☎ 318/449-1793

Description: This cemetery was established in 1867 as a burial site for Civil War soldiers. It contains graves of soldiers from every American war since the Spanish-American War.

Open to Public: Daily 8am–4pm.

Admission Fees: Free.

Visitor Services: None.

Directions: Located on U.S. Hwy. 165, north of Alexandria (across Red River Bridge).

Tangipahoa

25 Site: CAMP MOORE/CONFEDERATE CEMETERY, U.S. Hwy. 51, Tangipahoa, LA 70465, ☎ 504/229-2438

Description: Established in the summer of 1861, Camp Moore, named after Civil War Governor Thomas Moore, served as one of the largest Confederate training bases in the Southern states. The Confederate cemetery, adjacent to Camp Moore, contains the remains of more than 400 Confederate soldiers.

Open to Public: Tues–Sat 10am–4pm.

Admission Fees: Adults $2, children $1, children under 6 free.

Visitor Services: Museum, trails, information.

Directions: From Hammond: follow U.S. 51 north. Camp Moore is located on U.S. 51, .5 mile north of the village of Tangipahoa.

Vinton

26 **Site:** NIBLETT'S BLUFF, Rte. 1, P.O. Box 358, Vinton, LA 70668, ☎ 318/589-7117

Description: Overlooking the Old Sabine River, Niblett's Bluff is the site of an old Civil War encampment. Confederate breastworks may still be seen.

Open to Public: Daily 6am–10pm.

Admission Fees: Overnight RV $10, tent with electricity $10, cabins $20, tent $5. Tax is not included.

Visitor Services: Trails, lodging, camping, rest rooms.

Directions: From I-10: take exit at Tommey Starks, follow 109, and go north for 2.9 miles. At yellow light, look for directional sign on left.

White Castle

27 **Site:** NOTTOWAY PLANTATION, P.O. Box 160, White Castle, LA 70788, ☎ 504/545-2730

Description: This is the largest plantation home in the South, an outstanding example of the opulent lifestyle enjoyed by the wealthy sugar planter before the Civil War. The three-story mansion has 64 rooms and was considered immense even by the standards of the antebellum "Golden Age."

Open to Public: Daily 9am–5pm.

Admission Fees: Adults $8, children 5–12 $3, children 4 and under free.

Visitor Services: Restaurant (open daily 11am–3pm and 6–9pm), overnight accommodations with reservations, tours.

Directions: From I-10: go over Mississippi River Bridge at Baton Rouge; take Plaquemine exit south to LA 1. Continue south on LA 1 for 18 miles. Nottoway Plantation is on the left.

Zachary

28 **Site:** PORT HUDSON STATE COMMEMORATIVE AREA. Mailing address: 756 West Plains-Port Hudson Rd., Zachary, LA 70791, ☎ 504/654-3775

Description: Port Hudson was the longest siege in U.S. military history. The Union force of 30,000 to 40,000 was held off by 6,800 Confederate soldiers from May 23 to July 9, 1863. This conflict is also one of the first in which free black soldiers fought on the side of the Union.

Open to Public: Daily 9am–5pm.

Admission Fees: Adults $2, seniors and children under 12 free.

Visitor Services: Trails, interpretive center, rest rooms, picnic area.

Regularly Scheduled Events: *Last weekend in Mar:* Reenactment.

Directions: Located 14 miles north of Baton Rouge on Hwy. 61. Take I-10 to U.S. 61 (to Natchez), take St. Francisville exit (I-10 intersects with U.S. 61 at this point), and turn right. Port Hudson is 14–17 miles straight ahead on the left.

THOUSAND MILE FRONT: CIVIL WAR IN THE LOWER MISSISSIPPI VALLEY

The Lower Mississippi River Valley was a critical theater of the Civil War. The Mississippi River served as the major interstate highway of 19th-century America for transporting goods and people from St. Louis and Pittsburgh, through New Orleans, and to the world. Control of the Mississippi was a key strategic objective for Union and Confederate forces during the Civil War. The states of Arkansas, Illinois, Kentucky, Louisiana, Mississippi, Missouri, and Tennessee have created a seven-state map and guide to the Civil War in this region.

Follow Union and Confederate forces as they struggle to control the Lower Mississippi River Valley. Explore the lifestyles of people and places in this Valley during a troubled time when neighbor fought neighbor, brother fought brother, and father fought son. Visualize the clash of the Blue and the Gray along the mighty Mississippi River. Experience the broad scope of the Civil War from Lincoln's home in Springfield, Illinois; from the mountains of the Cumberland Gap through Shiloh, Tennessee; from St. Louis down the river to New Orleans; and throughout all the states of the Lower Mississippi River Valley—a rich path of history one thousand miles long. The map and guide provide an overview of events and a list of significant military, cultural, and historical sites in each state.

For your free copy of Thousand Mile Front: Civil War in the Lower Mississippi River Valley, contact one of the state tourism offices in the Lower Mississippi Valley region. Arkansas: ☎ 800/872-1259, Illinois: ☎ 800/2CONNECT, Kentucky: ☎ 800/225-TRIP, Louisiana: ☎ 800/695-1638, 504/342-8119 or 800/33-GUMBO, Mississippi: ☎ 800/WARMEST, Missouri: ☎ 800/877-1234, Tennessee: ☎ 800/TENN-200.

MAINE

*M*AINE'S ABOLITIONIST SENTIMENTS RENDERED it a Republican state that favored the war as a way to end slavery. Harriet Beecher Stowe penned *Uncle Tom's Cabin,* her novel indicting slavery, in Brunswick, Maine, in 1851. In 1860, Maine supported Abraham Lincoln for president and Maine native son Hannibal Hamlin for vice president. The state contributed more than 67,000 men to fight for the Union cause. Of these, approximately 9,000 lost their lives, and approximately 11,000 suffered illness or injury.

Two prominent generals were from Maine. Bvt. Maj. Gen. Joshua L. Chamberlain is probably best known as the college professor who with the 20th Maine became the hero of Little Round Top at Gettysburg. Chamberlain and the 20th Maine served with the Army of the Potomac from Antietam to Gettysburg to Appomattox. Chamberlain had the honor of accepting the surrender of Robert E. Lee's Confederate troops at Appomattox. After the war, Chamberlain returned to Maine and served four terms as governor and then became president of Bowdoin College.

Another important Maine officer, Maj. Gen. Oliver O. Howard, led Maj. Gen. William T. Sherman's right wing through Georgia on his March to the Sea. Howard later ran the Freedmans Bureau and helped establish Howard University in Washington, D.C., also serving as its president.

Brunswick

1   **Site:** JOSHUA LAWRENCE CHAMBERLAIN MUSEUM (a museum of the Pejepscot Historical Society). Mailing address: Pejepscot Historical Society, 159 Park Row, Brunswick, ME 04011. Physical address: 226 Maine St., ☎ 207/729-6606

Description: The Chamberlain Museum occupies the former home of Gen. Joshua Lawrence Chamberlain (1828–1914). Wounded six times in 24 engagements, Chamberlain, a former Bowdoin college professor, is best known for leading the heroic charge of the 20th Maine regiment down Little Round Top at Gettysburg. He was later selected by Grant to accept surrender of the Confederate infantry at Appomattox. Chamberlain returned to Maine, served four terms as Governor, and

more than a decade as president of Bowdoin College. Saved from demolition in 1983, the Chamberlain Museum continues to undergo extensive restoration.

Open to Public: June–Sept: Tues–Sat 10am–4pm. Oct: Museum open on a reduced schedule. Tours leave on the half hour.

Admission Fees: Adults $4, children $2. Combination tickets for the Society's other museums are available at a discount, and Society members receive free admission.

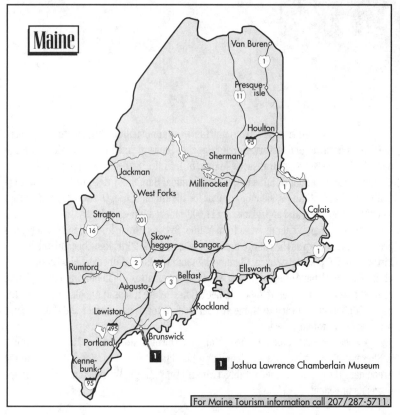

Maine

Van Buren
1
Presque-isle
11
Houlton
95
Sherman
Jackman
Millinocket
West Forks
1
Stratton
201
Calais
16
Skow-hegan
Bangor
1
Rumford
2
95
Belfast
Ellsworth
9
Augusta
3
Rockland
1
Lewiston
495
1
Portland
Brunswick
Kenne-bunk
1
95

1 Joshua Lawrence Chamberlain Museum

For Maine Tourism information call 207/287-5711.

Visitor Services: Guided museum tours; book shop (mail orders welcome); information on Chamberlain-related sites nearby, including his grave and Bowdoin College.

Regularly Scheduled Events: *Aug:* Chamberlain Days (including bus tours, lectures, and special programs); Specialty tours; "Chamberlain's Brunswick" walking tour.

Directions: From I-95: take exit 22; proceed toward downtown, following signs for Maine St. Turn right on Maine St. Museum is at 226 Maine St., opposite Bowdoin campus.

Joshua Lawrence Chamberlain Museum, the former home of Gen. Joshua Lawrence Chamberlain, Brunswick, ME (Photograph courtesy of the Pejepscot Historical Society.)

MARYLAND

*A*T THE OUTBREAK OF THE CIVIL WAR, Maryland could be described as both a Northern and a Southern state. Strong unionist sentiment was present, but there was also a great deal of sympathy for the Confederacy. Maryland relied on both free and slave labor and contained large plantations, small farms, and a great city.

On April 19, 1861, Maryland's two sides came to blows in the streets of Baltimore when Massachusetts troops, marching through the city, engaged a crowd of Southern sympathizers. To safeguard the national capital, Maryland had to be secured to the Union. Federal troops turned the guns of Fort McHenry on the city itself and imprisoned public officials with known secessionist tendencies. Gen. Ben "Beast" Butler seized the railroads around Annapolis, while John Garrett, president of the B & O Railroad, promised his company's support to Lincoln. Meanwhile, Governor Hicks moved the General Assembly to unionist Frederick to ensure the imprisoned legislators could not participate. In response, thousands of Marylanders headed south to join the Confederate army.

Larger numbers of Marylanders served in the Union forces than in the Confederate army. They confronted each other at such battles as Front Royal and Culps Hill (Gettysburg). Maryland witnessed the bloodiest day of the Civil War at the Battle of Antietam on September 17, 1862, with more than 23,000 killed or wounded that day. Lee's army invaded the state on two other occasions—on his way to Pennsylvania in 1863 and during General Early's 1864 raids on Washington, which included the Battle of Monocacy. Lee's setback at Antietam may have given Lincoln the opportunity to announce his Emancipation Proclamation; but his executive order did not apply to Maryland, which had abolished slavery with a state law about a year before the 13th Amendment. Many African Americans from Maryland served in the Union forces, fighting to gain or ensure their freedom. When soldiers of both sides returned home, Maryland healed its wounds more easily than the rest of the nation.

Baltimore

1 **Site:** CAMDEN STATION, Oriole Park at Camden Yards, 333 W. Camden St., Ste. 500, Baltimore, MD 21201-2435, ☎ 410/333-1560

Description: On April 19, 1861, the first casualties of the Civil War occurred when the 6th Massachusetts Infantry fought its way from President St. Station to Camden Station. President Lincoln went from Camden Station to Gettysburg, where he gave the Gettysburg Address, and then returned to the Station on November 19,

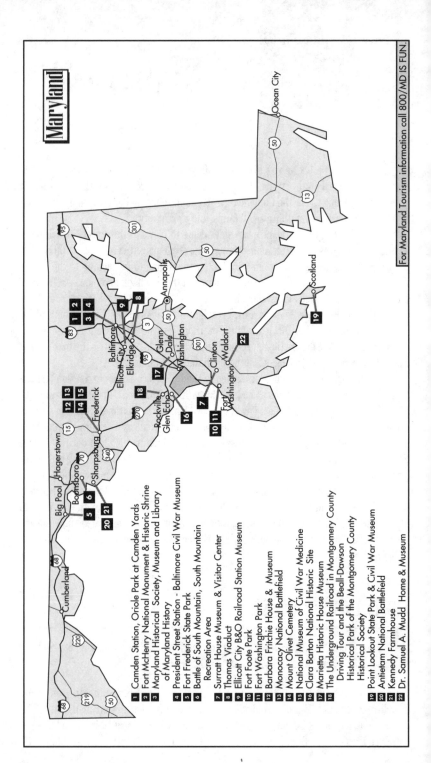

Maryland

For Maryland Tourism information call 800/MD IS FUN.

1 Camden Station, Oriole Park at Camden Yards
2 Fort McHenry National Monument & Historic Shrine
3 Maryland Historical Society, Museum and Library
    of Maryland History
4 President Street Station - Baltimore Civil War Museum
5 Fort Frederick State Park
6 Battle of South Mountain, South Mountain
    Recreation Area
7 Surratt House Museum & Visitor Center
8 Thomas Viaduct
9 Ellicott City B&O Railroad Station Museum
10 Fort Foote Park
11 Fort Washington Park
12 Barbara Fritchie House & Museum
13 Monocacy National Battlefield
14 Mount Olivet Cemetery
15 National Museum of Civil War Medicine
16 Clara Barton National Historic Site
17 Marietta Historic House Museum
18 The Underground Railroad in Montgomery County
    Driving Tour and the Beall-Dawson
    Historical Park of the Montgomery County
    Historical Society
19 Point Lookout State Park & Civil War Museum
20 Antietam National Battlefield
21 Kennedy Farmhouse
22 Dr. Samuel A. Mudd Home & Museum

1863. Lincoln's funeral train, carrying his body to Springfield, Illinois, stopped at Camden Station.

Open to Public: Daily 9am–5pm.

Admission Fees: Free.

Visitor Services: Historical information, handicapped access, rest rooms, food. Tours of Camden Yards and Historic Camden Station are available from the tour office at Camden Yards. Baseball and Babe Ruth museums will open in 1999 in the restored Camden Station and will feature historical exhibits.

Directions: Take I-95 to downtown Baltimore; follow signs to Oriole Park at Camden Yards.

---

2 **Site:** FORT MCHENRY NATIONAL MONUMENT & HISTORIC SHRINE, East Fort Ave., Baltimore, MD 21230-5393, ☎ 410/962-4290 or 410/962-4291

Description: The fort was made famous during the War of 1812 as the inspiration of Francis Scott Key's poem, "The Star Spangled Banner." The present-day fort reflects the Civil War period when Brig. Gen. William Morris commanded this heavily fortified (72-gun) harbor fort. With the suspension of Habeous Corpus in 1861, 31 members of the Maryland legislature were imprisoned here; and during the battles of Antietam and Gettysburg, guns could be heard. Nearly 8,000 Confederate soldiers were detained after Gettysburg as prisoners of war. The nation's largest display of 15-inch Rodman coastal guns may also be seen here.

Open to Public: Daily 8am–5pm. Call for extended summer hours.

Admission Fees: Adults $5, children under 17 free.

Visitor Services: Exhibits, a computer database guide to the 15,000 Confederate prisoners held here during the war, rest rooms, handicapped access.

Regularly Scheduled Events: *Last weekend in Apr:* "The Encampment at Fort McHenry: A Civil War Weekend, April 1864," a Union living history event; *June 14:* Flag Day festivities; *Second Tues in Sept:* Defenders Day (commemorates the Battle of Baltimore).

Directions: From I-95: take exit 55 (Key Hwy.) and follow posted signs.

---

3 **Site:** MARYLAND HISTORICAL SOCIETY, Museum and Library of Maryland History, 201 West Monument St., Baltimore, MD 21201, ☎ 410/685-3750

Description: This site is the home of Francis Scott Key's original handwritten version of "The Star-Spangled Banner," the nation's largest 19th-century silver collection, Peale family paintings, and a superb fine and decorative arts collection.

Open to Public: *Museum:* Tues–Fri 10am–5pm, Sat 9am–5pm, Sun 1–5pm. *Library:* Tues–Fri 10am–4:30pm, Sat 9am–4:30pm. Closed Mondays, major holidays, and Sundays in July and August.

Admission Fees: Adults $4, seniors $3, children 12 and over $3, students with ID $3, family rate (2 adults and 2 children) $6. Free admission: Sat 9am–11am.

Visitor Services: Handicapped access.

Directions: From I-95: take exit 53 (395N); stay to the right and follow signs to Martin Luther King Blvd. Go north on Martin Luther King for 1.5 miles, turn right on Druid Hill Ave., and turn left on Park Ave. Parking lot is on left.

---

4 **Site: PRESIDENT STREET STATION—BALTIMORE CIVIL WAR MUSEUM, 601 President St., Baltimore, MD 21202, ☎ 410/385-5188**

Description: Built in 1849 as the terminus of the Philadelphia, Wilmington & Baltimore Railroad, President St. Station was an important junction for the Under-ground Railroad and the Civil War. It was the site of the first bloodshed of the war on April 19, 1861, when Baltimore secessionists clashed with Massachusetts volunteers en route to Washington just 1 week after Fort Sumter. It was also an avenue for fleeing oppression, beginning with Frederick Douglass and including the claustrophobic journey of Henry "Box" Brown, on the P W & B.

Open to Public: Daily 10am–5pm. Closed Thanksgiving Day and Christmas Day.

Admission Fees: Adults $2, children $1, seniors $1.

Visitor Services: Museum, tours, gift shop, visitors center, rest rooms, handicapped access.

Regularly Scheduled Events: *Apr 19:* Commemoration of first bloodshed of the Civil War. Call for other events.

Directions: From I-95: take exit 53 and follow signs to downtown. Turn right on Pratt St., proceed approximately .75 mile to President St., and turn right. Museum is at corner of President and Fleet sts. From I-83: follow 83 to its end, where it becomes President St. Follow President St. to Fleet St.

Big Pool

---

5 **Site: FORT FREDERICK STATE PARK, 11100 Fort Frederick Rd., Big Pool, MD 21711, ☎ 301/842-2155**

Description: This restored stone fort, built in 1756, was the cornerstone of Maryland's defense during the French and Indian War. It served as a prison camp for Hessian and British soldiers during the American Revolution and as an outpost for Union infantry during the Civil War. Exhibits interpret the history of the park from the English Colonial period through the Civilian Conservation Corps restoration in the 1930s.

Open to Public: *Fort:* Weekends, Sept and May. Daily, Memorial Day–Labor Day: 9–4:30pm. *Park:* Daily year round: Apr–Oct 31: 8am–sunset. Nov–Mar 31: Mon–Fri 8am–sunset; Sat, Sun, and holidays 10am–sunset.

Admission Fees: *Fort:* Adults $2, children 6–12 $1, children under 6 free. *Park:* Free, except small charge during special events.

Visitor Services: Historic interpretation, camping, picnicking, hiking, visitors center and orientation film, exhibits, snacks and gifts, boat rentals, fishing, C & O Canal towpath, rest rooms, handicapped access.

Regularly Scheduled Events: *Apr:* Market fair and rifle frolic; *May:* French and Indian War Rendezvous; *Last full weekend* *in July:* Military field days; *Third week of Sept:* Governor's invitational firelock match; *Oct:* Ghost walk. Call about military reenactments and other events throughout the year.

Directions: Located 18 miles west of Hagerstown, MD. From I-70: take exit 12 at Big Pool, MD; follow signs.

Boonsboro

6 **Site:** BATTLE OF SOUTH MOUNTAIN, South Mountain Recreation Area. Mailing address: Greenbrier State Park, 21843 National Pike, Boonsboro, MD 21713, ☎ 310/791-4656

Description: The Battle of South Mountain, fought on September 14, 1862, is considered to be where Gen. Robert E. Lee's first invasion of the North was stopped. It was also the first battle of the war fought in Maryland. A 17-stop driving tour leads visitors through the battle that was a prelude to Antietam. The free driving-tour brochure, "Battle of South Mountain," is available from the above address or at Greenbrier and Gathland state parks. Also request a brochure called "Maryland Civil War Crossroads" for other Washington County sites. Gathland State Park has a museum with Civil War exhibits.

Open to Public: *Greenbrier State Park:* Park open daily year-round: 8am–sunset. *Visitors center (for brochure pickup):* Mon–Fri 8am–4:30pm. *Gathland State Park Museum:* Apr–Oct: Weekends only, noon–4pm.

Admission Fees: There is no charge for the brochure or for admission to Gathland State Park or museum. Greenbrier State Park charges admission from Memorial Day to Labor Day: $2/person on weekdays, $3/person on weekends.

Visitor Services: *Greenbrier State Park:* Rest rooms, camping. *Gathland Museum:* Exhibits, rest rooms, living history, tours.

Regularly Scheduled Events: *Sept, first weekend after Labor Day:* Civil War living history weekend.

Directions: To Greenbrier State Park: From I-70 take exit 32 (Rte. 40 east) 6 miles to Greenbrier State Park. To Gathland State Park (near Burkittsville): From I-70: take exit 32 (40 west); turn right on Hwy. 66 and proceed to Boonsboro; turn left on Alt. 40 and travel through Boonsboro; turn right on Rte. 67 south and travel 6 miles; turn left on Gapland Rd. and follow signs to Gathland State Park. To site of the Battle of South Mountain: From I-70: take exit 49 (Alt. 40 west) for 10 miles to Turner's Gap on South Mountain. Battle sites are marked with historic markers.

Clinton

7 **Site:** SURRATT HOUSE MUSEUM & VISITOR CENTER, 9118 Brandywine Rd., Clinton, MD 20735, ☎ 301/868-1121

Description: This historic house museum presents a variety of programs and events that capture the history of mid-19th-century life and focus on the fascinating web of the Lincoln conspiracy.

Open to Public: Mar–Dec: Thurs–Fri 11am–3pm, Sat–Sun noon–4pm. Open other days for special group tours.

Admission Fees: Adults $3, children 5–18 $1, seniors $2.

Visitor Services: Library, gift shop, museum, handicapped access to first floor.

Regularly Scheduled Events: *Feb:* Antique Valentine exhibit; *Apr and Sept:* John Wilkes Booth escape route tour; *Nov:* Annual open house; *Dec:* Victorian Christmas.

Directions: From I-95: take exit 7A (Rte. 5) south, exit at Rte. 223 west, and take a left onto Brandywine Rd.

Elkridge

8 **Site:** THOMAS VIADUCT, West of U.S. 1, Levering Ave., Elkridge, MD 21227, ☎ 410/313-1900

Description: Built in 1835, this bridge was part of the main railroad between Baltimore and Washington, which allowed boat and rail transport to move troops and supplies during the Civil War. It is the oldest multiarched curved bridge in the world and is still in use.

Open to Public: Daily from dawn to dusk.

Admission Fees: Free.

Visitor Services: None.

Directions: From I-95: take exit 41 (Rte. 175), go east to Rte. 1 (1 block), and go north on Rte. 1 to Elkridge (about 5 miles). Go past Harbor Tunnel Hwy. sign, turn at next left, and follow signs for Patapsco State Park. Road goes under the viaduct.

Ellicott City

9 **Site:** ELLICOTT CITY B & O RAILROAD STATION MUSEUM, 2711 Maryland Ave., Ellicott City, MD 21043, ☎ 410/461-1945

Description: This railroad station is the oldest in America, built in 1831. The station was a vital supply line to the west, and thousands of soldiers, prisoners of war, and

casualties were moved through this building. The museum's award-winning Civil War living history program emphasizes the Maryland story. Historians portray soldiers, civilians, and musicians of the Civil War in an interactive setting.

Open to Public: Days and hours of operation change with each exhibit and program; call for detailed information.

Admission Fees: A nominal fee is charged.

Visitor Services: Museum, gift shop, rest rooms, special events.

Directions: From I-95: take Rte. 32 west to Rte. 29 north. Take exit for Rte. 40 east, stay to right, turn right at first traffic light on Rogers Ave., and follow signs to the Ellicott City historic district.

Fort Washington

10 **Site:** FORT FOOTE PARK, 13551 Ft. Washington Rd., Ft. Washington, MD 20704, ☎ 310/763-4600

Description: Fort Foote is the only fort in the "Circle Forts" (defenses around Washington, D.C.) that remained active after the Civil War. It displays two mounted 15-inch Rodman cannons and is one of the best examples of undisturbed earthworks in the system of forts that were built to defend the nation's capital.

Open to Public: Daily 9am–sunset.

Admission Fees: None.

Visitor Services: None.

Regularly Scheduled Events: Special group tours by request.

Directions: From I-495: take exit #A (MD 210 south); proceed 3 miles to Old Fort Rd.; turn right and travel 1 mile. At the second traffic light, turn left on Fort Foote Rd. and travel approximately 2 miles. Fort is on the left.

11 **Site:** FORT WASHINGTON PARK, 13551 Fort Washington Rd., Fort Washington, MD 20744, ☎ 301/763-4600

Description: This site is an outstanding example of 19th-century seacoast fortifications and the only permanent fortification ever constructed to defend the nation's capital. During the first year of the Civil War, the fort controlled river access to Alexandria, Georgetown, and Washington, D.C.; and maintained a training base for state militia troops from the North. The site was an active military post from 1808 through the end of World War II, but there was never a shot fired in anger here. Military and civilian living history are presented from February to November.

Open to Public: Daily 9am–sunset.

Admission Fees: Cars $4.

Visitor Services: Trails, museum, gift shop, rest rooms, handicapped access.

Regularly Scheduled Events: Torchlight tours, Civil War garrison weekends, and cannon firing demonstrations. Call for special events.

Directions: From I-95: take Indian Head Hwy. (Hwy. 210 south) until you see Fort Washington Rd.; follow to the end.

Frederick

12 **Site:** BARBARA FRITCHIE HOUSE & MUSEUM, 154 West Patrick St., Frederick, MD 21701, ☎ 301/698-0630

Description: On September 10, 1862, as Gen. "Stonewall" Jackson and his troops were leaving Frederick, Barbara Fritchie, at age 95, earned her place as a legendary American heroine by defying those she believed to be wrong. This replica of the Barbara Fritchie House preserves many of her belongings.

Open to Public: Apr–Sept 30: Mon, Thurs, Fri, and Sat 10am–4pm; Sun 1–4pm. Oct–Nov: Sat 10am–4pm, Sun 1–4pm.

Admission Fees: Adults $2, children under 12 $1.50, seniors $1.50.

Visitor Services: Tours, gift shop.

Directions: From I-70: take exit 54 toward Frederick; in Frederick, turn left onto Patrick St.

13 **Site:** MONOCACY NATIONAL BATTLEFIELD, 4801 Urbana Pike, Frederick, MD 21701-7307, ☎ 301/662-3515

Description: Site of July 9, 1864, battle where Confederate forces, under Lt. Gen. Jubal Early, en route to Washington D.C., were delayed for a day by Union forces under Maj. Gen. Lew Wallace. This battle allowed time for General Grant to deploy Union troops around the defenseless capital, saving it from Confederate invasion.

Open to Public: *Visitors center:* Memorial Day–Labor Day: Daily 8am–4:30pm. Rest of the year: Wed–Sun 8am–4:30pm.

Admission Fees: Free.

Visitor Services: Visitors center, one-half mile loop trail, self-guided auto tour, rest rooms, handicapped access.

Directions: From I-270: take exit 26 (Rte. 80 north), travel .2 mile, and turn left on Rte. 355 north. Battlefield is 3.7 miles.

14 **Site:** MOUNT OLIVET CEMETERY, 515 South Market St., Frederick, MD 21701, ☎ 301/662-1164

Description: This cemetery contains the Francis Scott Key Monument as well as the graves of Governor Thomas Johnson, Barbara Fritchie, and more than 800 Confederate Civil War soldiers.

Open to Public: Daily from dawn to dusk.

Admission Fees: Free.

Visitor Services: None.

Directions: From I-70: take exit 54 (Rte. 355) toward Frederick and follow the signs. Cemetery is .25 mile west of Rte. 355.

15 Site: NATIONAL MUSEUM OF CIVIL WAR MEDICINE, 48 East Patrick St. Mailing address: P.O. Box 470, Frederick, MD 21705, ☎ 301/695-1864

Description: This is the only museum in the world devoted exclusively to Civil War Medicine. During the Civil War, more than 600,000 soldiers died, and countless others were maimed. Widespread disease, casualties, and bone-shattering wounds left a legacy of brutality and horror, but the resulting medical advances paved the way for modern medical practices. The museum features the only known surviving Civil War surgeon's tent. Exhibits inlcude a Civil War ambulance, a holding coffin, and a traveling medical chest that belonged to Dr. E. R. Squibb, medical and dental instruments, uniforms, documents, photos, books, and an amputation video.

Open to Public: Mon–Sat 10am–5pm, Sun 11am–5pm.

Admission Fees: Adults $4, seniors $3, children 10–16 $1, children 9 and under free, museum members free, guided tours (10-person minimum) $6.

Visitor Services: Museum, museum store, group tours (schedule 2 weeks in advance), Kid's Corner, rest rooms, handicapped access.

Regularly Scheduled Events: *First weekend in Aug:* Annual Conference on Civil War Medicine; Living history scheduled throughout the year.

Directions: From I-270 and I-70: travel north on Market St. (Rte. 355 and 85). Turn right on Church St., go 1 block, and turn right on Maxwell Ave. Museum is on Patrick St. at the end of the alley.

Glen Echo

16 Site: CLARA BARTON NATIONAL HISTORIC SITE, 5801 Oxford Rd., Glen Echo, MD 20812, ☎ 301/492-6245

Description: Built in 1891, this house was the final home of Clara Barton, founder of the American Red Cross. The house also served as the headquarters and warehouse space for the American Red Cross from 1897 to 1904. The museum houses a collection of furnishings used by Clara Barton in her Glen Echo home.

Open to Public: Daily 10am–5pm. Tours hourly on the hour; house shown by guided tour only; last tour at 4pm.

Admission Fees: Free.

Visitor Services: Tours, handicapped access to first floor.

Regularly Scheduled Events: *Apr and Sept:* Biannual Lamplight open house.

Directions: From I-495: take exit 40 on outer loop or exit 41 on the inner loop; follow signs for MacArthur Blvd.; turn left onto MacArthur Blvd.; go east past Glen Echo Park on left; take next left onto Oxford Rd.

Clara Barton

"Men have worshipped war till it has cost a million times more than the whole of the earth is worth . . . Deck it as you will, war is Hell . . . Only the desire to soften some of its hardships and allay some of its miseries ever induced me . . . to face its pestilent and unholy breath."

—*Clara Barton*

Clara Barton, founder of the American Red Cross, promoter of the right to vote for former slaves, and strong supporter of the early feminist movement, was born on Christmas Day, 1821, in North Oxford, Massachusetts. She began her career as a school teacher and opened one of the first free (public) schools in 1852 in Bordentown, New Jersey. However, she was not destined to remain a teacher.

During the Civil War, Barton dedicated herself to nursing and comforting the soldiers. She worked to ease the pain of the men and to lessen the unsanitary conditions that were considered normal during the war. At Antietam, Barton arrived with a wagon of much needed supplies and set up a hospital. Surgeons there had been using corn husks for bandages.

Though she worked alongside members of the U.S. Sanitary Commission and the U.S. Christian Commission, she never became closely allied with either group. She preferred to work alone, unhampered by organizations and outside interference with her work. A true perfectionist, she hated to delegate authority for fear that the job would not be well performed.

Because of her drive, Barton often suffered from poor health. After the war, she went to Europe for a rest tour; and it was during this trip that she learned of the work of the International Red Cross, which had been operating in Europe since 1863. She worked with the Red Cross in Europe during the Franco-Prussian War and was so impressed that she vowed to bring its ideals to the United States. An apathetic public, an uncooperative government, and her own poor health made this no easy task; however, her efforts were rewarded in 1882, when the United States Senate ratified the Treaty of Geneva, creating the American Red Cross.

Barton spent the rest of her life working with the group and served as its president until 1904. On April 12, 1912, she died at her home in Glen Echo, Maryland.

Credit: National Park Service

Glenn Dale

17 **Site:** MARIETTA HISTORIC HOUSE MUSEUM, Prince George's County Historical Society, 5626 Bell Station Rd., Glenn Dale, MD 20769, ☎ 301/464-5291

Description: Marietta is a Federal-style brick house (1812) built by Supreme Court Justice Gabriel Duvall (1752–1844). Its furnishings date from 1812 to 1900, and the home is interpreted during the years of the Duvall family.

Open to Public: *Library:* Sat noon–4pm. *Museum:* Fri 11am–3pm, Sun noon–4pm and by appointment. Call for expanded hours.

Admission Fees: Adult $3, students $1, seniors $2.

Visitor Services: Tours, gift shop, rest rooms.

Directions: From I-95: take exit 20A (Annapolis Rd. Rte. 450 east), proceed 4 miles, turn left on Rte. 193W, and turn left on Bell Station Rd.

Rockville

18 **Site:** THE UNDERGROUND RAILROAD IN MONTGOMERY COUNTY DRIVING TOUR AND THE BEALL-DAWSON HISTORICAL PARK OF THE MONTGOMERY COUNTY HISTORICAL SOCIETY, 111 W. Montgomery Ave., Rockville, MD 20850-4212, ☎ 310/340-6534

Description: Montgomery County was an active part of the Underground Railroad. Located close to Pennsylvania, with the District of Columbia as its southern border, Montgomery County was a natural place for Underground Railroad activity. "The Underground Railroad in Montgomery County, Maryland: A History and Driving Guide," published by the Montgomery County Historical Society, documents some of that activity and the places and sites that still stand and tell the story. The Beall-Dawson Historical Park includes the 1815 Beall-Dawson House, the Stonestreet Museum of 19th Century Medicine, and the Society's research library and museum shop.

Open to Public: Tues–Sat and the first Sun of the month: noon–4pm.

Admission Fees: The Underground Railroad tour booklet costs $7.00. It may be purchased at the museum shop or ordered by mail (add $3 S/H). *Beall-Dawson House and Stonestreet Museum:* Adults $3, students $1, seniors $2, children under 6 free.

Visitor Services: Library, tours, museums, museum shop, rest rooms.

Regularly Scheduled Events: *First Sun after Labor Day in Sept.:* Birthday celebration; *Dec:* Holiday tour; call for lectures, tours, workshops.

Directions: From I-270: take Rte. 28 east, turn left on W. Montgomery Ave., and proceed 1 block. Historical Society complex is on left. Park in back.

Scotland

19 **Site:** POINT LOOKOUT STATE PARK & CIVIL WAR MUSEUM, Rte. 5, Scotland, MD 20687, ☎ 301/872-5688

Description: Museum documents local history during the Civil War era. The site originally functioned as a Civil War Union hospital and then became a Union prisoner-of-war camp. More than 52,000 prisoners passed through the facility.

Open to Public: *Park:* Daily 8am–sunset. *Museum:* May–Sept: Daily 10am–6pm.

Admission Fees: *Museum:* Free. *Fort Lincoln and picnic area:* $2.

Visitor Services: Handicapped access, trails, boat rentals, camping, visitors center.

Regularly Scheduled Events: *Second weekend in June:* Confederate POW days; *Third weekend in June:* Blue & Gray days; *Last weekend in Oct:* Ghostwalk; *First weekend in Nov:* Lighthouse tour.

Directions: From I-95: take exit 7 and follow Rte. 5 south for 65 miles.

Sharpsburg

20 **Site:** ANTIETAM NATIONAL BATTLEFIELD, Sharpsburg Pike, Sharpsburg, MD 21782, ☎ 301/432-5124

Description: Site of the bloodiest single-day battle in American history. An 8.5-mile tour road leads through the battlefield with more than 300 markers, monuments, and Civil War cannons.

Open to Public: Daily 8:30am–5pm. *Summer:* 8:30am–6pm.

Admission Fees: Adults $2, family $4.

Visitor Services: Civil War Explorer, trails, museum, rest rooms, handicapped access, visitors center.

Regularly Scheduled Events: *First weekend in Dec:* The Illumination; *First Sat in July:* Maryland symphony and fireworks.

Directions: From I-70: take exit 29 to Rte. 65 south for approximately 10 miles.

ANTIETAM

The Battle of Antietam (or Sharpsburg) on September 17, 1862, climaxed the first of Confederate Gen. Robert E. Lee's two attempts to carry the war into the North. About 40,000 Southerners were pitted against the 87,000-man Federal Army of the Potomac under Union Gen. George B. McClellan. And when the fighting ended, the course of the American Civil War had been greatly altered.

After his great victory at Manassas in August, Lee had marched his Army of Northern Virginia into Maryland, hoping to find vitally needed men and supplies. McClellan followed, first to Frederick (where through rare good fortune a copy of the Confederate battle plan, Lee's Special Order No. 191, fell into his hands), then westward 12 miles to the passes of South Mountain. There on September 14, at Turner's, Fox's, and

continues

Antietam National Battle-field, Sharpsburg, MD. (Photograph by Dennis Kan, courtesy of The Civil War Trust.)

Crampton's gaps, Lee tried to block the Federals. But because he had split his army to send troops under Gen. Thomas J. "Stonewall" Jackson to capture Harpers Ferry, Lee could only hope to delay the Northerners. McClellan forced his way through, and by the afternoon of September 15, both armies had established new battle lines west and east of Antietam Creek near the town of Sharpsburg. When Jackson's troops reached Sharpsburg on the 16th, Harpers Ferry having surrendered the day before, Lee consolidated his position along the low ridge that runs north and south of the town.

The battle opened at dawn on the 17th when Union Gen. Joseph Hooker's artillery began a murderous fire on Jackson's men in the Miller cornfield north of town. Hooker's troops advanced, driving the Confederates before them, and Jackson reported that his men were "exposed for near an hour to a terrific storm of shell, canister, and musketry."

At about 7am, Jackson was reinforced and succeeded in driving the Federals back. An hour later, Union troops under Gen. Joseph Mansfield counterattacked and by 9 o'clock had regained some of the lost ground. Then, in an effort to extricate some of Mansfield's men from their isolated position near the Dunker Church, Union Gen. John Sedgwick's division of Edwin V. Sumner's corps advanced into the West Woods. There Confederate troops struck Sedgwick's men on both flanks, inflicting appalling casualties.

Meanwhile, Union Gen. William H. French's division of Sumner's corps moved up to support Sedgwick but veered south into Confederates under Gen. D. H. Hill posted along an old sunken road separating the Roulette and Piper farms. For nearly four hours, from 9:30am to 1pm, bitter fighting raged along this road (afterward known as Bloody Lane) as French, supported by Union Gen. Israel B. Richardson's division, also of Sumner's corps, sought to drive the Southerners back. Confusion and sheer exhaustion finally ended the battle here and in the northern part of the field generally.

Southeast of town, Union Gen. Ambrose E. Burnside's troops had been trying to cross a bridge over Antietam Creek since 9:30am. Some 400 Georgians had driven

continues

them back each time. At 1pm, the Federals finally crossed the bridge (now known as Burnside Bridge) and, after a 2-hour delay to reform their lines, advanced up the slope beyond. By late afternoon, they had driven the Georgians back almost to Sharpsburg, threatening to cut off the line of retreat for Lee's decimated Confederates. At about 4pm, Confederate Gen. A. P. Hill's division, left behind by Jackson at Harpers Ferry to salvage the captured Federal property, arrived on the field and immediately entered the fight. Burnside's troops were driven back to the heights near the bridge they had earlier taken. The Battle of Antietam was over. The next day Lee began withdrawing his army across the Potomac River.

More men were killed or wounded at Antietam on September 17, 1862, than on any other single day of the Civil War. Federal losses were 12,410; Confederate losses, 10,700. Although neither side gained a decisive victory, Lee's failure to carry the war effort effectively into the North caused Great Britain to postpone recognition of the Confederate government. The battle also gave President Abraham Lincoln the opportunity to issue the Emancipation Proclamation, which, on January 1, 1863, declared free all slaves in states still in rebellion against the United States. Now the war had a dual purpose: to preserve the Union and end slavery.

by Julie K. Fix, The Civil War Trust

---

21 **Site:** KENNEDY FARMHOUSE, 2406 Chestnut Grove Rd., Sharpsburg, MD 21783,
☎ 301/432-2666

Description: Kennedy Farm was used during the summer of 1859 by John Brown and his "Provisional Army of the United States" as a staging area for its forthcoming raid on Harpers Ferry, West Virginia. The Kennedy Farm is a restored and furnished National Historic Landmark.

Open to Public: *Farmhouse:* May–Oct: Sat–Sun 9am–5pm. *Grounds:* open all year

with interpretive recordings on the second floor porch.

Admission Fees: Free.

Visitor Services: None. Special guided tours for groups—call Capt. South T. Lynn, ☎ **301/515-4890.**

Directions: From I-70: take U.S. Rte. 340 west and follow the signs.

Waldorf

22 **Site:** DR. SAMUEL A. MUDD HOME & MUSEUM, P.O. Box 1043, LaPlata, MD 20646,
☎ 301/645-6870 or 310/934-8464

Description: St. Catherine on the Zechia is the home and plantation of Dr. Samuel A. Mudd, who set the leg of John Wilkes Booth, assassin of President Lincoln. For this deed, Dr. Mudd was sent to Fort Jefferson Prison, Dry Tortugas Island, Florida, for life, but was pardoned in 1869 by President Andrew Johnson.

Open to Public: Apr–Nov: Wed 11am–3pm, Sat–Sun noon–4pm.

Admission Fees: Adults $3, children $1.

Visitor Services: Handicapped access, rest rooms.

Regularly Scheduled Events: *Apr and Sept:* John Wilkes Booth escape route tour.

Directions: From U.S. Rte. 301 at Waldorf: take Rte. 5, go left on Rte. 205, and then go right on Poplar Hill Rd. for approximately 4 miles. Turn right on Dr. Samuel Mudd Rd. and travel .4 mile to the house.

Massachusetts

1 Robert Gould Shaw and 54th Regiment Memorial

MASSACHUSETTS

*T*HE ABOLITIONIST MOVEMENT WAS BORN in Boston in 1831 when William Lloyd Garrison began publishing the *Liberator*, his antislavery newspaper. Massachusetts remained the center of the antislavery movement. The state was prepared to go to war for its beliefs, and its military movement was well organized in the Massachusetts Volunteer Militia. Massachusetts sent the first troops in response to Lincoln's call to arms. On the way to Washington, Baltimore secessionists clashed with Massachusetts volunteers at President Street Station in Baltimore, claiming the first casualties of the war. This both angered the people of Massachusetts and strengthened their resolve, resulting in the doubling of their troop commitment.

In all, Massachusetts contributed more than 152,000 troops to the Union cause, including the second largest number of any state to the Union navy. The 54th Massachusetts Colored Regiment was organized in Massachusetts and became the most famous black regiment of the Civil War. The Regiment ended northern opposition to the recruitment of black troops, leading to the enlistment of nearly 179,000 black soldiers. In the brave attack on Battery Wagner at Morris Island, South Carolina, the 54th lost its commander, Robert Gould Shaw, and 272 of its 650 men.

Boston

1 **Site:** ROBERT GOULD SHAW AND 54TH REGIMENT MEMORIAL. Mailing address: c/o Boston African American National Historic Site and Museum of Afro-American History, 14 Beacon St., Ste. 506, Boston, MA 02108. Physical address: corner of Beacon and Park streets, on Boston Common, ☎ 617/742-5415

Description: The Robert Gould Shaw and 54th Regiment Memorial, a part of the Black Heritage Trail, commemorates Col. Robert Gould Shaw and the 54th Regiment of Massachusetts Volunteer Infantry, the first African American Regiment to be recruited from the North to fight in the Civil War.

Open to Public: Daily 24 hours.

Admission Fees: Free.

Visitor Services: A National Park Service ranger is stationed at the monument from Memorial Day to Labor Day 10am–4pm.

Regularly Scheduled Events: Abolitionist March and Rally. Call for details, ☎ 617/742-5415.

Directions: From I-93: exit at North Station and turn left; follow Causeway St. and stay left. Causeway turns into Staniford St., and Staniford ends at Cambridge St. Turn right and then left; follow Cambridge St. toward Government Center. Cambridge St. turns into Tremont St. Turn right on

Park St. Monument is on Boston Common at the corner of Park and Beacon streets.

Robert Gould Shaw and 54th Regiment Memorial, Boston Common, Boston, MA. (Photograph courtesy of the National Park Service.)

MINNESOTA

*M*INNESOTA WAS THE FIRST STATE TO OFFER TROOPS to President Lincoln following the outbreak of the Civil War at Fort Sumter. The 1st Minnesota Infantry left Fort Snelling for Washington, D.C., and arrived to fight in the First Battle of Bull Run. In that discouraging defeat, the 1st Minnesota Regiment suffered more casualties than any other Union regiment in that battle; but Minnesotans continued to volunteer for military service. Among the places Minnesota regiments saw action were Corinth, Vicksburg, Chickamauga, Chattanooga, Nashville, and Gettysburg.

But there was a crisis brewing back home as well. White settlement in Minnesota, home to the Sioux Indians, had expanded rapidly prior to 1861. Despite the fact that the army had traveled east to fight the Civil War, the white population continued to increase during this period. The displacement of the Sioux Indians and conditions on the reservations led to the Sioux uprising of 1862. During the summer, the Sioux launched a series of raids up and down the Minnesota River Valley. More than 800 white settlers were massacred.

Settlers sought refuge and protection at Fort Ridgely. Chief Little Crow unsuccessfully attacked the fort on August 20 and 22. At the instigation of the Governor, Col. Henry Hastings Sibley led a force of volunteers to quell the attacks and defeated Little Crow at the Battle of Wood Lake on September 23. While many of the Sioux forces fled, some 1,500 were captured and tried. Approximately 300 Sioux were convicted of the deaths of white settlers in the attacks. Lincoln pardoned all but 38, who were executed on December 26.

Some 24,000 Minnesota troops fought in the Union army and against the Indians. The Minnesotans were noted for special gallantry in the victory at Gettysburg, which cost the 1st Minnesota Regiment 215 of its 262 men.

St. Paul

1 **Site:** HISTORIC FORT SNELLING, Fort Snelling History Center, St. Paul, MN 55111, ☎ 612/726-1171

Description: This site, a restored and reconstructed massive stone fortress, is where Minnesota's Civil War troops were trained. Fort Snelling features extensive displays and living history programs, plus numerous special events.

Open to Public: *Fort Snelling:* May–Oct: Mon–Sat 10am–5pm, Sun noon–5pm. *Fort Snelling History Center:* May–Oct: Mon–Sat 9:30am–5pm, Sun 11:30am–5pm. Nov–Apr: Mon–Fri 9am–4:30pm.

Minnesota

Baudette
Thief River Falls
Big Falls
Cook
Ely
Hibbing
Silver Bay
Grand Rapids
Wadena
Hassman
Cloquet
Duluth
Brain
Alexandria
Milaca
Ortonville
St Paul
Minneapolis
Marshall
Lamberton
Owatonna
Pipestone
Austin
Jackson
Harmony

1 Historic Fort Snelling,
Fort Snelling History
Center

For Minnesota Tourism information call 800/657-3700 or 612/296-5029.

Admission Fees: *Fort Snelling:* Adults $4, children 6–15) $2, seniors $3. *Fort Snelling History Center:* Free.

Visitor Services: Living history programs, tours, museum, gift shop, rest rooms, handicapped access.

Regularly Scheduled Events: *June:* Civil War weekend.

Directions: From the junction of I-35W and I-494: travel east 6 miles on Hwy. 5 past the Mall of America and the International Airport to the Historic Fort Snelling exit.

Historic Fort Snelling, St. Paul, Minnesota (Photo courtesy of the Minnesota Historical Society.)

MISSISSIPPI

*I*N LATE APRIL 1862, FOLLOWING THE BATTLE OF SHILOH, a Union army besieged a smaller Confederate force entrenched at Corinth in defense of the vital crossroads of the Memphis & Charleston and the Mobile & Ohio railroads. The Federals built some 14 miles of offensive earthworks between Shiloh and Corinth, and during the night of May 29, the Confederates, whose defensive works had by then become untenable, secretly slipped out of Corinth, abandoning the crossroads to the North. Following the Confederate failure to recapture Corinth in October, Gen. Ulysses S. Grant led his army into northwestern Mississippi from his camp in Tennessee. Grant's first attempt to get to Vicksburg to wrest control of the Mississippi River from the Confederacy failed due to Union defeats at Coffeeville, Holly Springs, and Chickasaw Bayou in December 1862.

After failing to approach Vicksburg from the north, through the bayous of the Mississippi Delta in the winter of 1863, Grant decided to attempt yet another invasion of Mississippi, this time from the south. At the end of April he sent two-thirds of his army down the western shore of the Mississippi, while the Union navy, which had run the batteries of Vicksburg on the evening of April 22, attacked the Rebel fortress at Grand Gulf on the 29th. This assault failed, but the persistent Grant landed his troops even farther south at Bruinsburg on April 30. During the following 200 days, Grant's soldiers marched over a triangular route more than 200 miles long and defeated Confederate forces commanded by Gen. John Pemberton at Port Gibson on the 1st, Raymond on the 12th, Jackson on the 14th, and Champion Hill, the major battle of the campaign, on the 16th. Then, as Pemberton withdrew into Vicksburg's formidable works, his rear guard was routed at the Big Black River Bridge. When two bloody attempts to take the city by storm failed, Grant laid siege to Vicksburg for six weeks. Cut off from the rest of the Confederacy, the besieged had all but run out of food and medical supplies by early July, and Pemberton was forced to surrender on July 4, 1863.

During 1864, Mississippi suffered a number of Union raids, most significantly the Meridian Expedition, in which the Federals marched from Vicksburg eastward across the state to Meridian, destroying everything of military value in their path. During the remainder of 1864, as William T. Sherman marched on Atlanta, his lengthening supply lines were threatened by Confederate cavalry leader Nathan Bedford Forrest. To divert the aggressive Forrest from those lines, Sherman ordered three successive Union expeditions into North Mississippi. Battles at Brices Cross Roads and Tupelo, skirmishing at Oxford, and a celebrated raid by Forrest on Memphis ensued between June 10 and August 11, 1864. Of these, the battle at Brices Cross Roads, in which Forrest's force totally defeated their more numerous Union enemy, was the most significant.

by Michael F. Beard, Mississippi Department of Archives and History

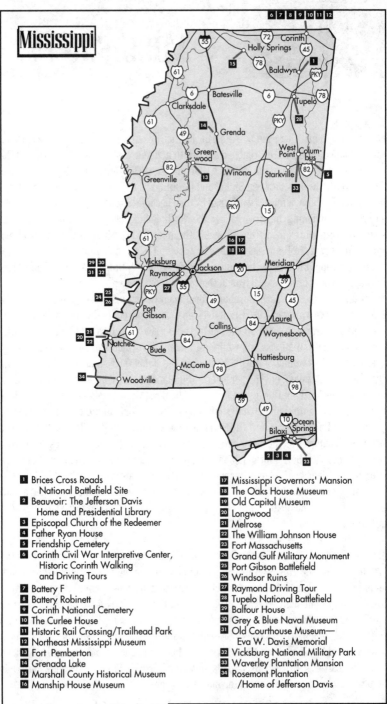

Mississippi

1 Brices Cross Roads
  National Battlefield Site
2 Beauvoir: The Jefferson Davis
  Home and Presidential Library
3 Episcopal Church of the Redeemer
4 Father Ryan House
5 Friendship Cemetery
6 Corinth Civil War Interpretive Center,
  Historic Corinth Walking
  and Driving Tours
7 Battery F
8 Battery Robinett
9 Corinth National Cemetery
10 The Curlee House
11 Historic Rail Crossing/Trailhead Park
12 Northeast Mississippi Museum
13 Fort Pemberton
14 Grenada Lake
15 Marshall County Historical Museum
16 Manship House Museum

17 Mississippi Governors' Mansion
18 The Oaks House Museum
19 Old Capitol Museum
20 Longwood
21 Melrose
22 The William Johnson House
23 Fort Massachusetts
24 Grand Gulf Military Monument
25 Port Gibson Battlefield
26 Windsor Ruins
27 Raymond Driving Tour
28 Tupelo National Battlefield
29 Balfour House
30 Grey & Blue Naval Museum
31 Old Courthouse Museum—
  Eva W. Davis Memorial
32 Vicksburg National Military Park
33 Waverley Plantation Mansion
34 Rosemont Plantation
  /Home of Jefferson Davis

For Mississippi Tourism information call 800/WARMEST.

℘or More Information

Mississippi's annual *Travel Planner* contains a Civil War section, organized regionally, that gives visitor contact information for approximately 75 sites, including battlefields and fortifications, cemeteries, historic communities, homes, and sites associated with the political history of the war. The guide also contains a general essay on the war in the state, a chronology of significant events from secession to surrender, a selected reading list, and photographs. It is available free by writing Mississippi Department of Tourism Development, P.O. Box 1705, Ocean Springs, MS 39566-1705 or by calling ☎ **800/WARMEST.**

Baldwyn

1 **Site:** BRICES CROSS ROADS NATIONAL BATTLEFIELD SITE. Mailing address: 2680 Natchez Trace Pkwy., Tupelo, MS 38801, ☎ 800/305-7417 or 601/680-4025

Description: At Brices Cross Roads in June 1864, a battle was fought that served to keep Confederate Gen. Nathan Bedford Forrest from altering the supply line that was essential to the success of Union Gen. William T. Sherman. While this battle was considered a Confederate victory, Sherman persevered and went on to win the Atlanta campaign.

Open to Public: Daily from dawn to dusk.

Admission Fees: Free.

Visitor Services: Interpretive panel, brochures.

Directions: From I-45: proceed north to Baldwyn, MS, and go west on MS 370 about 6 miles to park.

Biloxi

2 **Site:** BEAUVOIR: THE JEFFERSON DAVIS HOME AND PRESIDENTIAL LIBRARY, 2244 Beach Blvd., Biloxi, MS 39531, ☎ 800/570-3818 or 601/388-1313

Description: Beauvoir was the seaside retirement estate of Confederate President Jefferson Davis. The estate served as the Mississippi Confederate Soldiers' Home from 1903 to 1957. See the restored home and outbuildings, soldiers' home hospital (Confederate Museum), and cemetery and Tomb of the Unknown Confederate Soldier. Beauvoir is the site of the Jefferson Davis Presidential Library, containing a biographical exhibit on Jefferson Davis, and a research library on 19th-century southern history, opening in May of 1998.

Open to Public: Mar–Aug: Daily 9am–5pm. Sept–Feb: Daily 9am–4pm.

Admission Fees: Adults, $6, children $3.50, seniors $5.50. Group rates available.

Visitor Services: Museum, gift shop, library, information, rest rooms, handicapped access.

Regularly Scheduled Events: *Mar:* Spring Pilgrimage; *Apr:* Confederate Memorial Day; *Oct:* Fall Muster; *Dec:* Candlelight Christmas Tour.

Directions: From I-10 east: exit onto Lorraine-Cowan Rd. traveling south; turn left (east) on U.S. Hwy. 90 (Beach Blvd.) to Beauvoir at the intersection of U.S. Hwy. 90 and Beauvoir Ave. (Beauvoir is 8 miles from I-10.) From I-10 west: exit onto I-110, proceed toward the Gulf to U.S. Hwy. 90., and turn right (west) on U.S. 90 to Beauvoir Ave. (Beauvoir is 9 miles from I-10.)

---

3 **Site:** EPISCOPAL CHURCH OF THE REDEEMER, Corner of Hwy. 90 (Beach Blvd.) and Bellman St., 610 Water St., Biloxi, MS 39530, ☎ 601/436-3123

Description: Confederate President Jefferson Davis worshipped here and was a member of the vestry. Other Confederate generals who were church members during the time they lived in Biloxi were Lt. Gen. Alexander P. Stewart, Brig. Gen. Joseph Davis, and Brig. Gen. Samuel W. Ferguson. The church offers an exhibit of Confederate and Davis memorabilia, featuring the Davis pew, Confederate flag and cross, and a letter from Davis.

Open to Public: Daily 9am–2pm; open for viewing; tours by appointment.

Admission Fees: Free.

Visitor Services: Information.

Regularly Scheduled Events: *Mar:* Spring Pilgrimage; *Third Sun in May:* Police Remembrance and Appreciation; *First Sun in Oct:* Blessing of the Animals.

Directions: From I-10: take I-110 to Hwy. 90 east (exit 1A). Church is on Hwy. 90 at Bellman St. Distance to Church is 5.5 miles from I-10.

---

4 **Site:** FATHER RYAN HOUSE, 1196 Beach Blvd., Biloxi, MS 39539, ☎ 800/295-1189 or 601/435-1189

Description: This is the former home of Father Abram Ryan, Poet Laureate of the Confederacy. Here Father Ryan wrote some of his best-known poetry, including "Sea Rest," and "Sea Reverie." The home is now a bed-and-breakfast.

Open to Public: Daily 11am–5pm.

Admission Fees: Free.

Visitor Services: Tours, lodging.

Directions: From I-10: take exit 46A (I-110) south to Hwy. 90 west. Located 6 blocks west of the I-110 off ramp and 4 blocks west of the Biloxi Lighthouse.

Columbus

---

5 **Site:** FRIENDSHIP CEMETERY, P.O. Box 1408, Columbus, MS 39703, ☎ 601/328-2565

Description: This cemetery is the burial site of four Confederate generals, more than 2,000 Confederate soldiers, and veterans from every war the United States has fought, as well as distinguished authors, legislators, and people from all walks of life. It is also the site of America's first Decoration Day (1866), inspiring the writing of the poem "The Blue and the Gray." This site relates to the theme of reconciliation after the Civil War because the Ladies of Columbus put flowers on the graves of both Confederate and Union soldiers who had been buried there during the war.

Open to Public: Daily 7am–sunset.

Admission Fees: Free.

Visitor Services: Locator service is available.

Regularly Scheduled Events: Spring Pilgrimage includes "Tales from the Crypt."

Directions: 69 miles from I-55 on 82 E; 68 miles from I-20 on 45 N.

---

6 **Site:** CORINTH CIVIL WAR INTERPRETIVE CENTER, HISTORIC CORINTH WALKING AND DRIVING TOURS. Mailing address: P.O. Box 45, Corinth, MS 38835-0045, ☎ 601/287-9501 or 601/287-1328, www.corinth.org

Description: The Corinth Civil War Interpretive Center is located in the cottage at the rear of the historic Curlee House. A video, maps for the self-guided walking tour and Corinth Campaign driving tour, photo exhibits, and information about the Siege and Battle of Corinth National Historic Landmark Sites are available at the visitors center.

The **walking tour** includes: Corinth Civil War Interpretive Center, Curlee House, Historic Rail Crossing/Trailhead Park, Oak Home, Fishpond House, Duncan House.

The **driving tour** includes: Battery Robinett, Battery D, Battery F, Union Siege Lines, Army of the Tennessee (Brig. Gens. Thomas McKean's and Thomas W. Sherman's Divisions) and Army of the Ohio (Brig. Gens. T. J. Wood's and William Nelson's Divisions); Union Siege Lines, (Maj. Gen. William T. Sherman's and Brig. Gen. Thomas A. Davies' Divisions); Union Siege Line, Army of the Mississippi (Brig. Gen. E. A. Paine's Division); Union Earthworks, Harper Road; Confederate Fieldwork (rifle pit); Corona College; and First Phase—Battle of Corinth—October 3, 1862.

Open to Public: *Interpretive Center:* Mon–Sat 9am–5pm, Sun 1–5pm. Dec–Mar: Closes at 4pm. *Walking and driving tours:* Daily during daylight hours.

Admission Fees: Free.

Visitor Services: Information, exhibits, video, maps, gifts, free refreshments, rest rooms, handicapped access.

Directions: From I-40 at Jackson, TN: exit onto Hwy. 45 south, drive to Corinth (50 miles), and exit onto Hwy. 72 (Memphis exit) east. Turn left on Fulton Dr. at shopping center with Kroger store. Follow the brown Civil War Center banners mounted on light posts to Waldron St. Turn right on Waldron and continue to follow banners to Jackson St. Turn left on Jackson St. and proceed 2 blocks to Childs St. Turn left. The Interpretive Center is located at 301 Childs St. behind the Curlee House and across from City Hall.

THE CORINTH CAMPAIGN TRAIL

The Corinth Campaign Trail includes nationally significant sites associated with the struggle between Union and Confederate forces for control of the vital crossroads of the Memphis & Charleston and the Mobile & Ohio railroads at Corinth, Mississippi (April–October 1862). The trail includes primary sites in northeast Mississippi at Corinth, Iuka, Booneville, and Rienzi, and in central Tennessee in and around Shiloh.

For more information: "A Guide to the Corinth Campaign," which provides a self-guided driving tour of these sites is available free from the Corinth Civil War Interpretive Center, 310 Childs St., P.O. Box 45, Corinth, MS 38835-0045, ☎ **601/287-9501;** and from Mississippi Division of Tourism Development, P.O. Box 1705, Ocean Springs, MS 39566-1705, ☎**800/WARMEST.**

THE CAMPAIGN FOR CORINTH

Because of its location at the intersection of the Memphis and Charleston and the Mobile and Ohio railroads, Corinth was a city of strategic importance during the Civil War. The Siege and Battle of Corinth, Mississippi, are events that had a decisive effect on the outcome of the American Civil War. The Siege of Corinth (April 28–May 30, 1862) resulted in the severing of the vital Memphis and Charleston Railroad (the only railroad connecting Memphis and Richmond in the South) and the Mobile and Ohio (a north-south railroad connecting Mobile, Alabama, with Cairo, Illinois). For 3 months in 1862, the junction of these two railroads was the most strategic location in the Confederacy.

The Battle of Shiloh, the largest battle of the Corinth Campaign, was fought over the Corinth railroad crossing. After the Battle of Shiloh in May 1862, the Union troops laid siege and took Corinth from the Confederates and held it through 1864. In October 1862, the Confederates attacked, seeking to take Corinth back, but failed in this attempt.

Corinth was occupied by one force or the other from 1861 to 1865. A conservative estimate of troops stationed in or around Corinth during the war years numbered more than 300,000. At least 200 top Confederate or Federal generals were stationed in Corinth, and more than 100 skirmishes or raids occurred in the area.

Analysts consider the Siege and Battle of Corinth to be the beginning of the end of the war in the West. The Union occupation of Corinth led to the fall of Fort

continues

Pillow; Union control of central and west Tennessee; the surrender of Memphis; and the opening of the upper Mississippi River, in turn allowing ironclads to cooperate in the movements on Vicksburg. The Union advance on Corinth has been described as the "most extraordinary display of entrenchment under offensive conditions witnessed in the entire war." Today, the surviving earthworks, dating to early 1862, are one of the largest and best-preserved groups of field fortifications in the United States.

In the fall of 1862, the Confederate armies were on the offensive, moving north along a 1,000-mile front. The Battle of Antietam, September 17, 1862, gave President Lincoln the opportunity to issue the Emancipation Proclamation. Union victories followed at Iuka, Mississippi, September 19, 1862; Corinth, October 3–4, 1862; and Perryville, Kentucky, October 8, 1862. These victories ended the Confederate offensive, gave support to the tenuously issued proclamation, and convinced the Federal government that recognition of the Confederacy was not appropriate at that time. Confederate losses at the Battle of Corinth equaled the percentage of losses the Army of Northern Virginia sustained at Antietam, the bloodiest single day in American history.

After the Emancipation Proclamation, slaves from all over the South sought the protection of the Union Army. A camp set up in Corinth by the army to house the freed men became home to more than 4,000 African Americans from Mississippi, Tennessee, and Alabama. A regiment of black soldiers raised to guard the camp was originally called the 1st Alabama Infantry of African Descent; later it became the 55th U.S. Colored Infantry.

by Rosemary Taylor Williams

---

7   **Site: BATTERY F, P.O. Box 45, Corinth, MS 38835-0045, ☎ 601/287-9501**

Description: Battery F is one of the six outer batteries built by the Union army in a position to provide support fire on October 3, 1862. It was captured the evening of October 3, 1862. Battery F is a well-preserved earthwork about 150 feet long with a parapet between 3 feet and 6 feet high. Facing northwest, Battery F protected the Memphis & Charleston Railroad. The battery was the northernmost of the detached batteries protecting approaches along roads and railroads.

Open to Public: Daily during daylight hours.

Admission Fees: Free.

Visitor Services: Information.

Directions: From I-40 at Jackson, TN: exit onto Hwy. 45 south to Corinth (50 miles). From Hwy. 45, take Memphis exit onto Hwy. 72 east. Turn north at the intersection of Hwy. 72 and Alcorn Dr.; turn at the first right onto Smithbridge Rd. to Pinelake subdivision. Battery F is located at the corner of Bitner and Davis sts. in the subdivision.

8   **Site:** BATTERY ROBINETT, P.O. Box 45, Corinth, MS 38835-0045, ☎ 601/287-9501

Description: Battery Robinett is a reconstruction of one of seven batteries constructed by the Federal army following the Siege of Corinth in the spring of 1862. It was the scene of the most famous event of the Battle of Corinth.

Open to Public: Daily from dawn to dusk.

Admission Fees: Free.

Visitor Services: Trails, information.

Directions: From I-40 at Jackson, TN: exit onto Hwy. 45 south to Corinth (50 miles). From Hwy. 45, take Memphis exit onto Hwy. 72 east. From Hwy. 72 E, turn left onto Fulton Dr. at shopping center with Kroger Store; follow Fulton Dr. to Linden St.; turn left at this intersection. Battery Robinett will be on the left. Entrance is on the left at top of hill approximately .25 mile from the intersection of Fulton Dr. and Linden St.

9   **Site:** CORINTH NATIONAL CEMETERY, Horton St., Corinth, MS 38834, ☎ 901/386-8311

Description: On April 13, 1866, the Secretary of War authorized immediate action to provide a final resting place for the honored dead who died in Civil War battles for control of the railroad in and around Corinth, Mississippi. This beautiful 20-acre cemetery is the resting place for 1,793 known and 3,895 unknown Union soldiers.

Open to Public: Mon–Fri 8am–4:30pm.

Admission Fees: Free.

Visitor Services: Information, rest rooms.

Regularly Scheduled Events: Veterans Day and Memorial Day events.

Directions: From I-40 at Jackson, TN: exit onto Hwy. 45 south, drive to Corinth (50 miles), and exit onto Hwy. 72 (the Memphis exit) east. Follow signs off Rte. 72 in Corinth.

10   **Site:** THE CURLEE HOUSE, 705 Jackson St., Corinth, MS 38834, ☎ 601/287-9501

Description: Built in 1857 by one of Corinth's founders, the home is a significant example of Greek Revival architecture. The Curlee House was used in the Civil War as headquarters for Generals Braxton Bragg, H. W. Halleck, and John B. Hood.

The restored home-museum contains a collection of Boehme edition Audubon prints; 18th- and 19th-century antiques; paintings; and an exhibit of replicas of Civil War soldiers furnishings, made by Corinth's C & D Jarnigan Co.

Open to Public: Daily 1–4pm, sometimes 9am–1pm. Call ahead for morning appointments.

Admission Fees: Adults $2.50, children $1.50.

Visitor Services: Home-museum tour, information.

Directions: From I-40 at Jackson, TN: exit onto Hwy. 45 south, drive to Corinth (50 miles), and exit onto Hwy. 72 (Memphis exit) east. Turn left on Fulton Dr. at shopping center with Kroger store. Follow the brown Civil War Center banners mounted on light posts to Waldron St. Turn right on Waldron and continue to follow banners to Jackson St. Turn left on Jackson St. and proceed 2 blocks to Childs St. The house is at the corner of Jackson and Childs sts.

---

11 **Site:** HISTORIC RAIL CROSSING/TRAILHEAD PARK, P.O. Box 45, Corinth, MS 38835-0045, ☎ 601/287-9501

Description: This park was the viewing area for the crossing of the historic Memphis and Charleston and the Mobile and Ohio Railroads in 1862. The Battle of Shiloh was fought for control of this crossing. The park serves as the trailhead for the historic Corinth hiking and biking trail, which connects many of the Civil War Corinth National Historic Landmark sites.

Open to Public: Daily from dawn to dusk.

Admission Fees: Free.

Visitor Services: Rest rooms, handicapped access, drinking fountain, picnic area.

Directions: From I-40 at Jackson, TN: exit onto Hwy. 45 south, drive to Corinth (50 miles), and exit onto Hwy. 72 (Memphis exit) east. Turn left on Fulton Dr. at shopping center with Kroger store. Follow the brown Civil War Center banners mounted on light posts to Waldron St. Turn right on Waldron and continue to follow banners to the park located at the corner of Jackson and Waldron sts. in downtown Corinth.

---

12 **Site:** NORTHEAST MISSISSIPPI MUSEUM, 204 Fourth St., Corinth, MS 38834, ☎ 601/287-3120

Description: The Northeast Mississippi Museum has displays of Civil War artifacts and photographs, a model of the historic railroad crossing, and other information on Civil War Corinth.

Open to Public: *Summer:* Mon–Sat 10am–5pm, Sun 2–5pm. *Winter:* Mon–Sat 10:30am–4:30pm, Sun 2–4:30pm.

Admission Fees: Free.

Visitor Services: Museum, gift shop, information, rest rooms.

Directions: From I-40 at Jackson, TN: exit onto Hwy. 45 south, drive to Corinth (50 miles), and exit at MS Hwy. 2. Turn left on MS Hwy. 2 and turn right on Bus. Hwy. 45. Then turn right on 4th St. and proceed 1 block. Museum is on the left.

Greenwood

---

13 **Site:** FORT PEMBERTON, c/o Greenwood Convention and Visitors Bureau, P.O. Drawer 739, Greenwood, MS 38935-0739, ☎ 601/453-9197

Description: Located on Hwy. 82 West on the banks of the Yazoo Pass connecting the Yazoo and Tallahatchie rivers, Fort Pemberton was a hastily constructed fortification consisting of cotton bales and timber logs. A significant military battle occurred here when the Confederate forces successfully drove back three Union ironclads, forcing Grant to seek another route to Vicksburg. A brochure is available at the Convention and Visitors Bureau. The Cottonlandia Museum contains artifacts from Fort Pemberton.

Open to Public: Daily from dawn to dusk.

Admission Fees: Free.

Visitor Services: Trails, information.

Directions: From I-55: take Greenwood/Winona exit. Take State Hwy. 82 west to Greenwood. Pick up brochure at Greenwood Convention and Visitors Bureau located on Hwy. 82 at Leflore Ave. on left. To Cottonlandia Museum: travel west on Hwy. 82. Museum is located on the right, east of Fort Pemberton. To Fort Pemberton: travel west on Hwy. 82 and proceed past Wal-Mart. Fort is located on the right, just east of the 49E intersection.

Grenada

14 **Site:** GRENADA LAKE, 2151 Scenic Loop 333, Grenada, MS 38901, ☎ 601/226-5121

Description: Grenada was to be Pemberton's defense line against Grant's approach on the Mississippi Central Railroad against Vicksburg. Eight forts were built here; two of them are restored on Grenada Lake property. Only a skirmish was actually fought because Grant turned back after Dorn's raid.

Open to Public: *Forts:* Daily during daylight hours. *Visitors center:* Daily 9am–noon and 1–5pm.

Admission Fees: Free.

Visitor Services: Lodging, gas, camping, trails, food, museum, gift shop, information, rest rooms, handicapped access.

Regularly Scheduled Events: *Summer:* "Thunder on Water" music festival and boat race.

Directions: From I-55: take Grenada exit for Hwy. 8. Take Hwy. 8 east from Grenada to Scenic Rte. 333, which goes to Grenada Lake.

Holly Springs

15 **Site:** MARSHALL COUNTY HISTORICAL MUSEUM, 220 East College, P.O. Box 806, Holly Springs, MS 38635, ☎ 601/252-3669

Description: The Civil War hit Holly Springs hard. The town changed hands 62 times. Holly Springs served as a headquarters for General Grant in his first campaign against

Vicksburg. Van Dorn's raid on December 20, 1862 destroyed Grant's supply base and ended this campaign. Marshall County produced 10 Confederate generals, 8 adjutant generals, and 9 members of the Confederate Congress. The town boasts 61 antebellum homes. Arms for the Confederacy were manufactured at the armory in Holly Springs. The Marshall County Museum features a Civil War room with a variety of exhibits and artifacts.

Open to Public: Mon–Fri 10am–5pm, Sat 10am–2pm.

Admission Fees: $3.

Visitor Services: Museum, gift shop, information, rest rooms, handicapped access.

Regularly Scheduled Events: Annual history tours of local Civil War sites (call for schedule); Spring Pilgrimage.

Directions: From I-55 at Senatobia: travel east on Hwy. 4 for 32 miles to Holly Springs and the museum. Located 42 miles southeast of Memphis on U.S. 78; 60 miles northwest of Tupelo on U.S. 78; 17 miles southwest of Ashland on Hwy. 4; 30 miles north of Oxford on Hwy. 7.

Jackson

16 **Site:** MANSHIP HOUSE MUSEUM, 420 E. Fortification St., Jackson, MS 39202-2340, ☎ 601/961-4724

Description: The Manship House was the home of Charles Henry Manship, the mayor who surrendered Jackson to General Sherman on July 21, 1863.

Open to Public: Tues–Fri 9am–4pm, Sat 10am–4pm.

Admission Fees: Free.

Visitor Services: Museum, information, rest rooms, handicapped access.

Regularly Scheduled Events: *July:* Summer workshops for children; *Dec:* Christmas at the Manship House.

Directions: From I-55: take Fortification St. exit; continue west on Fortification and turn right (north) onto Congress St. The first driveway on the left belongs to the Manship House parking lot. Visitors should enter the cream-colored visitors center for information and a guided tour.

17 **Site:** MISSISSIPPI GOVERNORS' MANSION, 300 Capitol St., Jackson, MS 39201, ☎ 601/359-6421

Description: When the first occupation of Jackson occurred in May 1863, then Governor John Pettus abandoned the mansion. He returned in July, only to have to leave again. He moved the capital to Meridian, Macon, and finally, Columbus, where Governor Charles Clark was inaugurated in November 1863. Clark moved the capital to Macon and then to Columbus before the legislature reconvened in Jackson in May 1865. The mansion was not reoccupied by a governor until Governor Benjamin Humphreys moved there in October 1865. During the 2½-year absence of a governor in the mansion, the house was used as a temporary shelter for wounded soldiers, and General Sherman held a dinner there in July 1863, while using the house as his headquarters.

Open to Public: Tues–Fri 9:30–11am. Closed two weeks in Dec during public school vacation.

Admission Fees: Free.

Visitor Services: Museum, handicapped access.

Regularly Scheduled Events: *First Fri in Dec:* Candlelight tour.

Directions: From I-55: take Pearl St. exit (exit 96A) and bear right onto Pearl St. viaduct. Cross South State St., drive west to the intersection with West St., and turn right. The mansion is at the corner of West and Capitol sts.

---

18 **Site:** THE OAKS HOUSE MUSEUM, 823 North Jefferson St., Jackson, MS 39202, ☎ 601/353-9339

Description: This house museum interprets the life of the James Boyd family from the 1840s to the 1860s. General Grant's troops raided the house, and General Sherman and his troops briefly used the house as a headquarters.

Open to Public: Tues–Sat 10am–3pm.

Admission Fees: Adults $2, children $1, groups (10 or more) $1.25/person.

Visitor Services: Museum, information.

Directions: From I-55: take High St. exit (96B) west to North Jefferson St. and turn north on Jefferson St. The museum is #823, on the west side of the street. A white picket fence is in front of the house.

---

19 **Site:** OLD CAPITOL MUSEUM, Mississippi Department of Archives & History, P.O. Box 571, State St. at Capitol St., Jackson, MS 39205-0571, ☎ 601/359-6920

Description: This building was the site of Mississippi's Secession Convention, January 1861. It continued as the seat of state government until May 1863, when it was evacuated before the Battle of Jackson. Vandalized by Federal troops, it remained in Confederate hands, although legislative and state offices were removed to Macon, Mississippi. In October 1864, the building served as a Confederate military headquarters.

Open to Public: Mon–Fri 8am–5pm, Sat 9:30am–4:30pm, Sun 12:30–4:30pm.

Admission Fees: Free.

Visitor Services: Museum, gift shop, information, rest rooms, handicapped access.

Regularly Scheduled Events: *Autumn:* Social studies teachers workshop (annual training session on varied topics for social studies teachers); *Dec:* Christmas films, period trees, decorations, and electric train.

Directions: From I-55: take Pearl St. exit to downtown Jackson, turn right at first light onto State St., pass in front of building, and turn right on Amite St. to enter parking lot behind building.

Natchez

20 Site: LONGWOOD, 140 Lower Woodville Rd., Natchez, MS 39120, ☎ 601/442-5193

Description: Longwood provides a visitor with eloquent testimony to the devastating impact of the Civil War on the cotton economy of the American South. The tragic story of the hardships of the family who lived there "reared in the lap of luxury and reduced to poverty" has all the tragedy and pathos of *Gone With the Wind* but with a double reverse twist. First, it is true. Second, the family who lost everything was loyal to the Union. Work on the house, begun in 1860, stopped after war was declared in 1861. The northern workmen made their way home to Philadelphia through the blockade that was put on the South, leaving their tools on the workbench, where they remain.

Open to Public: *Tours:* Daily 9am–5pm; last tour at 4:30pm.

Admission Fees: Adults $5, children $2.50, groups $4/person.

Visitor Services: Gift shop, information, rest rooms, handicapped access.

Regularly Scheduled Events: Spring, Fall, and Christmas Pilgrimages. Call for dates.

Directions: From I-120 at Vicksburg, MS: turn south on Hwy. 61 and go approximately 75 miles to Natchez. From I-55 at Brookhaven, MS: turn west on Hwy. 84 and go approximately 60 miles to Natchez.

21 Site: MELROSE, P.O. Box 1208, Natchez, MS 39121, ☎ 601/442-7047

Description: The home of John T. McMurran, Melrose is an excellent example of an antebellum Greek Revival estate. McMurran was a well-known Natchez lawyer and planter from the 1830s to 1865, controlling cotton plantations in Mississippi, Arkansas, Louisiana, and Texas. Melrose's story tells of the effect of the Civil War on the cotton-based economy and on the political and social life of the South.

Open to Public: Daily 8:30am–5pm.

Admission Fees: *Grounds:* Free. *Guided tours of mansion:* Adults $5, children $2.50, seniors $2.50.

Visitor Services: Museum, gift shop, information, rest rooms, handicapped access.

Regularly Scheduled Events: *Mar:* Spring pilgrimage; *Oct:* Fall pilgrimage; *Dec:* Christmas program.

Directions: From I-20 at Vicksburg: take U.S. 61 to Natchez. Turn right on Melrose Pkwy. and follow signs. From I-10 at Baton Rouge: take U.S. 61 to Natchez. Turn left on Melrose Pkwy. and follow signs.

22 Site: THE WILLIAM JOHNSON HOUSE, P.O. Box 1208, Natchez, MS 39121, ☎ 601/442-7047

Description: The home of a free black entrepreneur and diarist in antebellum Natchez, the William Johnson House provides a unique opportunity to glimpse a seldom-interpreted part of Southern history. Born a slave, Johnson was freed by his father. He was educated and became a well-known Natchez businessman and slaveholder himself.

Open to Public: As staffing permits; call for information.

Admission Fees: Free.

Visitor Services: Information.

Directions: From I-20 at Vicksburg: take U.S. 61 to Natchez. Turn right on U.S. 84 toward the bridge. At Canal St. (just before the bridge), turn right. Follow Canal St. to State St. and turn right. Johnson House is on the right. From I-10 at Baton Rouge: take U.S. 61 to Natchez. Turn left on U.S. 84; follow it to Canal St. and turn right. Follow Canal St. to State St. and turn right. Johnson House is on the right.

Ocean Springs

23 **Site:** FORT MASSACHUSETTS, Gulf Islands National Seashore, 3500 Park Rd., Ocean Springs, MS 39564, ☎ 601/875-9057

Description: With hostilities under way in 1861, Ship Island and Fort Massachusetts witnessed Confederate occupation; a brief land-naval battle; Federal occupation; creation of western Gulf Union navy headquarters and depot; military prisons, including prisoner-of-war camp; and the staging of 20,000 troops used to capture Confederate New Orleans and Mobile.

Open to Public: Fort Massachusetts is normally open from arrival of the first ferryboat to the departure of the last vessel. This includes 4 hours at midday during spring and autumn and approximately 8 hours in summer. Call for schedule.

Admission Fees: *Ship Island entrance fee:* $2/person. Free with Gulf Islands National Seashore Annual Pass, Golden Age or Golden Access Pass.

Visitor Services: Snack bar, rest rooms, water fountains, ranger station, picnic area. Visitors are advised to wear a hat and sun protection.

Directions: From I-10: take Hwy. 49 south to Gulfport, MS, Small Craft Harbor. Board the ferry to Ship Island via Pan Isles Excursions; trip is approximately 1 hour.

Port Gibson

24 **Site:** GRAND GULF MILITARY MONUMENT, Rte. 2, Box 389, Port Gibson, MS 39150, ☎ 601/437-5911

Description: The river batteries at Grand Gulf were the southernmost leg of the

Vicksburg defenses. Grant tried to land his army at Grand Gulf but was driven off by the Confederate batteries. After the Battle of Port Gibson, Grand Gulf became Grant's base of operations.

Open to Public: Mon–Sat 8am–5pm, Sun 9am–6pm.

Admission Fees: Adults $1.50, children 75¢, seniors $1. Groups: Adults $1, children $.50.

Visitor Services: Camping, trails, museum, gift shop, information, rest rooms, handicapped access.

Regularly Scheduled Events: Civil War artillery demonstrations several times a year.

Directions: From I-20 at Vicksburg: take Hwy. 61 south for 22 miles, turn right at Grand Gulf Rd., and proceed 7.5 miles to the site.

---

25 **Site:** PORT GIBSON BATTLEFIELD, P.O. Box 491, Port Gibson, MS 39150, ☎ 601/437-4351 (Chamber of Commerce)

Description: The Shaifer House was the site of the opening shots in the Battle of Port Gibson. The house was used by Maj. Gen. John A. McClernand for his headquarters and later used as a hospital. Confederate forces were entrenched at Magnolia Church. Part of the battle was fought on the Bruinsburg Road at Point Lookout. Restoration of the site is in progress.

Open to Public: Daily from dawn to dusk.

Admission Fees: Free.

Visitor Services: None.

Directions: From I-20 at Vicksburg: travel south on Hwy. 61 for 28 miles to Port Gibson. Turn right on Carrol St. and continue on Rodney Rd. and Bessie Weathers Rd. to Shaifer Rd., a distance of 4.5 miles. For additional details, see "A Guide to the Campaign and Siege of Vicksburg," listed under "The Vicksburg Campaign Trail" in this chapter.

Shaifer House, Port Gibson, MS. (Photograph courtesy of The Civil War Trust.)

---

26 **Site:** WINDSOR RUINS. Mailing address: Department of Archives & History, 400 Jefferson Davis Blvd., Natchez, MS 39120, located approximately 10 miles outside the town of Port Gibson, ☎ 601/446-6502

Description: The Windsor Ruins are located near the extinct town of Bruinsburg, where Grant's army crossed the Mississippi River from April 30 to May 1, 1863, to begin the campaign for the capture of Vicksburg. The mansion was located along the route of Grant's army on its march inland toward Jackson. Windsor Mansion was destroyed by accidental fire in 1890.

Open to Public: Daily from dawn to dusk.

Admission Fees: Free.

Visitor Services: Interpretive sign.

Directions: From I-20: take the Natchez Trace Pkwy. south to the exit for County Hwy. 552; follow Hwy. 552, past the turnoff for Alcorn State University; follow the signs to the site entrance.

Raymond

27 | **Site:** RAYMOND DRIVING TOUR, P.O. Box 10, Raymond, MS 39154, ☎ 601/857-8041

Description: The Raymond Driving Tour features three structures that stand as a reminder of the Battle of Raymond, fought outside this small community. The Raymond Courthouse, built from 1857 to 1859 by the Weldon Brothers's skilled slave crew, is on the National Register of Historic Places and is an excellent example of Greek Revival architecture. It was used as a hospital for Union wounded following the 6-hour Battle of Raymond. St. Mark's Episcopal Church was organized in 1837, built in 1854, and is still an active church. Used as a hospital for Union wounded after the battle, the church contains bloodstains that can still be seen on the floor of the sanctuary. The tour also includes 1831–1834 Waverly, used as a temporary headquarters for Generals McPherson and Grant, and the Confederate cemetery.

Open to Public: Brochure and map are available from the city hall on Mon–Fri from 8am–12pm and 1–5pm. *Driving tour:* Daily during daylight hours. Interior tours of church and courthouse by appointment.

Admission Fees: Free.

Visitor Services: Information.

Regularly Scheduled Events: *First Sat of May:* Raymond Country Fair (Revival of Southern Culture with food, entertainment, crafts, and history); First Annual Reenactment of Grant's Overland Campaign will be held in May 1998. Call for future dates.

Directions: From I-20 at Jackson: take exit 40A (Hwy. 18 south) 8 miles to Raymond. Turn right on Hinds Blvd., turn left on Main St., and proceed to courthouse. City hall is a small building behind the courthouse. Park near the water tower; pick up a brochure at city hall.

Tupelo

28 | **Site:** TUPELO NATIONAL BATTLEFIELD. Mailing address: 2680 Natchez Trace Pkwy., Tupelo, MS 38801, ☎ 800/305-7147 or 601/680-4025

Description: Tupelo National Battlefield is a 1-acre site off the Natchez Trace Pkwy. In July 1864, a battle was fought here that served to keep Confederate Gen. Nathan Bedford Forrest from altering the supply line that was essential to the success of Union Gen. William T. Sherman. Neither side could claim victory.

Open to Public: Daily from dawn to dusk.

Admission Fees: Free.

Visitor Services: Interpretive signs, brochure.

Directions: Take Hwy. 78 to the Natchez Trace Pkwy. and go south on the Natchez Trace Pkwy. for 4 miles to MS Hwy. 6 (Main St.) exit. Turn left onto MS Hwy. 6 and go 1 mile to battlefield site.

Vicksburg

29 Site: BALFOUR HOUSE, 1002 Crawford St., P.O. Box 781, Vicksburg, MS 39181, ☎ 800/294-7113 or 601/638-7113

Description: Balfour House was the home of famous siege diarist Emma Balfour. It was also the Union headquarters after the fall of Vicksburg.

Open to Public: Mon–Sat 9am–5pm.

Admission Fees: *Tours:* Adults $5, children $3, seniors $4, groups (15 or more) $4 each person.

Visitor Services: Lodging, food, information, rest rooms, handicapped access.

Regularly Scheduled Events: *Second Sat in Dec:* Reenactment of 1862 Christmas Ball.

Directions: From I-20 west: take Halls Ferry Rd. exit, turn left, go to Cherry St., and turn right. From I-20 east: take Clay St. exit, proceed to Cherry St., turn left, and go 1 block to site. Located at corner of Cherry and Crawford sts.

THE CAMPAIGN FOR VICKSBURG

Between Cairo, Illinois, and the Gulf of Mexico, the Mississippi River meanders over a course nearly 1,000 miles long. During the Civil War, control of this stretch was of vital importance to the Federal government. Command of that waterway would allow an uninterrupted flow of Union troops and supplies into the South. It would also have the desired effect of isolating the states of Texas, Arkansas, and most of Louisiana—nearly half the land area of the Confederacy, and a region on which the South depended heavily for supplies and recruits.

From the beginning of the war in 1861, the Confederates erected fortifications at strategic points along the river to protect this vital lifeline. Federal forces,

continues

however, fighting their way southward from Illinois and northward from the Gulf, captured post after post, until by late summer of 1862, only Vicksburg and Port Hudson posed major obstacles to Union domination of the Mississippi. Of the two posts, Vicksburg was the stronger and more important. It sat on a high bluff overlooking a bend in the river, protected by artillery batteries along the riverfront and by a maze of swamps and bayous to the north and south. President Lincoln called Vicksburg "the key" and believed that "the war can never be brought to a close until that key is in our pocket." So far, the city had defied Union efforts to force it into submission.

In October 1862, Ulysses S. Grant was appointed commander of the Department of the Tennessee and charged with clearing the Mississippi of Confederate resistance. That same month, Lt. Gen. John C. Pemberton, a West Point graduate and a Pennsylvanian by birth, assumed command of the 50,000 widely scattered Confederate troops defending the Mississippi. His orders were to keep the river open. Vicksburg became the focus of military operations for both men.

During the winter of 1862–1863, Grant conducted a series of amphibious operations (often referred to as Bayou Expeditions) aimed at reducing Vicksburg. All of them failed. By spring, Grant had decided to march his army of approximately 45,000 men down the west (Louisiana) bank of the Mississippi, cross the river well below Vicksburg, and then swing into position to attack the city from the south.

On March 31, 1863, Grant moved his army south from its encampments at Milliken's Bend, 20 miles northwest of Vicksburg. By April 28, the Northerners were established at Hard Times on the Mississippi above Grand Gulf. On the 29th, Adm. David D. Porter's gunboats bombarded the Confederate forts at Grand Gulf to prepare the way for a crossing, but the attack was repulsed. Undaunted, Grant marched his troops a little farther south and, on April 30, stormed across at Bruinsburg.

Striking rapidly eastward to secure the bridgehead, the Northerners met elements of Pemberton's Confederate forces near Port Gibson on May 1. The Southerners fought a gallant holding action, but they were overwhelmed and fell back toward Vicksburg. After meeting and defeating a small Confederate force near Raymond on May 12, Grant's troops attacked and captured Jackson, the state capital, on May 14, scattering the Southern defenders.

Turning his army westward, Grant moved toward Vicksburg along the line of the Southern Railroad of Mississippi. At Champion Hill on May 16 and at Big Black River Bridge on May 17, his soldiers attacked and overwhelmed Pemberton's disorganized Confederates, driving them back into the Vicksburg fortifications. By May 18, advance units of the Federal army were approaching the bristling Confederate defenses.

Believing that the battles of Champion Hill and Big Black River Bridge had broken the Confederate morale, Grant immediately scheduled an assault on the Vicksburg lines. The first attack took place against the Stockade Redan on May 19. It failed. A second attack, launched on the morning of May 22, was also repulsed.

Realizing that it was useless to expend further lives in attempts to take the city by storm, Grant reluctantly began formal siege operations. Batteries of artillery were

continues

established to hammer the Confederate fortifications from the land side, while Admiral Porter's gunboats cut off communications and blasted the city from the river. By the end of June, with little hope of relief and no chance to break out of the Federal cordon, Pemberton knew that it was only a matter of time before he must "capitulate upon the best attainable terms." On the afternoon of July 3, he met with Grant to discuss terms for the surrender of Vicksburg.

Grant demanded unconditional surrender; Pemberton refused. The meeting broke up. During the afternoon, the Federal commander modified his demands and agreed to let the Confederates sign paroles not to fight again until exchanged. In addition, officers could retain sidearms and a mount. Pemberton accepted these terms, and at 10am on July 4, 1863, Vicksburg officially surrendered.

When Port Hudson surrendered 5 days later, the great Northern objective of the war in the West—the opening of the Mississippi River and the severing of the Confederacy—was at last realized. For the first time since the war began, the Mississippi was free of Confederate troops and fortifications. As President Lincoln put it, "The Father of Waters again goes unvexed to the sea."

Credit: National Park Service

---

30 **Site:** GRAY & BLUE NAVAL MUSEUM, 1102 Washington St., Vicksburg, MS 39180, ☎ 601/638-6500

Description: This museum houses the world's largest collection of Civil War gunboat models, plus a 8'×20' diorama of the Siege of Vicksburg, and dioramas of the battles of Chickasaw Bayou and Big Black.

Open to Public: Mon–Sat 9am–5pm. Evening hours are available for groups.

Admission Fees: Adults $2, children under 12 $1. Maximum charge per family $6.

Visitor Services: Guided tour for groups; individuals are given a self-guided tour book for the museum.

Directions: From I-20: take Clay St. west, turn right on Cherry St., turn left on Grove St., and turn left on Washington St. Museum is on the right in the first block.

---

31 **Site:** OLD COURT HOUSE MUSEUM—EVA W. DAVIS MEMORIAL, 1008 Cherry St., Vicksburg, MS 39180, ☎ 601/636-0741

Description: During the Siege of Vicksburg in 1863, Union prisoners were housed in this courthouse. The U.S. flag was raised, and Grant reviewed his troops. In earlier years (1843), Jefferson Davis launched his political career on the grounds.

Open to Public: Mon–Sat 8:30am–5pm, Sun 1:30–5pm. *Note:* Oct–Apr: closes at 4:30pm.

Admission Fees: Adults $2, children $1, seniors $1.50. Groups (10 or more): Adults $1.25, children 75¢.

Visitor Services: Museum, gift shop, information, rest rooms, handicapped access.

Directions: From I-20: take Clay St. exit to Cherry St. and turn right.

THE VICKSBURG CAMPAIGN TRAIL

Nationally significant sites associated with Union Maj. Gen. Ulysses S. Grant's brilliant Campaign and Siege of Vicksburg (April–July 1863).

Primary sites include: Big Black Battlefield sites, Champion Hill Battlefield sites, Confederate Cemetery—Raymond, Grand Gulf Military Monument Park, Jackson Battlefield sites, Port Gibson Battlefield sites, Raymond Battlefield sites, Vicksburg National Military Park, Windsor Ruins, and Wintergreen Cemetery—Port Gibson.

For more information: See "A Guide to the Campaign & Siege of Vicksburg," which provides a self-guided driving tour of these sites. The guide is available free from Mississippi Division of Tourism Development, P.O. Box 1705, Ocean Springs, MS 39566-1705, ☎ 800/WARMEST. The guide can also be purchased at the Old Capitol Museum, Shiloh National Military Park, and Vicksburg National Military Park.

---

32 **Site:** VICKSBURG NATIONAL MILITARY PARK, 3201 Clay St., Vicksburg, MS 39180, ☎ 601/636-0583

Description: Vicksburg National Military Park was established in 1899 to commemorate the Campaign, Siege, and Defense of Vicksburg that took place in 1863. The focus of Union land and naval operations along the Mississippi River, the city fell on July 4, 1863, to Gen. Ulysses S. Grant after a lengthy campaign and 47-day siege. The fall of Vicksburg gave the North control of the river, severed a major Confederate supply line that ran east-west through Vicksburg, achieved a major objective of the Anaconda Plan, and effectively sealed the doom of Richmond.

Open to Public: Daily 8am–5pm.

Admission Fees: Cars $4; school groups free.

Visitor Services: Visitors center, U.S.S. Cairo Museum, bookstore, trails, rest rooms, handicapped access.

Directions: From I-20: take exit 4B and follow signs.

West Point

33 Site: WAVERLEY PLANTATION MANSION, Rte. 2, P.O. Box 234, West Point, MS 39773, ☎ 601/494-1399

Description: Waverley is a National Historic Landmark Greek Revival home that commemorates the antebellum South. The plantation was a self-sustaining community complete with gardens, orchards, and livestock. In later years, Waverley had its own lumber mill, tannery, and hat-manufacturing operation. Gen. Nathan Bedford Forrest was a friend and frequent visitor of the owner, Col. George Hampton Young. General Forrest spent 3 weeks recuperating at Waverley during the Civil War. He resided in the Egyptian Room and used the place as a headquarters. The octagonal cupola of the home served as an observation point for watching the river and the prairie for troop movement. Waverley features 20 acres of landscaped gardens with peacocks and black swans.

Open to Public: *Summer:* Daily 9am–6:30pm. *Winter:* Daily 9am–5:30pm.

Admission Fees: Adults $7.50, children under 6 free, groups (25 or more) $6/person, school groups $5/person.

Visitor Services: Tours, trails, gift shop, information, rest rooms.

Regularly Scheduled Events: Spring Pilgrimage of Homes and Garden Ball (call for schedule); *Dec:* Antebellum Christmas.

Directions: Located 15 minutes from Columbus; 1 mile off Hwy. 50 between Columbus and West Point, near the Tenn-Tom Waterway on the west side of river.

Woodville

34 Site: ROSEMONT PLANTATION/HOME OF JEFFERSON DAVIS, P.O. Box 814, Hwy. 24 East, Woodville, MS 39669, ☎ 601/888-6809

Description: This was the family home of President Jefferson Davis. It was built by his parents in 1810 and served as the family home until 1895. Many articles of furniture and family portraits of the Davis family are still in the home. Rosemont is the headquarters of the Davis Family Association, and reunions are held there biannually. The home is an early "cottage style" planter's home. Five generations of the Davis family lived here. His mother,

Jane Davis, is buried in the family cemetery on the grounds.

Open to Public: Mar–Dec 15: Mon–Fri 10am–5pm. Open daily during the Natchez Spring Pilgrimage and during October.

Admission Fees: Adults $6, children $3.

Visitor Services: Museum, information, rest rooms.

Directions: One mile off U.S. 61 on Hwy. 24; marked by state highway signs.

Missouri

1 Battle of Athens State Historic Site
2 Battle of Carthage State Historic Site
3 Confederate Memorial State Historic Site
4 Missouri State Capitol and State Museum
5 Battle of Westport
6 Forest Hill Cemetery
7 Battle of Lexington State Historic Site
8 Newtonia Battlefield

9 Fort Davidson State Historic Site
10 General Sweeny's Museum
11 Wilson's Creek National Battlefield
12 Bellefontaine Cemetery
13 Calvary Cemetery
14 Jefferson Barracks Historic Site
15 Ulysses S. Grant National Historic Site
16 Springfield National Cemetery

For Missouri Tourism information call 800/877-1234.

MISSOURI

*A*T THE OUTSET OF THE CIVIL WAR, Missouri was a peninsula of slavery surrounded on three sides by free states. It was in every sense and at every level a true border state, racked by conflicting loyalties and deep internal divisions. Missouri's star adorned the flags of both sides; while a provisional unionist government ruled from the capital, Jefferson City, an exiled Confederate government held sway first from Arkansas and then from Marshall, Texas. Early in 1861, a specially elected state convention determined that Missouri should remain in the Union but participate in no actions to coerce the seceding states of the South. This hardly settled the issue, and competing secessionist and unionist factions waged a vigorous contest to determine Missouri's eventual loyalties. The North won this contest in the sense of gaining nominal control over the political and military administration of the state, but deep-seated southern loyalties on the part of much of the state's population were never successfully suppressed.

Although the conflict in Missouri was, by and large, a sideshow of the main war being conducted east of the Mississippi, the struggle within the state was a singularly vicious one that included not only large battles on the scale of Wilson's Creek, Pilot Knob, or Westport, but also hundreds of smaller conflicts. With nearly 1,200 battles and skirmishes of record, Missouri ranks third in total number of conflicts behind Virginia and Tennessee. Every year of the war saw armed challenges to Union occupation in the form of Confederate invasions, raiding and recruiting parties launched from Arkansas; and from guerrilla warfare, fought under the black flag with no quarter, that grew more vicious with each passing season.

Sixty percent of Missouri's men of military age marched off to fight for one side or the other. There were 110,000 men, including 8,400 black troops, who fought for the North, while some 30,000 to 40,000—the exact number is not known—donned Confederate gray.

by James M. Denny, Missouri Department of Natural Resources

Athens

1 **Site:** BATTLE OF ATHENS STATE HISTORIC SITE, located off State Hwy. 81 on Hwy. CC in Clark Co. Mailing address: Revere, MO 63465, ☎ 800/334-6946 (state park toll-free number, Mon–Fri, 8am–5pm) or 816/877-3871

Description: Athens is the site of the northernmost Civil War battle west of the Mississippi, fought on August 5, 1861. The Thome-Benning House (open to public) was struck by Southern artillery fire during the battle and has since been known as the Cannonball House.

Open to Public: *Grounds:* Dawn to dusk. *Thome-Benning House:* Mon–Sat 10am–4pm; Sun and holiday hours vary.

Admission Fees: Free.

Visitor Services: Trails, tours, museum (in Thome-Benning House), information, rest rooms, camping, picnicking, hiking, fishing, boating.

Regularly Scheduled Events: *Every three years:* Major Civil War reenactment of the battle; *Spring and Christmas:*

Open house; annual celebration of the battle and ice-fishing contest. Call for schedule. To receive free schedule of Special Events and Programs for parks and historic sites and other information, call ☎ **800/334-6946,** Mon–Fri 8am–5pm.

Directions: From I-70: take State Hwy. 61 (Wentzville) exit, exit 210; go north on Hwy. 61 to Wayland; take Hwy. 136 west to Kahoka; turn north on Hwy. 81 to Hwy. CC; follow Hwy. CC 4 miles to Athens.

Carthage

2   **Site:** BATTLE OF CARTHAGE STATE HISTORIC SITE, located in Carthage on the north side of East Chestnut Street, next to Carter Park; managed by Harry S. Truman Birthplace State Historic Site, 1009 Truman St., Lamar, MO 64759, ☎ 800/334-6946 (state park toll-free number, Mon–Fri 8am–5pm) or 417/682-2279

Description: This 7.4-acre tract was the site of the final confrontation of the Battle of Carthage—a day-long running skirmish that began on July 5, 1861, some 9 miles northeast of Carthage. An interpretive shelter with displays explains the history of this early armed confrontation. (It preceded the first Battle of Bull Run by 17 days.)

Open to Public: Daily from dawn to dusk.

Admission Fees: Free.

Visitor Services: Information.

Directions: From I-44: take State Hwy. 71 (Carthage) exit, exit 18; proceed north on Hwy. 71 for 6 miles to Hwy. 571 at Carthage; and travel east on Chestnut St. 10 blocks to site.

Higginsville

3   **Site:** CONFEDERATE MEMORIAL STATE HISTORIC SITE, Route 1, P.O. Box 221-A, Higginsville, MO 64037, ☎ 800/334-6946 (state park toll-free number, Mon–Fri 8am–5pm) or 816/584-2853

Description: This 191-acre site includes the grounds of the Confederate veterans home, a historic chapel, and a cemetery containing more than 800 graves. The site serves as a memorial to the 30,000 to 40,000 Missourians who fought for the Stars and Bars. There are picnic tables and several small fishing lakes on the grounds.

Open to Public: *Grounds:* Daily from dawn to dusk. *Chapel and museum:* Mon–Sat 10am–4pm; Sun and holiday hours vary; call for schedule.

Admission Fees: Free.

Visitor Services: Information, rest rooms, fishing, picnicking.

Regularly Scheduled Events: To receive a free schedule of Special Events and Programs for parks and historic sites and other information, call ☎ 800/334-6946, Mon–Fri 8am–5pm.

Directions: From I-70: take Lexington-Higginsville exit (exit 49); proceed north on State Hwy. 13 for approximately 7 miles to Bus. Hwy. 13. Proceed on Bus. Hwy. 13 1.5 miles to junction of Hwys. 20, 213, and Bus. 13. Entrance is on the left.

Jefferson City

4   **Site:** MISSOURI STATE CAPITOL AND STATE MUSEUM, Room B-2, State Capitol, Jefferson City, MO 65101, ☎ 800/334-6946 (state park toll-free number, Mon–Fri 8am–5pm) or 573/751-2854

Description: The capitol, built between 1913 and 1918, contains the legislative chambers and state offices. Flanking either side of the magnificent rotunda is the Missouri State Museum. The museum features several exhibits on the Civil War and a collection of battle flags as well as other displays pertaining to the state's history and natural resources.

Open to Public: Daily except Jan 1, Easter, Thanksgiving, and Christmas. Tours are available 8am–11am and 1–4pm, every half hour weekdays and every hour on Sat, Sun, and some holidays. For reservations for group tours, call ☎ 573/751-4127.

Admission Fees: Free.

Visitor Services: Guided tours, museum, information, rest rooms, food, gift shop, handicapped access.

Directions: From I-70: take State Hwy. 63 (Jefferson City) exit, exit 128a; proceed south on Hwy. 63 to Jefferson City. Take first exit after crossing Missouri River and east on West Main St. to Capitol.

Kansas City

5   **Site:** BATTLE OF WESTPORT, c/o Monnett Battle of Westport Fund, Inc., of the Civil War Round Table of Kansas City, 1130 Westport Road, Kansas City, MO 64111, ☎ 816/931-6620

Description: The Battle of Westport, fought on October 21–23, was the largest battle west of the Mississippi River and the decisive battle of Price's 1864 Missouri Campaign. Directions (see below) guide the visitor to the first of 25 narrative markers on a 32-mile, self-guided automobile tour and a self-guided walking tour of Byram's Ford and the Big Blue Battlefield, where a major part of the battle occurred.

Each marker provides directions to the next stop on the tour. A written brochure is available from the address listed above. Tour brochures are available at Wornall House Museum, 146 W. Terrace and Harris Kearney House, 4000 Baltimore.

Open to Public: Daily from dawn to dusk.

Admission Fees: Free.

Visitor Services: Self-guided tour, information, guided bus tours available on request.

Directions: From I-70: take I-435 south, then west; or take I-470 west to I-435. Exit State Line Rd. north and proceed north to 43rd Ave. Travel east on 43rd Ave. to Westport Rd. and Tour Stop No. 1, at the northeast corner of Westport Rd. and Broadway.

---

6 | **Site:** FOREST HILL CEMETERY, 6901 Troost Ave., Kansas City, MO 64131, ☎ 816/523-2114

Description: This cemetery is on the site of Gen. J. O. Shelby's heroic stand that saved Price's army. A large Confederate monument in the cemetery is surrounded by graves of the Confederate dead, including the celebrated Confederate cavalryman Gen. J. O. Shelby.

Open to Public: Daily from dawn to dusk.

Admission Fees: Free.

Visitor Services: None.

Directions: From I-70: take I-435 from west or I-470 from east to State Hwy. 71. Go north on Hwy. 71 to 75th St., proceed west on 75th St. to Troost Ave., and go north on Troost Ave. to cemetery.

Lexington

7 | **Site:** BATTLE OF LEXINGTON STATE HISTORIC SITE, located on 13th St. Mailing address: P.O. Box 6, Lexington, MO 64067, ☎ 800/334-6946 (state park toll-free number, Mon–Fri 8am–5pm) or 816/259-4654

Description: This is the site of the famous "Battle of the Hemp Bales" fought on September 18–20, 1861. Victorious Southerners under Gen. Sterling Price besieged and captured a Union garrison. A 106-acre section of the battlefield is preserved as is the Anderson House, a brick mansion that served as a field hospital and was occupied by both sides during the battle.

Open to Public: *Battlefield grounds:* Daily from dawn to dusk. *Visitors center and Anderson House:* Mon–Sat 10am–4:20pm; Sun and holiday hours vary.

Admission Fees: *Tour:* Adults $2, children 6–12 $1.25.

Visitor Services: Self-guided walking tour of battlefield, tours, museum, information, gift shop, visitors center, rest rooms. Visitors center is handicapped accessible.

Regularly Scheduled Events: *Every three years:* Major Civil War reenactment of the battle; *Sept:* Old Homes tour; *Dec:* Christmas candlelight tour of Anderson House. To receive a free schedule of

Special Events and Programs for parks and historic sites and other information, call ☎ **800/334-6946**, Mon–Fri 8am–5pm.

Directions: From I-70: take Lexington-Higginsville exit (Hwy. 13 north), proceed north on State Hwy. 13 for 20 miles to Lexington, and take 13th St. to site.

Newtonia

8 **Site:** NEWTONIA BATTLEFIELD, P.O. Box 106, Newtonia, MO 64850, ☎ 417/472-6216 (ask for Tom Higdon) or 417/451-3415 (ask for Kay Hively)

Description: Two major Civil War battles were fought at Newtonia—one on September 30, 1862, and the other on October 28, 1864. The first battle pitted Brig. Gen. James Blunt against Col. J. O. Shelby. Confederate forces numbered about 4,000; Union forces numbered about 6,500. The 1862 battle was one of the very few Civil War encounters in which Native Americans fought on both sides. Southern forces had Choctaw, Cherokee, and Chickasaw soldiers, while other Cherokee soldiers fought with the North. The 1864 battle was a delaying action by Shelby to protect Gen. Sterling Price's retreat to Arkansas. It was the last battle of the Civil War fought west of the Mississippi.

Open to Public: Daily during daylight hours.

Admission Fees: Free.

Visitor Services: Trails, information (brochure available at Dillion's store in Newtonia), tours by appointment.

Directions: From I-44: take Alternate 71 south and proceed to Hwy. 86, just south of Granby. Hwy. 86 leads straight into Newtonia. Turn left on County Rd. M., proceed 1 block, and turn right on Mill. Dillion's is 3 blocks down on Mill, just past the Ritchey Mansion. Pick up brochure and begin tour.

Pilot Knob

9 **Site:** FORT DAVIDSON STATE HISTORIC SITE, P.O. Box 509, Pilot Knob, MO 63663, ☎ 800/334-6946 (state park toll-free number, Mon–Fri 8am–5pm) or 573/546-3454

Description: This site consists of earthwork remnants of Fort Davidson, which was assaulted by the forces of Maj. Gen. Sterling Price on September 27, 1864, during the 2-day Battle of Pilot Knob. Some 1,200 Confederates fell within an hour in an unsuccessful effort to capture the fort held by Gen. Thomas Ewing Jr. and 1,450 men.

Open to Public: *Fort and surrounding grounds:* Daily from dawn to dusk. *Visitors center:* Mon–Sat 10am–4pm; Sun and holiday hours vary; call for schedule.

Admission Fees: Free.

Visitor Services: Tours, museum, information, visitors center, rest rooms, handicapped access.

Regularly Scheduled Events: *Every three years:* Major Civil War reenactment of the battle.

Directions: From I-55 at Cape Girardeau: take State Hwy. 72 (exit 99) and proceed west approximately 70 miles to Ironton. Turn north on State Hwy. 21, go 2 miles to Rte. V, and turn right to site.

Republic

10 **Site:** GENERAL SWEENY'S MUSEUM, 5228 S. State Hwy. ZZ, Republic, MO 65738, ☎ 417/732-1224

Description: The museum displays more than 5,000 artifacts. The focus is the Trans-Mississippi Theater. The exhibits are arranged chronologically, from John Brown and the 1850s, to the last battle between Missourians at Fort Blakeley, Alabama, in April, 1865. Highlights include a rare Confederate Indian flag of the "Cherokee Braves"; sash and sword belt of Gen. Pat Cleburne; Civil War medical exhibits; freshwater naval displays; and the presentation sword and binoculars of Gen. Thomas W. Sweeny, namesake of the museum.

Open to Public: Mar–Oct: Wed–Sun 10am–5pm. Nov and Feb: Weekends only 10am–5pm. Closed Dec–Jan.

Admission Fees: Adults $3.50, children under 12 $2, seniors $3.

Visitor Services: Handicapped access, guided tours for groups.

Directions: From I-44: exit onto State Hwy. MM and travel south for 8 miles to a traffic signal at the intersection with Hwy. 60, where Hwy. MM becomes Hwy. M. Continue south through the intersection on Hwy. M to Hwy. ZZ, turn right on Hwy. ZZ, and proceed south 1 mile to the museum. Located next to Wilson's Creek National Battlefield.

11 **Site:** WILSON'S CREEK NATIONAL BATTLEFIELD, 6424 West Farm Road 182, Republic, MO 65738, ☎ 417/732-2662

Ray House at Wilson's Creek National Battlefield, Republic, MO. (Photograph courtesy of National Park Service.)

Description: Wilson's Creek National Battlefield preserves 1,750 acres of the battle fought here on August 10, 1861. Called "Oak Hills" by the Confederates, the bloody 6-hour battle pitted 5,400 Union troops under Gen. Nathaniel Lyon against more than 10,000 Confederates under the combined commands of Generals Sterling Price and Ben McCulloch in the first major battle in the Trans-Mississippi region. Following the death of Lyon, Federal forces withdrew to Springfield. The failure of Confederate forces to consolidate the gains of this hard-earned victory resulted in their losing control of Missouri in the early spring of 1862.

Open to Public: Daily 8am–5pm; call for extended spring and summer hours. Closed Christmas and New Year's Day.

Admission Fees: Adults $2, family $4 maximum.

Visitor Services: Trails, tours, museum, information, gift shop, visitors center, rest rooms, handicapped access to the visitors center and the Ray House.

Regularly Scheduled Events: *Weekends June–Labor Day:* Historic Ray House; *Weekends in summer:* Musket and artillery demonstrations; *Aug 10:* Anniversary celebration; *Weekend in Aug after the anniversary:* Moonlight Bloody Hill tour.

Directions: From I-44: take exit 70 (MO MM, which becomes MO M) south to U.S. 60; cross U.S. 60, drive .75 mile to MO ZZ, and turn south. The battlefield is located 2 miles south on MO ZZ. From U.S. 60 and U.S. 65: take the James River Expressway to MO FF; turn left (south) on FF, proceed to MO M, and turn right (west). Proceed to MO ZZ, turn south, and travel 2 miles to the park.

St. Louis

12 **Site:** BELLEFONTAINE CEMETERY, 4947 West Florissant, St. Louis, MO 63115, ☎ 314/381-0750

Description: Many Civil War notables are buried in this beautiful cemetery: Edward Bates, Lincoln's attorney general; Union Major Generals Frank P. Blair Jr. and John Pope; Confederate Maj. Gen. Sterling Price; Confederate senator and later U.S. senator George Graham Vest; unionist provisional governor Hamilton Gamble; ironclad boatbuilder James B. Eads; and many others.

Open to Public: *Grounds:* Daily 8am–5pm. *Cemetery office:* Mon–Fri 8:30am–4:30pm.

Admission Fees: Free.

Visitor Services: Information on burial locations available in office.

Directions: From I-70: take West Florissant exit (exit 245B) and proceed north approximately .7 mile to cemetery (next to Calvary Cemetery).

13 **Site:** CALVARY CEMETERY, 5239 West Florissant, St. Louis, MO 63115, ☎ 314/381-1313

Description: This Catholic cemetery contains the grave of Gen. William T. Sherman.

Several other prominent Civil War per-sonages are interred here, including

Thomas Reynolds, Confederate governor-in-exile.

Open to Public: *Grounds:* Daily 8am–5pm. *Office:* Mon–Fri 8:30am–4:30pm, Sat 8:30am–12:30pm.

Admission Fees: Free.

Visitor Services: Information on burial locations available in the office.

Directions: From I-70: take West Florissant exit (exit 245B) and proceed north approximately 1.1 miles to cemetery (next to Bellefontaine Cemetery).

---

14 **Site:** JEFFERSON BARRACKS HISTORIC SITE, 533 Grant Rd., St. Louis, MO 63125-4121, ☎ 314/544-5714 or 314/544-5790

Description: In 1861, troops from Jefferson Barracks, led by Nathaniel Lyon, participated in the "Camp Jackson Affair," which saved the St. Louis Arsenal from pro-secessionist state forces. In 1862, Jefferson Barracks was turned over to the Medical Department of the U.S. Army and became one of the largest and most important Federal hospitals in the country. Sick and wounded soldiers were brought to Jefferson Barracks by riverboat and railroad car. In 1864, Jefferson Barracks became a concentration point for the defense of St. Louis during "Price's Raid," the last major Confederate invasion of Missouri. In 1866, a national cemetery was established at Jefferson Barracks.

Open to Public: Tues–Fri 10am–4:30pm, Sat–Sun noon–4:30pm. Closed Thanksgiving, Christmas, and New Year's Day.

Admission Fees: Free. *Note:* There may be a small charge for special events and exhibits.

Visitor Services: Trails, tours, museum, information, gift shop, visitors center, rest rooms, camping. Improvements for handicapped access are under way—call for status.

Regularly Scheduled Events: *Held throughout year:* Native American pow-wows; *Spring:* World War II weekend; *Dec:* Holiday at Barracks. Other events include Civil War battle reenactments and living history and French Colonial weekends. Call for schedule.

Directions: From I-255: exit at Telegraph Rd. and proceed north. At a "Y" intersection, take the right fork (straight) onto Kingston. Follow Kingston to South Broadway and turn right. South Broadway leads to the park. At the park, go through the left opening in the gate and proceed on Grant Rd. to the historic area and the stone buildings that house the museum.

---

15 **Site:** ULYSSES S. GRANT NATIONAL HISTORIC SITE, 7400 Grant Road, St. Louis, MO 63123, ☎ 314/842-3298

Description: The Ulysses S. Grant National Historic Site encompasses five historic structures from the core of a 1000-acre plantation owned by General Grant. His personal life and partnership

with his wife, Julia Dent Grant, provide the context for understanding his military leadership as Union General during the Civil War and his subsequent presidency.

Open to Public: Daily 9am–5pm. Closed Thanksgiving Day, Christmas Day, and New Year's Day.

Admission Fees: Free.

Visitor Services: Tours, information, gift shop, visitors center, handicapped access.

Regularly Scheduled Events: *First Sat of each month:* Special programs (call for schedule); *Apr:* Grant's birthday celebration; *Aug:* Past residents of White Haven living history; *Dec:* Christmas and New Year's holiday celebration.

Directions: Located in suburban St. Louis County, immediately across from the Anheuser-Busch "Grant's Farm" attraction. From I-270: exit at Gravois Rd. and go northeast approximately 2.5 miles. Turn left onto Grant Rd. The site is approximately .5 mile down on the right. Enter via the one-lane drive over an abandoned railroad berm. Limited parking for passenger vehicles; drivers of motor homes and buses should call the visitors center concerning access.

Springfield

16 **Site:** SPRINGFIELD NATIONAL CEMETERY, 1702 E. Seminole, Springfield, MO 65804, ☎ 417/881-9499

Description: The cemetery was established in 1876 because of the critical need for suitable burial space for the remains of the men who fell at the Battle of Wilson's Creek. Other remains removed from original burial sites at Forsyth, Newtonia, Carthage, Pea Ridge, and Springfield were among the early interments. There are 1,514 Union burials in the cemetery, of which 719 are unknown; and 566 Confederate grave sites in the Confederate section, most of which are unknown. Adjoining the original site was the only Confederate cemetery in Missouri; the two sites are now united. There are monuments to Confederate Gen. Sterling Price; to the Federal troops who fought in the Battle of Springfield; and to Union Gen. Nathaniel Lyon, who died in the Battle of Wilson's Creek. A memorial stone in memory of Confederate soldiers is placed where many unknown soldiers are buried.

Open to Public: Daily 8am–dusk.

Admission Fees: None.

Visitor Services: Grave site locator available.

Directions: From I-44: take Hwy. 65 south (Branson exit) and proceed to the Sunshine exit. Travel west on Sunshine into Springfield. Proceed to Glenstone Ave. and travel south to Seminole St.; proceed on Seminole St. to cemetery.

New Mexico

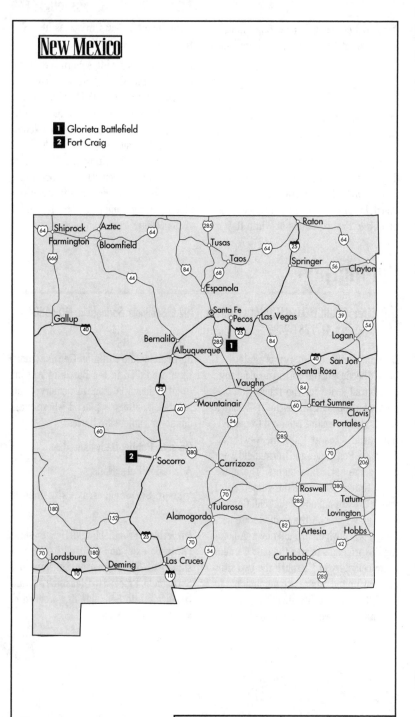

1 Glorieta Battlefield
2 Fort Craig

NEW MEXICO

$\mathcal{B}$ECAUSE OF CENTURIES OF COLONIAL ISOLATION under Spanish dominion and its comparatively recent ascension to the United States (in 1846), New Mexico was never outwardly courted by the Union and Confederacy. Also, the territory was poor, and its population was sparse.

New Mexico's role in the Civil War was comparatively minor. However, vital business partnerships with the prosperous North—brought about by the influence of the Santa Fe Trail—were an important factor in rallying sympathy for the North. The territory helped thwart an 1862 invasion by Texas Confederates who were intent on capturing Fort Union, located on the Santa Fe Trail in northeast New Mexico, and then on leaping into Colorado Territory to seize the gold fields for the struggling Confederacy.

At the outbreak of the Civil War, the commander of Fort Union, Henry H. Sibley, resigned his commission and returned to his native Texas. He was placed in command of a force of Texas Confederates, which he then led into New Mexico. The territory's populace, however, did not flock to the Confederate cause. If anything, it stayed away, leaving the invasion force to forage for supplies as it continued up the Rio Grande Valley.

Initially, the Texans defeated a U.S. force at the Battle of Valverde in February 1862. Shortly afterward, the Confederates seized Albuquerque, then Santa Fe. Meanwhile, a ragtag army of Colorado volunteers marched into New Mexico and strengthened a force of U.S. troops from Fort Union. The combined force then met and defeated the Texas Confederates at the decisive battle of Glorieta Pass in March 1862. Soon afterward, the Texans retreated south to El Paso, the lone invasion of New Mexico having ended.

Historians regard this as the westernmost campaign of the Civil War.

by Michael E. Pitel, New Mexico Department of Tourism

Pecos

1 **Site: GLORIETA BATTLEFIELD, Glorieta Unit, Pecos National Historical Park,**
P.O. Drawer 418, Pecos, NM 87552-0418, ☎ 505/757-6032

Description: Pecos National Historical Park preserves two sites associated with the Civil War Battle of Glorieta Pass: Apache Canyon (also called Canoncito) and Pigeon's Ranch. Texan and Colorado volunteers skirmished at Apache Canyon on March 26, 1862. The final encounter took place at Pigeon's Ranch on March 28, 1862. Texan troops withdrew after their supplies were destroyed at Apache Canyon on the 28th. The battle ended the Confederate attempt to gain Federal supplies at

Fort Union and the plans to invade Colorado and California. The park also preserves Kozlowski's Ranch—the site of the Union field headquarters during the battle. Much of the Glorieta Battlefield is still in private ownership. The sites are currently closed to public visitation. The visitor center at Pecos National Historical Park contains exhibits and information relating to the battle. Rangers can orient visitors to battle sites. Special talks and tours can also be arranged.

Open to Public: *Visitors Center:* Daily 8am–5pm. Memorial Day–Labor Day: Open daily until 6pm. Closed Christmas.

Admission Fees: $2/person.

Visitor Services: Ruins trail, museum, visitors center, rest rooms. Ruins trail is 80% wheelchair accessible.

Regularly Scheduled Events: *Early Aug:* Civil War encampment.

Directions: From I-25, southeast of Santa Fe: take exit 299 or 307.

View of Glorieta Battlefield looking northeast from present-day landmark Sharpshooter's Ridge. (Photograph courtesy of Pecos National Historical Park.)

Socorro

2 Site: FORT CRAIG, BLM Special Management Area, c/o U.S. Bureau of Land Management, Socorro Resource Area, 198 Neal St., Socorro, NM 87801, ☎ 505/835-0412

Description: In February 1862, the fort supplied U.S. troops to thwart the invasion of Texas Confederates under the command of Gen. Henry H. Sibley. Troops from the fort, under the command of Col. R. S. Canby, bolstered by a contingent of New Mexico volunteers commanded by Kit Carson, engaged Sibley's invasion force at a nearby crossing of the Rio Grande. The day-long Battle of Valverde on February 21, 1862, was a decisive Confederate victory. However, the U.S. troops retreated into the fort, which was never attacked. Sibley's Confederates pressed northward to siege Albuquerque and

Santa Fe. Their goal was the capture of Fort Union and the Colorado gold fields. Sibley's troops were defeated 1 month later, southeast of Santa Fe. Today, Fort Craig is in ruins.

Open to Public: Daily from dawn to dusk.

Admission Fees: Free.

Visitor Services: Trails, tours, information. *Note:* gravel paths, primitive conditions.

Directions: From I-25: take San Marcial exit; take Hwy. 1 and follow the signs. Fort Craig is approximately 10 miles from I-25 and located 32 miles from Socorro and 121 miles from Las Cruces.

NEW YORK

*N*EW YORK, THE 11TH STATE IN THE UNION, was home to a diverse population whose varied European heritage and interests made for lively and controversial state politics. Although political parties were divided in their support for the war, the majority of New Yorkers opposed slavery. War Democrats supported the Union and the Republican party. Other Democrats were not unsympathetic with the notion of states' rights.

The Republicans supported the war, although some wanted a more immediate end to slavery. New York began the war with a Republican governor and then elected a Democrat in 1862.

Congress passed the Federal Enrollment Act on March 3, 1863. When the draft began in New York, violent riots erupted, fueled by the frustration over rising inflation and military losses. Many of the working class resented fighting to free blacks with whom they would then compete for jobs. A mob of more than 50,000 swarmed the draft office, setting it on fire. Blacks were lynched, abolitionists' homes were attacked and burned, and property was destroyed in a rampage that left 12 dead and more than $1.5 million dollars in property destroyed. Federal troops returning from Gettysburg were called in to quell the riots. Before it was over, more than 1,000 people had been killed or injured. The draft was temporarily postponed.

In spite of the controversies and clashes, New York's contribution to the Union effort was the largest among all the states in the number of troops sent, the quantity of supplies provided, and the financial contributions raised. New York sent approximately 500,000 troops to fight for the Union and suffered 50,000 deaths among those men.

---

1 **Site:** General Grant National Memorial. Mailing address: 26 Wall St., New York, NY 10005. Physical address: W. 122nd St. and Riverside Dr., Manhattan.
☎ 212/666-1640

Description: This grand memorial to Ulysses S. Grant commemorates the great Union commander and the nation's 18th President. The mausoleum is the final resting place of President Grant and his wife, Julia Dent Grant.

Open to Public: Daily 9am–5pm.

Admission Fees: Free.

Visitor Services: Tours, exhibits.

Regularly Scheduled Events: April 27: Ceremony commemorating Ulysses S. Grant's birthday.

Directions: Accessible by 5th Ave. bus; IRT subway to 116th or 125th and Broadway; or 125th St. crosstown bus. Riverside Dr. is also accessible from the Henry Hudson Pkwy.

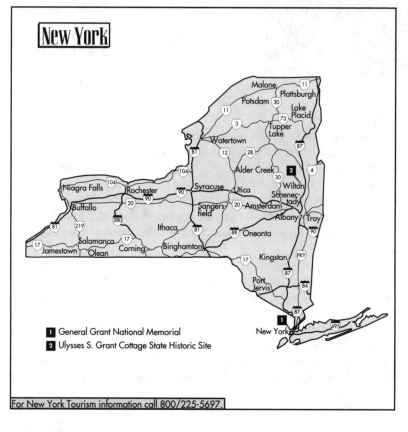

New York

■1 General Grant National Memorial
■2 Ulysses S. Grant Cottage State Historic Site

For New York Tourism information call 800/225-5697.

Wilton

2 **Site:** ULYSSES S. GRANT COTTAGE STATE HISTORIC SITE, P.O. Box 990, Saratoga Springs, NY 12866, ☎ 518/587-8277

Description: Here, at the summit of Mt. McGregor, Ulysses S. Grant spent the last weeks of his life completing his memoirs. On July 23, 1885, Grant died, surrounded by his family, in the parlor of this Adirondack cottage. Visitors find that the furnishings, decorations, and personal effects remain where they were when Grant was here. The cottage first opened to the public in 1890.

Open to Public: Memorial Day–Labor Day: Wed–Sun 10am–4pm. Labor Day–Columbus Day: Sat–Sun 10am–4pm.

Admission Fees: Adults $2.50, children 6–16 $1, children 5 and under free, seniors $2.

Visitor Services: Tours, gift shop, overlook with view of Hudson Valley, handicapped access.

Regularly Scheduled Events: *June:* Adirondack Day; *July:* Grant Remembrance Day; *Aug:* Victorian Picnic.

Directions: From I-87, the Northway: take exit 16 and follow the signs.

Ulysses S. Grant Cottage State Historic Site, Wilton, NY (Photograph courtesy of the Friends of the Ulysses S. Grant Cottage.)

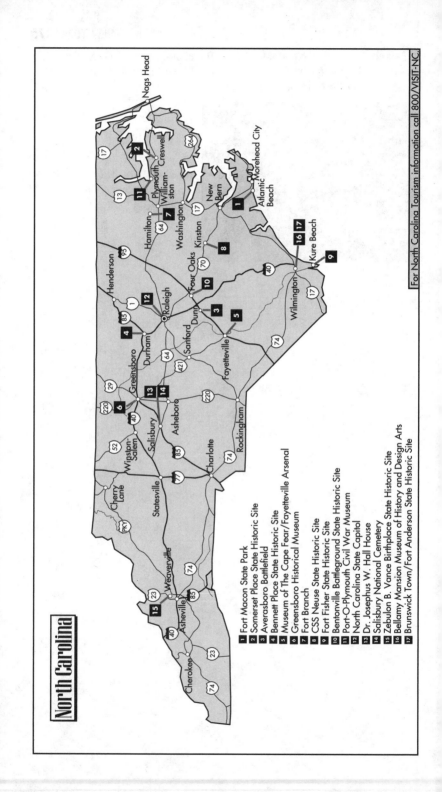

North Carolina

1 Fort Macon State Park
2 Somerset Place State Historic Site
3 Averasboro Battlefield
4 Bennett Place State Historic Site
5 Museum of The Cape Fear/Fayetteville Arsenal
6 Greensboro Historical Museum
7 Fort Branch
8 CSS Neuse State Historic Site
9 Fort Fisher State Historic Site
10 Bentonville Battleground State Historic Site
11 Port-O-Plymouth Civil War Museum
12 North Carolina State Capitol
13 Dr. Josephus W. Hall House
14 Salisbury National Cemetery
15 Zebulon B. Vance Birthplace State Historic Site
16 Bellamy Mansion Museum of History and Design Arts
17 Brunswick Town/Fort Anderson State Historic Site

For North Carolina Tourism information call 800/VISIT-NC.

NORTH CAROLINA

$\mathscr{A}$LTHOUGH AMONG THE LAST STATES to join the Confederacy, North Carolina suffered greatly during the war years. The state served as a vital supply center, furnishing the South's armies with food, arms, and medical equipment. More important, the state also provided 125,000 men, one-sixth of all Confederate soldiers. North Carolina's total loss in battle and from disease was greater than any other Southern state.

Eleven battles and approximately 74 skirmishes were fought on Tar Heel soil. There were four major military operations: the conquest of the sound region, the capture of Fort Fisher and Wilmington, Stoneman's raid, and Sherman's invasion.

The war resulted in 40,000 lost Tar Heel lives, destroyed factories and railroads, and a shattered state economy. At the war's end, the long task of rebuilding was begun in earnest. By 1868, sufficient progress had been made, and the state was readmitted to the Union.

$\mathscr{F}$or More Information

For a map and guide to Civil War sites in North Carolina, call ☎ 800/VISIT-NC and ask for the "North Carolina Civil War Trails" brochure.

Atlantic Beach

1 **Site:** FORT MACON STATE PARK, P.O. Box 127, Atlantic Beach, NC 28512, ☎ 919/726-8598

Description: Construction of this brick fort began in 1826. The fort was garrisoned in 1834 and named after U.S. Senator Nathaniel Macon. At the start of the Civil War, North Carolina seized Fort Macon from Union forces. The Confederate force was later attacked in 1862, and the fort fell into Union hands. For the duration of the war, the fort protected ships recoaling in Beaufort. Fort Macon was a Federal prison from 1867 to 1876, garrisoned during the Spanish-American War, and closed in 1903.

Open to Public: *Fort:* Daily 9am–5:30pm. *Park:* Open extended hours; call for schedule.

Admission Fees: Free.

Visitor Services: Trails, museum, gift shop, information, rest rooms.

Regularly Scheduled Events: *Three times a year:* Reenactment teams.

Directions: From I-40 or I-95: take Hwy. 70 east to Morehead City, NC; turn off Hwy. 70 onto the Atlantic Beach Bridge; follow road to stoplight at the intersection with 58 and turn left onto 58 south. Park is at the end of the road.

Creswell

2 **Site:** SOMERSET PLACE STATE HISTORIC SITE, Rte. 1, P.O. Box 337, Creswell, NC 27928, ☎ 919/797-4560

Description: At the dawn of the Civil War, Somerset Place was a wealthy planter's estate and home to more than 300 enslaved men, women, and children. The war transformed it into a shadowy remnant, home to no one. The stories surrounding that transformation provide a microscopic view of social, emotional, economic, and legal impacts of the war on individual Southerners of different races and genders.

Open to Public: Apr 1–Sept 30: Mon–Sat 9am–5pm, Sun 1–5pm. Oct 1–Apr 1: Tues–Sat 10am–4pm, Sun 1–4pm.

Admission Fees: Free.

Visitor Services: Gift shop, information.

Regularly Scheduled Events: Annual Christmas open house program; Biannual Somerset homecomings. Call for schedule.

Directions: From I-95: take NC 64 east to Creswell, NC; follow highway signage, proceeding 7 miles south to site.

Dunn

3 **Site:** AVERASBORO BATTLEFIELD, P.O. Box 1811, Dunn, NC 28335 ☎ 901/733-4994

Description: This is the site of the 1865 Battle of Averasboro, where Confederate General Hardee sought to check the advance of the left wing of Gen. W. T. Sherman's army as it made its way through eastern North Carolina. The Battle of Averasboro was fought March 15–16, 1865. Although initially successful, the Confederates were no match for the larger Union force and did not slow it enough to prevent its eventual union with the right wing at the Battle of Bentonville, fought 25 miles to the north on March 19–21, 1865.

Open to Public: *Cemetery and marker:* Daily from dawn to dusk.

Admission Fees: Free.

Visitor Services: None.

Directions: From I-95: take Long Branch Rd. exit, continue east for approximately 4 miles to its intersection with NC Hwy. 82, and turn left on 82. The site is approximately 4 miles down 82 toward the town of Godwin.

Durham

4   **Site:** BENNETT PLACE STATE HISTORIC SITE, 4409 Bennett Memorial Rd., Durham, NC 27705, ☎ 919/383-4345

Description: At the Bennett farmhouse, Generals Joseph E. Johnston and William T. Sherman met in April 1865 and signed an agreement that surrendered all the Confederate troops in North Carolina, South Carolina, Georgia, and Florida—almost 90,000 men. This surrender on April 26, 1865, followed Gen. Robert E. Lee's surrender at Appomattox by 17 days and was the largest surrender of the Civil War.

Open to Public: Apr–Oct: Mon–Sat 9am–5pm, Sun 1–5pm. Nov–Mar: Tues–Sat 10am–4pm, Sun 1–4pm.

Admission Fees: Free.

Visitor Services: Museum, gift shop, information, rest rooms, handicapped access.

Regularly Scheduled Events: *Weekend closest to Apr 26:* Annual Surrender; *First Sun in Dec:* Annual Christmas open house.

Directions: From I-85 north: take exit 170 onto U.S. 70 east; go east on U.S. 70 approximately .5 mile and turn right onto Bennett Memorial Rd. Site is .5 mile down Bennett Memorial Rd. on the right. From I-85 south: take exit 173 and follow the signs.

Fayetteville

5   **Site:** MUSEUM OF THE CAPE FEAR/FAYETTEVILLE ARSENAL, 801 Arsenal Ave., P.O. Box 53693, Fayetteville, NC 28305, ☎ 910/486-1330

Description: The North Carolina Arsenal was under construction by the Federal government from 1838 to 1858. Built in response to woeful national defenses following the War of 1812, the arsenal was originally intended for construction and deposit. The installation was surrendered to a local militia in April 1861 and shortly thereafter became a significant producer of arms and ammunition for the Confederacy. It was destroyed by Sherman's army in March 1865. Today, extant tower and building foundations as well as a 35-foot-high steel facsimile of an original tower represent the focal points of the public presentation.

Open to Public: Tues–Sat 10am–5pm, Sun 1–5pm.

Admission Fees: Free.

Visitor Services: Museum, gift shop, information, rest rooms, handicapped access.

Regularly Scheduled Events: Military demonstrations throughout the year.

Directions: From I-95: take exit 56 (Hwy. 301) south to Grove St., turn right onto Grove St., and follow Grove to Bragg Blvd. Turn left on Bragg Blvd. and follow Bragg to Hay St. Turn right onto Hay St. and take the second left onto Bradford. The site is on the first street on the right.

Greensboro

6 **Site:** GREENSBORO HISTORICAL MUSEUM, 130 Summit Ave., Greensboro, NC
27401-3004, ☎ 336/373-2943

Description: This local history museum has
an extensive military history exhibit and
Civil War–related items. The collection
includes a rare Tarpley carbine, made in
Greensboro during the Civil War; haversack
contents; weapons; a display featuring the
Guilford Grays; a Confederate school text;
a bust of Stephen A. Douglas; and excerpts
from a local resident's Civil War diary about
life in Greensboro.

Open to Public: Tues–Sat 10am–5pm, Sun
2–5pm. Closed city holidays.

Admission Fees: Free.

Visitor Services: Museum shop, handicapped access.

Directions: From I-85/I-40: take S. Elm-
Eugene exit, turn north toward downtown,
and go several miles to Bellemeade St. Turn
right and proceed 4 blocks. The museum
is on the right.

Hamilton

7 **Site:** FORT BRANCH, P.O. Box 355, Hamilton, NC 27840, ☎ 800/776-8566 or
919/792-6605

Description: Fort Branch protected the
Roanoke River Valley farms, the Ram
Albemarle construction site, and the
Weldon Railroad bridge from destruction
by Federal gunboats. The Weldon Railroad
bridge was critical to the Army of Northern Virginia in receiving supplies from the
port of Wilmington via the Wilmington and
Weldon Railroad. Fort Branch features
7 of the 11 original cannons and well-
preserved earthworks.

Open to Public: Apr–Nov: Sat–Sun
1:30–5:30pm; extended hours for reenactment weekend. Other times by
appointment.

Admission Fees: Free except on reenactment weekend: $5/car, $10/bus or 15-
passenger van.

Visitor Services: Museum, gift shop, information, rest rooms, handicapped access.

Regularly Scheduled Events: *First full
weekend in Nov:* Annual battle reenactment weekend.

Directions: From I-95: take exit 138 at
Rocky Mount, follow U.S. 64 east to
Robersonville, and take NC 903 north.
When you are .5 mile south of Hamilton,
turn right on the Fort Branch Rd. and go
2 miles. The site is on the left.

Kinston

8 **Site:** CSS *NEUSE* STATE HISTORIC SITE, P.O. Box 3043, 2612 West Vernon Ave., Hwy. 70 Bus., Kinston, NC 28502-3043, ☎ 919/522-2091

Description: The CSS *Neuse* State Historic Site houses and interprets the archaeological remains of the Confederate ironclad *Neuse,* one of the only three Civil War ironclads on display in the United States. The CSS *Neuse* was an integral factor in preventing Union forces from moving from New Bern to Goldsboro.

Open to Public: Apr–Oct: Mon–Sat 9am– 5pm, Sun 1–5pm. Nov–Mar: Tues–Sat 10am–4pm, Sun 1–4pm.

Admission Fees: Free.

Visitor Services: Museum, gift shop, information, rest rooms, handicapped access.

Regularly Scheduled Events: North Carolina History Bowl competition for eighth-grade students (call for schedule); *Second weekend in Nov:* Annual living history reenactment.

Directions: From I-95: take Smithfield/ Selma, NC exit and take U.S. 70 east to Kinston approximately 45 miles. In Kinston, take U.S. 70 Bus. The site is .5 mile on right.

Kure Beach

9 **Site:** FORT FISHER STATE HISTORIC SITE, P.O. Box 169, Kure Beach, NC 28449, ☎ 910/458-5538

Shepherd's Battery at Fort Fisher, Kure Beach, NC. (Photo courtesy of North Carolina Division of Archives and History.)

Description: Fort Fisher was an earthen fort built on New Inlet (Atlantic Ocean inlet to Cape Fear River) to protect it for blockade-running into the port of Wilmington. It kept the port open until early 1865. Wilmington fell on February 22, 1865.

Open to Public: Apr–Oct: Mon–Sat 9am– 5pm, Sun 1–5pm. Nov–Mar: Tues–Sat 10am–4pm, Sun 1–4pm.

Admission Fees: Free.

Visitor Services: Tour, museum, gift shop, information, rest rooms, handicapped access.

Regularly Scheduled Events: *Jan:* Annual commemorative anniversary program; *Summer:* Interpretive program.

Directions: Take I-40 to Wilmington, NC; then take U.S. 421 south approximately 20 miles to Kure Beach. Fort Fisher is on the right side of U.S. 421, 1 mile past Kure Beach.

Newton Grove

10 Site: BENTONVILLE BATTLEGROUND STATE HISTORIC SITE, 5466 Harper House Rd., Four Oaks, NC 27524, ☎ 910/594-0789

Description: Bentonville was the site of the last major battle of the Civil War, March 19–21, 1865, nearly 3 weeks before Lee's surrender to Grant at Appomattox. The battle is also significant as the largest ever fought on North Carolina soil, the last Confederate offensive operation of the war, and the only significant attempt to stop the march of Sherman's army after the fall of Atlanta.

Open to Public: Apr–Oct: Mon–Sat 9am–5pm, Sun 1–5pm. Nov–Mar: Tues–Sat 10am–4pm, Sun 1–4pm.

Admission Fees: Free.

Visitor Services: Tours of Harper House field hospital, trails, gift shop, information, rest rooms.

Regularly Scheduled Events: *July–Sept:* Summer seasonal living history program; *Every fifth year:* Anniversary commemoration reenactments; *Every year:* Living history.

Directions: From I-95: take exit 90, travel 15 miles south on U.S. 70; go left onto State Rte. 1008, and travel 3 miles east to site. From I-40: take exit 343, travel 6 miles north on U.S. 701 to State Rte. 1008, and travel 3 miles east to site.

Plymouth

11 Site: PORT-O-PLYMOUTH CIVIL WAR MUSEUM, 302 Water St., Plymouth, NC 27962, ☎ 919/793-1377

Description: In 1862, Union troops stationed a garrison in the town of Plymouth to control the mouth of the Roanoke River. With the aid of northern sympathizers, free blacks, and runaway slaves, they built four forts. In the second largest Civil War battle in North Carolina, on April 17–20, 1864, Confederate forces recaptured Plymouth from Union forces. The *Charlotte Observer*

named this museum dedicated to Plymouth's Civil War history, "one of the top ten Civil War sites in the Carolinas."

Open to Public: Tues–Sat 8am–5pm.

Admission Fees: Adults $1, children 50¢.

Visitor Services: Book sales, free printed material, lectures.

Regularly Scheduled Events: *Third weekend in Apr:* Living History Weekend.

Directions: From I-95: take U.S. 64 east for 50 miles to Plymouth. In Plymouth, proceed to Washington St. and turn left. This street ends at the river. Turn right on Water St. and proceed to the museum.

Raleigh

12 **Site:** NORTH CAROLINA STATE CAPITOL (1 East Edenton St.). Mailing address: 109 East Jones St., Raleigh, NC 27601-2807, ☎ 919/733-4994

Description: The building is virtually unaltered from its Civil War–era appearance. Completed in 1840, the capitol's house chamber was the site of the 1861 Secession Convention, and the building served several sessions of the war-era Confederate legislators. The capitol was occupied by staff officers of Sherman's army from April to May 1865 and was peacefully surrendered. The capitol's dome was the site of one of the last U.S. Army signal stations. The legislative chambers contain the original 1840 desks and chairs. The interior is now being restored to its 1840–1865 appearance.

Open to Public: Mon–Fri 8am–5pm, Sat 9am–5pm, Sun 1–5pm. Closed New Year's Day, Thanksgiving Day, and Christmas Day.

Admission Fees: Free.

Visitor Services: Tours, information, rest rooms, handicapped access.

Regularly Scheduled Events: *Last weekend in Apr:* 1865 occupation of Raleigh Civil War living history; *July:* Traditional July 4 celebration and Civil War encampment; *Third weekend in Sept:* Secession Experiences, 1861.

Directions: From 1-40: take Person St. exit into Raleigh and turn left on Edenton St. The capitol is located at the third block on the left. Parking is available beneath the N.C. Museum of History at the corner of Wilmington and Jones sts.

Salisbury

13 **Site:** DR. JOSEPHUS W. HALL HOUSE, P.O. Box 4221, Salisbury, NC 28145-4221, ☎ 704/636-0103

Description: A symbol of Old Salisbury, this beautiful house was built in 1820. In 1859, Dr. Hall moved his family into the house. Dr. Hall served as chief surgeon at the Salisbury Confederate Prison during the Civil War. The house was used as headquarters for the Union commander George Stoneman following the war.

Open to Public: Sat–Sun 1–4pm.

Admission Fees: Adults $3, children $1.

Visitor Services: Museum, gift shop, rest rooms.

Regularly Scheduled Events: *Second weekend in Oct:* Annual tour; *Two weekends before Christmas and on Christmas*

Eve: Annual Victorian Christmas at the Hall House.

Directions: From I-85: take exit 76B, travel on Innes St. for about 1 mile, turn left at the Confederate Monument onto Church St., proceed 2 blocks, and turn right onto West Bank St. The house is in the second block.

---

14 **Site:** SALISBURY NATIONAL CEMETERY, 202 Government Rd., Salisbury, NC 28144, ☎ 704/636-2661

Description: This site is the final resting place for the remains of 11,700 Union soldiers who died in the Confederate prison in Salisbury from 1864 to 1865. The cemetery contains the largest number of unknown burials of any of the national cemeteries.

Open to Public: *Cemetery:* Daily from dawn to dusk. *Office and museum:* Mon–Fri 7:30am–4:30pm.

Admission Fees: Free.

Visitor Services: Museum, information, rest rooms.

Regularly Scheduled Events: *May:* Memorial Day event; *Nov:* Veterans Day event.

Directions: From I-85: take exit 76B, travel west on Innes St. to Long St., proceed south on Long St. to Monroe St., turn west on Monroe to Railroad St., and turn south on Railroad St. The cemetery is on the left.

Weaverville

15 **Site:** ZEBULON B. VANCE BIRTHPLACE STATE HISTORIC SITE, 911 Reems Creek Rd., Weaverville, NC 28787, ☎ 704/645-6706

Description: This reconstructed log house with six log outbuildings depicts the 1830 farmstead where the Civil War governor of North Carolina, Zebulon B. Vance, and his brother, Confederate Brig. Gen. Robert B. Vance, were born. Exhibits in the visitors center trace their careers.

Open to Public: Apr–Oct: Mon–Sat 9am–5pm, Sun 1–5pm. Nov–Mar: Tues–Sat 10am–4pm, Sun 1–4pm.

Admission Fees: Free.

Visitor Services: Museum, gift shop, information, rest rooms.

Regularly Scheduled Events: *Spring:* Pioneer Day; *Autumn:* Pioneer days and militia encampment; *Dec:* Christmas open house.

Directions: From I-240: take Weaverville exit onto U.S. 19-23 north, take New Stock Rd. exit, and follow signs to site.

Wilmington

16 **Site:** BELLAMY MANSION MUSEUM OF HISTORY AND DESIGN ARTS. Mailing address: P.O. Box 1176, Wilmington, NC 28402. Physical address: 503 Market St., ☎ 910/251-3700

Description: Built as the city residence of prominent planter John D. Bellamy, the Bellamy Mansion is a premier architectural and historical treasure in North Carolina. The mansion was completed in 1861, but fear of the raging yellow fever and the threat of invasion by Union forces soon displaced the Bellamys from their new home. The mansion was commandeered as a Union headquarters, but the Bellamys were able to return in the summer of 1865.

Open to Public: Wed–Sat 10am–5pm, Sun 1–5pm.

Admission Fees: Adults $6, children $3, children under 6 free.

Visitor Services: Tours, changing exhibitions, archaeological dig, gift shop.

Regularly Scheduled Events: *May:* Civil War encampment; *Oct:* Halloween History-Mystery Tour; *Dec:* Candlelight tour.

Directions: From the north: take I-40 to 17 south to downtown Wilmington. From the south: take 17 north to downtown Wilmington. The mansion is on the corner of 5th and Market sts.

17 **Site:** BRUNSWICK TOWN/FORT ANDERSON STATE HISTORIC SITE, 8884 St. Philips Rd., SE, Winnabow, NC 28479, ☎ 910/371-6613

Description: Fort Anderson was constructed in March 1862 as part of the overall Cape Fear defense system. This system was to protect the Cape Fear River channel to the port of Wilmington, which was a major supply line to the Confederate forces. On February 19, 1865, a month after Fort Fisher's fall, a severe bombardment by the Union navy and an encircling movement by Union land forces caused the abandonment of Fort Anderson by the Confederates, who fled northward to Wilmington.

Open to Public: Apr–Oct: Mon–Sat 9am–5pm, Sun 1–5pm. Nov–Mar: Tues–Sat 10am–4pm, Sun 1–4pm.

Admission Fees: Free.

Visitor Services: Trails, museum, gift shop, information, rest rooms, handicapped access.

Regularly Scheduled Events: *Mid-Feb:* Civil War encampment.

Directions: Take I-40 into Wilmington; I-40 becomes South College. Stay on S. College to the Oleander intersection, turn right on Oleander, travel westbound on U.S. 74-76 until you come to NC 133. Take a left off exit and travel southbound on NC 133 approximately 18 miles.

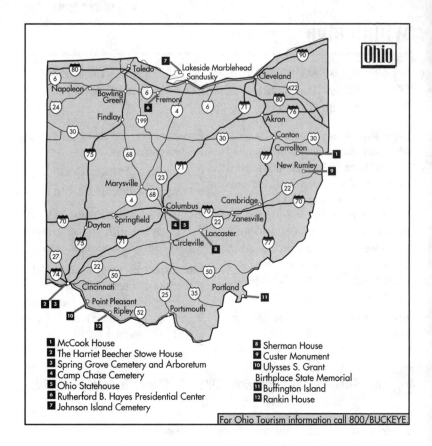

Ohio

1. McCook House
2. The Harriet Beecher Stowe House
3. Spring Grove Cemetery and Arboretum
4. Camp Chase Cemetery
5. Ohio Statehouse
6. Rutherford B. Hayes Presidential Center
7. Johnson Island Cemetery
8. Sherman House
9. Custer Monument
10. Ulysses S. Grant Birthplace State Memorial
11. Buffington Island
12. Rankin House

OHIO

*T*HE MAJORITY OF THE BATTLES FOUGHT during the Civil War occurred in Confederate territory. Ohio troops, however, fought in every major theater of the war, and 34,591 Ohioans gave their lives. Three out of every five Ohio males between 18 and 45 served in the Union army and navy. A considerable number of Ohioans also served in Confederate armies; seven became Confederate generals.

According to *Ohio and Its People*, by George W. Knepper, Ohio supplied the third largest number of troops to the Union, exceeded only by the more populous states of New York and Pennsylvania. In proportion to state population, Ohio's contribution ranked number one. Distinguished generals, including Ulysses S. Grant, William Tecumseh Sherman, Philip Sheridan, and George McClellan, came from Ohio. Five Ohio-born officers in the Union army became president of the United States.

More than 5,000 African American troops from Ohio served in state or federal units, and others served in the units of other states. Ohio stood fourth among the 20 states and the District of Columbia in the number of African Americans serving in the Union army.

Carrollton

1 **Site:** MCCOOK HOUSE, P.O. Box 174, Public Square, Carrollton, OH 44615, ☎ 330/627-3345

Description: This house is a memorial to the "Fighting McCooks," a nickname given to the family because of their military service. During the Civil War, Daniel McCook's family contributed three major generals, two brigadier generals, one colonel, two majors, and one private to the Union cause. Brother John's side of the McCooks produced one major general, one brigadier general, two lieutenants, and a lieutenant in the navy. Four of Daniel's family, including Daniel himself, lost their lives in the conflict.

Open to Public: Memorial Day weekend–Labor Day: Fri–Sat 9am–5pm, Sun 1–5pm.

Labor Day–mid-Oct: Sat 9am–5pm, Sun 1–5pm. Tours other times by appointment.

Admission Fees: Adults $3, children $1, Ohio Historical Society members free.

Visitor Services: Museum, information, rest rooms.

Directions: From I-77 south: take Rte. 39 east to Carrollton. From I-77 north: take Rte. 43 from Canton. Located on the west side of the public square in Carrollton, Carroll County.

Cincinnati

2 **Site:** THE HARRIET BEECHER STOWE HOUSE, 2950 Gilbert Ave., Cincinnati, OH 45206, ☎ 513/632-5120

Description: The Harriet Beecher Stowe House was built by Lane Seminary in 1833 to serve as the residence of that institution's president. Harriet Beecher Stowe moved to Cincinnati from Connecticut in 1832 with her father, Dr. Lyman Beecher, who had been appointed president of the seminary. During her stay in Cincinnati, she learned of the evils of slavery and wrote of them in her influential novel *Uncle Tom's Cabin.* The Stowe House has been restored by youth workers of the Cincinnati Citizens Committee on Youth. Recent renovations were funded by the Ohio Historical Society and the City of Cincinnati.

Open to Public: Tues–Thurs 10am–4pm.

Admission Fees: Free.

Visitor Services: Rest rooms.

Directions: From I-71 south: take William Howard Taft exit, turn right onto Reading Rd., travel north to Martin Luther King Dr., and turn right onto Gilbert Ave. House is located on the corner of Gilbert and Martin Luther King.

3 **Site:** SPRING GROVE CEMETERY AND ARBORETUM, 4521 Spring Grove Ave., Cincinnati, OH 45232, ☎ 513/681-6680

Description: Spring Grove Cemetery and Arboretum, serving the community for more than 150 years, encompasses 733 acres. It is known worldwide for its beautiful landscaping and unique "lawn plan." Preserved within this "museum without walls" are exquisite illustrations of art, statuary, and architecture. Among its notable burials are 999 Civil War soldiers; 40 are generals, including Gen. Robert McCook of the "Fighting McCooks" and Gen. Joseph Hooker.

Open to Public: Daily 8am–6pm.

Admission Fees: Free.

Visitor Services: Information, rest rooms, self-guided walking tour brochure and map. Guided tours available for groups of 20 or more.

Directions: From I-75: take Mitchell Ave. exit and go south on Spring Grove Ave. to entrance.

Columbus

4 **Site:** CAMP CHASE CEMETERY, 2900 Sullivant Ave., Columbus, OH, ☎ 614/276-0060

Description: Camp Chase, the largest camp in the area, was used for training Union soldiers. Later, it served as a prison for captured Confederates. Camp Chase is the largest Confederate cemetery in the north, with 2,260 Confederates buried there.

Open to Public: Daily.

Admission Fees: Free.

Visitor Services: None.

Regularly Scheduled Events: *First Sun in June:* Annual Confederate memorial services.

Directions: From I-70: exit at Broad St. and proceed west on Broad St. to Hague Ave. Turn left on Hague, turn right on Sullivant Ave., and proceed 1 block to cemetery.

---

5 **Site:** OHIO STATEHOUSE, Corner of Broad and High streets, Columbus, OH 43215, ☎ 614/752-9777

Description: The Ohio Statehouse is the finest example of Greek Revival architecture in the United States. Built between 1839 and 1861, it is a National Historic Landmark and has been restored to its 1861 appearance. President Abraham Lincoln visited the statehouse three times: first, in 1859, shortly after his involvement with the Lincoln-Douglas debates; second, in 1861, when he spoke to a joint session of the Ohio legislature in the House chamber; and third, in 1865, when he was laid in state in the rotunda. A monument, These Are My Jewels, pays tribute to seven Ohioans who played key roles in the Civil War, including Ulysses S. Grant, Philip Sheridan, Edwin M. Stanton, James A. Garfield, Rutherford B. Hayes, Salmon P. Chase, and William Tecumseh Sherman.

Open to Public: Mon–Fri 8am–7pm, Sat–Sun 11am–5pm. Tours can be scheduled by calling ☎ 614/752-6350.

Admission Fees: Free.

Visitor Services: Museum, information, rest rooms, handicapped access.

Regularly Scheduled Events: *Aug:* Annual G.A.R. Civil War encampment features 1860s baseball game between Ohio Village Muffins and Lady Diamonds and the Ohio legislators. Call for a schedule of other events.

Directions: From I-71: take Broad St. exit and go west until you reach Third St. Parking is available underground; turn south onto Third St.

Fremont

6 **Site:** RUTHERFORD B. HAYES PRESIDENTIAL CENTER, Spiegel Grove, 1337 Hayes Ave., Fremont, OH 43420, ☎ 800/998-PRES

Description: This site features a museum, the first presidential library, and the 33-room Victorian mansion of Rutherford B. Hayes, 19th president of the United States. The tomb of the president and his wife, Lucy Webb Hayes, are located on the 25-acre Spiegel Grove estate. Hayes was decorated as a Civil War officer and served three terms as Ohio governor and one term as president. The two-story museum has Civil War artifacts and one of the nation's finest antique weapons collections. The library contains works of American history from the Civil War to the 20th century.

Open to Public: Mon–Sat 9am–5pm, Sun and holidays noon–5pm. Extended hours July–Aug: Daily 9am–7pm.

Admission Fees: *House and museum:* Adults $7.50, children $2, seniors $6.50. *House or museum:* Adults $4, children $1, seniors $3.25.

Visitor Services: Trails, museum, gift shop, information, rest rooms, handicapped access.

Directions: Located at the intersection of Buckland and Hayes Avenues in Fremont, Sandusky County. Exit 6 on the Ohio Turnpike or via SR 20, 53, 12, or 6.

Lakeside–Marblehead

7 **Site:** JOHNSON ISLAND CEMETERY, Lakeside-Marblehead, OH 43440, ☎ 800/441-1271

Description: This cemetery holds the graves of 206 Confederates who died while imprisoned here.

Open to Public: Daily from dawn to dusk.

Admission Fees: Free; $1 toll to cross causeway.

Visitor Services: None.

Directions: From I-80/90: take exit 6A north on State Rte. 4 to State Rte. 2 west; then take State Rte. 269 north to Danbury and Bay Shore Rd. Travel east on Bay Shore Rd. to Johnson Island entrance; cross the causeway to Johnson Island.

Lancaster

8 **Site:** SHERMAN HOUSE, 137 E. Main St., Lancaster, OH 43130, ☎ 614/687-5891

Description: Sherman House is the birthplace of William Tecumseh Sherman and a museum with war memorabilia and artifacts from the general's collection.

Open to Public: Apr–Nov: Tues–Sun 1–4pm.

Admission Fees: Adults $2.50, children 6–17 $1.

Regularly Scheduled Events: *Early Feb:* Sherman's birthday celebration.

Directions: From I-270: travel south on State Rte. 33 to downtown Lancaster, turn left on State Rte. 22, and proceed 2 blocks to house.

New Rumley

9 **Site:** CUSTER MONUMENT, Ohio Historical Society, 1982 Velma Ave., Columbus, OH 43211-2497, ☎ 1-800/BUCKEYE or 614/297-2630

Description: This 8½-foot bronze statue stands on the site of George Armstrong Custer's birthplace. Custer, born in 1839, became famous as a daring young cavalryman in the Civil War, fighting in the battles of Bull Run, Shenandoah, Waynesboro, Appomattox, and many others.

Open to Public: Daily from dawn to dusk.

Admission Fees: Free.

Directions: Located on the north side of State Rte. 646, at the west edge of New Rumley, north of Cadiz, in Harrison County.

Point Pleasant

 Site: ULYSSES S. GRANT BIRTHPLACE STATE MEMORIAL, 1591 State Rte. 232, Point Pleasant, OH 45153, ☎ 513/553-4911

Description: Ulysses S. Grant, 18th president of the United States, was born in this small frame cottage in Point Pleasant, Ohio. Today, Grant's birthplace is restored and open to the public.

Open to Public: Apr–Oct: Wed–Sat 9:30am–noon and 1–5pm, Sun noon–5pm.

Admission Fees: Adults $1, children 6–12 50¢, seniors 75¢. Groups: $10/bus or 50¢/person.

Visitor Services: Tours.

Directions: Located in the Clermont County Village of Point Pleasant, off State Rte. 52 near the intersection with State Rte. 132.

Portland

 Site: BUFFINGTON ISLAND, Ohio Historical Society, 1982 Velma Ave., Columbus, OH 43211-2497, ☎ 1-800/BUCKEYE or 614/297-2630

Description: This site commemorates the only significant Civil War battle that took place on Ohio soil. Here a Union army routed a column of Confederate cavalry commanded by Gen. John Hunt Morgan in 1863.

Open to Public: Daily from dawn to dusk.

Admission Fees: Free.

Visitor Services: Picnic area, handicapped access.

Directions: The memorial is approximately 20 miles east from Pomeroy, Meigs County, on State Rte. 124, at Portland, OH.

Ripley

12 **Site:** RANKIN HOUSE, P.O. Box 176, Rankin Hill Rd., Ripley, OH 45167, ☎ 937/392-1627

Description: The Rankin House was an important way station on the Underground Railroad by which slaves escaped from the South to freedom. John Rankin was a Presbyterian minister and educator who devoted his life to the antislavery movement. From 1825 to 1865, Rankin and his wife, Jean, with their Brown County neighbors, sheltered more than 2,000 slaves escaping to freedom, with as many as 12 escapees being hidden in the Rankin home at one time. The Rankins prided themselves on never having lost a "passenger."

Open to Public: Memorial Day Weekend–Labor Day: Wed–Sun noon–5pm. After Labor Day–Oct: Sat–Sun noon–5pm.

Admission Fees: Adults $2, children 6–12 $1.

Visitor Services: Rest rooms, limited handicapped access.

Directions: The entrance road (Race St. or Rankin St.) to the Rankin House runs northeast off of State Rte. 52 at the northwest edge of Ripley, Brown County.

The Rankin House, a way station on the "Underground Railroad," Ripley, OH. (Photograph courtesy of the Ohio Historical Society.)

THE UNDERGROUND RAILROAD

"I's hoping and praying all the time I meets up with that Harriet Tubman woman. She the colored woman what takes slaves to Canada. She always travels the underground railroad, they calls it, travels at night and hides out in the day. She sure sneaks them out the South, I think she's a brave woman."

—Thomas Cole, born a slave in Alabama in 1845

The Underground Railroad was perhaps the greatest protest against slavery in the United States. It was not really a railroad, with trains and stations, but rather a network of secret routes that slaves could use to escape to freedom in the northern states and Canada. Sometimes there was a guide, called a conductor, who led the escaped slaves to freedom. Other times, slaves just followed the North Star or used directions, passed from person to person by word of mouth or through songs, to freedom.

continues

The runaway slaves were in great danger, so they traveled at night and slept during the day to avoid being captured by the "slave catchers." People of all races and religious backgrounds helped the slaves along the way, offering shelters to hide in during the day and providing food and water for the travelers.

Most of the escaped slaves were men between the ages of 16 and 35, though some women and children escaped too. Many of them had been field hands in the South, working under harsh conditions.

One famous conductor was known simply as "Moses," and the slave catchers spent years searching for him. Very few people knew that "Moses" was really a woman named Harriet Tubman, herself an escaped slave from Maryland. She led thousands of slaves to freedom in the North, and towards the end of the Civil War she went south to tell the slaves that they had been freed by the Emancipation Proclamation, issued by President Lincoln on January 1, 1863.

Credit: National Park Service

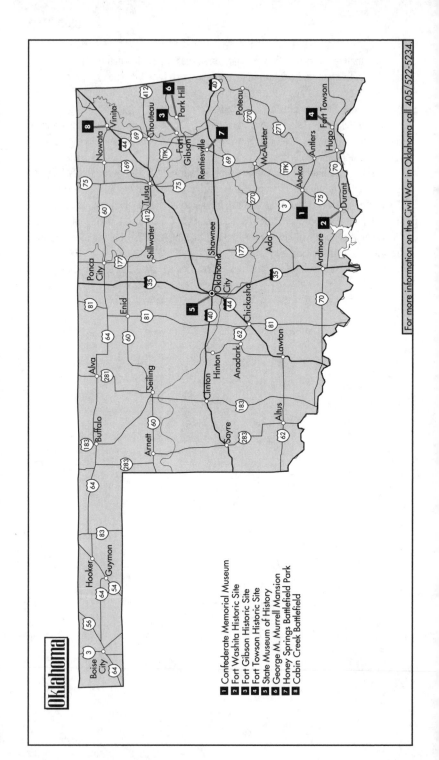

Oklahoma

1 Confederate Memorial Museum
2 Fort Washita Historic Site
3 Fort Gibson Historic Site
4 Fort Towson Historic Site
5 State Museum of History
6 George M. Murrell Mansion
7 Honey Springs Battlefield Park
8 Cabin Creek Battlefield

For more information on the Civil War in Oklahoma call 405/522-5234.

OKLAHOMA

$\mathcal{I}$N 1861 THE FLAME OF THE CIVIL WAR SPED across Indian Territory, an area that would become the state of Oklahoma 46 years later. And when the war came, it struck with such a fury that left the lands of the Five Civilized Tribes in shambles.

All five tribes—the Cherokee, Creek, Choctaw, Chickasaw, and Seminole—officially sided with the Confederacy in 1861, but in reality, only the Choctaw and Chickasaw were united in their support of the South. All-Indian regiments were formed, and by the end of the war, thousands of Indians would serve on both sides, brother against brother, tribe against tribe.

Located between the unionist states of Kansas and Missouri, and the Confederate states of Arkansas and Texas, the Indian Territory was both a crossroads for armies and a source of men, mules, and material. From 1861 to 1865 the boys in blue and gray fought 89 battles and skirmishes on the soil that would become Oklahoma. In all, the people of the Five Civilized Tribes suffered more destruction and death per capita than any state of the South, including the states of Virginia, Tennessee, and Missouri.

Today, the remnants of that life and death struggle await the observant traveler.

by Dr. Bob Blackburn, Oklahoma Historical Society

Atoka

1 **Site:** CONFEDERATE MEMORIAL MUSEUM, P.O. Box 245, Atoka, OK 74525, ☎ 405/889-7192

Description: Confederates maintained camps nearby along the Middle Boggy River in the Choctaw Nation of Indian Territory. Some died of disease and were buried on the grounds where the museum exists now. The Battle of Middle Boggy was fought on February 13, 1864, when Col. William Phillips and 350 Union troops surprised about 90 Confederates about where the Texas Road crossed the Middle Boggy River. Forty-seven Confederates were killed in the Union victory. The museum includes memorabilia from that Civil War battle. Grounds include cemetery and a section of the Butterfield Mail Route. The Battle of Middle Boggy is reenacted every third year at a nearby site by the Oklahoma Historical Society and Atoka County Historical Society.

Open to Public: Mon–Sat 9am–4pm.

Admission Fees: Free. *Note:* Admission fee charged for the reenactment.

Visitor Services: Museum, information, gift shop, visitors center, rest rooms. Grounds inside stockade and buildings have handicapped access.

Directions: From I-40: travel south on U.S. 69 to Atoka. Museum is located 1 mile north of Atoka on the east side of U.S. 69 with the Oklahoma Travel Information Center.

Durant

2 Site: FORT WASHITA HISTORIC SITE, Star Rte. 213, Durant, OK 74701-9443, ☎ 405/924-6502

Description: Fort Washita was established in 1842 in the Choctaw Nation of Indian Territory and was used as a staging ground for the Mexican War. In the 1850s, it was a United States Army Artillery School. Famous Civil War leaders who served earlier at Fort Washita included Randolph B. Marcy, George McClellan, William G. Belknap, Theophylus H. Holmes, and numerous others. Federal troops abandoned Fort Washita in 1861, and it was occupied by Confederate troops during the Civil War as the headquarters of Brig. Gen. Douglas Cooper. Fort Washita National Historic Landmark today includes ruins, restored barracks, and the parade ground.

Open to Public: Mon–Sat 9am–5pm, Sun 1–5pm.

Admission Fees: Free.

Visitor Services: Information, gift shop, visitors center, rest rooms. Grounds and buildings have handicapped access.

Regularly Scheduled Events: *Third weekend in Feb:* Mexican War living history; *First and third weekends of Mar:* Civil War living history; *First weekend in Apr:* 1840s Fur Trade Rendezvous (admission charge); *First weekend of Nov:* Candlelight tours (admission charge); *Mid-Nov:* Instruction Camp for male reenactors (admission charge); *Dec:* Mexican and Civil War Christmas living history.

Directions: From I-35: travel east on U.S. 70 to Madill; continue 11 miles East on State Hwy. 199 to Fort Washita Historic Site.

Fort Gibson

3 Site: FORT GIBSON HISTORIC SITE, 907 North Garrison, P.O. Box 457, Fort Gibson, OK 74434, ☎ 918/478-4088

Description: Fort Gibson was constructed in 1824 to keep peace between warring Indian tribes in the area and was a base of operations for many expeditions. The fort was abandoned in 1857, but reactivated during the Civil War and used as a base for postwar Reconstruction activities. The fort lies 25 miles north of Honey Springs Battlefield. The battle of Honey Springs was the largest Civil War engagement in Indian Territory and protected Fort Gibson from Confederate attack. The site was permanently abandoned by the Army in 1890. This National Historic Landmark includes seven original structures and a reconstructed 1830s log garrison. A new museum and gift shop are housed in the 1840s Commissary. A hiking trail connects the early fort with the post–Civil War fort. Restoration is under way on the 1871 hospital.

Open to Public: Mon–Sat 9am–5pm, Sun 1–5pm.

Admission Fees: Adults $3, students 6–18 $1, children 5 and under free, seniors $2.50. Call for group rates.

Visitor Services: Tours, museum, information, gift shop, visitors center, rest rooms.

Grounds inside stockade and buildings have handicapped access.

Regularly Scheduled Events: Educational tours by reservation; *Mar:* Public Bake Day; *Armed Forces Day:* Military History Timeline living history; *First Sat in Oct:* Mexican War Encampment;*Last Sat in Oct:* Ghost Stories; *Mid-Nov:* Ladies Camp of Instruction; *Second weekend in Dec:* Candlelight tour.

Directions: From I-40: travel north at Checotah on U.S. 69 to Muskogee. Go east on U.S. 62 and north on State Hwy. 80 to Fort Gibson Military Park in the town of Fort Gibson.

Fort Towson

4 **Site:** FORT TOWSON HISTORIC SITE, HC 63, Box 1580, Fort Towson, OK 74701-9443, ☎ 405/873-2634

Description: Fort Towson was established in 1824 by Col. Matthew Arbuckle near the Red River in Indian Territory. The town of Doaksville was founded 1 mile away in 1831 and became the capital of the Choctaw Nation during the Civil War. The fort was expanded for the Mexican War but closed by the Federal army in 1854. Confederate Maj. Gen. Sam Bell Maxey established his command post at Fort Towson during the Civil War. The last surrender of the Civil War by an officer was completed near Doaksville on June 23, 1865, by Brig. Gen. Stand Watie, a Cherokee who commanded the Indian Brigade for the Confederates. Today, Fort Towson consists of extensive masonry ruins of barracks, officers' quarters, a bakery, a powder magazine, and other buildings.

Archaeological excavations at Doaksville are part of a development plan that will see it merged and linked by a trail to Fort Towson by the end of 1997. A sutler's store has been replicated at Fort Towson.

Open to Public: Mon–Fri 9am–5pm, Sat–Sun 1–5pm.

Admission Fees: Free. *Note:* Small fees may be charged for special events.

Visitor Services: Information, gift shop, visitors center, rest rooms. Grounds and buildings have handicapped access.

Regularly Scheduled Events: *Feb or Mar:* 1830s Fur Trade Rendezvous;*Sept:* Antique Auto Show;*Oct:* Choctaw Cultural Festival. Call for full calendar of events.

Directions: From I-35: go east on U.S. 70 through Hugo to town of Fort Towson; drive east out of town for .5 mile and proceed north for 1 mile, following signs. From I-40: go south on Indian Nation Turnpike to Hugo; then go east on U.S. 70 to town of Fort Towson; drive east out of town for .5 mile and proceed north for 1 mile, following signs.

Oklahoma City

5 Site: STATE MUSEUM OF HISTORY, 2100 Lincoln Blvd., Oklahoma City, OK 73105, ☎ 405/521-2491

Description: The State Museum of History, which is managed by the Oklahoma Historical Society, tells the comprehensive story of Oklahoma from the beginning. It has separate rooms for the Union and the Confederacy to commemorate the Civil War and its impact on Oklahoma. Both rooms include artifacts, relics, paintings, exhibits, and interpretations of the Civil War in Indian Territory and what became the State of Oklahoma. The same building houses the Oklahoma Historical Society Division of Archives and Manuscripts and the Oklahoma Historical Society Research Library, including extensive holdings of Indian units that fought in the Civil War.

Open to Public: Mon–Sat 8am–5pm.

Admission Fees: Free.

Visitor Services: Museum, information, gift shop, visitors center, rest rooms, handicapped access.

Directions: From I-40: travel north on I-235 in the middle of Oklahoma City; exit on Lincoln Blvd.; then go north to State Museum in Wiley Post Historical Building on the east side of Lincoln Blvd., just south of the State Capitol. From I-235: exit on NE 23d St., go east to Lincoln Blvd., and go south on Lincoln to Wiley Post Building as just described.

Park Hill

6 Site: GEORGE M. MURRELL MANSION, HC-69, Box 54, Park Hill, OK 74451-9601, ☎ 918/456-2751

Description: George M. Murrell, of Lynchburg, Va., married Minerva Ross, niece of principal chief John Ross of the Cherokee Nation. The Murrells built their home in Park Hill starting in 1844. It became known as Hunter's Home, a social center for Cherokee Nation leaders and Fort Gibson officers. After Minerva died, George married her younger sister, Amanda. During the Civil War, the Cherokee nation split. Murrell, a slave owner with strong family ties in Virginia and Louisiana, was married into the Ross family, which was led by strong unionists. The Murrell home was one of the few in Indian Territory not burned by one side or the other. The homes of John Ross, leader of the pro-Union faction, and Gen. Stand

Watie of the Confederates were both burned. Restoration of the Murrell Mansion is under way.

Open to Public: Mar: Fri–Sat 10am–5pm, Sun 1–5pm. Sept–Oct: Fri–Sat 10am–5pm, Sun 1–5pm. Nov–Feb: Sat 10am–5pm, Sun 1–5pm.

Admission Fees: Free. *Note:* A small fee is charged for the Ghost Story sessions during Halloween week.

Visitor Services: Trails, information, visitors center, rest rooms. Grounds and lower floor of mansion have handicapped access.

Regularly Scheduled Events: *First week of June:* 1858 Lawn Social living history; *Oct, Halloween week:* Ghost Stories.

Directions: From I-40: go north on U.S. 69 to Muskogee, then east on U.S. 62 to 4 miles short of Tahlequah, and then south on State Hwy. 82 to Park Hill. From I-44: travel south on U.S. 69, proceed east on U.S. 62, and go south on State Hwy. 82 to Park Hill.

Rentiesville

7 **Site:** HONEY SPRINGS BATTLEFIELD PARK, c/o Oklahoma Historical Society, 2100 Lincoln Blvd., Oklahoma City, OK 73105, ☎ 405/522-5241

Reenactment at Honey Springs Battlefield in Oklahoma. (Photograph by Jeff Briley, courtesy of Oklahoma Historical Society.)

Description: On July 17, 1863, 3,000 Union troops under Maj. Gen. James Blunt defeated 6,000 Confederates under Brig. Gen. Douglas Cooper in the Battle of Honey Springs. It was one of the first Civil War battles in which African Americans fought as a unit—the First Regular Kansas Volunteers (Colored). They carried the day, defeating two Texas cavalry units. It was also the largest battle in which Native Americans fought on both sides, and it was a turning point of the war in Indian Territory. The Union controlled the Cherokee Nation, the upper Arkansas River, and most of Indian Territory for the rest of the war. The current site includes monuments to the battle, as well as woods and pastures with a few structures. A project to develop a visitors center is under way and scheduled for completion by 1998.

Open to Public: Daily from dawn to dusk.

Admission Fees: Free. *Note:* An admission fee is charged for the reenactment of the battle, held every 3 years in mid-July.

Visitor Services: Information.

Regularly Scheduled Events: *Mid-July, every 3 years (1999, 2002, etc.):* Battle of Honey Springs reenactment; *Mid-July:* Battle of Honey Springs memorial service.

Directions: From I-40: go north on U.S. 69 4 miles to exit marked Rentiesville and go 2 miles east to Rentiesville; just after Rentiesville, at the edge of town, turn north (left) to the monuments and battle site.

Vinita

8 **Site:** CABIN CREEK BATTLEFIELD, c/o Oklahoma Historical Society, 2100 Lincoln Blvd., Oklahoma City, OK 73105, ☎ 405/522-5241

Description: Two Civil War battles were fought at Cabin Creek—both Confederate raids on Union supply wagon trains moving from Fort Scott toward Fort Gibson. On July 1, 1863, Stand Watie and the Confederates failed to stop the wagon train as it crossed Cabin Creek about 10 miles south of what is today, Vinita. It was one of the first battles in which African Americans fought as a unit west of the Mississippi River. On September 18, 1864, Watie and the Confederates won the Second Battle of Cabin Creek, capturing 740 mules, 130 wagons, and more than $1 million in supplies. Monuments to the leaders and soldiers of both sides were erected by the United Daughters of the Confederacy and are maintained by the Oklahoma Historical Society and the Friends of Cabin Creek at the battle site.

Open to Public: Daily from dawn to dusk.

Admission Fees: Free.

Visitor Services: Information, handicapped access.

Regularly Scheduled Events: *Last weekend in Sept, every 3 years (1998, 2001, etc.):* Battle of Cabin Creek reenactment.

Directions: From I-44: exit at Vinita onto U.S. 60/State Hwy. 82. Proceed east for 3 miles until these roads split; turn right and continue to follow Hwy. 82 for another 10 miles south to State Hwy. 28. Turn right onto Hwy. 28 and proceed 5 miles to Pensacola. Turn right onto a county road and proceed about 2.5 miles to the monument site. From I-40: take U.S. 69 north to OK 28; turn right (east) and travel 8 miles to Pensacola; turn left on county road and travel 2.5 miles to monument site.

PENNSYLVANIA

*G*EOGRAPHIC, POLITICAL, AND ECONOMIC CIRCUMSTANCES PLACED a reluctant Pennsylvania at the forefront of the Union coalition of states during the Civil War.

Because of Pennsylvania's geographic location and advanced railroad network, a transportation estuary was developed for the campaigns in Virginia and Maryland and, via the Ohio River and railroad extensions, for the west operations as well. In the end, Pennsylvania supplied one-sixth of the combatants and a leading share of the metal, textile, fuel, and food products. The relatively small Confederate forays to Chambersburg in October 1862 and July 1864 and the climactic Gettysburg campaign of June and July 1863 were the only periods of fighting on Pennsylvania soil. At Gettysburg one-third of the Union army was from Pennsylvania, commanded by two Pennsylvanians—John F. Reynolds and George G. Meade.

Politically, at the outset of the Civil War, there was less than a consensus in Pennsylvania for abolition, but political leaders from the newly arisen Republican Party convinced the public that the Union must be preserved. Later, ghastly casualties and the failures of the army, even as reorganized by the Pennsylvanian Gen. George B. McClellan, swelled antiwar sentiment. The possibility of a negotiated peace allowing Confederate independence haunted the North's wartime government. Pennsylvania's Congressman Thaddeus Stevens led the Congressional Radical Republicans, who prosecuted the war vigorously. Stevens worked uncompromisingly for the equality of African Americans.

Economically, Philadelphia banker Jay Cooke was commissioned to float government loans to finance the war. Free-enterprise economics prevailed, although political pressure forced private business into cooperating with military goals.

The Gettysburg and Vicksburg victories of July 1863 did not destroy the Confederacy; Pennsylvanians served on through Grant's Virginia campaigns, and Sherman's march through Georgia, South Carolina, and Tennessee. Former army commander George McClellan of Philadelphia was the Democratic candidate for president. Although reputed to be popular with the common soldiers, the soldiers as well as a slim Pennsylvania civilian majority voted for Lincoln, who carried the state by a mere 3.5 percent.

by Louis M. Waddell, Division of History,
Pennsylvania Historical and Museum Commission

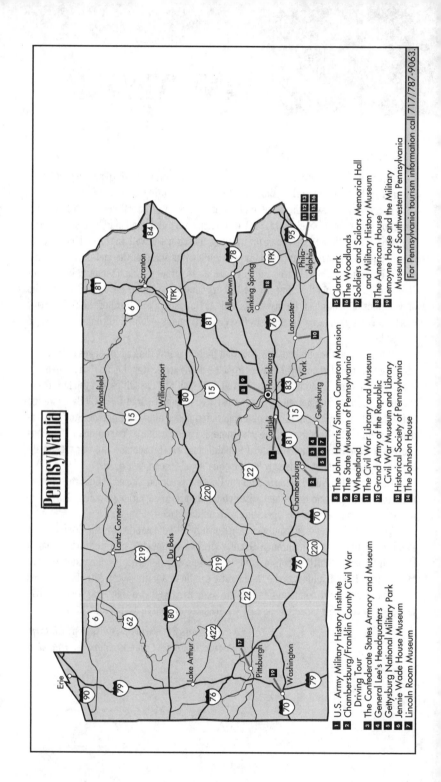

Pennsylvania

1 The John Harris/Simon Cameron Mansion
2 The State Museum of Pennsylvania
3 Wheatland
4 The Civil War Library and Museum
5 Grand Army of the Republic
   Civil War Museum and Library
6 Historical Society of Pennsylvania
7 The Johnson House

1 U.S. Army Military History Institute
2 Chambersburg/Franklin County Civil War
   Driving Tour
3 The Confederate States Armory and Museum
4 General Lee's Headquarters
5 Gettysburg National Military Park
6 Jennie Wade House Museum
7 Lincoln Room Museum

15 Clark Park
16 The Woodlands
17 Soldiers and Sailors Memorial Hall
   and Military History Museum
18 The American House
19 Lemoyne House and the Military
   Museum of Southwestern Pennsylvania

For Pennsylvania tourism information call 717/787-9063.

Carlisle

 Site: U.S. ARMY MILITARY HISTORY INSTITUTE, Upton Hall, Carlisle Barracks, Carlisle, PA 17013-5008, ☎ 717/245-3103 (books), 717/245-3434 (photos), 717/245-3601 (manuscripts), carlisle-www.army.mil/usamhi/

Description: The Institute is the Army's central historical repository, with vast holdings on many aspects of military history. These holdings include one of the greatest Civil War research collections in the world: 64,000 Civil War books, including 16,000 regimental histories; 85,000 Civil War photographs, drawings, and paintings; and unpublished letters, diaries, or memoirs of 4,500 Federal and Confederate soldiers.

Some papers and pictures concern generals; most cover U.S. and C.S. Army junior officers and enlisted men: regular, volunteer, and militia; national, state, and territorial. A few are from other Armed Services or from civilians. All these Civil War holdings are available for study. The Institute is a public institution that welcomes and encourages public usage of its holdings.

Open to Public: Weekdays 8am–4:30pm. Closed on weekends and Federal holidays.

Admission Fees: Free.

Visitor Services: Library, archives, small museum, information, exhibits, rest rooms, handicapped access.

Regularly Scheduled Events: *One evening a month, Sept–May:* Guest lecturer speaks on a military history topic.

Directions: From I-81: take exit 17 and proceed south on U.S. 11 about 3 miles to the third stop light after passing under Pennsylvania Turnpike. From I-76: take exit 16 and proceed south on U.S. 11 about 2 miles to the third stop light. Via either route, turn left at that light and proceed into Carlisle Barracks to the first stop sign. Upton Hall is to the right front.

Chambersburg

2 **Site:** CHAMBERSBURG/FRANKLIN COUNTY CIVIL WAR DRIVING TOUR, c/o Greater Chambersburg Chamber of Commerce, 75 S. Second St., Chambersburg, PA 17201, ☎ 717/264-7101

Description: The Chambersburg area saw more sustained military action during the war than any other place in Pennsylvania. In 1861, it was the staging point for Union Gen. Robert Patterson's unsuccessful Shenandoah Valley Campaign. Following the Battle of Antietam in 1862, the town was an important supply and hospital center. Jeb Stuart raided Chambersburg on

October 10, 1862, destroying warehouses and railroad yards. Approximately 65,000 Confederate troops camped around the town in June 1863 during the "Great Invasion." From there, Robert E. Lee made the decision to move toward Gettysburg. Chambersburg suffered its worst Confederate visitation on July 30, 1864, when cavalry under Gen. John McCausland burned the town after a ransom of $100,000 in gold ($500,000 cash) was not met. The fire destroyed more than 500 structures and gave Chambersburg the dubious distinction of being the only town in the North burned by the Confederates during the war. A driving tour features 50 Civil War sites in the area.

Open to Public: *Chamber office:* Mon–Fri 8am–5pm.

Admission Fees: Free driving tour brochure available from the Chamber of Commerce; write, call, or stop by the office at the address listed above.

Visitor Services: The free brochure "Franklin County: Civil War Country" features 50 Civil War sites in the area. Information on dining, lodging, and recreation is also available. Sales items include a Blue and Gray magazine driving tour of the 1864 Chambersburg Raid and a walking tour booklet and audio tape of historic sites in downtown Chambersburg.

Directions: From I-81: take exit 5 to Wayne Ave., which turns into 2nd St. Proceed through 4 traffic lights. The Chamber of Commerce office is at the corner of 2nd and Queen sts.

Gettysburg

3 **Site:** THE CONFEDERATE STATES ARMORY AND MUSEUM, 529 Baltimore St., Gettysburg, PA 17325, ☎ 717/337-2340

Description: The museum features a large collection of rare and original Confederate small arms, edged weapons, and memorabilia, as well as some Union weapons. Each artifact displayed is carefully and accurately described, and a tour through the facility is truly an educational experience.

Open to Public: Mon noon–7pm. Wed–Sun noon–7pm.

Admission Fees: $1.50. AAA discount available. Children under 6 are free.

Visitor Services: Museum, gift shop.

Directions: From Rte. 15: take Baltimore Pike exit and travel 2–3 miles. Museum is on the left, across from the Holiday Inn.

F or More Information

For Gettysburg visitor information, contact Gettysburg Convention and Visitors Bureau, Dept. 702, 35 Carlisle St., Gettysburg, PA 17325, ☎ **717/334-6274.**

---

4 **Site:** GENERAL LEE'S HEADQUARTERS, 401 Buford Ave., Gettysburg, PA 17325, ☎ 717/334-3141

Description: This stone house was used by Gen. Robert E. Lee as his personal

headquarters on July 1, 1863, during the Battle of Gettysburg.

Open to Public: *Summer:* Daily 9am–9pm. *Spring and Fall:* Daily 9am–5pm.

Admission Fees: Adults $2, children free.

Visitor Services: Museum, gift shop, rest rooms.

Directions: Located 23 miles east of I-81 on U.S. 30. From Harrisburg: take U.S. 15 south for 36 miles to U.S. 30 west.

---

5 **Site:** GETTYSBURG NATIONAL MILITARY PARK, 97 Taneytown Rd., Gettysburg, PA 17325, ☎ 717/334-1124

Description: Gettysburg National Military Park is the site of a major battle of the Civil War. The 3 days of fighting on July 1, 2, and 3, 1863, are considered a turning point in the war and marked the second and final invasion of the North by the Confederate forces.

Open to Public: *Battlefield:* Daily 6am–10pm. *Visitors Center:* 8am–5pm.

Admission Fees: Free; Orientation Map is $2.50.

Visitor Services: Civil War Explorer, museum, bookstore, information, rest rooms, handicapped access.

Regularly Scheduled Events: *June 15–Sept 1:* Ranger-guided walks; *Mar:* Battle seminar.

Directions: Located 78 miles north of Washington, DC; take I-270 west to Frederick, MD; take U.S. 15 north directly to the park. From Harrisburg, PA: take U.S. 15 south for approximately 36 miles directly into the park.

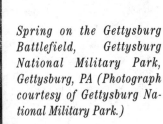

Spring on the Gettysburg Battlefield, Gettysburg National Military Park, Gettysburg, PA (Photograph courtesy of Gettysburg National Military Park.)

THE BATTLE OF GETTYSBURG

On June 3, 1863, a month after his dramatic victory at Chancellorsville, Confederate Gen. Robert E. Lee began marching his Army of Northern Virginia westward from its camps around Fredericksburg, Virginia. Once through the gaps of the Blue Ridge Mountains, the Southerners trudged northward into Maryland and

continues

Pennsylvania. They were followed by the Union Army of the Potomac under Gen. Joseph Hooker, but Lee, whose cavalry under J. E. B. Stuart was absent on a brash raid around the Federal forces, had no way of knowing his adversary's whereabouts.

The two armies touched by chance at Gettysburg on June 30. The main battle opened on July 1 with Confederates attacking Union troops on McPherson Ridge west of town. Though outnumbered, the Federal forces (now commanded by Gen. George G. Meade) held their position until afternoon, when they were finally overpowered and driven back to Cemetery Hill south of town. The Northerners labored long into the night over their defenses while the bulk of Meade's army arrived and took up positions.

On July 2 the battle lines were drawn up in two sweeping arcs. The main portions of both armies were nearly one mile apart on parallel ridges: Union forces on Cemetery Ridge; Confederate forces on Seminary Ridge to the west. Lee ordered an attack against both Union flanks. James Longstreet's thrust on the Federal left turned the base of Little Round Top into a shambles, left the Wheatfield strewn with dead and wounded, and overran the Peach Orchard. Farther north, Richard S. Ewell's evening attack on the Federal right at East Cemetery Hill and Culp's Hill, though momentarily successful, could not be exploited to Confederate advantage.

On July 3 Lee's artillery opened a two-hour bombardment of the Federal lines on Cemetery Ridge and Cemetery Hill. This for a time engaged the massed guns of both sides in a thundering duel for supremacy, but did little to soften up the Union defensive position. Then, in a desperate attempt to recapture the partial success of the previous day, some 12,000 Confederates under George E. Pickett advanced across the open fields toward the Federal center. Only one Southerner in three retired to safety.

With the repulse of Pickett's assault, the Battle of Gettysburg was over. The Confederate army that staggered back into Virginia was physically and spiritually exhausted. Never again would Lee attempt an offensive operation of such magnitude. And Meade, though criticized for not pursuing Lee's troops, would forever be remembered as the man who won the battle that has come to be known as the "High Watermark of the Confederacy."

by Julie K. Fix, The Civil War Trust

---

6 **Site:** JENNIE WADE HOUSE MUSEUM, 548 Baltimore St., Gettysburg, PA 17325, ☎ 717/334-4100

Description: During the Battle of Gettysburg, 20-year-old Mary Virginia "Jennie" Wade and her family took shelter at the home of her sister, Mrs. J. Lewis McClellen, who had just given birth to her first child. While Jennie Wade was baking bread for the Union troops, a stray bullet passed through two doors striking and killing her. Jennie Wade became Gettysburg's heroine. The 1863 home is now a museum that tells the story and life of Jennie Wade.

Open to Public: Mar–May: Daily 9am–5pm. End of May and June: 9am–7pm. July–Aug: 9am–9pm. Sept–Oct: 9am–7pm. End of Oct and Nov: 9am–5pm. Closed Dec–Feb.

Admission Fees: Adults $5.25, children $3.25, seniors $4.75. Groups (10 or more): Adults $3, children $1.50.

Visitor Services: Museum, gift shop, information.

Directions: Located along Baltimore St. (Rte. 97 South).

---

7   **Site:** LINCOLN ROOM MUSEUM, 12 Lincoln Sq., Gettysburg, PA 17325, ☎ 717/334-8188

Description: The "Lincoln Room" is located in the historic Wills House, where President Lincoln stayed the night before he gave his Gettysburg Address on November 19, 1863. The house was used as a hospital after the Battle of Gettysburg. The actual bedroom is preserved, and an audio program is presented to visitors. In addition, there is a display of Lincoln items period artifacts.

Open to Public: Daily 9am–5pm.

Admission Fees: Adults $3.25, children $1.75, seniors $3. Groups 15% off regular admission.

Visitor Services: Museum, gift shop, information.

Regularly Scheduled Events: *Nov 19:* Anniversary of the Gettysburg Address.

Directions: In the center of the Borough of Gettysburg at the intersection of Rte. 30 and Bus. Rte. 15 on Lincoln Square.

Harrisburg

8   **Site:** THE JOHN HARRIS/SIMON CAMERON MANSION, 219 South Front St., Harrisburg, PA 17104, ☎ 717/233-3462

Description: From 1863 to 1889, this was the home of Simon Cameron, Lincoln's first secretary of war. Cameron was a controversial figure who had proposed arming blacks early in the war effort and was forced to resign as a result. He also established Harrisburg as a central location for the movement of Union troops and material. Among the mansion tour highlights are the exhibition "Simon Cameron: In the

Eye of the Civil War" and General and Mrs. Cameron's 1863 Drawing Room.

Open to Public: Tues–Sat 10am–4pm. Reservations suggested.

Admission Fees: Adults $7, children $4, seniors $6. Group rates available.

Visitor Services: Museum, gift shop, rest rooms.

Regularly Scheduled Events: *Presidents' Day:* "Presidents at the Mansion."

Directions: From I-83: take the Second St. exit. Get in the left lane and turn left on Washington St. Turn right onto River St. at the "Mansion Tours" sign and then turn left into the parking lot.

---

9 | **Site:** THE STATE MUSEUM OF PENNSYLVANIA, P.O. Box 1026, Harrisburg, PA 17108-1026, ☎ 717/787-4980

Description: Among the museum's collections is a large and important collection of Civil War materials, many of which are exhibited in a second-floor gallery, "Keystone of the Union," which illustrates the role of the Commonwealth in the war. The collection includes flags, uniforms, firearms, swords, accoutrements, and soldiers' personal gear.

Open to Public: Tues–Sat 9am–5pm, Sun noon–5pm.

Admission Fees: Free.

Visitor Services: Museum, gift shop, information, rest rooms, handicapped access.

Directions: From I-83 south: take Second St. exit, turn right on North St., and proceed 2 blocks to Third and North. Museum is on opposite corner. From I-81: take exit 22 (Front St.) and turn left on North St.

Lancaster

10 | **Site:** WHEATLAND, 1120 Marietta Ave., Lancaster, PA 17603, ☎ 717/295-8825

Description: Wheatland was the home of President James Buchanan, 15th president of the United States, 1857–1861.

Open to Public: Apr 1–mid-Dec: Daily 10am–4pm.

Admission Fees: Adults $5.50, students $3.50, children $1.75, seniors $4.50, groups (15 or more by reservation) $3.50/person.

Visitor Services: Museum, snacks, gift shop, information, rest rooms.

Regularly Scheduled Events: *May–June:* Old-Fashioned Sunday; *June–Aug:* Children's Story Hour, Boy Scout Merit Badge; *Oct:* Halloween tours; *Dec:* Evening Christmas candlelight tours.

Directions: Located 1.5 miles west of Lancaster on Rte. 23 (Marietta Ave.) near the intersection of President Ave.

Philadelphia

11 | **Site:** THE CIVIL WAR LIBRARY AND MUSEUM, 1805 Pine St., Philadelphia, PA 19103, ☎ 215/735-8196

Description: Founded in 1888, the Civil War Library and Museum is the oldest chartered Civil War museum in the country. Three floors of exhibits include extensive George G. Meade, Ulysses S. Grant, and John F. Reynolds collections. Research library includes more than 2,000 photographs, microfilm, manuscripts, and 12,000 books.

Open to Public: Wed–Sun 11am–4:30pm.

Admission Fees: Adults $5, children under 12 $2, seniors $4, groups (up to 30 by reservation) $2/person.

Visitor Services: Museum, gift shop, information, rest rooms, limited handicapped access.

Regularly Scheduled Events: Special exhibits change annually; *Second Thurs of the month:* Meeting place of Civil War Round Table.

Directions: From I-76 east: take South St. exit (left-hand exit). At the top of the ramp, turn left, follow South St. to 18th St., turn left, and follow 18th St. 2 blocks to the corner of 18th and Pine sts. From I-95 north or south: take I-676 (Vine St. Expressway) and follow I-676 to merge with the Schuylkill Expressway, I-76. Follow I-76 east and get into the left lane; take the South St. exit, as before.

---

12 **Site:** GRAND ARMY OF THE REPUBLIC CIVIL WAR MUSEUM AND LIBRARY, 4278 Griscom St., Philadelphia, PA 19124-3954, ☎ 215/289-6484

Description: The museum contains an extensive collection of Civil War artifacts, battle relics, personal memorabilia, paintings, documents, and photographs that were initially assembled by the veterans who formed Post 2 of the Grand Army of the Republic.

Open to Public: Third Mon of every month: 7–9pm. Second Tues of every month: 7–9pm. First Sun of every month and by appointment.

Admission Fees: Free.

Visitor Services: Museum, gift shop, rest rooms, handicapped access.

Regularly Scheduled Events: Programs are presented the first Sun of every month. Call for schedule.

Directions: From I-95: exit at Bridge St. and go west on either Bridge or Wakeling St.; follow to Griscom St. and turn left to museum.

---

13 **Site:** HISTORICAL SOCIETY OF PENNSYLVANIA, 1300 Locust St., Philadelphia, PA 19107, ☎ 215/732-6201, www.libertynet.org/~pahist

Description: HSP is one of the nation's largest nongovernmental repositories of documentary materials, housing more than 500,000 books, 30,000 graphics, and 15 million manuscript items. The collection contains Union muster rolls, consolidated reports, returns, enlistment certificates,

some correspondence, and reminiscences. Among the major groups of regimental papers are enlistment certificates. There is a wealth of diaries written by soldiers during their service. The James Buchanan and Salmon P. Chase collections contain papers, correspondence, and other documents on political trends, economic conditions, and social history before, during, and after the Civil War. The Civil War collections are described in more depth on the Society's Web site.

Open to Public: Tues and Thurs–Sat 10am–5pm; Wed 1–9pm.

Admission Fees: *Research library:* Adults $5/day, students $2. All researchers must present photo ID.

Visitor Services: Research library, rest rooms, handicapped access.

Directions: From I-95: take I-676 (Vine St. Expressway) exit and go south on 15th St. After 5 blocks, turn left onto Locust St. Museum is located at 13th and Locust sts.

---

14 **Site:** THE JOHNSON HOUSE, 6306 Germantown Ave., Philadelphia, PA 19144, ☎ 215/438-1768

Description: The Johnson House was a station on the Underground Railroad. At this time, the Johnson House is the only site in Philadelphia that interprets the Underground Railroad.

Open to Public: Apr–Oct: Sat 1–4pm. All other times by appointment. Call to confirm reservation.

Admission Fees: Adults $3, children $1.50, seniors $1.50.

Visitor Services: Museum, information.

Directions: From Pennsylvania Turnpike: take exit 25 at Norristown and follow Germantown Pike east for 8 miles. From I-76: take the Lincoln Dr. exit. Just beyond the second stoplight, turn onto Harvey St. and follow to the end; turn left onto Germantown Ave.

---

15 **Site:** CLARK PARK, located in downtown Philadelphia

Description: Clark Park is located on the former Satterlee Hospital site. A stone from the battlefield at Gettysburg was placed in the park in 1916 to commemorate the Satterlee Hospital; a plaque rests at the base of the stone.

Open to Public: Daily from dawn to dusk.

Admission Fees: Free.

Visitor Services: Handicapped access.

Directions: From I-76: exit on University Ave. Proceed straight for about 3 blocks to the first large intersection. Turn left onto Baltimore Ave. and continue from 38th St. to 43rd St. Clark Park and the Gettysburg stone are on the left between 43rd and 44th sts.

---

16 **Site:** THE WOODLANDS, 4000 Woodland Ave., Philadelphia, PA 19104-4560, ☎ 215/386-2181

Description: The Woodlands Cemetery, incorporated in 1840 on the grounds of the historic Hamilton Mansion, built about 1788, is the grave site of many individuals associated with the Civil War. Among those veterans buried at the Woodlands are Maj. Gen. David Bill Birnay; John Hill Briton, M.D.; Sidney George Fisher; Adm. Charles Stewart; Mary Grew; and Emily Bliss Souder. The graves of other Civil War veterans are marked by GAR markers. The cemetery grounds overlook the Schuylkill River, used to transport Union soldiers wounded at Gettysburg to nearby Satterlee Hospital, the largest U.S. Army hospital in the Civil War. The hospital was located in nearby Clark Park.

Open to Public: *Grounds:* Daily 9am–5pm. *Office:* Mon–Fri 10am–4:30pm.

Admission Fees: Free.

Visitor Services: A map of grave sites is available at the office.

Regularly Scheduled Events: *Apr, at The Woodlands:* Adopt-a-Grave picnic and walkabout; *Nov, at Clark Park:* Veterans Day commemoration.

Directions: To The Woodlands: From I-76: exit at University Ave., turn left on Baltimore Ave., turn left on Woodland Ave., and proceed left through gates at 40th St. Follow white arrows.

Pittsburgh

17 **Site:** SOLDIERS AND SAILORS MEMORIAL HALL AND MILITARY HISTORY MUSEUM, 4141 Fifth Ave., Pittsburgh, PA 15213, ☎ 412/621-4253

Description: Soldiers and Sailors Memorial Hall opened in 1910 to commemorate Allegheny County veterans who served in the Civil War. The museum's Civil War holdings include flags, uniforms, weapons, battlefield memorabilia, photographs, artwork, and an extensive collection of GAR post records. A fine Civil War library complements the museum's holdings. Memorial Hall's military collection spans the period from the 1860s to Desert Storm and also contains a Hall of Valor, honoring area residents who earned the Silver Star or higher decorations in American wars.

Open to Public: Mon–Fri 9am–4pm, weekends 1–4pm.

Admission Fees: Free.

Visitor Services: Museum, gift shop, information, rest rooms, handicapped access.

Directions: From Pennsylvania Turnpike: take I-376 west to Oakland exit, continue in right lane up hill to second traffic light, and turn left. Then turn right at next light onto Forbes Ave. and turn left on Bigelow Blvd. From I-79: take exit I-279 to I-376, take Forbes Ave. exit, and turn left on Bigelow Blvd.

Sinking Spring

18 **Site:** THE AMERICAN HOUSE, 737 Fritztown Rd., Sinking Spring, PA 19608; Berks County Visitors Bureau: ☎ 610/670-8880

Description: The American House operated under the proprietorship of Civil War veteran John J. K. Gittelman. Upon the outbreak of the war, Gittelman, on October 19, 1862, became Corporal of Company E, 17th Pennsylvania Volunteer Cavalry, Second Brigade, First Division, Army of the Potomac. Today, the American House contains specialty shops, featuring a crafts gallery, gift shop, restaurant, and ice-cream parlor.

Open to Public: Tues–Fri 11am–8pm, Sat 11am–5pm, Sun noon–5pm.

Admission Fees: Free.

Visitor Services: Ice-cream parlor, retail specialty shops, historic information, rest rooms. Victorian-style lunch served Tues–Sat 11am–3pm; candlelight dinners served Fri 5–9pm; high noon tea served Sat by reservation.

Regularly Scheduled Events: Annual Civil War encampment weekend. Call for dates.

Directions: From Pennsylvania Turnpike: take exit 22 (Morgantown) and take I-176 north to Rte. 422 west. At traffic light, Sinking Springboro Hall, fork to left off 422 west onto Columbia Ave. (which turns into Fritztown Rd.). American House is located 1.8 miles on the right.

Washington

---

19 **Site:** LEMOYNE HOUSE AND THE MILITARY MUSEUM OF SOUTHWESTERN PENNSYLVANIA, Washington County Historical Society, 49 East Maiden St., Washington, PA 15301, ☎412/225-6740

Description: The LeMoyne House is the 1812 home of Dr. F. Julius LeMoyne, a physician, abolitionist, and humanitarian. The house was a stop on the Underground Railroad and is designated a National Historic Landmark. Dr. LeMoyne was a candidate for governor of Pennsylvania on the platform of antislavery. His son, Dr. Frank LeMoyne, was a surgeon for the Union during the Civil War. The military museum occupies one room within the LeMoyne House. The core collection contains Civil War artifacts, including military equipment and uniforms and a military history library.

Open to Public: Tues–Fri 11am–4pm, Sat–Sun noon–4pm. Closed mid-Dec–Jan.

Admission Fees: Adults $4, children $2, groups $3.50/person.

Visitor Services: Museum, gift shop, information.

Regularly Scheduled Events: *Third weekend in May:* National Pike festival (museum open extended hours); *Dec:* Christmas tours (first-person interpretation; extended hours).

Directions: Located 25 miles south of Pittsburgh, at the intersection of interstates 70 and 79. From I-70/79: exit at Rte. 19 south and turn right at Rte. 40 west. LeMoyne House is in the first block on the right.

SOUTH CAROLINA

*S*OUTH CAROLINA PLAYED A MAJOR ROLE in the Civil War from the beginning—indeed, in the more than 30 years of tension between the North and South before the war. When Abraham Lincoln was elected president in 1860, many South Carolinians were among the most prominent and most enthusiastic proponents of secession from the Union. The South Carolina General Assembly called a secession convention and on December 20 became the first state to secede.

Three Federal forts in Charleston Harbor—Fort Sumter, Fort Moultrie, and Castle Pinckney—were crucial to the interests of both the United States and the new republic of South Carolina. When Maj. Robert Anderson moved a small Federal garrison from Fort Moultrie to Fort Sumter in late December, the South Carolinians responded by taking Castle Pinckney and Fort Moultrie, making war a distinct possibility. In March 1861, Lincoln decided to send provisions to Fort Sumter. In the early morning of April 12, Confederate troops demanded the surrender of Fort Sumter and ordered the artillery bombardment that began the Civil War. Anderson surrendered the next day after a prolonged bombardment.

The Palmetto State was not a major battleground during the Civil War, though it did see a few major campaigns and several minor engagements. Most notable were the occupation of the Sea Islands; the long siege of Charleston, which lasted until the end of the war; and the march of Federal troops commanded by Gen. William T. Sherman from Savannah to Columbia and into North Carolina in early 1865. The Federal blockade of Southern ports was headquartered at Port Royal after its capture by a large naval expedition in November 1861. Sea Islands were used for the training and education of thousands of ex-slaves whom the Federal authorities considered to be freed by virtue of the military occupation of the area.

Federal attempts to capture Charleston began in June 1862 at Secessionville, on James Island, and continued through the bloody assault on Battery Wagner in July 1863. Fort Sumter withstood three major bombardments and only surrendered in February 1865 after the city was evacuated by Confederate troops. After Sherman captured Savannah in December 1864, he marched his Federals into South Carolina. Sherman's march left considerable devastation and lasting bitterness that lingered for years.

One of the more obvious costs of the war was the 12,000 lives lost or ruined. Perhaps the most significant consequence of Union victory, however, was the emancipation of 400,000 slaves and their subsequent attempt to adjust to their new place in South Carolina society. As in so much of the South, the end of the war raised as many new questions as the old ones it had been fought to answer.

by J. Tracy Power, South Carolina Department of Archives and History

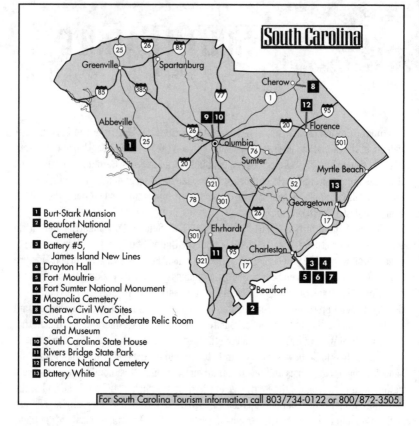

South Carolina

- **1** Burt-Stark Mansion
- **2** Beaufort National Cemetery
- **3** Battery #5, James Island New Lines
- **4** Drayton Hall
- **5** Fort Moultrie
- **6** Fort Sumter National Monument
- **7** Magnolia Cemetery
- **8** Cheraw Civil War Sites
- **9** South Carolina Confederate Relic Room and Museum
- **10** South Carolina State House
- **11** Rivers Bridge State Park
- **12** Florence National Cemetery
- **13** Battery White

For South Carolina Tourism information call 803/734-0122 or 800/872-3505.

Abbeville

1 **Site:** BURT-STARK MANSION, 306 North Main St. at Greenville St., Abbeville, SC 29620, ☎ 864/459-4600

Description: This house was the site of the last Council of War held by Confederate President Jefferson Davis, on May 2, 1865. Davis, along with a few members of his cabinet and several Confederate generals, was on his way south after the fall of Richmond and hoped to rally support. Though Davis still clung to the hope of military success, he was persuaded by subordinates that further resistance was futile, and the war was over.

Open to Public: Fri–Sat 1–5pm; any day by appointment.

Admission Fees: $4.

Visitor Services: Tours.

Directions: From I-26 east or west: take exit 54 and then take SC Hwy. 72; go 3 miles west to Clinton, 24 miles SW to Greenwood, and 14 miles west to Abbeville. Turn right onto South Main St., travel around square, and follow signs on North Main St. to house.

From I-85: take exit 27 and then take SC Hwy. 81 South to Anderson, SC Hwy. 28 for 30 miles to Abbeville. SC Hwy. 28 becomes North Main St. in Abbeville; follow signs on North Main St. to house.

Beaufort

2 Site: BEAUFORT NATIONAL CEMETERY, 1601 Boundary St., Beaufort, SC 29902, ☎ 803/524-3925

Description: This national cemetery was established in 1863 for the burial of Union soldiers who died during the Federal occupation of Beaufort and for the reinterment of Union soldiers' remains from various locations in South Carolina, Georgia, and Florida. More than 9,000 Union soldiers or veterans are buried here—4,400 of them unknown—including 2,800 prisoners of war from the camp at Millen, Georgia, as well as 1,700 black Union soldiers. There are 117 Confederate soldiers buried here.

Open to Public: *Office:* Mon–Fri 8am–4:30pm. *Cemetery:* Daily from dawn to dusk.

Admission Fees: Free.

Visitor Services: None.

Directions: From I-95: take exit 33 to Beaufort; take U.S. Hwy. 21 south through Pocotaligo, Sheldon, and Garden's Corner; and proceed past the U.S. Marine Corps Air Station on left. Cemetery is on the left approximately 2 miles after the air station.

Charleston

3 SITE: BATTERY #5, James Island Seige Line. Mailing address: South Carolina Battleground Preservation Trust, P.O. Box 12441, James Island, SC 29422, ☎ 803/762-3563

Description: Battery #5, a Confederate earthwork constructed in 1863 under the direction of Gen. P. G. T. Beauregard, commander of the Departments of South Carolina, Georgia, and Florida, was the eastern terminus of the James Island Siege Line. Intended to anchor the Confederate defenses of James Island and overlooking Seaside Creek and the Secessionville peninsula, this battery is an excellent intact example of a Civil War earthwork.

Open to Public: Daily from dawn to dusk.

Admission Fees: Free.

Visitor Services: None.

Directions: From I-26: take exit for U.S. Hwy. 17 south toward Savannah, cross over Ashley River, take Hwy. 171 for 5 miles, turn left onto Burclair Dr., and cross Secessionville Rd. to Seaside Plantation. Take the second road on the right.

4 Site: DRAYTON HALL, A National Trust Historic Site, 3380 Ashley River Rd., Charleston, SC 29414, ☎ 803/766-0188

Description: Begun in 1738, Drayton Hall is an authentic plantation house that tells the story of the rise, fall, and recovery of the South after the Civil War. The museum offers excellent guided tours that describe the lifestyles of the Draytons, who supported the Confederacy, and of African Americans before and after freedom. Drayton Hall is the only antebellum plantation in the Charleston area that is open to the public.

Open to Public: Mar–Oct: Daily 9:30am–4pm. Nov–Feb: Daily 9:30am–3pm. Closed Thanksgiving Day, Christmas Day, and New Year's Day.

Admission Fees: Adults $8, children 12–18 $4, children 6–11 $4, children 5 and under free. Call for group rates.

Visitor Services: Guided house tour, self-guided walks of the marsh and the river, gift shop, picnic area, handicapped access, free parking.

Regularly Scheduled Events: *Spring:* Oyster Roasts; Candlelight Concert; *Spring and Fall weekends:* Nature Walks; *Dec:* Spirituals Concert.

Directions: From I-526: take Hwy. 61 (Ashley River Rd.) north. Drayton Hall is located on Hwy. 61, 9 miles northwest of Charleston.

5 Site: FORT MOULTRIE, a unit of Fort Sumter National Monument, 1214 Middle St., Sullivan's Island, SC 29484, ☎ 803/883-3123

Description: Fort Moultrie is administered by the Fort Sumter National Monument. Fort Moultrie's history covers more than 220 years of seacoast defense, from the first decisive victory in the American Revolution to protecting the coast from U-boats in World War II. The present fort, built in 1809, was occupied by Maj. Robert Anderson and 85 Federal soldiers before they moved to Fort Sumter. During the first battle of the Civil War (April 12–13, 1861), Confederates at Fort Moultrie fired on Union troops in Fort Sumter. Confederate forces successfully used both forts to protect Charleston from a combined Union navy and army siege from 1863 to 1865.

Open to Public: Daily 9am–5pm. Closed Christmas Day.

Admission Fees: *User fee for admission to the fort:* Adults $2, children 15 and under $1, family $5, annual pass $20. No fee for school groups.

Visitor Services: Orientation film, museum, rest rooms, bookstore, information, handicapped access.

Directions: From Charleston: take U.S. 17 north toward Mount Pleasant. Just over the Cooper River Bridge, turn right onto U.S. Hwy. 703. Stay on this road to Sullivan's Island; at the stop sign, turn right onto Middle St. The fort is 1.5 miles from this intersection.

6 Site: FORT SUMTER NATIONAL MONUMENT, 1214 Middle St., Sullivan's Island, SC 29482, ☎ 803/883-3123. Accessible by private boat or through Fort Sumter Tours, 803/722-1691

Fort Sumter, Charleston, SC. (Photograph courtesy of the National Park Service, Fort Sumter National Monument.)

Description: Fort Sumter National Monument includes Fort Sumter, a coastal fortification whose construction was begun in 1829 but was still not completed by the time the Civil War started here in April 1861. Confederate and South Carolina troops under the direction of Gen. P. G. T. Beauregard bombarded the Union garrison commanded by Maj. Robert Anderson for 34 hours on April 12–13 until Major Anderson surrendered the fort. Fort Sumter was occupied by a Confederate garrison for most of the war. During the Siege of Charleston, from 1863 to 1865, Fort Sumter was reduced to one-third of its original size. After the war, Fort Sumter was repaired but was never rebuilt to its original height.

Open to Public: Daily except Christmas. Easter weekend and April–Labor Day: 10am–5:30pm. Dec 26–Jan 1, Mar, and the day after Labor Day through Feb: 10am–4pm. Dec–Feb 2–4pm.

Admission Fees: Free. *Tour boat:* Adults $10.50, children 6–12 $5.50, seniors and military $1 discount.

Visitor Services: Museum, museum shop, rest rooms, information, handicapped access.

Directions: To the City Marina: take I-26 to Charleston, take U.S. Hwy. 17 south toward Savannah, turn left onto Lockwood Blvd., and turn right at the first traffic light; City Marina is on the right. To Patriots Point: take I-26 to Charleston and take U.S. Hwy. 17 north toward Mt. Pleasant. Just over the Cooper River Bridge, turn right onto U.S. Hwy. 703 (Coleman Blvd.). At the first traffic light, turn right into Patriots Point. For private boaters: Fort Sumter is 3.3 miles from Charleston at the harbor entrance.

---

7 **Site:** MAGNOLIA CEMETERY, 70 Cunnington Ave., Charleston, SC 29405,
☎ 803/722-8638

Description: Magnolia Cemetery, established in 1850, includes the graves of several prominent Confederate civilian and military leaders. Capt. Horace Hunley and the crew of the CSS *H. L. Hunley,* the Confederate submarine that was the first to sink a warship, are also buried here. A monument to South Carolina's Civil War dead stands in the Confederate section of the cemetery, which contains the graves of many officers and enlisted men, many of whom died during the siege of Charleston.

Open to Public: *Grounds:* Winter 8am–5pm. Summer 8am–6pm. *Office:* Mon–Fri 9am–4pm.

Admission Fees: Free.

Visitor Services: None.

Regularly Scheduled Events: *Second Sat in May:* Confederate Memorial Day observance; *Second Fri and Sat in Oct:* Confederate Ghost Walk (purchase tickets in advance, $10).

Directions: From I-26: take exit 219B (Meeting St.), turn left at second light, and then turn right at Cunnington Ave. Cemetery is at the end of the block.

Cheraw

8 Site: CHERAW CIVIL WAR SITES, c/o Cheraw Visitors Bureau, 221 Market St., Cheraw, SC 29520, ☎ 843/537-8425

Description: Cheraw was the home of John Inglis, who introduced the resolution that South Carolina secede from the Union. This 18th-century river town became a place of refuge and a storehouse of valuables, including an official repository of C.S.A. gold. In March 1865, Gen. William T. Sherman visited Cheraw, with more Union troops than occupied any other South Carolina city. They found it "a pleasant town and an old one with the southern aristocratic bearing." Of particular interest are the St. David's Church (ca. 1770), used as a hospital during the Civil War, the cemetery with the earliest known Confederate monument (1867), and the Cheraw Lyceum Museum.

Open to Public: *Chamber of Commerce:* Mon–Thurs 9am–5pm, Fri 9am–noon.

Admission Fees: A free historic district tour brochure and keys to St. David's Church and the museum are available from the Cheraw Chamber of Commerce at 221 Market St.

Visitor Services: Tour brochure, museum, information, rest rooms, dining, lodging, shopping, and recreation in town.

Regularly Scheduled Events: *Apr:* Cheraw Spring Festival features historic home tours, a Confederate encampment and skirmish for the bridge, a period church service, lantern tours, arts, and entertainment.

Directions: From I-95 at Florence: take U.S. 52 north for 35 miles. Chamber of Commerce office is located at 221 Market St., which is also U.S. 1, U.S. 52, and SC 9.

Columbia

9 Site: SOUTH CAROLINA CONFEDERATE RELIC ROOM AND MUSEUM, 920 Sumter St., Columbia, SC 29201, ☎ 803/734-9813

Description: The military collection was established in 1895 to honor South Carolina's Confederate veterans. The museum contains exhibits from the American

Revolution through Desert Storm, with an emphasis on the Confederate period.

Open to Public: Mon–Fri 8:30am–5pm. First Sat each month: 10am–4pm. Closed holidays.

Admission Fees: Free.

Visitor Services: *Note:* Museum is not handicapped accessible.

Directions: Located in downtown Columbia at the corner of Sumter and Pendleton sts., on the University of South Carolina campus. Follow signs to USC.

---

10 **Site:** SOUTH CAROLINA STATE HOUSE, Gervais St. and Main St., Columbia, SC 29201, ☎ 803/734-2430

Description: The South Carolina State House, begun in 1855 and unfinished until after the Civil War, witnessed the Federal occupation of Columbia on February 17–18, 1865. Union artillery batteries seeking to find their range fired on this building from across the Congaree River, and bronze stars mark the places where their shells hit the state house. Gen. William T. Sherman's Federals also raised the United States flag over the unfinished building, looted the existing state house, and repealed the Ordinance of Secession. Several Civil War–related monuments are on the state house grounds.

Open to Public: Opening Summer 1998 after renovation; call for hours.

Admission Fees: Free.

Visitor Services: None.

Directions: From I-26, which becomes Elmwood Ave.: turn right onto Main St., which dead-ends at the state house at Gervais St. From I-77: travel south to 277, which becomes Bull St.; take Bull St. to Gervais St.; turn right on Gervais St.; proceed 3 blocks; and turn onto Main St. The state house is on the left at the end of Main St.

Ehrhardt

---

11 **Site:** RIVERS BRIDGE STATE PARK, Rte. 1, Box 190, Ehrhardt, SC 29081, ☎ 803/267-3675

Description: The only significant engagement in South Carolina during Gen. William T. Sherman's advance through the state in early 1865 took place on February 2–3 at the still-intact earthworks overlooking Rivers Bridge, on the Salkehatchie River Sherman's Federals, some 8,000 troops, were delayed briefly by 900 Confederates under the overall command of Gen. Lafayette McLaws. Sherman's troops soon outflanked the Confederate position upstream at Buford's Bridge and downstream at Broxton's Bridge, forcing a Confederate withdrawal and clearing the way for a Federal advance to Columbia.

Open to Public: Access to battlefield closes at 6pm Apr–Aug. Daily 9am–9pm. Sept–Oct: Thurs–Mon 9am–9pm. Nov–Mar: Thurs–Mon 9am–6pm.

Admission Fees: Free.

Visitor Services: Battlefield tours, camping, trails, rest rooms, handicapped access.

Regularly Scheduled Events: Annual battle reenactment and living history exhibit.

Directions: From I-95: take exit 57 (SC 64) west to SC 641 west. Follow signs to Rivers Bridge State Park.

Florence

12 **Site:** FLORENCE NATIONAL CEMETERY, 803 East National Cemetery Rd., Florence, SC 29501, ☎ 803/669-8783

Description: This national cemetery was established in 1865 and is associated with the nearby Union prisoner-of-war camp, Florence Stockade, which held as many as 12,000 prisoners between September 1864 and February 1865. The prisoner cemetery formed the nucleus of the new national cemetery. Some 3,000 Union soldiers who died in the prison, as many as 2,000 of them unknown, are buried here.

Open to Public: *Office:* Mon–Fri 8am–5pm. *Cemetery:* Daily from dawn to dusk.

Admission Fees: Free.

Visitor Services: None.

Directions: From I-95: travel on U.S. 52 (Lucas St.) to North Irby St. and turn right. North Irby St. becomes South Irby St. Continue on South Irby St. and turn left onto National Cemetery Rd.

Georgetown

13 **Site:** BATTERY WHITE, Belle Isle Yacht Club, Georgetown, SC 29440, ☎ 803/546-1423

Description: Battery White, a Confederate earthwork constructed in 1862 under the direction of Gen. John C. Pemberton, commander of the Departments of South Carolina and Georgia, was built on Mayrant's Bluff to defend the entrance to Winyah Bay and the Santee River.

Open to Public: Daily from dawn to dusk.

Admission Fees: Free.

Visitor Services: None.

Directions: From I-95: take Rt. 521, at Alcolu, east for 50 miles and cross Santee River; follow signs to Belle Isle Garden.

TENNESSEE

*T*HE OUTCOME OF THE CIVIL WAR WAS DECIDED in the heartland of the Confederacy known as the Western Theater. Tennessee, one of the strongholds of this region, was the last of the Southern states to secede from the Union, yet it would become the second most embattled, with more than 1,462 military encounters on its soil. One of the reasons for such intense fighting within Tennessee's borders was its strategic importance for the new Confederacy. Besides being an important defensive perimeter state, Tennessee was a leader among other Southern states in production of raw materials, manufacturing facilities, and agricultural goods, and it was the second most populated state in the Confederacy. Tennessee was a major link in the South's overall transportation system with more than a dozen railroads and four major rivers essential to the Confederacy for the placement of troops and material.

Splitting the Confederacy and destroying the South's natural resources were two of the Federal government's major war objectives. These could only be accomplished by gaining control of the Mississippi, Tennessee, and Cumberland rivers. The eventual capture of Tennessee's river and rail systems, and the Federal occupation of its major cities, thwarted Confederate hopes for victory.

by Fred M. Prouty, Administrator, Tennessee Wars Commission

---

*F*or More Information

For a free guide to Civil War sites in Tennessee, call ☎ **800/836-6200.**
    "Quiet Places: The Burial Sites of Civil War Generals in Tennessee," is available from the East Tennessee Historical Society, P.O. Box 1629, Knoxville, TN 37901-1629, ☎ **423/544-5732** ($10 + S/H). This book locates the burial sites and gives a brief history of the 63 Tennessee Civil War generals.

Chattanooga/Lookout Mountain

1 **Site:** BATTLES FOR CHATTANOOGA MUSEUM, 1110 E. Brow Rd., Lookout Mountain, TN 37350, ☎ 423/821-2812

Description: Experience the Battles for Chattanooga through the sights and sounds of a three-dimensional, 480 square-foot electronic battle map. More than 5,000 miniature soldiers and dramatic sound effects show troop movements during the 1863 battles.
Open to Public: Daily 8am–5pm. *Summer:* Daily 8:30am–8pm.

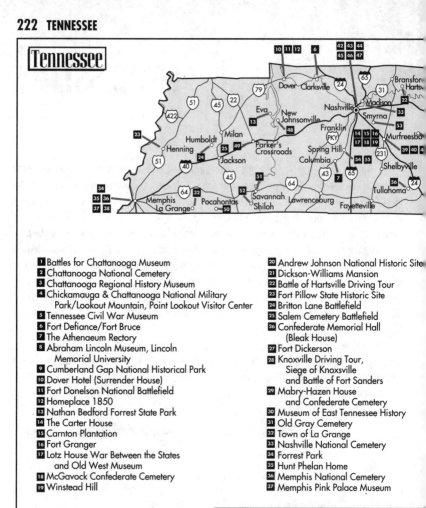

Tennessee

■1 Battles for Chattanooga Museum
■2 Chattanooga National Cemetery
■3 Chattanooga Regional History Museum
■4 Chickamauga & Chattanooga National Military
   Park/Lookout Mountain, Point Lookout Visitor Center
■5 Tennessee Civil War Museum
■6 Fort Defiance/Fort Bruce
■7 The Athenaeum Rectory
■8 Abraham Lincoln Museum, Lincoln
   Memorial University
■9 Cumberland Gap National Historical Park
■10 Dover Hotel (Surrender House)
■11 Fort Donelson National Battlefield
■12 Homeplace 1850
■13 Nathan Bedford Forrest State Park
■14 The Carter House
■15 Carnton Plantation
■16 Fort Granger
■17 Lotz House War Between the States
   and Old West Museum
■18 McGavock Confederate Cemetery
■19 Winstead Hill

■20 Andrew Johnson National Historic Site
■21 Dickson-Williams Mansion
■22 Battle of Hartsville Driving Tour
■23 Fort Pillow State Historic Site
■24 Britton Lane Battlefield
■25 Salem Cemetery Battlefield
■26 Confederate Memorial Hall
   (Bleak House)
■27 Fort Dickerson
■28 Knoxville Driving Tour,
   Siege of Knoxville
   and Battle of Fort Sanders
■29 Mabry-Hazen House
   and Confederate Cemetery
■30 Museum of East Tennessee History
■31 Old Gray Cemetery
■32 Town of La Grange
■33 Nashville National Cemetery
■34 Forrest Park
■35 Hunt Phelan Home
■36 Memphis National Cemetery
■37 Memphis Pink Palace Museum

For Tennessee Tourism information call 800/TENN-20(

Admission Fees: Adults $5, children $3.

Visitor Services: Gift shop, rest rooms, handicapped access.

Directions: From I-24: take exit 178 and follow signs to Point Park atop Lookout Mountain.

**2   Site: CHATTANOOGA NATIONAL CEMETERY, 1200 Bailey Ave., Chattanooga, TN 37404,
☎ 423/855-590**

Description: Chattanooga National Cemetery was established during the Civil War in December 1863 by an order from Gen. George Thomas to provide a proper burial for Union soldiers killed in battles around Chattanooga. Eight Andrews' Raiders are buried in the cemetery, four of whom were the first to receive the Medal of Honor.

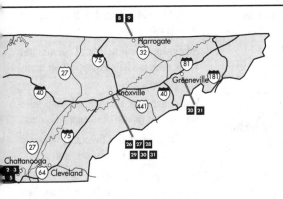

38 Mississippi River Museum at Mud Island
39 Fortress Rosecrans, Stones River
          National Battlefield
40 Oaklands Historic House Museum
41 Stones River National Battlefield
42 Battle of Nashville Driving Tour
43 Belle Meade Mansion
44 Belmont Mansion
45 Historic Travellers Rest
46 Mount Olivet Cemetery
47 Tennessee State Capitol and State Museum
48 Johnsonville State Historic Area
49 Parker's Crossroads Battlefield Self-Guided Tour
50 Davis Bridge Battlefield
51 Tennessee River Museum
52 Shiloh National Military Park
53 Sam Davis Home
54 Rippavilla Plantation
55 Tennessee Antebellum Trail
56 Tullahoma Campaign Civil War Trail

For information on Civil War sites in Tennesse, call 615/741-2158.

Open to Public: Daily 24 hours.

Admission Fees: Free.

Visitor Services: Information, rest rooms, handicapped access.

Regularly Scheduled Events: *May:* Memorial Day ceremony; *Nov:* Veterans Day ceremony.

Directions: From I-24: take the Fourth Ave. exit. Turn right at the first traffic light, turn left at the next traffic light, turn right at Holtzclaw Ave., and continue to the main entrance of the cemetery. Proceed into the cemetery and turn right to the cemetery office to pick up brochure.

3 **Site:** CHATTANOOGA REGIONAL HISTORY MUSEUM, 400 Chestnut St., Chattanooga, TN 37402, ☎ 423/265-3247

Description: The Chattanooga Regional History Museum has an extensive Civil War collection numbering more than 500 pieces, including a mountain howitzer; Grant's headquarter's chair; dozens of muskets, rifles, swords, knives, and pistols; projectiles; minié balls; various accouterments; uniforms; original photographs taken by R. M. Linn, George N. Bernard, and others; diaries and letters; and veterans' and National Park memorabilia. These artifacts are on display in the museum's permanent collection or stored in its archives.

Open to Public: Mon–Sat 10am–4:30pm, Sun 11am–4:30pm.

Admission Fees: Adults $2.50, children $1.50, seniors $1.75, groups (10 or more) $1.50/person.

Visitor Services: Museum, gift shop, information, rest rooms, handicapped access.

Regularly Scheduled Events: Programs on Civil War history. Call for schedule.

Directions: From I-24: take exit 178 to I-124 north, take exit 1C, and turn right on Chestnut St. Take first left turn into museum parking lot.

---

4 **Site:** CHICKAMAUGA AND CHATTANOOGA NATIONAL MILITARY PARK/LOOKOUT MOUNTAIN, Point Lookout Visitor Center, Lookout Mountain, TN 37350, ☎ 423/821-7786

Description: The Lookout Mountain district of Chickamauga and Chattanooga NMP preserves land on which the Battle of Lookout Mountain was fought, November 24, 1863, as part of the Battles for Chattanooga.

Open to Public: *Visitors center:* Daily 8am–4:45pm; summer 8am–5:45pm. *Point Park:* Daily 9am–sunset.

Admission Fees: Free.

Visitor Services: Museum, gift shop, rest rooms, handicapped access.

Regularly Scheduled Events: Anniversary of the Battles for Chattanooga: Living history regiment demonstrations; Special tours of Missionary Ridge and other battle sites. Call for schedule.

Directions: From I-24: take exit 74; turn onto U.S. 41 east, then onto State Hwy. 148 up Lookout Mountain. After ascending approximately 3 miles, turn right onto East Brow Rd. At the end of East Brow Rd. is Point Park.

---

5 **Site:** TENNESSEE CIVIL WAR MUSEUM, 3914 St. Elmo Ave., Chattanooga, TN 37409, ☎ 423/821-4954

Description: The museum interprets the Western Theater of the Civil War in and around the Tennessee Valley. It focuses on the common soldier and civilian of the Civil War with special exhibits and multimedia presentations on infantry, cavalry, artillery, specialty troops (medical, signal corps, etc.), African Americans in the Civil War, and the role of women in the war. A film provides an overview of the Civil War, and visitors can use the interactive Civil War Explorer to pursue specific areas of interest or search for an ancestor who fought in the war. The museum features a collection of guns, swords, soldiers' personal items, an archaeology exhibit, and more. A living history demonstration takes place every hour on the hour.

Open to Public: Planned museum opening in spring of 1998; Tues–Sun 10am–7pm.

Admission Fees: Adults $7.50, children 12 and under $5, children under 2 free, seniors and military $6.50.

Visitor Services: Museum, Civil War Explorer, living history, gift shop.

Directions: From I-24: take exit 178. Turn south on Broad St. toward Lookout Mountain. Bear left onto Tennessee Ave./Hwy. 58 toward the Incline Railway. Museum is .25 mile on the right, across from the Incline Railway at the base of Lookout Mountain.

Clarksville

6 Site: FORT DEFIANCE/FORT BRUCE, 200 South Second St., Clarksville, TN 37040, ☎ 615/648-5780

Description: During the capture of Clarksville, Fort Defiance was burned and abandoned by Confederate forces, leading to the fall of Nashville. The recapture of the city by Confederate troops in August 1862 renewed interest in the fort. During the rest of the war, the fort was commanded by Col. Sanders D. Bruce of Kentucky, for whom it was renamed.

Open to Public: Daily 8am–5pm.

Admission Fees: Free.

Visitor Services: For tours, call Clarksville-Montgomery Co. Museum at ☎ 615/648-5780.

Directions: From I-24 west from Clarksville: take exit 4, turn left onto Hwy. 79, and cross the bridge to Kraft St. Turn right (41A north) across bridge and turn left onto B St.; then turn left onto Walker St. and turn left at A St.

Columbia

7 Site: THE ATHENAEUM RECTORY, 808 Athenaeum St., Columbia, TN 38401, ☎ 615/381-4822

Description: The Athenaeum Rectory was headquarters for Generals Negley and Schofield during the Civil War. Gen. Nathan Bedford Forrest was a frequent visitor. The owner of the house, the Reverend F. G. Smith, the rector of a girls' school, outfitted a company of Confederate soldiers, the Maury Rifles. The Reverend Smith also designed a submarine and worked on a hot

air balloon for the South. The Rectory is owned and operated by APTA.

Open to Public: Feb–Dec: Tues–Sat 10am–4pm, Sun 1–4pm.

Admission Fees: Adults $3, children $1, seniors $2.

Visitor Services: Tours, museum, gift shop, rest rooms, handicapped access.

Regularly Scheduled Events: *First week-end in May:* Ladies' 1861 weekend; *First full week after the Fourth of July:* 1861 Girls' summer school; *Sept:* Tour of homes, by special reservation.

Directions: From I-65 South: take Saturn Pkwy. to Hwy. 31 south (take Columbia exit from Saturn Pkwy.). Travel approximately 8 miles into Columbia to West Seventh St. and turn right. Proceed 3 blocks to West Seventh St. Church of Christ. Turn left immediately past the church on Athanaeum St. The house is at the end of the street and is marked by a blue sign.

Cumberland Gap/Harrogate

8 **Site:** ABRAHAM LINCOLN MUSEUM, Lincoln Memorial University, Harrogate, TN 37752, ☎ 423/869-6235

Description: From his humble birth in rural Kentucky to the dramatic years of the Civil War and his tragic death, Lincoln's life is recounted at the Abraham Lincoln Museum. You are invited to experience the events of his time—the events that shaped the future of this country in its fight for an identity amid the problems of slavery and sectionalism. The Abraham Lincoln Museum is a monument to regional and national history that allows visitors to get a glimpse of the Great Emancipator.

Open to Public: Mon–Fri 9am–4pm, Sat 11am–4pm, Sun 1–4pm.

Admission Fees: Adults $2, children 6–12 $1, seniors 60 and over $1.50. Groups welcome.

Visitor Services: Gift shop, rest rooms, information.

Directions: From I-81: take Hwy. 25E exit and travel south through Middlesboro, KY, on Hwy. 25E. The museum is located on the campus of Lincoln Memorial University.

9 **Site:** CUMBERLAND GAP NATIONAL HISTORICAL PARK, U.S. 25E South, P.O. Box 1848, Middlesboro, KY 40965, ☎ 606/248-2817

Description: Cumberland Gap is the historic mountain pass on the Wilderness Road that opened the pathway for westward migration. During the Civil War, Cumberland Gap was first held by the South and then captured by Union troops. Each side held the Gap twice.

Open to Public: Mid-June–Labor Day: Daily 8am–6pm. Labor Day–mid-June: Daily 8am–5pm.

Admission Fees: Free.

Visitor Services: Gift shop, rest rooms, trails, museum, information, camping, handicapped access.

Directions: From I-75 at the Caryville exit: take Hwy. 63 to 25E, turn left on 25E, and travel 5 miles to the park.

Dover

10 **Site:** DOVER HOTEL (SURRENDER HOUSE), P.O. Box 434, Dover, TN 37058,
☎ 615/232-5348

Description: The Dover Hotel was the site where Gen. Ulysses S. Grant accepted the Confederate surrender of Gen. Simon Bolivar Buckner after the Battle of Fort Donelson in February 1862. The house is the only original surrender structure remaining from the Civil War.

Open to Public: June–Sept: Daily noon–4pm.

Admission Fees: Free.

Visitor Services: Information, rest rooms, handicapped access.

Directions: From I-24: exit onto Hwy. 79 south at Clarksville, continue 35 miles to Dover, and turn left at Petty St. The hotel is 2 blocks down on the left.

11 **Site:** FORT DONELSON NATIONAL BATTLEFIELD, P.O. Box 434, Dover, TN 37058,
☎ 615/232-5706

Description: Fort Donelson was built by the Confederates to control the Cumberland River. The fort was captured in February 1862 by the Union army under the command of General Grant, and victory secured Union control of the Cumberland River, Nashville, Clarksville, and most of middle Tennessee.

Open to Public: Daily 8am–4:30pm.

Admission Fees: Free.

Visitor Services: Trails, museum, gift shop, information, rest rooms, handicapped access.

Directions: From I-24: take Rte. 79 to Dover; follow signs.

12 **Site:** HOMEPLACE 1850. Mailing address: Land Between the Lakes, 100 Van Morgan Dr., Golden Pond, KY 42211-9001. Physical location: 13 miles north of Dover, TN, on the Trace in Land Between the Lakes, ☎ 502/924-2054

Description: Homeplace 1850 is a living history, open-air museum that re-creates life on a mid-19th-century Tennessee farm. Authentically furnished houses and barns, along with demonstrations of daily chores, bring to life a typical Civil War soldier's boyhood. In the Civil War, the Cumberland and Tennessee rivers were a gateway to Nashville and the all-important railroads that fed the Confederacy its troops and supplies. Forts Henry and Donelson, located nearby, were critical to the defense of the region. Homeplace 1850 considers the impact the war had on the farmers of Tennessee.

Open to Public: Mar: Wed–Sat 9am–5pm, Sun 10am–5pm; Apr–Oct: Mon–Sat 9am–5pm, Sun 10am–5pm; Nov: Wed–Sat 9am–5pm, Sun 10am–5pm.

Admission Fees: Age 13 and over $3.50, children 5–12 $2, children 4 and under free. Call for group rates.

Visitor Services: Rest rooms, picnic area, camping, hunting, fishing, Fort Henry trail, cycling, horseback riding.

Regularly Scheduled Events: *Second weekend in June:* River Sounds; *July:*

Independence Day; *Third weekend in Sept:* Harvest Celebration; *Third weekend in Oct:* Homeplace Wedding. Call for a complete schedule.

Directions: From I-24: take exit 31 or 4 in TN, or take exit 65 in KY. Follow signs to Land Between the Lakes.

Eva

13 Site: NATHAN BEDFORD FORREST STATE PARK, Star Rte., Eva, TN 38333, ☎ 901/584-6356

Description: The park was named for Gen. Nathan Bedford Forrest, the intrepid Confederate cavalry leader who on November 4, 1864, attacked and destroyed the Federal supply and munitions depot at (old) Johnsonville at the mouth of Trace Creek. His operations were concentrated along the river near the park and the town of Eva. The park features a monument to General Forrest and a map delineating the action at Johnsonville.

Open to Public: *Park:* Daily 24 hours. *Museum:* Apr–Nov: 8am–4:30pm.

Admission Fees: Free.

Visitor Services: Camping, trails, museum, gift shop, information, rest rooms, handicapped access.

Regularly Scheduled Events: *Third Sat in Sept:* Civil War reenactment; *Second Sat in Oct:* Folklife festival.

Directions: Located north of I-40 on the Tennessee River. From I-40: take exit 126; travel north on Hwy. 641 (15 miles) to Hwy. 70 in Camden; go around courthouse and take Hwy. 191 north for 9 miles to the park. There are signs from Camden.

Franklin

14 Site: THE CARTER HOUSE, 1140 Columbia Ave., Franklin, TN 37065, ☎ 615/791-1861

Description: Built in 1830, the Carter House was the location of the 1864 Battle of Franklin. Serving as a Federal command post before the battle and as a hospital after, the house and grounds are today preserved on 10 acres. In this evening battle lasting only 5 hours, more Confederate soldiers, including 13 generals, were lost than in Pickett's Charge at Gettysburg.

Open to Public: Apr–Oct: Mon–Sat 9am–5pm, Sun 1–5pm. Nov–Mar: Mon–Sat 9am–4pm, Sun 1–4pm.

Admission Fees: Adults $6, children 6–12 $2, seniors $4, groups (25 or more) $1 off each ticket.

Visitor Services: Museum, gift shop, film, rest rooms.

Regularly Scheduled Events: *First weekend in Dec:* Candlelight tour of homes.

Directions: From I-65: take exit 65 and go on Hwy. 96 into Franklin. At Courthouse Sq., turn left on Main St.; then turn left on Columbia Ave. (State Rte. 31 South). Entrance is off W. Fowlkes St.

---

15 **Site:** CARNTON PLANTATION, 1345 Carnton Lane, Franklin, TN 37064, ☎ 615/794-0903

Description: Possibly the bloodiest 5 hours of the Civil War took place at the Battle of Franklin. On November 30, 1864, Carnton was engulfed by Confederate troops moving toward well-entrenched Federal troops and a devastating battle. Later, the mansion housed hundreds of the more than 6,000 Confederate casualties leaving the floors permanently bloodstained. Adjoining the property is the McGavock Confederate Cemetery.

Open to Public: Apr–Oct: Mon–Sat 9am–5pm, Sun 1–5pm. Nov–Mar: Mon–Sat 9am–4pm, Sun 1–4pm.

Admission Fees: Adults $7, children 4–12 $3, seniors $5.

Visitor Services: Museum, gift shop, rest rooms.

Directions: From I-65: take exit 65 (Hwy. 96), turn left on Mack Hatcher Bypass, turn left to Lewisburg Ave. (431), and turn left on Carnton Lane.

---

16 **Site:** FORT GRANGER, P.O. Box 305, Franklin, TN 37065, ☎ 615/791-3217

Description: In February 1863, General Rosecrans, in command of the Federal troops in middle Tennessee, ordered Maj. Gen. Gordon Granger to fortify Franklin. On November 30, 1864, Confederate General Hood attacked. The fort was abandoned when the Federals withdrew to Nashville during the night, but was reoccupied 2 weeks later as Hood's defeated army withdrew from the state.

Open to Public: Daily 8am–5pm.

Admission Fees: Free.

Visitor Services: Tours may be arranged through the Carter House Museum by calling ☎ 615/791-1861.

Directions: From I-65: take Franklin exit (Hwy. 96) west toward downtown Franklin for 2.5 miles. Turn right into Pinkerton Park and follow the signs to the fort. (The park is on the right just before the bridge over the Harpeth River, before you get into downtown Franklin.)

---

17 **Site:** LOTZ HOUSE WAR BETWEEN THE STATES AND OLD WEST MUSEUM, 1111 Columbia Ave., Franklin, TN 37064, ☎ 615/791-6533

Description: The Lotz House features rare Confederate and Union artifacts as well as Old West and Native American items. The house was built in 1858 by German woodworker Albert Lotz and still features much of his handiwork. Lotz House was used as a hospital after the Battle of Franklin.

Open to Public: Mon–Sat 9am–5pm, Sun noon–5pm.

Admission Fees: Adults $5, children $1.50, seniors $4. Groups (20 or more): Adults $4, seniors $3.

Visitor Services: Museum, gift shop, rest rooms.

Regularly Scheduled Events: *June 3:* Confederate Memorial Day celebration; *Nov 30:* Commemoration of the Battle of Franklin.

Directions: From I-65: take exit 65; travel west on Hwy. 96 to Franklin's town square; turn left (around square) on Main St. and proceed to the second light. Travel south approximately .25 mile on Hwy. 31 (Columbia Ave.) to 1111 Columbia Ave. House is on the left; look for signs and a cannon on the front porch.

---

18 **Site:** MCGAVOCK CONFEDERATE CEMETERY. Mailing address: 611 W. Main, Genealogy Dept., Franklin, TN 37064

Description: The largest private Confederate cemetery in the nation and a National Historic Landmark, this site adjoins the Carnton Plantation property. The cemetery is maintained by the Franklin UDC. Also visit the Confederate monument in the Franklin town square, unveiled by the UDC on November 30, 1899, which memorializes the Southern men who fought in the Battle of Franklin on November 30, 1864.

Open to Public: Daily 24 hours.

Admission Fees: Free.

Visitor Services: Informational sign, tours available by request. A booklet about the cemetery is available for $5 from the address above and at Carnton Plantation.

Regularly Scheduled Events: *First Sat in June:* Illumination; *First Sun in June:* Jefferson Davis Memorial Service.

Directions: From I-65 north: take exit 61; turn left on Goose Creek Bypass; at a 4-way stop, turn right on Lewisburg Pike; proceed to Carnton Lane and turn left; follow signs to cemetery. From I-65 south: take exit 65 (Hwy. 96); take Hwy. 96 to Mack Hatcher Bypass and turn left; proceed to Lewisburg Ave. and turn left; travel to Carnton Lane and turn left; follow signs to cemetery.

---

19 **Site:** WINSTEAD HILL. Mailing address: 4439 Peytonsville Rd., Franklin, TN 37064, ☎ 615/791-6533

Description: General Hood's troops formed on Winstead Hill before the Battle of Franklin. A memorial to the Army of the Tennessee stands on the hill today. The overlook features a large military map and memorials to the Confederate generals who died in the battle in 1864.

Open to Public: Daily 24 hours.

Admission Fees: Free.

Visitor Services: Access to the monument requires a climb up stairs to the top of the hill.

Regularly Scheduled Events: The Battle of Franklin Memorial March starts here and concludes at the Carter House. Call for information.

Directions: From I-65: take exit 65 and travel west on Hwy. 96 for .25 mile to Mack Hatcher Bypass. Turn left and proceed to the end of the bypass; then turn left on Hwy. 31. Winstead is the first hill on the right.

Greeneville

20 Site: ANDREW JOHNSON NATIONAL HISTORIC SITE, P.O. Box 1088, Greeneville, TN 37744-1088, ☎ 423/638-3551 or 423/638-1326

Description: This 16-acre site preserves two homes; the tailor shop; and the cemetery where President Andrew Johnson lived, worked, and is buried. When Tennessee seceded from the Union, Johnson became an avid opponent of secession and was appointed military governor of Tennessee by President Lincoln in 1862.

Open to Public: Daily 9am–5pm. Tours of the homestead at 9:30am, 10:30am, 11:30am, 1:30pm, 2:30pm, 3:30pm, and 4:30pm. Closed Thanksgiving Day, Christmas Day, and New Year's Day.

Admission Fees: $2 for ages 18–61, under 18 and over 61 free.

Visitor Services: Visitors center, bookstore, rest rooms, museum.

Directions: From I-81: follow 11E north if traveling north or TN 172 if traveling south. Follow directional signs to the visitors center, located at the corner of College and Depot sts. in Greeneville. Ranger will direct visitors to the homestead and national cemetery.

21 Site: DICKSON-WILLIAMS MANSION, Church and Irish streets, Greeneville, TN 37745, ☎ 423/787-7746

Description: This mansion, built between 1815 and 1821, hosted many notables: Marquis de Lafayette, Henry Clay, and Presidents Jackson and Polk. During the war, it served as headquarters for both Union and Confederate officers while they were in Greeneville. It was in this house that Gen. John Hunt Morgan, the "Rebel Raider," spent his last night, before he was killed in the garden on September 4, 1864. The room where

General Morgan slept contains the original furniture from when he occupied the room.

Open to Public: By appointment; call ☎ 423/638-4111.

Admission Fees: Adults $3, children $1.

Visitor Services: Tours.

Regularly Scheduled Events: *Oct:* Reenactment of Battle of Blue Springs; *Dec:* Christmas tours.

Directions: From I-81 northbound: take exit 23, turn right onto 11-E (4-lane), continue for 12 miles, and takeGreeneville Business exit (exit right). Turn right on Summer St.; at the third traffic light, turn left onto Irish St. The mansion is 2 blocks on the right at Church and Irish sts. From I-81 southbound: take exit 36, turn left onto Baileyton Rd. (State Rd. 172), proceed 10–11 miles to the first traffic light, and turn right onto Main St. Continue on Main St. through the first traffic light; turn right at the second traffic light onto Church St. The mansion is 1 block on the left.

Hartsville

 Site: BATTLE OF HARTSVILLE DRIVING TOUR, c/o Battle of Hartsville Preservation, 105 East Main St., Hartsville, TN 37074, ☎ 615/374-9243

Description: The Battle of Hartsville has been called "the most successfully executed cavalry raid of the War Between the States." From this battle, Col. John Hunt Morgan received his commission to Brigadier General. The 17-stop driving tour includes river crossings, rendezvous points, homes, buildings used as hospitals where Morgan rushed 1,834 prisoners after the 75-minute battle, and a cemetery.

Open to Public: Daily during daylight hours. *Chamber of Commerce office:* Mon–Fri 8:30am–4:30pm.

Admission Fees: Free.

Visitor Services: Informational brochure available from the Hartsville-Trousdale Co. Chamber of Commerce, 200 E. Main St., Ste. 11, Hartsville, TN 37074 (located in the courthouse); also available at Heath's Furniture and Appliance at 105 E. Main.

Directions: From I-40 at Lebanon: take Hwy. 231 to Hwy. 25. Turn right on Hwy. 25 and proceed to Hartsville. At the first traffic light, turn right on Broadway. Proceed 3 blocks and turn left on Main St. The Chamber of Commerce is located at 200 E. Main.

Henning

23 **Site:** FORT PILLOW STATE HISTORIC SITE, Rte. 2, P.O. Box 109-D, Henning, TN 38041, ☎ 901/738-5581

Description: Federal forces captured this important Confederate river defense in 1862. On April 12, 1864, Confederate Gen. N. B. Forrest attacked the fort and demanded immediate surrender of the garrison, but he was refused. The fort was then stormed and captured. Because of high Union casualties and the presence of black troops, controversy surrounding this battle still exists today.

Open to Public: *Grounds:* Daily 8am–10pm. *Visitors center:* Mon–Fri 8am–4:30pm.

Admission Fees: Free.

Visitor Services: Camping, trails, information, museum, gift shop, rest rooms, handicapped access.

Regularly Scheduled Events: *Every second weekend in Apr:* Living History Weekend; *First weekend in Nov:* Civil War lectures.

Directions: From I-40: take Brownsville exit, Hwy. 19, to Hwy. 51; travel south; and turn left to Hwy. 87 west. Follow signs to the park.

Humboldt

24 **Site:** BRITTON LANE BATTLEFIELD, c/o 461 Sanders Bluff Rd., Humboldt, TN 38343, ☎ 901/784-4227 or 901/935-2209

Description: On September 1, 1862, Confederate Col. William H. Jackson's 7th Tennessee Cavalry, Forrest's Brigade, attacked the 20th and 30th U.S. Infantry, Cavalry, and Artillery under the command of Colonel Dennis, near Jackson, Tennessee. The Battle of Britton's Lane resulted in the capture of a large Union wagon train, two pieces of artillery, and 213 prisoners. Monuments mark the site along with a mass grave of Confederates killed in the action. An extant cabin on the site was used as a Federal and a Confederate hospital site. After the battle, 87 Union prisoners were imprisoned in the Denmark Presbyterian Church near Britton Lane Battlefield. The

structure still contains graffiti left by the Union prisoners.

Open to Public: Daily 24 hours.

Admission Fees: Free.

Visitor Services: Trails, museum, information, handicapped access.

Regularly Scheduled Events: *Throughout the year:* Reenactments, living history, gun shows, Civil War church services. Call for information.

Directions: From I-40: take exit 76 (Hwy. 223 south) and travel on Hwy. 223 south 9 miles to Denmark. Turn left at Denmark Church onto Britton Lane Rd.

Jackson

25 **Site:** SALEM CEMETERY BATTLEFIELD, 35 Cotton Grove Rd., Jackson, TN 38301, ☎ 901/423-0512 (Mon–Fri) or 901/424-1279 (Sat–Sun)

Description: A self-guided tour with brochures is available at the cemetery's main gate. The site has two large monuments, flag pole, and battle map inlay showing the layout of the battle. A historical marker identifies the site. A battle occurred nearby on December 19, 1862, between General Forrest's cavalry and Union troops. Approximately 1,000 men were engaged in the 2-hour battle.

Open to Public: Daily during daylight hours.

Admission Fees: Free.

Visitor Services: Tour brochure.

Directions: From I-40 east of Jackson, TN: take Christmasville Rd. exit and travel south on Paul D. Wright Dr. (look for Salem Battlefield signs). Proceed 4 miles to Bendix Dr. and turn left. Proceed 2 miles to Cotton Grove Rd., turn left, and travel .75 mile. Cemetery and battlefield entrance are on the left.

Knoxville

26 | **Site:** CONFEDERATE MEMORIAL HALL (BLEAK HOUSE), P.O. Box 15012, Knoxville, TN 37901, ☎ 800/727-8045 or 423/523-2316

Description: Bleak House is a Victorian mansion built in 1858 by prominent Knoxvillian Robert H. Armstrong, using slave labor to mold the bricks on-site. During the Siege of Knoxville and the Battle of Fort Sanders in November and December 1863, the home served as headquarters for Confederate Generals James Longstreet and Lafayette McLaws. Three soldiers using the house's tower as a sharpshooters post were killed here by Federal cannon fire. A comrade sketched their likenesses on the wall of the tower. Two cannonballs are still embedded in the walls. Artillery was also used on the lawn to fire on the Federals.

Open to Public: Tues–Fri 1–4pm. Group tours by appointment.

Admission Fees: Adults $3, children $1.50, seniors $2.

Visitor Services: Museum, tours, gift shop, rest rooms.

Regularly Scheduled Events: *Dec:* Christmas open house; *Apr:* Extended hours and gardens open during Knoxville dogwood arts festival.

Directions: From I-40: take Kingston Pike exit and turn right (west) on Kingston Pike. Confederate Memorial Hall is on left at 3148 Kingston Pike.

27 | **Site:** FORT DICKERSON, P.O. Box 15012, Knoxville, TN 37901, ☎ 800/727-8045 or 423/523-2316

Description: Fort Dickerson was one of 16 earthen forts and battery emplacements built by the Federal army to protect Knoxville during the Civil War. The fort, atop a 300-foot-high ridge across the Tennessee River from Knoxville, was begun in November 1863 and completed in January or February 1864. The position was attacked by Confederate cavalry under Gen. Joseph Wheeler on November 15, 1863, but the assault was canceled because of the formidable terrain, artillery, and unexpected strong force guarding the approaches to Knoxville. There is a highway marker at the fort; future plans call for this to be a part of a Knoxville Civil War driving tour.

Open to Public: Daily during daylight hours.

Admission Fees: Free.

Visitor Services: None.

Directions: From I-40: take the Downtown or Hwy. 441 exit, go south on Hwy. 441 (also called Henley St. and then Chapman Hwy. after the bridge), cross the Henley St. bridge, and continue for approximately 1 mile. A Gulf station is on the left; the drive to the fort is on the right and is marked by a sign.

---

28 Site: KNOXVILLE DRIVING TOUR, Siege of Knoxville and Battle of Fort Sanders, c/o Knoxville Visitors Welcome Center, 810 Clinch Ave., Knoxville, TN 37901, ☎ 423/523-2316

Description: This driving tour features sites associated with the November 1863 attempt by Confederate Gen. James Longstreet to capture Knoxville and the army of Union Gen. Ambrose E. Burnside. Tour sites include Longstreet's headquarters, Fort Dickerson, cemeteries, hospitals, the site of the mortal wounding of Gen. William P. Sanders, and the site of the unsuccessful attack on Fort Sanders.

Open to Public: *Knoxville Visitors Welcome Center:* Mon–Fri 8:30am–5pm, Sat 10am–4pm.

Admission Fees: Free.

Visitor Services: Brochure for the self-guided driving tour is available at the Knoxville Visitors Welcome Center in the Candy Factory downtown, or by writing to the address listed above.

Directions: The Knoxville Visitors Welcome Center is located off I-75 in downtown Knoxville in the Candy Factory. Tour brochure includes map and driving directions.

---

29 Site: MABRY-HAZEN HOUSE AND CONFEDERATE CEMETERY, 1711 Dandridge Ave., Knoxville, TN 37915, ☎ 423/522-8661

Description: The Mabry-Hazen House was occupied by Union and Confederate troops alternately. From 1861 to 1863, Knoxville was occupied by Confederate troops under Gen. Felix Zollicoffer, who set up headquarters in the home. In 1863, Knoxville and the Mabry home were taken over by Union troops while the family continued to live upstairs. The grounds were fortified, and Mrs. Mabry's sketch of the trenches surrounding the house survives. Hundreds of artifacts help create a personal picture of family life during the Civil War and Reconstruction. The Knoxville Confederate Cemetery contains the remains of 1,600 Confederate troops plus 60 Union soldiers killed between 1861 and 1864. The centerpiece of the cemetery is a 12-foot-square, 48-foot-high monument dedicated in 1891.

Open to Public: Mon–Fri 10am–5pm, Sat 1–5pm. Open Sun for holidays and special events only.

Admission Fees: Adults $3, children $1.50, seniors $2.50, groups $2.50/person.

Visitor Services: Museum, gift shop, information, rest rooms, limited handicapped access.

Regularly Scheduled Events: *Spring:* Civil War reenactment weekend; *June:* Confederate Memorial Day observance; *Dec:* Christmas tour (Victorian holiday decor).

Directions: From I-40: take exit 388 to James White Pkwy., take first exit off Pkwy., and turn left on Summit Hill Dr. At second traffic light, Summit Hill Dr. becomes Dandridge Ave. Turn left on Rosedale and take the first gravel drive to the right.

---

30 **Site:** MUSEUM OF EAST TENNESSEE HISTORY, P.O. Box 1629, 600 Market St., Knoxville, TN 37901, ☎ 423/544-5732

Description: The museum interprets and preserves the history of East Tennessee and its people. The museum dedicates a section of "The East Tennesseeans" permanent exhibit to the crucial role the Civil War played in this region's history. A Union stronghold in a secessionist state, East Tennessee has a unique story to tell. The historical society attempts to give a balanced presentation relating the events and debate of the time, while focusing on the East Tennessee men, women, and children who lived during the period.

Open to Public: Tues–Sat 10am–4pm, Sun 1–5pm.

Admission Fees: Free.

Visitor Services: Museum, gift shop, information, rest rooms, handicapped access.

Regularly Scheduled Events: The East Tennessee Historical Society holds lectures once a month, brown bag lunches in summer, and evening events in autumn and spring; call for details.

Directions: From I-275 south: take "Downtown" exit to Summit Hill exit, turn left at traffic light, and proceed through Henley St. and Summit Hill intersection. Turn right on Locust, turn left on Union, turn right on Market, and proceed to museum at corner of Market and Clinch. From I-40 west: take exit #387 to Ailor Ave., turn right on Western Ave., and proceed on Western to Henley St. (Western Ave. becomes Summit Hill at this intersection.) Turn right on Locust, turn left on Union, turn right on Market, and proceed to museum at corner of Market and Clinch. From I-40 east: take exit #388, following Rte. 62 to Western Ave./Summit Hill. At traffic light, turn left on Western Ave./Summit Hill intersection. Turn right on Locust, turn left on Union, turn right on Market, and proceed to museum at corner of Market and Clinch.

---

31 **Site:** OLD GRAY CEMETERY, P.O. Box 806, Knoxville, TN 37901. Physical address: 543 North Broadway, ☎ 423/522-1424

Description: Old Gray Cemetery reflects the sympathies of East Tennessee during the Civil War with gravestones and sculpted monuments honoring both Union and Confederate dead. Col. Henry M. Ashby, Gen. William R. Caswell, and Tennessee wartime governor William G. "Parson" Brownlow are among those buried in this Victorian cemetery in the heart of Knoxville.

Open to Public: Daily from dawn to dusk.

Admission Fees: Free.

Visitor Services: Self-guided tour brochure.

Directions: From I-275: take exit 1A east to Baxter Ave., proceed up the hill to N. Central Ave., turn right on N. Central, and proceed .4 mile to N. Broadway. Turn right and travel 2 blocks. Old Gray is opposite St. John's Lutheran Church.

La Grange

32 **Site:** TOWN OF LA GRANGE, P.O. Box 621, La Grange, TN 38046, ☎ 901/878-1246

Description: La Grange was occupied by Federal troops from 1862 until the Civil War ended. In 1863, Grierson's Raid originated here. Immanuel Episcopal Church was a hospital. See the birthplace of Lucy Holcombe Pickens, the "Queen of the Confederacy," and many antebellum homes. Pick up brochure for the driving and walking tour.

Open to Public: Daily during daylight hours. Pick up driving tour brochure at Cogbill's Store and Museum (☎ 901/878-1235) or city hall (☎ 901/878-1246). Cogbill's Store and Museum is open Thurs–Sun except in winter, when it is open only on Sun 1–5pm; call ahead for schedule.

Admission Fees: Free; brochure costs $3.

Visitor Services: *In town:* gas, food, museum (in Cogbill's Store), gift shop, antique shop.

Directions: From I-40: take exit 56; drive south toward Somerville on TN Hwy. 76, which intersects TN Hwy. 57 in Moscow. Turn east onto TN Hwy. 57 and drive approximately 10 miles to La Grange. Hwy. 57 becomes Main St. Cogbill's Store and the city hall are located on the corner of Main St. and La Grange Rd.

Madison

33 **Site:** NASHVILLE NATIONAL CEMETERY, 1420 Gallatin Rd. South, Madison, TN 37115-4619, ☎ 615/736-2839

Description: In 1867, 16,489 interments were brought from all over the area and reinterred in the Nashville National Cemetery. Of these, 4,156 are unknown.

Open to Public: *Office:* Mon–Fri 8am–4:30pm. *Grounds:* Daily during daylight hours.

Admission Fees: Free.

Visitor Services: Information, restrooms.

Directions: From I-65 at Nashville: take I-65 north and exit at Briley Pkwy. Follow Briley Pkwy. 2 miles to Gallatin Rd. and take second exit (Gallatin Rd. North, Madison). The national cemetery is located .25 mile on the left.

Memphis

34 **Site:** FORREST PARK, P.O. Box 241813, Memphis, TN 38124, ☎ 901/576-4500 (ask for county historian)

Description: This park in downtown Memphis is the site where Gen. Nathan Bedford Forrest is buried. The park features a large, bronze equestrian statue of the general that was erected in 1905, as well as the granite monument that serves as the grave marker for the general and his wife, Mary Montgomery Forrest. After the Civil War, General Sherman said of Forrest, "He was the most remarkable man our Civil War produced on either side." General Lee, when asked to identify the greatest soldier under his command, said, "a man I have never seen sir . . . Forrest." The monument is located 2 blocks from the scene of Forrest's death in 1877.

Open to Public: Daily 24 hours.

Admission Fees: Free.

Visitor Services: Trails, handicapped access.

Regularly Scheduled Events: *Sun closest to July 13:* Forrest's birthday celebration.

Directions: From I-240 north: take the Union Ave. westbound exit. Forrest Park is on the north side of Union between Dunlap and Manassas sts. From I-240 south and I-40: take the Madison St. westbound exit. Forrest Park is on the south side of Madison between Dunlap and Manassas sts.

35 **Site:** HUNT PHELAN HOME, 533 Beale St., Memphis, TN 38104, ☎ 901/344-3166

Description: Built from 1828 to 1832 by slaves and Chickasaw Indians, this home hosted many well-known Tennesseans, including President Andrew Jackson, President Jefferson Davis, and Gen. Nathan Bedford Forrest. Union Gen. Ulysses S. Grant used the home as his headquarters and planned the Battle of Vicksburg in the library. After the war, the first school in the county for African Americans was built on the property by the Freedmen's Bureau. A large family archive contains many Civil War–related papers and books.

Open to Public: Jan–Mar and Sept–Dec: Mon, Thurs, Fri, and Sat 10am–4pm; Sun noon–4pm. Apr–May: Mon–Sat 10am–4pm, Sun noon–4pm. June–Aug: Mon–Fri 10am–4pm, Sat 10am–5pm, Sun noon–5pm. Closed Thanksgiving Day, Christmas Eve, Christmas Day, and New Year's Day.

Admission Fees: Adults $10, children 5–12 $6, children under 5 free, seniors and students $9. Call for group rates.

Visitor Services: Museum, gift shop, information, rest rooms, handicapped access to first floor of home and gardens.

Directions: Located at 533 Beale St., on the corner of Beale and Lauderdale. From I-240: take Union St. exit and proceed west on Union St. to Lauderdale St. Turn left on Lauderdale St., continue to Beale St., and turn right on Beale St. The home is on the left.

36 **Site:** MEMPHIS NATIONAL CEMETERY, 3568 Townes Ave., Memphis, TN 38122,
☎ 901/386-8311

Description: Strong Union land and river forces captured Memphis on June 6, 1862, and with the surrender, the city became the location of several Federal hospitals serving the Western theater of war. The dead from these hospitals were buried in private cemeteries and in 1866 were reinterred in the Mississippi National Cemetery. In 1867, the name was changed to the Memphis National Cemetery. Of the 13,965 soldiers buried at this site, 8,866 are unknown. Other burials include those from the USS *Sultana*, which sank in April, 1865, and ranks as one of the nation's deadliest maritime disasters with 1,700 soldiers and crew lost.

Open to Public: *Office:* Mon–Fri 8am–4:30pm. *Grounds:* Daily 24 hours.

Admission Fees: Free.

Visitor Services: Information, rest rooms.

Regularly Scheduled Events: *May:* Memorial Day program; *Nov:* Veterans Day program.

Directions: From I-240: take exit 8B/Jackson Ave. and travel south approximately 2 miles. After crossing railroad viaduct, take first left onto Townes Ave. Cemetery gate is at the intersection of Jackson and Townes aves.

37 **Site:** MEMPHIS PINK PALACE MUSEUM, 3050 Central Ave., Memphis, TN 38111-3399,
☎ 901/320-6320

Description: The Civil War exhibit displays artifacts, documents, and photographs of civilian Memphis; arms and equipment; and currency. It provides material on the war around Memphis, the battle of Memphis, Gen. Nathan Bedford Forrest, and Confederate veterans. A vignette of an artillery crew serving an ordnance rifle is the centerpiece of the exhibit. The Civil War exhibit is part of a larger museum.

Open to Public: Memorial Day–Labor Day: Mon–Wed 9am–5pm, Thurs 9am–9pm, Fri–Sat 9am–10pm, Sun noon–5pm. Day after Labor Day–day before Memorial Day:

Mon–Wed 9am–4pm, Thurs 9am–8pm, Fri–Sat 9am–9pm, Sun noon–5pm.

Admission Fees: Adults $5.50, children $4. Call for group rates.

Visitor Services: Food, museum, gift shop, information, rest rooms, handicapped access.

Directions: From I-40: take Sam Cooper Blvd. to the Highland exit and travel south on Highland for 2 miles to the Central Ave. intersection. Turn west on Central and continue for 1 mile. The museum is located on the north side of Central Ave.

38 **Site:** MISSISSIPPI RIVER MUSEUM AT MUD ISLAND, 125 North Front St., Memphis, TN 38103-1713, ☎ 901/576-7232

Description: Within the Mississippi River Museum are five galleries dedicated to the significant role of the Mississippi River in the Civil War. A life-size replica of a Union City ironclad gunboat is featured. Also included are a half-dozen boat models, displays of Civil War uniforms, field equipment, weapons, and personal items.

Open to Public: *Spring:* Tues–Sun 10am–5pm. *Summer:* Daily 10am–8pm. *Autumn:* Tues–Sun 10am–5pm. Closed Nov–early Apr; call for dates.

Admission Fees: Adults $6, children $4, seniors $4.

Visitor Services: Museum, gift shop, information, rest rooms, handicapped access.

Directions: From I-40 east: take Front St. exit, turn right (south), and proceed 2 blocks.

Murfreesboro

39 **Site:** FORTRESS ROSECRANS, STONES RIVER NATIONAL BATTLEFIELD, 3501 Old Nashville Hwy., Murfreesboro, TN 37129-3094, ☎ 615/893-9501

Description: After the Confederates had withdrawn from Murfreesboro at the conclusion of the Battle of Stones River in January 1863, the Federal army, under Gen. William Rosecrans, began fortifying Murfrees-boro. Fortress Rosecrans became one of the Union's largest earthen fortifications of the Civil War. The features that remain include Redoubt Brannan, Lunettes Palmer and Thomas, and Curtain Wall #2.

Open to Public: Redoubt Brannan and Lunette Thomas are being readied for visitor access. Lunette Palmer and Curtain Wall #2 are open during daylight hours. Closed December 25.

Admission Fees: Free.

Visitor Services: Trail, exhibits, handicapped access.

Directions: From I-24: take exit 78B and turn left on Golf Lane into the Old Fort Park of Murfreesboro. See Park officials for the location of Redoubt Brannan.

40 **Site:** OAKLANDS HISTORIC HOUSE MUSEUM, 900 North Maney Ave., Murfreesboro, TN 37130, ☎ 615/893-0022

Description: Oaklands was one of the largest plantations in Rutherford County during the Civil War. It was the home of the Maney family, one of the wealthiest families in the county. The plantation was used by the Union army in June of 1862 as a camp. On July 13, 1862, Confederate Gen. Nathan Bedford Forrest and his cavalry raided the city of Murfreesboro and recaptured it. The surrender was negotiated at Oaklands.

Open to Public: Tues–Sat 10am–4pm, Sun 1–4pm.

Admission Fees: Adults $4, children $2.50, seniors $3, groups $3/person.

Visitor Services: Museum, gift shop, information.

Regularly Scheduled Events: *May:* Annual antique show; *Dec:* Candlelight tour of homes.

Directions: From I-24: take exit 81B, proceed to third traffic light, turn right on Broad St., and go to next traffic light. Turn left on Maney Ave. and follow Maney Ave. to Oaklands.

---

41 **Site: STONES RIVER NATIONAL BATTLEFIELD, 3501 Old Nashville Hwy., Murfreesboro, TN 37129, ☎ 615/893-9501**

Description: Stones River National Battlefield commemorates the battle that began a Federal offensive to trisect the Confederacy. More than 81,000 soldiers fought in this midwinter battle. With more than 23,000 casualties, it was one of the bloodiest battles fought west of the Appalachians. The Union victory allowed the army to construct Fortress Rosecrans and set the stage for the advance on Chattanooga.

Open to Public: Daily 8am–5pm. Closed Christmas Day.

Admission Fees: Free.

Visitor Services: Museum, gift shop, information, rest rooms, handicapped access.

Regularly Scheduled Events: *May:* Memorial Day ceremony; *Weekend following July 4:* Artillery encampment weekend; *Weekend closest to Dec 31 and Jan 1–2:* Anniversary programs.

Directions: From I-24: take exit 78B onto Hwy. 96 and take Hwy. 96 east to intersection with Hwy. 41/70. Turn left on Hwy. 41 north and travel about 2 miles to Thompson Lane. Turn left, exit onto Old Nashville Hwy., and follow signs.

Nashville

42 **Site: BATTLE OF NASHVILLE DRIVING TOUR, c/o Metropolitan Historical Commission, 209 Tenth Ave. South, Ste. 414, Nashville, TN 37203, ☎ 615/862-7970**

Description: Historians have called the Battle of Nashville one of the most decisive of the Civil War. Union forces had held this strategically important city since February 1862. After losing Atlanta to Sherman, Gen. John Bell Hood moved his Army of Tennessee north, hoping to reclaim Nashville. On December 15–16, 1864, the Confederacy's last offensive action ended in the loss of the Army of Tennessee as an effective fighting force. The tour brochure includes a map and pertinent background information.

Open to Public: Daily from dawn to dusk.

Admission Fees: Free.

Visitor Services: Information.

Directions: Write or call for brochure at the address listed above or pick up a brochure at the Cumberland Science Museum. To Cumberland Museum: From I-65: take Wedgewood Ave. exit. Proceed west on Wedgewood Ave. and turn right onto Eighth Ave. South; proceed to the next traffic light and turn right on Chestnut; cross over the interstate to Ft. Negley Blvd. and turn left onto Ft. Negley Blvd. Fort Negley is on the right. Continue to curve around on this road, and the Cumberland Science Museum is just past Fort Negley on the right.

---

43 **Site:** BELLE MEADE PLANTATION, 5025 Harding Rd., Nashville, TN 37205, ☎ 615/356-0501

Description: The Belle Meade plantation house was built in 1853 by William J. Harding. When Tennessee entered the Civil War, Governor Isham G. Harris appointed Harding to the Military and Financial Board. During the Battle of Nashville in December 1864, Confederate Gen. James R. Chalmers made his headquarters at Belle Meade. Bullet scars from a cavalry skirmish on the front lawn are visible on the limestone columns of the front porch. After the war, Belle Meade became one of the nation's finest stables for thoroughbred horses.

Open to Public: Mon–Sat 9am–5pm, Sun 1–5pm.

Admission Fees: Adults $8, children $3, seniors $7.50, groups $7/person.

Visitor Services: Tours, museum, gift shop, information, rest rooms, handicapped access on first floor.

Regularly Scheduled Events: *Third weekend in Sept:* Fall Fest (antiques, music, crafts, food, and children's activities*); Mid-Nov–New Year:* Plantation Christmas.

Directions: From I-440: take 70S exit and proceed approximately 4 miles on 70S. Belle Meade is on the left.

---

44 **Site:** BELMONT MANSION, 1900 Belmont Blvd., Nashville, TN 37212, ☎ 615/386-4459

Description: Belmont Mansion was built by Joseph and Adelicia Acklen in 1853 and enlarged between 1859 and 1860. During the Civil War, the house served as headquarters for General Stanley and for Gen. Thomas J. Wood, commander of the Fourth Army Corps. At Belmont, Wood gave orders to all division commanders for the first day of the Battle of Nashville.

Open to Public: June–Aug: Mon–Sat 10am–4pm, Sun 2–5pm. Sept–May: Tues–Sat 10am–4pm.

Admission Fees: Adults $5, children $2, children under 6 free, seniors $4.50, groups $4.50/person.

Visitor Services: Tours, gift shop, rest rooms, handicapped access.

Regularly Scheduled Events: *Day after Thanksgiving–Dec:* Christmas at Belmont.

Directions: From I-65: take Wedgewood exit and travel west on Wedgewood Ave. Turn left on Magnolia, turn left onto 18th Ave., and turn left onto Acklen.

---

45 **Site:** HISTORIC TRAVELLERS REST, 636 Farrell Pkwy., Nashville, TN 37220, ☎ 615/832-8197

Description: This is one of the oldest residences in Nashville, built in 1799 by Judge John Overton. In the Civil War, Union troops camped on the grounds during the Federal occupation of Nashville. For 2 weeks before the Battle of Nashville, Travellers Rest was the headquarters of Confederate Comdr. Gen. John Bell Hood. Riding from Murfreesboro to confer with Hood, Gen. Nathan Bedford Forrest spent the night on December 11, 1864. During the second day of the Battle of Nashville, December 16, 1864, Federal forces charged the Confederate right flank on Peach Orchard Hill, located on the Overton property and within sight of the house. It was the scene of several charges by the U.S. Colored Infantry.

Open to Public: Tues–Sat 10am–5pm, Sun 1–5pm. Last tour at 4pm.

Admission Fees: Adults $6, children 6–12 $3, seniors $5. Group tours $5/person; AAA discount off admission only.

Visitor Services: Gift shop, information, rest rooms.

Regularly Scheduled Events: *June:* Summer Solstice and Celtic Music Festival; *Oct:* Civil War Encampment; *Dec:* Twelfth Night.

Directions: From I-65: take Harding Place. west exit, turn left onto Franklin Rd., proceed 1 mile, turn left onto Farrell Rd., and turn right onto Farrell Pkwy. Entrance is on the left.

---

46 **Site:** MOUNT OLIVET CEMETERY, 1101 Lebanon Rd., Nashville, TN 37210, ☎ 615/255-4193

Description: This cemetery is the final resting place of nearly 1,500 Confederate soldiers. The Confederate Circle Monument marks the remains of individuals of all ranks. Mount Olivet is also the burial place for seven generals.

Open to Public: Daily from dawn to dusk.

Admission Fees: Free.

Visitor Services: Information.

Regularly Scheduled Events: Annual tour of cemetery with living history; call for schedule.

Directions: From I-40: exit at Fesslers Lane and proceed north on Fesslers Lane until it dead-ends into Hermitage Ave./Lebanon Rd. Turn right onto this road and continue to Mount Olivet Cemetery, which is on the right, past Calvary Cemetery.

---

47 **Site:** TENNESSEE STATE CAPITOL AND STATE MUSEUM, 505 Deaderick St., Nashville, TN 37243-1120, ☎ 615/741-2692

Description: The capitol was completed in 1859. The fortifications around the capitol consisted of four earthworks connected by a stockade with loopholes. The Tennessee State Museum traces the history of the state from prehistoric Indians until the early 1900s, including a large section on the Civil War. This section includes descriptions and

artifacts from each major battle in Tennessee, audiovisual presentations, firearms, uniforms, paintings of notable soldiers, and a large collection of battle flags.

Open to Public: *State Museum:* Tues–Sat 10am–5pm, Sun 1–5pm. *State Capitol:* Mon–Fri 9am–4pm.

Admission Fees: Free.

Visitor Services: *State Museum:* museum, gift shop, information, rest rooms, handicapped access. *State Capitol:* Information, guided tours.

Directions: From I-40: take Broadway exit and travel toward downtown. From Broadway, turn left onto Fifth Ave. and go past the third intersection. Museum is on left at Fifth and Deaderick. State Capitol is located 1 block away at Sixth and Charlotte.

New Johnsonville

48 **Site:** JOHNSONVILLE STATE HISTORIC AREA, Rte. 1, P.O. Box 37-4, New Johnsonville, TN 37134, ☎ 615/535-2789

Description: On November 4, 1864, at Johnsonville, Gen. Nathan Bedford Forrest's cavalry took up artillery positions on the west bank of the Tennessee River. The Confederates destroyed the Federal depot at Johnsonville. Union losses in the raid were 4 gunboats, 14 steamboats, 17 barges, 33 cannons, and more than 75,000 tons of supplies valued at $6.7 million. Two large Civil War field fortifications are interpreted at the park.

Open to Public: Daily 8am–sunset.

Admission Fees: Free.

Visitor Services: Trails, museum, information, rest rooms, handicapped access, picnic areas and shelters.

Regularly Scheduled Events: *Every other year:* Reenactment; Living history. Call for schedule.

Directions: From I-40 at Memphis: travel to Hwy. 13, go north to Waverly, proceed to Hwy. 70 west, and follow signs.

Parker's Crossroads

49 **Site:** PARKER'S CROSSROADS BATTLEFIELD SELF-GUIDED TOUR, c/o The Cotton Patch Restaurant, I-40 & Hwy. 22, Parker's Crossroads, TN 38388, ☎ 901/968-5533

Description: The Battle of Parker's Crossroads was fought on December 31, 1862. Union forces sought to capture Confederate troops on their return from their "First West Tennessee Raid." When Confederate General Forrest found himself caught between two Union forces at Parker's Crossroads, each roughly the size of his own, he ordered his troops to "charge both ways" and made a successful escape.

Open to Public: Daily from dawn to dusk.

Admission Fees: Free.

Visitor Services: Rest rooms.

Regularly Scheduled Events: *Every 2 years in June (1998, 2000, etc.):* Reenactment of the Battle of Parker's Crossroads.

Directions: The site is traversed by I-40. Starts at I-40 and Hwy. 22. at exit 108.

Pocahontas

50 **Site:** DAVIS BRIDGE BATTLEFIELD, c/o Davis Bridge Memorial Foundation,
P.O. Box 280, Bolivar, TN 38008, ☎ 901/658-6272

Description: After the Battle of Corinth on October 5, 1862, the retreating Confederate army under Generals Sterling Price and Earl Van Dorn met General Ord and 8,000 Union troops at Davis Bridge over the Hatchie River. An all-day battle ensued for the bridge. The Confederates managed to hold off the attacking Union forces and cross the Hatchie at Crum's Mill, farther south.

Open to Public: Daily from dawn to dusk.

Admission Fees: Free.

Visitor Services: Interpretive signs, monument, and flag memorial.

Regularly Scheduled Events: Call for schedule of reenactments and living history.

Directions: From I-40 at Jackson: take Hwy. 45 south to Hwy. 18 and take Hwy. 18 south to Bolivar. At Bolivar, continue south on Hwy. 125 to Middleton. Turn left on Hwy. 57 east to Pochahontas, turn right on Pochahontas Rd., bear left on Essary Springs Rd., and travel approximately 1.5 miles. Look for signs.

Savannah

51 **Site:** TENNESSEE RIVER MUSEUM, 507 Main St., Savannah, TN 38372,
☎ 800-552-3866 or 901/925-2363

Description: The Tennessee River was the invasion route for the Union armies in the West. Exhibits at the museum include "The War on the River," which begins with a one-half scale model of the bow of the USS *Cairo*. The exhibit contains many artifacts from this ill-fated ironclad and other gunboats. The "Army" exhibit features a collection of Shiloh field artillery, firearms, and personal items. The "Johnsonville" exhibit features General Forrest's cavalrymen.

Open to Public: Mon–Sat 9am–5pm, Sun 1–5pm.

Admission Fees: Adults $2, under 18 free.

Visitor Services: Museum, gift shop, rest rooms, handicapped access, tourism information.

Directions: From I-40: take Hwy. 22 to Crump, stay on Hwy. 22/64, cross Tennessee River, and stay on Hwy. 64 into Savannah (becomes Main St.). Museum is at 507 Main St.

Shiloh

52 **Site:** SHILOH NATIONAL MILITARY PARK, Rte. 1, P.O. Box 9, Shiloh, TN 38376,
☎ 901/689-5275

Description: Gen. Albert Sidney Johnston's Army of the Mississippi (C.S.A.), marching north from its base at Corinth, attacked and partially overran Ulysses S. Grant's Federal Army of the Tennessee. Shiloh was the first large-scale battle of the Civil War, and the magnitude of casualties shocked the nation. There were 65,000 Federal troops at Shiloh and 13,000 casualties. Confederate troop strength was 44,700 with 10,700 casualties.

Open to Public: Daily 8am–5pm.

Admission Fees: Adults $2, families $4.

Visitor Services: Trails, museum, bookstore, information, rest rooms, handicapped access.

Regularly Scheduled Events: *First weekend in Apr:* Living history weekend.

Directions: From I-40 at Parker's Crossroads: travel south on Hwy. 22 for 57 miles to Shiloh Park entrance; follow signs.

Smyrna

53 **Site:** SAM DAVIS HOME, 1399 Sam Davis Rd., Smyrna, TN 37167, ☎ 615/459-2341

Description: The Sam Davis Home is the family home and farm of Tennessee's "Boy Hero of the Confederacy," Sam Davis. The land consists of 168 acres of the original 1,000-acre plantation. Sam Davis was serving as a member of the Coleman Scouts when he was captured by the Union army and accused of being a spy. He was executed at age 21.

Open to Public: June–Aug: Mon–Sat 9am–5pm, Sun 1–5pm. Sept–May: Mon–Sat 10am–4pm, Sun 1–4pm.

Admission Fees: Adults $4, children $2.50, seniors $3.50, groups (10 or more) 50¢ discount.

Visitor Services: Museum, gift shop, information, rest rooms, limited handicapped access.

Regularly Scheduled Events: *May:* Days on the Farm/living history demonstrations; *June:* Civil War Show; *Mid-Oct:* Heritage Days.

Directions: From I-24 east: take exit 66B and go approximately 5.5 miles to Sam Davis Rd. From I-24 west: take exit 70 and proceed approximately 5 miles to Sam Davis Rd.

Spring Hill

54 **Site:** RIPPAVILLA PLANTATION, P.O. Box 1076, Columbia, TN 38402, ☎ 800/381-1865 or 615/486-9037

Description: Rippavilla Plantation was completed in 1853. Early in the Civil War, its owner, Confederate Maj. Nathaniel Cheairs, had carried the white flag of surrender to Gen. Ulysses S. Grant at Fort Donelson. On November 30, 1864, Major

Rippavilla Plantation, Visitor Center for the Tennessee Antebellum Trail, Spring Hill, TN. (Photograph courtesy of the Tennessee Antebellum Trail.)

Cheairs welcomed Confederate General Hood and his ranking officers to breakfast. It was here that Hood angrily accused his staff of letting the entire Federal army escape to Franklin. Five Confederate generals at that breakfast were dead by evening in the bloody Battle of Franklin.

Open to Public: Mon–Sat 10am–4pm, Sun 1–4pm.

Admission Fees: Adults $5, children $2, groups $4/person.

Visitor Services: Museum, gift shop, information, rest rooms, handicapped access.

Regularly Scheduled Events: *Apr and Dec:* Home Pilgrimage; *Oct:* Balloon Festival; Civil War reenactments: ongoing—call for schedule.

Directions: From I-65: 25 miles south of Nashville, take Saturn Pkwy. to Columbia exit. Take Columbia exit and turn left immediately at the end of the ramp. Rippavilla Plantation is located 100 yards on the left.

---

55 **Site:** TENNESSEE ANTEBELLUM TRAIL, 5700 Main St., Spring Hill, TN 37174,
☎ 800/381-1865 or 615/486-9055

Description: This is a 90-mile, self-driving loop tour featuring more than 55 Civil War sites, battlefields, antebellum homes, and plantations. The route traces Gen. John Bell Hood's Nashville campaign from Spring Hill through Franklin, and north to Nashville. Nine historic homes are open to the public along the Trail, each playing an important role in the campaign. The homes include Belle Meade Plantation, Belmont Mansion, Travellers Rest, Carter House, Carnton Plantation, Rippavilla Plantation, The Athenaeum, Polk Home, and Rattle

and Snap. Other significant sites include McGavock Confederate Cemetery, Winstead Hill, and Spring Hill Battlefield.

Open to Public: The trail is open daily. The nine historic homes have varying hours but are generally open Mon–Sat 10am–5pm and Sun 1–5pm.

Admission Fees: Range from $3 to $8.50 at each of the nine sites. A discount admission ticket for all of the nine sites is available for $35.00 (a 28% savings off regular admission prices).

Visitor Services: The free map guide to the Trail is available from the address and phone number listed above. The nine historic homes have tours, gift shops, and rest rooms. The map guide includes bed-and-breakfasts, dining establishments, and antique shops along the Trail.

Regularly Scheduled Events: Spring Pilgrimage; Plantation Christmas; the map guide includes an extensive calendar of events.

Directions: The tour can be started at any point along the Trail. The map guide provides detailed directions.

Tullahoma

56 **Site:** TULLAHOMA CAMPAIGN CIVIL WAR TRAIL, Tennessee's Backroads, 300 S. Jackson St., Tullahoma, TN 37388, ☎ 800/799-6131 or 615/454-9446

Description: A driving tour includes important scenes of the Tullahoma Campaign. The trail features the battle sites of Liberty Gap and Hoover's Gap, the first battle to feature the Spencer repeating rifle. From battles to encampments to guerrilla-style encounters, the campaign followed the Battle of Stone's River and led to Chattanooga.

Open to Public: Daily from dawn to dusk.

Admission Fees: Free.

Visitor Services: The Tennessee Backroads Tullahoma Campaign Civil War Trail brochure is free and available from the Tennessee Backroads office at ☎ 800/799-6131. The trail is approximately 130 miles long. All sites are free and open to the public unless noted as private property.

Directions: The trail can be accessed at its beginning off I-24 at exit 97 (Beech Grove) or at its end at I-24 at the Monteagle/Sewanee exit.

TEXAS

*A*MERE 16 YEARS AFTER TEXAS HAD GIVEN UP its status as an independent nation and joined the Union, the American Civil War erupted. Despite the efforts of then Governor Sam Houston to keep Texas in the Union or at least to reestablish a neutral republic, voters overwhelmingly approved an ordinance of secession, and the state formally joined the Confederacy in early March 1861. On February 16, Ben McCulloch, a veteran Texas Ranger, captured the commander of the U.S. troops in Texas and took possession of a string of frontier forts from Ft. Bliss in El Paso to Ft. Brown in Brownsville. Although the great majority of Texans supported the Southern cause, there were notable exceptions as evidenced by the killing of 30 German settlers from the Comfort area of the Texas Hill Country who were caught as their party attempted to flee to Mexico in August 1862.

Although the largest battles of the war took place in theaters to the east, Texas saw some significant actions primarily related to the defense of its borders and ill-fated attempts to expand Confederate dominance into New Mexico and Arizona. Of the 90,000 Texans to see service in the war, only one-third were in action east of the Mississippi; however, these were represented by such distinguished units as Benjamin F. Terry's Texas Rangers and John Bell Hood's Texas Infantry Brigade of whom Lee once remarked, "I never ordered the Brigade to hold a place, that they did not hold it."

The Texas coast was the object of much Federal attention with a blockade beginning in July 1861. The major port city of Galveston was captured on October 4, 1862, and held until New Year's Day, 1863, when Gen. John B. Magruder recaptured it. Sabine Pass was also held for a short time by Union troops in late 1862, but a second major Union attack was repulsed by Lt. Richard W. Dowling and a handful of artillerymen on September 8, 1863. The Federals then focused their attention on southern Texas and the mouth of the Rio Grande, the major supply route to Mexico. Brownsville was captured in November 1863 but retaken by troops under the command of Col. John Salmond "Rip" Ford in the summer of 1864. Federal troops managed to hold Brazos Island at the mouth of the Rio Grande but were again defeated by Ford's troops on May 13, 1865, at Palmito Ranch near Brownsville, more than a month after Lee's surrender in Virginia, in what proved to be the last battle of the Civil War.

Gen. Edmund Kirby Smith, commander of the Trans-Mississippi Department and headquartered in Marshall, Texas, formally surrendered on board a Union ship in Galveston Bay on June 2, 1865, bringing an end to the Civil War.

by Stanley O. Graves, AIA, Texas Historical Commission

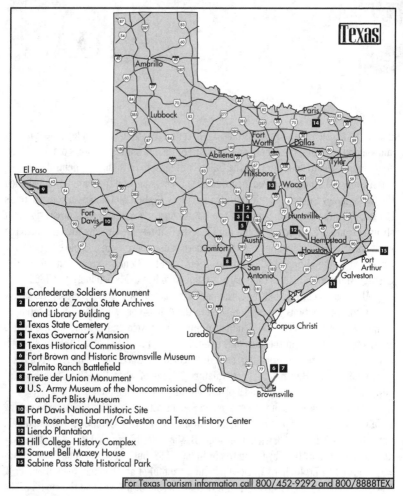

Texas

Amarillo
Lubbock
Fort Worth
Dallas
Paris **14**
El Paso **9**
Fort Davis **10**
Abilene
Hillsboro
13 Waco
Tyler
1 2
3 4
5
12 Hempstead
Comfort
Austin
Houston
8
San Antonio
Galveston
Port Arthur
15
Laredo
Corpus Christi
6 7
Brownsville
11

1 Confederate Soldiers Monument
2 Lorenzo de Zavala State Archives
and Library Building
3 Texas State Cemetery
4 Texas Governor's Mansion
5 Texas Historical Commission
6 Fort Brown and Historic Brownsville Museum
7 Palmito Ranch Battlefield
8 Treüe der Union Monument
9 U.S. Army Museum of the Noncommissioned Officer
and Fort Bliss Museum
10 Fort Davis National Historic Site
11 The Rosenberg Library/Galveston and Texas History Center
12 Liendo Plantation
13 Hill College History Complex
14 Samuel Bell Maxey House
15 Sabine Pass State Historical Park

For Texas Tourism information call 800/452-9292 and 800/8888TEX.

Austin

1 **Site:** CONFEDERATE SOLDIERS MONUMENT, Texas Capitol Grounds, 11th and Congress, Austin, TX 78701, ☎ 512/305-8400 (Capitol Complex Visitors Center), 512/463-0063 (Capitol Information and Guide Service)

Description: The Confederate Soldiers Monument, located on the historic south grounds of the Texas State Capitol near the Congress Ave. entrance gates, was begun in 1900 and completed around 1903. It consists of five bronze figures representing the infantry, cavalry, Confederate states, and battles fought between 1861 and 1865. Pompeo Coppini executed the bronze figures, and Frank Teich erected the monument.

Open to Public: Accessible 24 hours. *Visitors center:* Tues–Fri 9am–5pm, Sat 10am–5pm.

Admission Fees: Free.

Visitor Services: The Capitol Complex Visitors Center, located one-half block east of the monument at 112 E. 11th St., offers an exhibitions program, an educational video presentation, and a gift shop. The facility is accessible to people with disabilities. Public rest rooms, a drinking fountain, and pay telephones are located in the basement.

Directions: From I-35: take 11th St. exit to downtown Austin. Proceed west on 11th St. about .5 mile to the Capitol.

---

2   **Site:**   LORENZO DE ZAVALA STATE ARCHIVES AND LIBRARY BUILDING, P.O. Box 92927, Austin, TX 78711, ☎ 512/463-5455

Description: The Texas State Archives contain Civil War records related to the State of Texas. These records consist primarily of Confederate pension applications and records of Texas state troops and militias.

Open to Public: Mon–Fri 8am–5pm.

Admission Fees: Free.

Visitor Services: Information, rest rooms, handicapped access.

Directions: From I-35: take 12th St. exit in downtown Austin. Proceed west on 12th St. for about .25 mile. The State Archives Building is located directly east of the Texas State Capitol.

---

3   **Site:**   TEXAS STATE CEMETERY, Navasota St., Austin, TX 78702, ☎ 512/463-0605, www.gsc.state.tx.us/statecemetery

Description: The State Cemetery was established in 1851 with the burial of Edward Burleson. The southeast section of the cemetery has historically been referred to as The Confederate Plat. More than 2,047 Confederate veterans and their wives are buried and marked by row after row of simple white marble tablets. Each tablet contains the name of the soldier, with most also including the date of birth and death and the company with which he fought. The Confederates were first buried in the State Cemetery in 1871. In that year, the sexton was authorized by the state legislature to procure suitable monuments as long as the cost did not exceed $40 each.

In 1867, the state legislature authorized funds for the removal of Gen. Albert Sidney Johnston's remains from the State of Louisiana to the Texas State Cemetery. General Johnston was the strategic force behind the Confederate offensive at Shiloh, but he chose to lead the charge and was fatally wounded. Elisabet Ney, a noted sculptor, carved in white marble a recumbent statue of the general in 1902 and designed a metal Gothic-style tomb, located west of The Confederate Plat.

Open to Public: *Grounds:* Daily 8am–5pm. *Visitors center:* Mon–Sat 8am–5pm.

Admission Fees: Free.

Visitor Services: Internet access to biographies, photos, and Confederate records; trails, gift shop, visitor center, rest rooms, handicapped access at the Visitor Center on Navasota St.

Directions: From I-35: drive south of Austin, take Eighth St. exit, drive on frontage road, turn left on Seventh St., and drive under freeway 3 blocks to Navasota St. Turn left and drive past turn-of-century caretaker's cottage. Visitor center is on the right.

Gen. Albert Sidney Johnston's Tomb, carved by noted sculptor Elisabet Ney; State Cemetery, Austin, TX. (Photograph courtesy of the Texas Historical Commission.)

---

4 **Site:** TEXAS GOVERNOR'S MANSION, 1010 Colorado, Austin, TX 78701,
☎ 512/463-5518 or 512/463-5516 (24-hour tour info)

Description: The Greek Revival house was built in 1856, and every Texas governor since has lived in the mansion. Abraham Lincoln reputedly offered Governor Sam Houston Federal military assistance during the secession crisis to keep Texas in the Union. Houston may have burned Lincoln's letter in a mansion fireplace. He left office in March 1861 after refusing to sign an oath of allegiance to the Confederacy and was replaced by Lt. Governor Edward Clark. Clark was succeeded by Governor Francis R. Lubbock, who later resigned his office to join the Confederate army, becoming an aide-de-camp to Jefferson Davis.

Open to Public: Mon–Fri 10–11:40am; tours every 20 minutes. Call first to check availability; group reservations required.

Admission Fees: Free.

Visitor Services: Tours, handicapped access.

Directions: From I-35: take State Capitol exit.

---

5 **Site:** TEXAS HISTORICAL COMMISSION, P.O. Box 12276, Austin, TX 78711-2276,
☎ 512/463-6100

Description: Many of Texas's 11,500 historical markers are Civil War related. A high percentage of the historical marker files, which are located in the agency research center, contain documented narratives supporting the historical significance of the subject matter of each marker.

Open to Public: Mon–Fri 8am–5pm.

Admission Fees: Free.

Visitor Services: Information; rest rooms; the main floor and library have handicapped access; files are hand-delivered to the public.

Directions: From I-35: take the 15th St. exit in downtown Austin. Proceed west on 15th St. for approximately .5 mile to Colorado St. Turn right onto Colorado and proceed 1 city block to 16th St. The Texas Historical Commission is housed in the Carrington-Covert House at the southeast corner of Colorado and 16th.

Brownsville

6 **Site:** FORT BROWN AND HISTORIC BROWNSVILLE MUSEUM, c/o Historic Brownsville Museum, 641 East Madison St., Brownsville, TX 78520, ☎ 210/548-1313

Description: Fort Brown, established in 1846, housed Federal troops during the Mexican War. In 1861, Texas state troops occupied the fort. With the southern Atlantic coast blockaded, Brownsville became an important Confederate port, with cotton and war material flowing back and forth. To eliminate the trade, a Union army landed near the mouth of the Rio Grande in November 1863, occupying Fort Brown and Brownsville. Eight months later a strong Confederate army drove out Federal forces and held the fort until the end of the war. The original hospital building is now the administration building for Texas Southmost College. Other extant buildings include a medical laboratory, a guardhouse, and a morgue. The Historic Brownsville Museum houses materials related to Brownsville's long military history.

Open to Public: Mon–Fri 10am–4:30pm, Sat 9am–1pm, Sun 2–5pm (closed Sun in summer).

Admission Fees: *Grounds:* Free. *Museum:* Adults $2, children 50¢.

Visitor Services: Tours, museum, information, rest rooms.

Directions: Fort Brown/Texas Southmost College adjoins International Blvd. at Jefferson St. in Brownsville. Historic Brownsville Museum is in the restored Southern Pacific Depot at 641 E. Madison St.

7 **Site:** PALMITO RANCH BATTLEFIELD, c/o Brownsville Convention and Visitors Bureau, 650 Farm-to-Market 802, Brownsville, TX 78520, ☎ 800/626-2639

Description: More than 1 month after Lee's surrender to Grant at Appomattox, the battle at Palmito Ranch represented the last-known land engagement fought as part of the Civil War and the ongoing conflict between the Confederacy's Trans-Mississippi Department and the Union army. The battle was fought on May 12 and 13, 1865, as the Confederates sought to protect the center of their clandestine cotton shipping operation with Mexico and European mills. The battle was the Union's last unsuccessful attempt to seize control of the Lower Rio Grande region.

Open to Public: Daily from dawn to dusk. Visitors can drive or bicycle along Hwy. 4, Boca Chica Hwy., and view the battlefield and related historical markers. However, most of the property is private, and trespassing is strongly discouraged.

Admission Fees: Free.

Visitor Services: None.

Directions: From Brownsville: follow Hwy. 4 to the Gulf of Mexico.

Comfort

8 **Site:** TREÜE DER UNION MONUMENT (German for "True to the Union"), c/o Comfort Heritage Foundation, Box 433, Comfort, TX 78013, ☎ 830/995-3131 (Chamber of Commerce), 830/995-2398 (public library)

Description: The oldest Civil War monument in Texas (dedicated August 10, 1866), this limestone obelisk is inscribed with the names of the 36 men captured and killed in the Battle of the Nueces, in Kinney County, on August 10, 1862. The battle and ensuing pursuit were initiated when Confederate forces attacked a group of Hill Country Union sympathizers, mostly German immigrants, who were trying to make their way to Mexico rather than fight against their adopted homeland. The Treüe der Union monument is the only memorial to the Union (outside national cemeteries) in Confederate territory, and one of only six places in the nation permitted by Congress to fly the flag at half-mast in perpetuity (and the only one of these to fly a flag with 36 stars). The memorial is listed in the National Register of Historic Places, is a Texas State Historical Landmark, and is a Texas State Archaeological Landmark.

Open to Public: Daily 24 hours.

Admission Fees: Free.

Visitor Services: Information.

Regularly Scheduled Events: Ceremonies on major anniversaries.

Directions: The town of Comfort is approximately 40 miles northwest of San Antonio, just off I-10. Proceed through Comfort on State Hwy. 27 west, toward the towns of Center Point and Kerrville. The monument is on the right (west) side of the road, just past the intersection of High St. and Hwy. 27.

El Paso

9   **Site:** U.S. ARMY MUSEUM OF THE NONCOMMISSIONED OFFICER AND FORT BLISS
MUSEUM. Fort Bliss Museum mailing address and telephone: Attn.: ATZC-DPD-M,
Fort Bliss, TX 79916, ☎ 915/568-2804 or 915/568-6940. Noncommissioned
Officer Museum mailing address and telephone: Attn.: ATSS-S-M, USASMA,
Fort Bliss, TX 79918-5000, ☎ 915/568-8646

Description: Fort Bliss, a U.S. Army post established in 1848 to assert authority over lands acquired after the Mexican War, served as headquarters for Confederate forces in the Southwest during the Civil War. The U.S. Museum of the Noncommissioned Officer traces the history of the U.S. NCO Corps with some artifacts that pertain to the Civil War. The Fort Bliss Museum is an exact replica of the original adobe fort that was part of the frontier military era. The museum includes a small Civil War exhibit that focuses on Gen. Horace Hopkins Sibley's campaign into New Mexico to establish the Confederate Territory of New Mexico.

Open to Public: *Fort Bliss Museum:* Daily 9am–4:30pm. *U.S. Army Museum of the*

Noncommissioned Officer: Mon–Fri 9am–4pm. Sat–Sun noon–4pm.

Admission Fees: Free.

Visitor Services: Museum, information.

Directions: To Fort Bliss Museum: From I-10: go north on U.S. 54 to Pershing Dr. and turn right; proceed to Sheridan Rd. and turn right. The museum is at Sheridan Rd. and Pleasanton. To NCO Museum: From I-10: go north on U.S. 54 to Fred Wilson Rd. and turn right; proceed to Sergeant Major Blvd. and turn left; proceed to Biggs St. and turn left; travel to Simms St. and turn right. The museum is 3 blocks down on the right.

Fort Davis

10   **Site:** FORT DAVIS NATIONAL HISTORIC SITE, P.O. Box 1456, Fort Davis, TX 79734,
☎ 915/426-3224

Description: Fort Davis, established in 1854, was the first military post to guard the route westward and offer haven by the precious waters of Limpia Creek. Col. John R. Baylor's Confederate cavalry brigade reached Fort Davis on April 13, 1861, and Union troops withdrew in compliance with

orders already received from Brig. Gen. David E. Twiggs, commanding the Eighth United States Military District. The Confederates remained a few months, then vacated the post. Federal troops returned in June 1867, but little of value remained, and construction ensued.

Open to Public: Daily 8am–5pm. Closed on Christmas.

Admission Fees: $2/person or $4/vehicle. Free admission with Golden Passport.

Visitor Services: Trails, tours, museum, information, gift shop, visitors center, rest rooms.

Directions: From I-10: take Hwy. 17 south; this joins Hwy. 118. The site is located just before the town of Fort Davis, which is approximately 39 miles from I-10.

Galveston

11 **Site:** THE ROSENBERG LIBRARY/GALVESTON AND TEXAS HISTORY CENTER, 2310 Sealy, Galveston, TX 77550, ☎ 409/763-8854

Description: The Rosenberg Library contains Civil War artifacts in a museum-like setting. The Galveston and Texas History Center contains Civil War Muster Rolls; Civil War–era Galveston newspapers; Civil War maps; and a manuscript collection, which includes letters and diaries written by Civil War participants from Galveston.

Open to Public: *Rosenberg Library:* Mon–Thurs 9am–9pm, Fri–Sat 9am–6pm. Sun open Sept–May 1–5pm. *Galveston and Texas History Center:* Tues–Sat 9am–5pm.

Admission Fees: Free.

Visitor Services: Museum, information, rest rooms, handicapped access.

Directions: From I-45 (southeast from Houston): merge into Broadway Ave. in Galveston. Continue east on Broadway to 24th St., turn left (north) on 24th, and proceed about 2 city blocks. The Rosenberg Library and the History Center are located just past Ashton-Villa Historic House Museum.

Hempstead

12 **Site:** LIENDO PLANTATION, P.O. Box 454, Hempstead, TX 77445, ☎ 800/826-4371 or 409/826-4400

Description: This Greek Revival-style home was built by Leonard Waller Groce and is among the most famous and historic plantations in Texas. Liendo was built by slave labor and completed in 1853. During the Civil War, Camp Groce was established at Liendo, where cavalry, artillery, and infantry were recruited. Converted to a prisoner-of-war camp, it housed troops

captured at the Battle of Galveston. From September 1 to December 1, 1865, the plantation was the camp for Gen. G. A. Custer and his command.

Open to Public: First Sat of each month: Tours given at 10am, 11:30am, and 1pm; open to group tours with advance reservations.

Admission Fees: $5.

Visitor Services: Tours, information.

Regularly Scheduled Events: *Third weekend in Apr:* Old South Festival.

Directions: From Hwy. 290: take the FM 1488 exit, travel 1 mile northeast, and turn right on Wyatt Chapel Rd. The plantation is .5 mile on the right on Wyatt Chapel Rd.

Hillsboro

13 **Site:** HILL COLLEGE HISTORY COMPLEX, 112 Lamar Dr., Hillsboro, TX 76645, ☎ 817/582-2555

Description: The research center houses an extensive collection of archival materials and books, microfilm, and vertical files on the Civil War, with emphasis on Confederate military history. The museum displays a collection of military art, guns, photographs, original battle flags, and artifacts.

Open to Public: Mon–Fri 9am–noon and 1–3pm. Closed on college holidays.

Admission Fees: Free.

Visitor Services: Tours, museum, information, gift shop, visitors center, rest rooms, handicapped access.

Regularly Scheduled Events: *First Sat in Apr (except on Easter weekend):* Confederate History Symposium. *Note:* Reservations should be made before Mar 1 because space is limited.

Directions: Located .5 mile east of I-35 at Hillsboro on the Hill College campus, south of Dallas.

Paris

14 **Site:** SAMUEL BELL MAXEY HOUSE, 812 S. Church St., Paris, TX 75460, ☎ 903/785-5716

Description: The Samuel Bell Maxey House, a two-story residence, was constructed from 1866 to 1867 by General Maxey on his return to Paris, Texas, after the Civil War. The home, with a rear ell, is an excellent example of a late Greek Revival–style residence foreshadowing the Victorian era. General Maxey, born in Kentucky on March 30, 1825, graduated from West Point Military Academy and went on to fight in the Mexican War with Gen. Zachary Taylor. After resigning from the military to study law in 1849, Maxey married and moved to Texas. Advocating secession, Maxey headed to the field to fight for

the Confederacy. In the spring of 1865, he was promoted to Major General; but the war was coming to a close, and his army disbanded in May 1865. He returned to Paris, where he practiced law and later served in the United States Senate. Maxey died on August 16, 1895, in Eureka Springs, Arkansas, where he had gone to recover after a period of ill health. Some of General Maxey's Civil War items are on temporary and permanent display at his home.

Open to Public: Fri and Sun 1–5pm, Sat 8am–5pm; open by appointment on Wed and Thurs for large groups.

Admission Fees: Adults $2, children $1, children under 6 free.

Visitor Services: Tours, museum, information, gift shop, rest rooms, handicapped access to grounds and first floor only.

Regularly Scheduled Events: *Sept:* Civil War reenactment; *Dec:* Christmas open house.

Directions: From I-30: exit on State Hwy. 24 north and proceed to Paris. In Paris, State Hwy. 24 becomes Church St. Proceed approximately 1 mile past the railroad tracks. The Samuel Bell Maxey House is on the left.

Port Arthur

15 Site: SABINE PASS STATE HISTORICAL PARK, Sea Rim/Sabine Pass Battleground State Historical Park, Texas Parks and Wildlife Dept., P.O. Box 1066, Sabine Pass, TX 77655, ☎ 409/971-2559

Description: Two naval engagements, or battles, of the Civil War occurred at Sabine Pass. The first took place September 24–25, 1862, and the second on September 8, 1863. Sabine Pass was a major Confederate center for the shipment and trade of cotton in exchange for supplies and arms, and the Union forces attempted to blockade harbors and disrupt shipping along the Gulf coast. To protect Sabine Pass from Union incursions, the Confederates first constructed Fort Sabine and then constructed Fort Griffin, both earthworks along the Pass. Twice the Union forces attempted to overrun Confederate fortifications, briefly but successfully in 1862 in preparation for the invasion of Galveston and Houston, and then unsuccessfully in 1863. The 1863 engagement that repulsed the Union forces (22 ships and troops) is commemorated by a monument to Confederate Lt. Richard W. ("Dick") Dowling and

his men. Through time and erosion, there is no visible evidence of Confederate Forts Sabine and Griffin at the Sabine Pass State Historical Park.

Open to Public: Mon–Sat 8am–5pm.

Admission Fees: Free.

Visitor Services: Interpretive exhibits, historical markers, trails, rest rooms, camping.

Regularly Scheduled Events: *Sept 8:* Dick Dowling commemoration.

Directions: Sabine Pass State Historical Park is about 22 miles south of I-10, from either Orange or Beaumont. From I-10 at Orange: take State Hwy. 87 exit south through Beaumont to the Park. From I-10 at Beaumont: take the U.S. 69 exit south to State Hwy. 87 in Port Arthur (11 miles); follow State Hwy. 87 to the Park, about .5 mile south of the small town of Sabine Pass on FM 3322.

VIRGINIA

*V*IRGINIANS VOTED TO SECEDE FROM THE UNION on May 23, 1861. Before the vote, former U.S. President John Tyler, a native Virginian, chaired a peace conference in Washington, D.C., with the goal of resolving the nation's sectional crisis. Delegates to a convention called by the Virginia General Assembly had been leaning toward preserving the Union, but after the Washington Peace Conference failed, and Virginians reacted negatively to President Abraham Lincoln's inaugural address, public opinion changed. Edmund Ruffin, a Virginian, fired one of the first shots of the Civil War on April 12 at Fort Sumter, South Carolina, and when Lincoln called for troops to put down the Southern forces, the convention quickly voted for secession on April 17. The convention's action was ratified in a referendum on May 23.

The western Virginia counties opposed to secession formed a new state, West Virginia, which was admitted to the Union in 1863. Westerner Francis H. Pierpont, head of the pro-Union Restored Government of Virginia, established offices in Alexandria in 1863 and eventually moved to Richmond after the Union victory in 1865.

For four long years, the Union army's chief goal was to capture Richmond. Consequently, more of the major battles of the Civil War were fought in Virginia than in any other state. In 26 major battles and hundreds of smaller engagements, more men fought and died in Virginia than in any other state. Recently, the Civil War Sites Advisory Commission reported to Congress that one-third of the nation's most important battlefields are in Virginia. More Civil War sites are open to the public in Virginia than in any other state.

From 1861 to 1865, the Confederate strategy was essentially defensive. Until 1864, when Grant took command of Union forces, the Southern troops fighting in Virginia repulsed Northern attacks.

Many of the Civil War's greatest ironies unfolded in Virginia. Robert E. Lee was offered command of the Union army but refused before he accepted command of the Army of Northern Virginia. Fighting raged on the same bloody ground where the nation won its freedom from England at Yorktown. More African Americans were awarded the Medal of Honor in Virginia for their valor during the Civil War than in any other state. The Congress of the Confederate States of America took up residence in Virginia's State Capitol, meeting place of the oldest legislative body in the Western Hemisphere.

Perhaps one of the greatest ironies of all is the story of Wilmer McLean, who fled Northern Virginia where the first major land battle of the war was fought in July, 1861, at Manassas, to find peace at Appomattox Court House. On April 9, 1865, in McLean's home there, Confederate Gen. Robert E. Lee surrendered to Ulysses S. Grant.

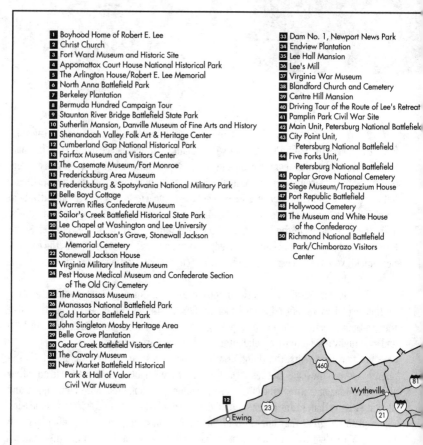

1. Boyhood Home of Robert E. Lee
2. Christ Church
3. Fort Ward Museum and Historic Site
4. Appomattox Court House National Historical Park
5. The Arlington House/Robert E. Lee Memorial
6. North Anna Battlefield Park
7. Berkeley Plantation
8. Bermuda Hundred Campaign Tour
9. Staunton River Bridge Battlefield State Park
10. Sutherlin Mansion, Danville Museum of Fine Arts and History
11. Shenandoah Valley Folk Art & Heritage Center
12. Cumberland Gap National Historical Park
13. Fairfax Museum and Visitors Center
14. The Casemate Museum/Fort Monroe
15. Fredericksburg Area Museum
16. Fredericksburg & Spotsylvania National Military Park
17. Belle Boyd Cottage
18. Warren Rifles Confederate Museum
19. Sailor's Creek Battlefield Historical State Park
20. Lee Chapel at Washington and Lee University
21. Stonewall Jackson's Grave, Stonewall Jackson Memorial Cemetery
22. Stonewall Jackson House
23. Virginia Military Institute Museum
24. Pest House Medical Museum and Confederate Section of The Old City Cemetery
25. The Manassas Museum
26. Manassas National Battlefield Park
27. Cold Harbor Battlefield Park
28. John Singleton Mosby Heritage Area
29. Belle Grove Plantation
30. Cedar Creek Battlefield Visitors Center
31. The Cavalry Museum
32. New Market Battlefield Historical Park & Hall of Valor Civil War Museum

33. Dam No. 1, Newport News Park
34. Endview Plantation
35. Lee Hall Mansion
36. Lee's Mill
37. Virginia War Museum
38. Blandford Church and Cemetery
39. Centre Hill Mansion
40. Driving Tour of the Route of Lee's Retreat
41. Pamplin Park Civil War Site
42. Main Unit, Petersburg National Battlefield
43. City Point Unit, Petersburg National Battlefield
44. Five Forks Unit, Petersburg National Battlefield
45. Poplar Grove National Cemetery
46. Siege Museum/Trapezium House
47. Port Republic Battlefield
48. Hollywood Cemetery
49. The Museum and White House of the Confederacy
50. Richmond National Battlefield Park/Chimborazo Visitors Center

Alexandria

1 Site: **BOYHOOD HOME OF ROBERT E. LEE,** 607 Oronoco St., Alexandria, VA 22314, ☎ 703/548-8454

Description: Lee lived here from age 5 until he entered West Point. The house is a splendid example of Federal architecture. The site interprets Lee's early life.

Open to Public: Mon–Sat 10am–4pm, Sun 1–4pm. Closed Dec 15–Feb 1.

Admission Fees: Adults $4, children 11–17 $2.

Visitor Services: Guided tours.

Directions: From I-395: take exit 1B (Rte. 1 north) to Old Town Alexandria. Turn right on Oronoco St.

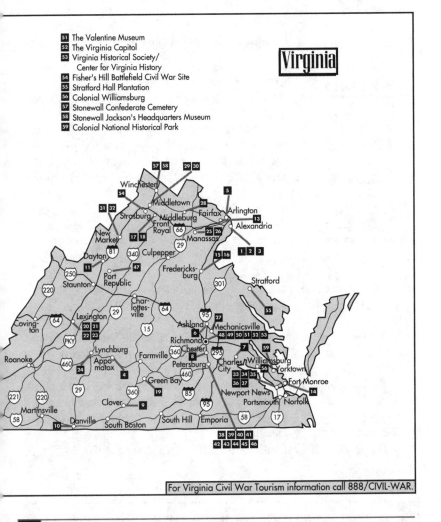

51 The Valentine Museum
52 The Virginia Capitol
53 Virginia Historical Society/
    Center for Virginia History
54 Fisher's Hill Battlefield Civil War Site
55 Stratford Hall Plantation
56 Colonial Williamsburg
57 Stonewall Confederate Cemetery
58 Stonewall Jackson's Headquarters Museum
59 Colonial National Historical Park

Virginia

For Virginia Civil War Tourism information call 888/CIVIL-WAR.

---

2 **Site:** CHRIST CHURCH, 118 North Washington St., Alexandria, VA 22314,
☎ 703/549-1450

Description: This lovely English-style church, built from 1767 to 1773, was attended by George Washington and Robert E. Lee. Washington's pew is marked, as is the communion rail where he was confirmed.

Open to Public: Mon–Sat 9am–4pm, Sun 1–3pm.

Admission Fees: Free.

Visitor Services: Gift shop.

Directions: From I-395: take exit 1B (Rte. 1 north) to Old Town Alexandria; turn right onto King St.; turn left onto Columbus. Church is on the right, at the corner of Cameron and North Washington sts.

VIRGINIA CIVIL WAR TRAILS

Virginia Civil War Trails is a five-phased effort to link Virginia's Civil War history through a combination of driving, biking and walking trails. The five trails are:

The 1862 Peninsula Campaign: Thirty-six markers line the route of the Federal Army's attempt to capture Richmond via the peninsula between the James and York rivers. Additional sites relay Tidewater Virginia's experience throughout the Civil War.

Lee vs. Grant: The 1864 Overland Campaign is interpreted by this 51-stop trail that follows the route taken by the Union Army of the Potomac as it moved from Culpeper toward Richmond. The trail ends at the Federal entrenchments surrounding Petersburg.

Lee's Retreat: This 26-stop trail traces the final footsteps taken by Robert E. Lee's Army of Northern Virginia as it marched from Petersburg to the Appomattox Court House.

Northern Virginia: Opening in May of 1998 and named the "crossroads of conflict," this trail explores the Manassas Campaigns; the defense of Washington, D.C.; and routes used by the Confederate cavalry commander John Mosby.

The Shenandoah Valley: Opening in September of 1998, this trail is called the "avenue of invasion." Interpretive stops highlight the events of "Stonewall" Jackson's "Valley Campaign" of 1862 and the bloody campaigns fought throughout the Shenandoah Valley in 1863 and 1864.

For more information: Call Virginia Civil War Trails at ☎ 888/CIVIL WAR.

---

3 | **Site:** FORT WARD MUSEUM AND HISTORIC SITE, 4301 West Braddock Rd., Alexandria, VA 22304, ☎ 703/838-4848

Description: This fort is one of the 68 major forts built to protect Washington, D.C., during the Civil War. The museum features a Civil War collection and a reference library.

Open to Public: *Museum:* Tues–Sat 9am–5pm, Sun noon–5pm. *Park:* Daily 9am–sunset.

Admission Fees: Free.

Visitor Services: Rest rooms, gift shop, handicapped access, trails, picnic area.

Regularly Scheduled Events: Annual Living History Day—call for date.

Directions: From I-395: take Seminary Rd. exit east. Follow signs to the fort (near Alexandria Hospital).

Appomattox

 Site: APPOMATTOX COURT HOUSE NATIONAL HISTORICAL PARK, State Rte. 24, Appomattox, VA 24522, ☎ 804/352-8987

Description: Gen. Robert E. Lee surrendered to Gen. Ulysses S. Grant here on April 9, 1865. The historic meeting of Lee and Grant at the McLean house is captured in the picturesque village of Appomattox Court House, which still reflects its 1865 appearance.

Open to Public: June–Aug: Daily 9am–5:30pm. Rest of the year: 8:30am–5pm.

Admission Fees: Memorial Day–Labor Day: Adults $4, children under 17 free.

Rest of the year: Adults $2, children under 17 free.

Visitor Services: Rest rooms, handicapped access, bookstore.

Directions: From I-81 at Lexington: travel east on VA Rte. 60 approximately 1½ hours to VA Rte. 24 south. Located on VA 24, 3 miles northeast of Appomattox.

Arlington

5 **Site:** THE ARLINGTON HOUSE/ROBERT E. LEE MEMORIAL, Arlington Cemetery, Arlington, VA 22211, ☎ 703/557-0613

Description: This was the home of General Lee and Mary Custis Lee, a great-granddaughter of Martha Washington. The Union seized the estate, converting it into a training center and later a cemetery.

Open to Public: Apr–Oct: Daily 9:30am–6pm. Oct–Mar: Daily 9:30am–4:30pm.

Admission Fees: Free; hourly parking fee for cemetery.

Visitor Services: Rest rooms, visitors center.

Directions: Located in Arlington National Cemetery.

Ashland

6 **Site:** NORTH ANNA BATTLEFIELD PARK, c/o Hanover Co. Parks and Recreation, 200 Berkley St., Ashland, VA 23005, ☎ 804/798-8062

Description: Here at the Ox Ford portion of the North Anna battlefield, Confederates turned back Union attacks on May 24 and 25, 1864. A 2.4 mile walking trail features

interpretive signs that detail the events of the battle. A brochure is also available from the address above or at the Ashland Visitor Center.

Open to Public: Daily from dawn to dusk.

Admission Fees: Free.

Visitor Services: Interpretive trails and signs.

Directions: Located on Verdon Rd. (Rte. 684), adjacent to the General Crushed Stone Quarry in Doswell (near King's Dominion).

Charles City

7 **Site:** BERKELEY PLANTATION, 12602 Harrison Landing Rd., Charles City, VA 23030, ☎ 804/829-6018

Description: The Berkeley Plantation was used by Gen. George B. McClellan as headquarters during his Peninsula Campaign. President Lincoln conferred with him here, and "Taps" was composed here by Gen. Daniel Butterfield during the campaign.

Open to Public: Daily 8am–5pm.

Admission Fees: Adults $8.50, students 13–16 $6.50, children 6–12 $4, groups (10 or more) $4.50/person, student groups $2.50/person. Seniors, military, AAA members 10% off the adult admission.

Visitor Services: Guided tours; gift shop; museum; Coach House Tavern open daily for lunch, including Sun brunch and dinner and by reservation on weekends (☎ 804/829-6003).

Regularly Scheduled Events: *First Sun of Nov:* First Thanksgiving festival.

Directions: From I-295: take Rte. 5. Located on Rte. 5, halfway between Richmond and Williamsburg.

Chester

8 **Site:** BERMUDA HUNDRED CAMPAIGN TOUR, c/o 4303 Pinewood Ct., Prince George, VA 23875

Description: Follow the Army of the James from May 5 to June 15, 1864, in the Bermuda Hundred Campaign. A self-guided tour brochure is available at Richmond National Battlefield and Petersburg National Battlefield visitors centers, or by mail from the above address.

Open to Public: Daily from dawn to dusk.

Admission Fees: Free.

Visitor Services: None.

Directions: Begin tour at Fort Darling at Richmond National Battlefield Park, off I-95, exit 64. Tour brochure provides driving directions.

Clover

9 **Site:** STAUNTON RIVER BRIDGE BATTLEFIELD STATE PARK, 1035 Fort Hill Trail, Randolph, VA 23962-9801, ☎ 804/454-4312 or 804/786-1712

Description: On June 25, 1864, a ragtag band of Confederate soldiers, boys, and old men, commanded by Capt. Benjamin L. Farinholt, repelled a Union force sent to burn the Southern Railroad bridge over the Staunton River. Brig. Gen. James H. Wilson and Brig. Gen. August V. Kautz led the Union cavalry. Today, the remains of Farinholt's fortification stands on the high bluff overlooking the river and bridge site, on the south side of the river.

Open to Public: *Park:* Daily 8am–dusk. *Visitors center:* Oct–Apr: Wed–Sat 9am–4pm, Sun 11am–4pm. May–Sept: Mon–Sat 9am–4:30pm, Sun 11am–4:30pm.

Admission Fees: Free.

Visitor Services: Visitors center, trails, tours in summer, museum, gift shop, information, picnic shelter, rest rooms, handicapped access to visitors center and part of trail. Handicapped access planned for earthworks.

Regularly Scheduled Events: Call for events, dates, and times.

Directions: Take Rte. 360 to Rte. 92. One mile north of Clover, turn right onto Rte. 600. Proceed about 2.5 miles to entrance. Turn right and follow signs.

Danville

10 **Site:** SUTHERLIN MANSION, Danville Museum of Fine Arts and History, 975 Main St., Danville, VA 24541, ☎ 804/793-5644

Description: For 1 week, April 3–10, 1865, Maj. William and Mrs. Sutherlin opened their home to Jefferson Davis and the Confederate government. The Confederate president wrote his final proclamation to the Confederacy on April 4 in this home. A new permanent exhibition, "Danville During the Civil War Years," opens in the fall of 1998.

Open to Public: Tues–Fri 10am–5pm, Sat–Sun 2–5pm.

Admission Fees: Free.

Visitor Services: Guided tours, gift shop, handicapped access.

Directions: Located on Rte. 29 Bus. (Main St.) in Danville.

Dayton

11 **Site:** SHENANDOAH VALLEY FOLK ART & HERITAGE CENTER, 382 High St., Dayton, VA 22821, ☎ 540/879-2681

Description: The museum, among other Civil War exhibits relating to the Shenandoah Valley, features Stonewall Jackson's "Valley Campaign" as explained through the narrative program of a 12-foot electronic relief map

where 300 lights follow the movements of the contending armies.

Open to Public: Mon and Wed–Sat 10am–4pm, Sun 1–4pm. Closed Tues.

Admission Fees: Adults $4, children under 18 $1, Harrisonburg/Rockingham Historical Society members free.

Visitor Services: Handicapped access, museum, gift shop, rest rooms, picnic area.

Directions: From I-81: take exit 245 at Harrisonburg and go west on Port Republic Rd. Turn left on VA Rte. 42, turn right on Rte. 732, and follow Rte. 732 as it turns sharply left. Site is on the right at the corner of Bowman Rd. and High St.

Ewing

 Site: CUMBERLAND GAP NATIONAL HISTORICAL PARK, U.S. 25E South, P.O. Box 1848, Middlesboro, KY 40965, ☎ 606/248-2817

Description: Cumberland Gap is the historic mountain pass on the Wilderness Road that opened the pathway for westward migration. During the Civil War, Cumberland Gap was first held by the South and then captured by Union troops. Each side held the gap twice.

Open to Public: Mid-June–Labor Day: Daily 8am–6pm. Labor Day–mid-June: Daily 8am–5pm. Visitors center closed Christmas and New Year's Day.

Admission Fees: Free.

Visitor Services: Bookstore, rest rooms, trails, museum, information, camping, handicapped access.

Directions: From I-75: take exit 29 at Corbin and follow signs on U.S. 25E (Cumberland Gap Pkwy.) through Middlesboro. The park is .25 mile south of Middlesboro, KY. From I-81 in TN: access U.S. 25E going north at Morristown. Park is approximately 50 miles north of Morristown. From I-81 at Bristol: follow U.S. 58 west to Cumberland Gap National Historical Park. Visitor Center is located 3 miles north on U.S. 25E.

Fairfax

Site: FAIRFAX MUSEUM AND VISITORS CENTER, 10209 Main St., Fairfax, VA 22030, ☎ 703/385-8414

Description: This local history museum is located in an 1873 school building. The museum features exhibits and information on Fairfax during the Civil War. Walking tours of Historic Fairfax are available during certain seasons and include the following Civil War–related sites:

Joshua Gunnell House (now a bed-and-breakfast and restaurant), now called **The**

Bailiwick Inn, open for lodging, lunch, tea, and dinner; call ☎ 1-800/366-7666). Open for walking tour. Address: 4023 Chain Bridge Rd., Fairfax, VA 22030. **Confederate Memorial at the Fairfax Cemetery.** Address: 10565 Main St., Fairfax, VA 22030. **Dr. William Gunnell House.** Open for walking tour. Address: 10520 Main St., Fairfax, VA 22030. **Fairfax County Courthouse.**

Open for walking tour. Address: 4000 Chain Bridge Rd., Fairfax, VA 22030.

Open to Public: *Museum:* Daily 9am–5pm. *Walking tours:* Apr–June and Sept–Nov: Sat mornings at 10am.

Admission Fees: *Museum:* Free. *Walking tours:* Adults $2, children $1.

Visitor Services: Tours, museum, gift shop, visitors center, rest rooms, handicapped access.

Directions: From I-66: exit onto Rte. 50 east. Follow until 50 becomes Main St. (Rte. 236). Proceed 4 miles, and museum is on the right.

Fort Monroe

14 **Site:** THE CASEMATE MUSEUM/FORT MONROE, P.O. Box 51341, Fort Monroe, VA 23651-0341, ☎ 757/727-3391

Description: This fort was never attacked by the Confederacy. Lee knew its strength; he helped build it. Fort Monroe denied the Confederacy access from the ocean to Norfolk and Richmond. Jefferson Davis was imprisoned here after being accused of plotting Lincoln's assassination.

Open to Public: Daily 10:30am–4:30pm.

Admission Fees: Free.

Visitor Services: Rest rooms, handicapped access, gift shop.

Regularly Scheduled Events: Guided tours.

Directions: From I-64: take exit 268 and follow signs to Fort Monroe.

Fredericksburg

15 **Site:** FREDERICKSBURG AREA MUSEUM. Mailing address: P.O. Box 922, Fredericksburg, VA 22404. Physical address: 907 Princess St., ☎ 540/371-5668

Description: This 1816 Town Hall/Market House was used as a hospital during the Civil War. Today, a portion of the permanent exhibit examines the civilian experiences during the war. The museum owns a large Civil War weapons collection as well as numerous letters and diaries from the period.

Open to Public: Mar–Nov: Mon–Sat 10am–5pm, Sun 1–5pm. Dec–Feb: Mon–Sat 10am–4pm, Sun 1–4pm.

Admission Fees: Adults $4, students $1, groups 20¢ off regular admission.

Visitor Services: Gift shop, rest rooms, handicapped access, elevator.

Directions: From I-95: take exit 130A and follow Rte. 3 east into downtown. Museum is at the corner of Rte. 3 (William St.) and Princess Anne St.

16 **Site:** FREDERICKSBURG AND SPOTSYLVANIA NATIONAL MILITARY PARK, 120 Chatham Lane, Fredericksburg, VA 22405, ☎ 540/371-0802

Description: Portions of four major Civil War battlefields (Fredericksburg, Chancellorsville, the Wilderness, and Spotsylvania Court House) and several other smaller historic sites (Chatham, Salem Church, and Guinia Station) make up the park. The four battlefields witnessed the death or wounding of more than 100,000 men over 2 years. It is the bloodiest ground in North America. The battles here reflect a continuum of war—the ebb and flow of a nation at war with itself—and the changing nature of the human experience (both civilian and military) during the 4 years of combat. The battles offer important insights into the minds and methods of great leaders, men like Lee, Jackson, and Grant. The battlefields reflect the changing nature of battlefield tactics as they evolved from open-field fighting to trench warfare. These changes had major implications for the soldiers' experience in battle, which changed dramatically between 1862 and 1864.

Open to Public: *Park and Visitors Center:* Daily 9am–5pm. Extended hours in summer: 8:30am–6:30pm.

Admission Fees: $3.

Visitor Services: Rest rooms, handicapped access, picnic area, trails.

Directions: From I-95: take exit 130A east on Rte. 3 to Fredericksburg battlefield.

Front Royal

17 **Site:** BELLE BOYD COTTAGE, 101 Chester St., Front Royal, VA 22630, ☎ 540/636-1446

Description: This site is an 1860 interpretation of a middle-class house, emphasizing the life of famed Confederate spy Belle Boyd. The information she gathered helped General Jackson win the Battle of Front Royal.

Open to Public: Mon–Fri 10am–4pm, Sat–Sun by appointment.

Admission Fees: Adults $2, children 12–16 $1.

Visitor Services: Guided tours, gift shop.

Regularly Scheduled Events: *Sat nearest May 23:* Battle of Front Royal Tour; *Second weekend in Oct:* Festival of Leaves.

Directions: From Washington, DC: take I-66 west; take exit 13 (Linden/Front Royal); then go 5 miles on Rte. 55 west to Rte. 522. Follow Rte. 522 (Commerce St.) into Front Royal; turn left onto Main St. and right onto Chester St.

18 **Site:** WARREN RIFLES CONFEDERATE MUSEUM, 95 Chester St., Front Royal, VA 22630, ☎ 540/636-6982 or 540/635-2219

Description: Exhibits include memorabilia of Belle Boyd, Mosby's Rangers, Stonewall Jackson, Robert E. Lee, Jefferson Davis, and others, together with arms, uniforms, and historic documents.

Open to Public: Apr 15–Oct 31: Mon–Sat 9am–4pm, Sun noon–4pm. Rest of the year: open by appointment.

Admission Fees: Adults $2, children under 12 free.

Visitor Services: None.

Directions: From I-66: take Front Royal exit; follow Main St. to Chester St.

Green Bay

19 **Site:** SAILOR'S CREEK BATTLEFIELD HISTORICAL STATE PARK, Rte. 2, P.O. Box 70, Green Bay, VA 23942, ☎ 804/392-3435

Description: Lee's ragged, hungry army fled Petersburg and Richmond, planning to converge and meet a supply train at Amelia. The expected supplies did not arrive. Then disaster struck. Lee's column bogged down along Sailor's Creek near Rice, and Federals overtook and decimated the stalled Confederates. Total Confederate losses have been estimated at approximately 8,000.

Open to Public: Daily from dawn to dusk.

Admission Fees: Free.

Visitor Services: Interpretive driving tour.

Directions: From Rte. 360: take Rte. 307; turn right onto Rte. 617, which goes through the park. From Rte. 460: take Rte. 307; turn left onto Rte. 617, which goes through the park.

Lexington

20 **Site:** LEE CHAPEL AT WASHINGTON AND LEE UNIVERSITY, Lexington, VA 24450, ☎ 540/463-8768

Description: Built in 1867 during Lee's term as president of Washington College, the Chapel contains his office, a museum with items belonging to Lee and his family, the Washington-Custis-Lee portrait collection, his tomb, and the famous recumbent statue of General Lee by Valentine. His horse, Traveller, is buried nearby.

Open to Public: Apr–Oct: Mon–Sat 9am–5pm, Sun 2–5pm. After Oct: Mon–Sat 9am–4pm.

Admission Fees: Free.

Visitor Services: Rest rooms, gift shop.

Regularly Scheduled Events: *Jan 19 at 11:30am:* Founders' Day celebrating Lee's birthday; *Oct 12 at noon:* Special service on the anniversary of General Lee's death.

Directions: From the intersection of I-81 and I-64: follow Rte. 11 south (Jefferson St.) 1 mile; campus is on the right.

21 Site: STONEWALL JACKSON'S GRAVE, STONEWALL JACKSON MEMORIAL CEMETERY, South Main St., Lexington, VA 22450, ☎ 540/463-2931

Description: Stonewall Jackson's grave is marked by Valentine's bronze statue of the General.

Open to Public: Daily from dawn to dusk.

Admission Fees: Free.

Visitor Services: None.

Directions: From I-64: take exit 55 to Rte. 11 south, which becomes Jefferson St. Follow Jefferson St. until it ends; turn left onto South Main, where the cemetery is located.

22 Site: STONEWALL JACKSON HOUSE, 8 East Washington St., Lexington, VA 24450, ☎ 540/463-2552

Description: This is the only home that famed Gen. Thomas "Stonewall" Jackson ever owned, restored to the time period of the Jackson occupancy, from 1859 to 1861. The house contains many of his personal possessions.

Open to Public: Mon–Sat 9am–5pm. June, July, and August: open until 6pm, Sun 1–5pm.

Admission Fees: Adults $5, youth (under 18) $2.50, children under 6 free. Groups (10 or more with advance reservation): Adults $4, youths $2.

Visitor Services: Orientation exhibits and changing exhibits, introductory slide show,

rest rooms, and museum shop are located on the ground floor and have handicapped access. Guided tours are given of the site, including the period rooms on the second floor, which are reached by a narrow stairway. A video tour of the second floor exhibit areas is available.

Regularly Scheduled Events: *Jan 21:* Stonewall Jackson's birthday.

Directions: From I-81: take 188N. From I-64: take exit 55. Follow the Historic Lexington Visitor Center signs to Washington St. in downtown Lexington. The Jackson House is located 1 block west of the visitors center.

23 Site: VIRGINIA MILITARY INSTITUTE MUSEUM, Jackson Memorial Hall, Lexington, VA 24450, ☎ 540/464-7232, www.vmi.edu/museum/museum.html

Description: This museum is rich in Civil War history; it includes "Stonewall" Jackson uniforms (one he was wearing when he was shot) and the mounted hide of his horse, Little Sorrel. Museum is in Jackson Memorial Hall, which features a mural of the heroic cadet charge in the Battle of New Market. The graves of six cadets killed

in the battle are on the grounds. VMI was shelled and burned by the Union army in June 1864.

Open to Public: Apr 1–Nov 30: Daily 9am–5pm. Dec 1–Mar 31: Mon–Sat 9am–5pm, Sun 2–5pm.

Admission Fees: Free.

Visitor Services: Handicapped access, rest rooms, food, tours.

Directions: Located on the Virginia Military Institute Campus. From I-81: take

Lexington exit (Rte. 11) 2 miles to VMI campus.

Lynchburg

24 Site: PEST HOUSE MEDICAL MUSEUM AND CONFEDERATE SECTION OF THE OLD CITY CEMETERY, 4th and Taylor sts. Mailing address: c/o Lynchburg Chamber Visitors Center, 216 12th St., Lynchburg, VA 24504, ☎ 804/847-1811

Description: The Confederate section of the historic Old City Cemetery contains the individually marked graves of more than 2,200 Confederate soldiers from 14 states. A monument at the entrance to the Confederate section remembers the 99 soldiers who died of smallpox at the nearby Pest House. Audio commentary at the Pest House Medical Museum describes medical conditions at this medical office of Dr. John J. Terrell during the Civil War. One room depicts conditions in the House of Pestilence quarantine hospital during the Civil War. The second room is furnished as Dr. Terrell's late 1800s medical office. An audio speaker is located outside the museum. For a tour inside the museum, call in advance.

Open to Public: *Cemetery and grounds of the Pest House:* Daily from dawn to dusk. Tours by appointment.

Admission Fees: Free.

Visitor Services: Information (brochures available at the gatehouse); interpretive markers; tours by appointment.

Directions: Located in the Old City Cemetery in downtown Lynchburg at 4th and Taylor sts.

Manassas

25 Site: THE MANASSAS MUSEUM, 9101 Prince William St., Manassas, VA 20110, ☎ 703/368-1873

Description: This museum interprets the history of the Northern Virginia Piedmont, emphasizing the Civil War. The museum grounds were the site of camps, fortifications, and Stonewall Jackson's raid.

Open to Public: Tues–Sun 10am–5pm. Closed Mon except federal holidays.

Admission Fees: Adults $2.50, children $1.50, seniors $1.50, groups $1.50/person. Tues: Free.

Visitor Services: Walking and driving tours, museum, gift shop, information, rest rooms, handicapped access.

Regularly Scheduled Events: *First weekend in Feb:* Anniversary weekend; *June–Oct:* Weekend programs/living history; *First Fri in Dec:* Holiday open house.

Directions: From I-66 east: take exit 47 to VA 234 south. Proceed south about 3 miles; bear right, following 234. Enter Old Town area, travel under the railroad overpass, turn left at the stoplight (Prince William St.), and proceed to the top of the hill. Museum is on the right. From I-66 west from Washington, DC: take exit 53, travel 7.5 miles on Rte. 28 south, and then follow signs.

---

26 **Site:** MANASSAS NATIONAL BATTLEFIELD PARK, 6511 Sudley Rd., Manassas, VA 22110, ☎ 703/361-1339

Description: Gen. Thomas J. "Stonewall" Jackson figured prominently in two Confederate victories here. Also known as "Bull Run," the First Battle of Manassas on July 21, 1861, ended any illusion of a short war. The Second Battle of Manassas, August 28–30, 1862, brought Southern forces to the height of their military power. The two battles are commemorated on this 5,000-acre battlefield park.

Open to Public: *Park:* Dawn to dusk. *Visitors Center:* Daily 8:30am–5pm.

Admission Fees: Adults $2, children under 17 free. Seniors may purchase a "Golden Age Pass," which is good for life, for $10.

Visitor Services: Trails, picnic area, rest rooms, handicapped access.

Directions: The park is 26 miles southwest of Washington, DC. The Visitors Center is on VA Rte. 234, .75 mile north of I-66 interchange (exit 47).

Mechanicsville

27 **Site:** COLD HARBOR BATTLEFIELD PARK, c/o Hanover Co. Parks and Recreation, 200 Berkley St., Ashland, VA 23005, ☎ 804/798-8062

Description: This County park with interpretive trails and National Park visitor center commemorate and interpret the battle fought here on May 31–June 12, 1864. The 50-acre park surrounds the historic Garthright House.

Open to Public: Daily from dawn to dusk.

Admission Fees: Free.

Visitor Services: Walking trail (approximately 1 mile) with interpretive signs; persons who would have difficulty on a gravel trail may call ahead for vehicle access. Rest rooms and other services available at Richmond National Battlefield Park, approximately .5 mile away.

Directions: Located on Cold Harbor Rd.(Rte. 156), 4 miles south of Mechanicsville business district.

Middleburg

28 **Site:** JOHN SINGLETON MOSBY HERITAGE AREA. Mailing address: P.O. Box 1178, Middleburg, VA 20116. Physical address: 207 E. Washington St., ☎ 540/687-6681

Description: Once the stage for Civil War activity in northern Virginia, the John Singleton Mosby Heritage area geographically encompasses what was commonly known as "Mosby's Confederacy," at the time Col. John Mosby led his Rangers in dramatic raids and cavalry battles. The scenic landscape is defined by the Blue Ridge, Bull Run, and Catoctin mountain ridges; and by Goose Creek, Little River, and the Shenandoah River. The heritage area features historic sites and landscapes, Virginia horse country, and recreational and cultural activities.

Open to Public: Hours vary by site.

Admission Fees: Individual sites within the area may charge admission.

Visitor Services: A free driving tour brochure, "Route 50: Drive Through History," is available from the address and telephone listed above; an audio tour tape, "Prelude to Gettysburg," is also available for $17.

Directions: From I-495: take Rte. 66 west to Rte. 50; take Rte. 50 west to Middleburg.

Middletown

29 **Site:** BELLE GROVE PLANTATION, 336 Belle Grove Rd., Middletown, VA 22645, ☎ 540/869-2028

Description: This 18th-century home, located on 100 acres, served as Sheridan's headquarters before and after the Battle of Cedar Creek in October 1864.

Open to Public: Mon–Sat 10am–4pm; last tour at 3:15pm. Sun 1–5pm; last tour at 4:15pm.

Admission Fees: Adults $5, children under 12 free, seniors $4.50, groups $4.50/person.

Visitor Services: Gift shop, quilt shop.

Directions: From I-66: take I-81 north to exit 302 (Rte. 627); go west on Rte. 627 to U.S. Rte. 11. Located 13 miles south of Winchester off Rte. 11; go 1 mile south of Middletown.

30 **Site:** CEDAR CREEK BATTLEFIELD VISITORS CENTER, P.O. Box 229, Middletown, VA 22645, ☎ 540/869-2064

Description: Cedar Creek Battlefield is the site of the last major battle in the Shenandoah Valley, which occurred on October 19, 1864. This dramatic conflict between Jubal Early and Phil Sheridan was the only Civil War battle where both sides experienced victory and defeat on the same day.

Open to Public: Mon–Sat 10am–4pm, Sun 1–5pm.

Admission Fees: Free.

Visitor Services: Interpretive center, bookstore, rest rooms, handicapped access.

Regularly Scheduled Events: *Oct:* Cedar Creek living history and reenactment weekend.

Directions: From I-66: take I-81 north to exit 302 (Rte. 627), go west on Rte. 627 to U.S. Rte. 11, and proceed 1 mile south to Cedar Creek.

New Market

31 Site: THE CAVALRY MUSEUM, 298 W. Old Crossroads, New Market, VA 22844, ☎ 540/740-3959

Description: The museum houses a collection of cavalry-related arms, armor, uniforms, and more, with special emphasis on the Civil War.

Open to Public: Apr–Nov: Daily 9am–5pm.

Admission Fees: Adults $5, children $2.50, children under 6 free.

Visitor Services: Gift shop, rest rooms, handicapped access.

Directions: From I-81: take exit 264, go west on Rte. 211, and make an immediate right onto Collins Dr. (Rte. 305). Museum is on the left.

32 Site: NEW MARKET BATTLEFIELD STATE HISTORICAL PARK AND HALL OF VALOR CIVIL WAR MUSEUM, P.O. Box 1864, New Market, VA 22844, ☎ 540/740-3101

Description: At New Market in 1864, about 6,000 Federals under Gen. Franz Sigel clashed with 4,500 Confederates led by Gen. John Breckinridge. The Hall of Valor, focal point of the 280-acre battlefield park, presents a survey of the entire Civil War through the exhibits.

Open to Public: Daily 9am–5pm.

Admission Fees: Adults (age 16 and over) $5, children $2, children under 5 free, adult

groups $4/person for self-guided tour, youth groups $1/person.

Visitor Services: Picnic areas, rest rooms, handicapped access.

Directions: From I-81: take exit 264 at New Market; turn onto Rte. 211 west and immediately turn right onto Rte. 305 (George Collins Pkwy.); travel to the end.

Newport News

33 Site: DAM NO. 1, NEWPORT NEWS PARK, 13560 Jefferson Ave., VA Rte. 143, Newport News, VA 23603, ☎ 757/886-7912

Description: To halt McClellan's march up the peninsula toward Richmond, General Magruder built three dams to create impassable lakes on the Warwick River and fortified the dams to prevent frontal assaults by Union forces.

Open to Public: *Park:* Daily from dawn to dusk. *Interpretive Center:* Memorial Day–Labor Day: Wed–Sun 9am–5pm. Rest of the year: Sat–Sun 9am–5pm.

Admission Fees: Free.

Visitor Services: Interpretive Center.

Directions: From I-64 east: take exit 250B, Fort Eustis Blvd. Turn left at junction of Eustis Blvd. and Rte. 143 (Jefferson Ave.). Park is on the right.

---

34 Site: ENDVIEW PLANTATION, 362 Yorktown Rd., Newport News, VA 23603, ☎ 757/887-1862

Description: Endview was built by Col. William Harwood around 1760. It was the pre–Civil War home of Capt. Humphrey Harwood Curtis, M.D., commander of the Warwick Beauregards (Co. H, 32nd Virginia Regiment). The house served as a Confederate and Union hospital during the Peninsula Campaign.

Open to Public: Mon–Sat 10am–4pm.

Admission Fees: Free; charge during special events.

Visitor Services: Guided tours, handicapped access to first floor.

Regularly Scheduled Events: *Mar and Dec:* Civil War reenactments; *June–Aug:* Summer camp for children; *Oct:* Night Walk; Living history programs throughout the year.

Directions: From I-64 east: take exit 247, turn left on Rte. 143 (Jefferson Ave.) and turn left at traffic light at Yorktown Rd. (Rte. 238). Endview is .25 miles on the right. From I-64 west: take exit 247, turn right on Yorktown Rd. (Rte. 238), and proceed straight through traffic light. Endview is on the right.

---

35 Site: LEE HALL MANSION, 163 Yorktown Rd., Newport News, VA 23603, ☎ 757/888-3371

Description: This Italianate plantation house was built around 1850 by affluent planter Richard Decatur Lee. The mansion was used as a headquarters during the 1862 Peninsula Campaign by Maj. Gen. John Bankhead McGruder and Gen. Joseph Johnston. A small redoubt on the lawn was the site of a Confederate hot-air observation balloon launching.

Open to Public: Mon–Sat 10am–4pm.

Admission Fees: $2.

Visitor Services: Guided tours, handicapped access to first floor.

Directions: From I-64 east: take exit 247, turn left on Rte. 143 (Jefferson Ave.), and turn right at traffic light at Yorktown Rd. (Rte. 238). Lee Hall is 1.4 miles on the right. From I-64 west: take exit 247 and turn left on Yorktown Rd. Lee Hall is 1.4 miles on the right.

36 Site: LEE'S MILL. Mailing Address: 9285 Warwick Rd., Newport News, VA 23607. Physical address: River's Ridge Circle, ☎ 757/247-8523

Description: These fortifications overlooking the Warwick River formed part of Maj. Gen. John Bankhead McGruder's 2nd Peninsula Defensive Line. On April 5, 1862, Lee's Mill was the scene of a brief skirmish that stopped Maj. Gen. George B. McClellan's march toward Richmond. The Lee's Mill fortifications prompted McClellan to besiege the Confederate defenses during the first phase of the Peninsula Campaign.

Open to Public: Daily from dawn to dusk.

Admission Fees: Free.

Visitor Services: Interpretive trail, guided tours by appointment.

Directions: From I-64 east: take exit 250 onto Rte. 105 south toward Ft. Eustis (second exit); turn right on Rte. 60 east. At first traffic light, turn right into Lee's Mill subdivision; then turn left on Riversridge Rd. Entrance is on the left past town houses. From I-64 west: take exit 250 onto Rte. 105 south toward Ft. Eustis (first exit); turn right on Rte. 60 east. At first traffic light, turn right into Lee's Mill subdivision; then turn left on Riversridge Rd. Entrance is on the left past townhouses.

---

37 Site: VIRGINIA WAR MUSEUM, 9285 Warwick Blvd., Newport News, VA 23607, ☎ 757/247-8523

Description: This museum offers a comprehensive review of U.S. military history since 1775. Within this context, the museum provides its visitors with a detailed survey of the Civil War.

Open to Public: Mon–Sat 9am–5pm, Sun 1–5pm.

Admission Fees: Adults $2, children 6–15 $1, seniors $1, active military $1. Group rates available.

Visitor Services: Picnic area, rest rooms, handicapped access.

Directions: From I-64: take the Mercury Blvd./James River Bridge exit (263A from east/263B from west); follow south on Mercury Blvd. to last traffic light before bridge. Turn right into Huntington Park and follow signs to museum.

Petersburg

38 Site: BLANDFORD CHURCH AND CEMETERY, 111 Rochelle Lane, Petersburg, VA 23803, ☎ 804/733-2396

Description: The church features 15 stained-glass windows, 13 of which were donated by states in memory of 30,000 Confederate soldiers buried in the cemetery. The church was used as a field hospital during the war.

Open to Public: Daily 10am–5pm; tours every half hour.

Admission Fees: Adults $3, children 7–12 $2, seniors $2, active military $2.

Visitor Services: Rest rooms, picnic area, book and gift shop, guided tours.

Regularly Scheduled Events: *June:* Confederate Memorial Day ceremony; *Oct:* Halloween cemetery tour.

Directions: From I-95 north: take the Wythe St. exit; turn right on Crater Rd.; turn left on Rochelle Lane. From I-95 south: take Crater Rd. exit from the interstate; turn right on Rochelle Lane.

---

39 **Site:** CENTRE HILL MANSION, Centre Hill Ct. Mailing address: 15 W. Bank St., Petersburg, VA 23803, ☎ 804/733-2401

Description: The mansion was built in 1823 by Robert Bolling and is a combination of Federal, Greek Revival, and Colonial architectural styles. The home was visited by two United States presidents, including Abraham Lincoln.

Open to Public: Daily 10am–5pm; tours every half hour.

Admission Fees: Adults $3, children 7–12 $2, seniors $2, active military $2.

Visitor Services: Rest rooms, gift shop.

Regularly Scheduled Events: *Jan:* Ghost Watch Night.

Directions: From I-95 south: take the Petersburg/Washington St. exit, go 1 stoplight, turn right onto Jefferson St., take first left onto Franklin St., and take immediate right to Centre Hill Ct.

---

40 **Site:** DRIVING TOUR OF THE ROUTE OF LEE'S RETREAT, P.O. Box 2107, Petersburg, VA 23804, ☎ 1-800/6-RETREAT

Description: The final days of the Civil War are interpreted on a 110-mile route of Lee's retreat from Petersburg to Appomattox through a 26-stop radio transmission tour. The route remains virtually unchanged since the Civil War. Call to receive a map of the tour.

Open to Public: Daily from dawn to dusk.

Admission Fees: Free.

Visitor Services: Rest rooms, information.

Directions: Start tour at Downtown Petersburg Visitor Center.

---

41 **Site:** PAMPLIN PARK CIVIL WAR SITE, 6523 Duncan Rd., Petersburg, VA 23803, ☎ 804/861-2408 or 804/861-2820

Description: Interpretive Center contains exhibits; fiber optic map; and interactive video displays on events leading to the April 2, 1865, battle resulting in the Union capture of Petersburg. Visit historic Tudor Hall plantation, an antebellum home and Confederate generals headquarters.

Open to Public: Daily 9am–5pm.

Admission Fees: Adults $3, children 7–11 $1.50, groups (10 or more) $2/person, children under 6 free.

Visitor Services: Rest rooms, handicapped access, 1.5 miles of interpretive trails, guided walks, living history.

Directions: From I-85: take exit 63A (U.S. 1 south) to Rt. 670 (Duncan Road). Park entrance on left 1 mile.

Living history at Pamplin Park Civil War Site, Petersburg, VA. (Photograph courtesy of Pamplin Park.)

---

42 **Site:** MAIN UNIT, PETERSBURG NATIONAL BATTLEFIELD, 1539 Hickory Hill Rd., Petersburg, VA 23803, ☎ 804/732-3531

Description: The Union army waged a 10-month campaign here from 1864–1865 to seize Petersburg, the center of railroads supplying Richmond and the Confederate Army of Northern Virginia.

Open to Public: *Battlefield:* Dawn to dusk. *Visitors Center:* Summer: Daily 8:30am–5:30pm. Winter: Daily 8am–5pm.

Admission Fees: June–Aug: Adults $5. Rest of the year: Adults $4.

Visitor Services: Bookstore, picnic area, trails, rest rooms, handicapped access.

Directions: From I-95: take exit 52; take Wythe St. (Rte. 36) east to park. The park is located 2.5 miles east of the center of Petersburg on State Rte. 36.

---

43 **Site:** CITY POINT UNIT, PETERSBURG NATIONAL BATTLEFIELD, 1539 Hickory Hill Rd., Petersburg, VA 23803, ☎ 804/458-9504

Description: Between June 1864 and April 1865, City Point was transformed from a sleepy village of fewer than 300 inhabitants into a bustling supply center for the 100,000 Federal soldiers on the siege lines in front of Petersburg and Richmond.

Open to Public: Daily 8:30am–4:30pm.

Admission Fees: *House tour:* Adults $1. Free with main park admission.

Visitor Services: Visitors center, books, rest rooms.

Directions: From I-95: take Hopewell exit; follow Rte. 10 east into Hopewell. At second traffic light, turn onto Main St., which becomes Appomattox St. Go 1 mile; turn left onto Cedar Lane and proceed approximately 2½ blocks to parking lot.

---

44 **Site:** FIVE FORKS UNIT, PETERSBURG NATIONAL BATTLEFIELD, 1539 Hickory Hill Rd., Petersburg, VA 23803, ☎ 804/265-8244

Description: On April 1, 1865, Union forces were able to capture this important crossroads that protected a nearby railroad supply line. The next evening, Petersburg was evacuated, and Lee began his retreat that ended at Appomattox Court House.

Open to Public: Daily during daylight hours. Brochure available outside contact station. *Contact station:* Summer: Wed–Sun 8:30am–5pm and as staffing permits.

Admission Fees: Free.

Visitor Services: Information, rest rooms, handicapped access.

Directions: From I-85: take Dinwiddie exit and follow signs to Five Forks Unit, approximately 6–7 miles.

---

45 **Site:** POPLAR GROVE NATIONAL CEMETERY, 1539 Hickory Hill Rd., Petersburg, VA 23803, ☎ 804/732-3531

Description: The cemetery was established in 1868 for Union soldiers who died during the Petersburg and Appomattox campaigns. Of the 6,178 interments, 4,110 are unknown. Others are buried in the City Point National Cemetery in Hopewell. Most Confederate soldiers who died during the siege are buried in Blandford Cemetery in Petersburg.

Open to Public: Daily from dawn to dusk.

Admission Fees: Free.

Visitor Services: Rest rooms.

Directions: From I-85: take Squirrel Level Rd. exit south to Wells Rd. and follow to Halifax Rd.; turn right. Proceed to Vaughn Rd.; turn right. Travel approximately 2 miles to cemetery; there is a sign on the left.

---

46 **Site:** SIEGE MUSEUM/TRAPEZIUM HOUSE, 15 West Bank St., Petersburg, VA 23803, ☎ 800/368-3595 or 804/733-2400

Description: The human side of the 10-month siege of Petersburg is portrayed in exhibits and in a film narrated by Petersburg native Joseph Cotton.

Open to Public: Daily 10am–5pm.

Admission Fees: Adults $3, children $2, seniors $2, groups $2/person.

Visitor Services: Rest rooms, handicapped access.

Regularly Scheduled Events: Special tours.

Directions: From I-95: take exit 52 (Washington St.). At third traffic light, turn right onto Sycamore St. and go to Petersburg Visitors Center at the end of the street for directions.

Port Republic

47 **Site:** PORT REPUBLIC BATTLEFIELD, Rockingham County, managed by the Association for the Preservation of Civil War Sites (APCWS), 11 Public Sq., Ste. 200, Hagerstown, MD 21740, ☎ 301/665-1400

Description: The last and most fiercely contested battle of Jackson's 1862 Valley campaign was fought here on June 9, 1862. The APCWS owns nine acres of the "Coaling" part of the Federal position.

Open to Public: Daily from dawn to dusk.

Admission Fees: Free.

Visitor Services: Walking trail, information.

Directions: From I-81 at Harrisonburg: take Port Republic Rd. (Rte. 659) south through Port Republic to Rte. 340. Turn left and drive 1.5 miles to Rte. 708. Turn right on Rte. 708. Park at the markers in front of the Episcopal church.

Richmond

48 **Site:** HOLLYWOOD CEMETERY, 412 South Cherry St., Richmond, VA 23220, ☎ 804/648-8501

Description: This most impressive and gorgeously landscaped cemetery contains graves of Confederate President Jefferson Davis, Gen. J. E. B. Stuart, Gen. George E. Pickett, and other Confederate notables, as well as President James Monroe and President John Tyler. Magnificent holly trees give the cemetery its name.

Open to Public: Daily 8am–6pm.

Admission Fees: Free.

Visitor Services: Information: Mon–Fri 8:30am–4:30pm.

Directions: From I-95: take exit 76B; proceed south on Belvedere St. and follow signs to Hollywood Cemetery.

49 **Site:** THE MUSEUM AND WHITE HOUSE OF THE CONFEDERACY, 1201 East Clay St., Richmond, VA 23219, ☎ 804/649-1861

Description: The Museum houses the world's most comprehensive collection of Confederate artifacts, documents, and art. The White House is the restored executive mansion of Confederate President Jefferson Davis.

Open to Public: Mon–Sat 10am–5pm, Sun noon–5pm.

Admission Fees: Adults $8, children 7–college $5, children 6 and under free, seniors 55 and over $7.

Visitor Services: Handicapped access, rest rooms, gift shop.

Directions: From I-95: take exit 74C (Broad St.) to 11th St. and turn right onto 11th. Museum is 2 blocks down on Clay St. Free parking in MCVH parking deck adjacent to the museum.

---

50 **Site:** RICHMOND NATIONAL BATTLEFIELD PARK/CHIMBORAZO VISITORS CENTER, 3215 East Broad St., Richmond, VA 23223, ☎ 804/226-1981

Description: This site commemorates several battles to capture Richmond, which was the Confederate capital during the Civil War. From the beginning of the war, "On to Richmond" was the rallying cry of Union troops, and the city was their primary objective for 4 years. Extensive remains of Union and Confederate earthworks are preserved. Included battlefields are Gaines' Mill, Malvern Hill, and Cold Harbor.

Open to Public: *Park:* Daily from dawn to dusk. *Visitors Center:* Daily 9am–5pm.

Admission Fees: Free.

Visitor Services: Handicapped access, rest rooms, picnic area, self-guided tours.

Directions: From I-95: take East Broad St. exit. Begin tour at Chimborazo Visitors Center.

---

51 **Site:** THE VALENTINE MUSEUM, 1015 East Clay St., Richmond, VA 23219, ☎ 804/649-0711

Description: The Valentine Museum collects, preserves, and interprets the materials of the life and history of Richmond, including the Civil War. The studio contains the bust statues of Robert E. Lee, "Stonewall" Jackson, Albert Sidney Johnston, Jefferson Davis, G. E. Pickett, and other Civil War figures, as well as the plaster cast of "Recumbent Lee." The 1812 Wickham House, a National Historic Landmark, illustrates the social and architectural history of that time period. The Valentine maintains the South's largest costume and textile collection, as well as extensive holdings in photographs, documents, industrial artifacts, and decorative arts. Lunch is served year-round in the garden.

Open to Public: *Museum:* Daily 10am–5pm, Sun noon–5pm.

Admission Fees: *Museum:* Adults $5, children $3, seniors $4.

Visitor Services: Food, rest rooms.

Directions: From I-95 north or south and I-64 east: take exit 74C (Broad St.), turn right onto Broad St., turn right onto 11th, turn left at Clay St., and turn left on 10th. The museum parking lot is on the left.

52 Site: THE VIRGINIA CAPITOL, Capitol Square, Richmond, VA 23219, ☎ 804/786-4344

Description: Designed by Thomas Jefferson, this officially became the capital of the Confederacy on May 21, 1861. A statue of Robert E. Lee and busts of Confederate heroes Stonewall Jackson, J. E. B. Stuart, Joseph E. Johnson, Fitzhugh Lee, among others, are located here.

Open to Public: Daily 9am–5pm.

Admission Fees: Free.

Visitor Services: Guided tours.

Directions: From I-95: take Third St. exit (Coliseum), continue straight, turn left onto Franklin St., and turn left onto Ninth St. Capitol Square is the first right.

53 Site: VIRGINIA HISTORICAL SOCIETY/CENTER FOR VIRGINIA HISTORY, The Battle Abbey, 428 N. Boulevard, Richmond, VA 23221, ☎ 804/358-4901

Description: The Museum of Virginia History offers seven galleries exhibiting rare Virginia treasures. Travel through Virginia history with the expanded exhibit "The Story of Virginia, an American Experience," opening in the fall of 1998. Explore the development of Virginia from the Colonial period and the Civil War, through World War I and World War II and into the present. Tour the exhibit, using handheld gallery guides that let you decide how much information you want about each object, and open drawers of "please touch" objects. Visit the Library of Virginia History for historical and genealogical research. See "The Four Seasons of the Confederacy," dramatic Civil War murals by Charles Hoffbauer; and the Maryland-Steuart collection of Confederate-made weapons, the largest and finest in the world. The Battle

Abbey, part of the VHS complex, is a memorial to the Confederate soldier. See the Civil War horse statue, a memorial to all horses and mules that were casualties of the war. Allow 1 hour minimum.

Open to Public: Mon–Sat 10am–5pm, Sun 1–5pm. Library closed Sun.

Admission Fees: *Museum:* Adults $4, seniors $3, students and children $2, Historical Society members free.

Visitor Services: Museum, gift shop, library, handicapped access, free parking, picnic area.

Regularly Scheduled Events: Call for information on lectures and special events held year-round.

Directions: From I-95: take exit 78 and follow signs to Virginia Historical Society.

Strasburg

54 Site: FISHER'S HILL BATTLEFIELD CIVIL WAR SITE, managed by the Association for the Preservation of Civil War Sites (APCWS), 11 Public Sq., Suite 200, Hagerstown, MD 21740, ☎ 301/665-1400

Description: APCWS maintains 194 acres of the Fisher's Hill Battlefield, where Gen. Jubal Early's Confederates were defeated on September 22, 1864.

Open to Public: Daily from dawn to dusk.

Admission Fees: Free.

Visitor Services: Walking trail, information.

Directions: From I-81: take exit 298 to Rte. 11, through Strasburg; go right from VA Rte. 1 to State Rte. 601 and follow signs.

Stratford

55 **Site:** STRATFORD HALL PLANTATION, Stratford, VA 22558, ☎ 804/493-8038

Description: Built in the 1730s, this magnificent Potomac River plantation was the home of four illustrious generations of Lees. It was also the birthplace of Robert E. Lee.

Open to Public: Daily 9am–4pm.

Admission Fees: Adults $7, children $3.

Visitor Services: Tours, gift shop.

Directions: From Richmond: take 360 through Tappahannock to Warsaw; take Rte. 3 west to State Rte. 214 and proceed to Stratford Hall. From I-95 at Fredericksburg: take Rte. 3 east to State Rte. 214 and go 1 mile.

Williamsburg

56 **Site:** COLONIAL WILLIAMSBURG, P.O. Box 1776, Williamsburg, VA 23187,
☎ 800/HISTORY

Description: Colonial Williamsburg is a historic restoration encompassing 186 acres and 88 original buildings of the colonial capital of 18th-century Virginia. Although the primary focus is the Colonial period, there is a great deal of Civil War history to be explored in the town. In addition to being the site of the Battle of Williamsburg (May 5, 1862), the town was a central mustering point for Confederates in 1861. Several Confederate hospitals were located here. Beginning in mid-1862, the town was occupied by Federal forces for 3 years. Much of the battlefield, several

Confederate redoubts, and many Civil War specific buildings survive.

Open to Public: Daily 9am–5pm, with seasonal variations. Civil War Tours offered on selected nights; call for schedule.

Admission Fees: *Basic Pass:* Adults $25, children $15. *Patriot's Pass:* Adults $33, children $19. Other options available.

Visitor Services: Tours, museums, gift shop, visitors center, rest rooms, food, lodging, handicapped access. Ask for Civil War brochure and guidebook.

Regularly Scheduled Events: Civil War walking tours on selected nights, with living history; Annual Civil War conference.

Directions: From I-64: take Camp Peary/Colonial Williamsburg exit. Follow signs to visitors Center.

Winchester

57 **Site:** STONEWALL CONFEDERATE CEMETERY, Mt. Hebron, 305 East Boscawen St., Winchester, VA 22601, ☎ 540/662-4868

Description: This cemetery contains the remains of 3,000 Confederate soldiers killed in nearby battles.

Open to Public: *Summer:* Daily 7:30am–6pm. *Winter:* Daily 7:30am–5pm.

Admission Fees: Free.

Visitor Services: A roster listing the Confederate burials is available from the office ($5).

Directions: From I-81: take Rte. 7, which turns into Berryville Ave.; turn left on Pleasant Valley Rd.; proceed 1 block and follow the iron fence to the gatehouse entrance.

58 **Site:** STONEWALL JACKSON'S HEADQUARTERS MUSEUM, 415 North Braddock St., Winchester, VA 22601, ☎ 540/667-3242

Description: From this brick house, Stonewall Jackson commanded his forces in defense of the strategic Shenandoah Valley.

Open to Public: Apr 1–Oct 31: Daily 10am–4pm.

Admission Fees: Adults $3.50, children 6–12 $1.75, seniors $3.

Visitor Services: Gift shop, rest rooms.

Directions: From I-81: take exit 313 and follow the signs.

Yorktown

59 **Site:** COLONIAL NATIONAL HISTORICAL PARK, P.O. Box 210, Yorktown, VA 23690, ☎ 757/898-3400

Description: Though established to commemorate the Colonial era, this park also possesses extensive vestiges of the Civil War related to the Siege of 1862 during the Peninsula Campaign.

Open to Public: *Visitors Center:* Winter: Daily 9am–5pm. Summer: Daily 8:30am–5:30pm.

Admission Fees: Adults $4, children 16 and under free.

Visitor Services: Information, visitors center, rest rooms.

Regularly Scheduled Events: *Memorial Day weekend:* Civil War weekend; *Spring:* Half-day Civil War tours by reservation only.

Directions: From I-64: take exit 242 and follow the signs to Colonial Pkwy.

WASHINGTON, D.C.

$\mathscr{I}$N 1861, THE CAPITAL OF THE UNITED STATES remained incomplete. The Capitol's dome was unfinished, sanitary conditions were horrible, and there were deep political divisions. The Civil War transformed the capital that antebellum Americans called Washington City.

From the firing on Fort Sumter, South Carolina, the war became the central fact of the city's life. During the conflict's early days, fear reigned as Southern sympathizers in Maryland attempted to isolate the city. Order returned when the first Union volunteers poured into the District, but in July, the Union rout at First Bull Run produced near panic. During the following months, thousands of drilling soldiers and an elaborate defensive perimeter that included 68 forts, 22 batteries, and sprawling earthworks brought security to the city. Washington, D.C., like its Confederate counterpart, Richmond, Virginia, 100 miles to the south, became a nation's symbol, the one place that could not be surrendered to the enemy.

The war brought growth, activity, and problems. The city's population, fueled in part by freed slaves who poured in from the South, quadrupled from 41,000 in 1860 to 160,000 at its wartime peak. With the arrival of Northerners, the city's distinctive antebellum Southern atmosphere changed. Besides the many soldiers, the city attracted lobbyists, speculators, inventors, and job seekers who came in droves, each looking for a share of the money to be made in the wartime economy.

The mood of the city's inhabitants reflected the fortunes of the Union army: euphoria after a victory, despair following a defeat. Government buildings, including the Capitol, the Treasury, and the Patent Office were used to house and supply the troops, and cattle grazed on the Mall. Numerous private residences, taken over by the Federal government, became hospitals teeming with wounded young men.

Workmen finally completed the Capitol's dome in time for Lincoln's second inaugural in March 1865. On April 14, 1865, just 5 days after Lee's surrender at Appomattox, the president was assassinated at downtown Ford's Theatre, delaying for a time the restoration of the American Union.

Washington, D.C.

1   **Site:** FORD'S THEATRE AND PETERSEN HOUSE NATIONAL HISTORIC SITE, 511 and 516 10th St., NW, Washington, DC 20004, ☎ 202/426-6924

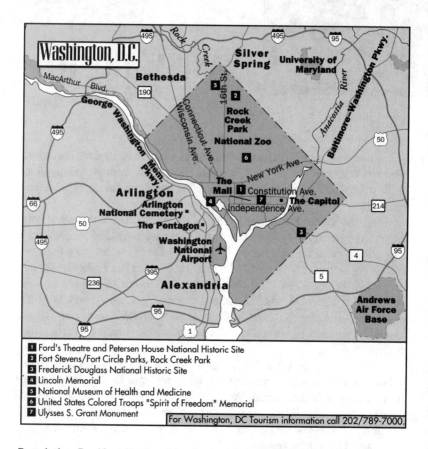

Washington, D.C.

1. Ford's Theatre and Petersen House National Historic Site
2. Fort Stevens/Fort Circle Parks, Rock Creek Park
3. Frederick Douglass National Historic Site
4. Lincoln Memorial
5. National Museum of Health and Medicine
6. United States Colored Troops "Spirit of Freedom" Memorial
7. Ulysses S. Grant Monument

For Washington, DC Tourism information call 202/789-7000.

Description: President Abraham Lincoln was shot while attending a play at Ford's Theatre on April 14, 1865. Following the shooting, he was moved to the Petersen House, a neighboring boardinghouse, where he died 9 hours later.

Open to Public: Daily 9am–5pm. Closed during matinees and rehearsals—call to confirm hours.

Admission Fees: Free.

Visitor Services: Museum, bookstore, limited handicapped access.

Directions: Located on 10th St., NW between E and F sts.

---

2 **Site:** FORT STEVENS/FORT CIRCLE PARKS, Rock Creek Park, Washington, DC, ☎ 202/426-6829 (Rock Creek Nature Center)

Description: At the outset of the Civil War, a system of flanking forts and batteries was constructed around Washington. One such spot was Fort Massachusetts, built along the Seventh Street Pike, a thoroughfare leading to and from Washington. The fort was enlarged on two occasions. In 1863, its name was changed to Fort Stevens, in memory of Brig. Gen. Isaac Ingalls Stevens, who lost his life at Chantilly, Virginia. On July 11, 1864, Fort Stevens was the site of the only battle within the District of Columbia. Fort Stevens is one of the defenses that today is part of the Fort Circle Parks in Washington, D.C.; Maryland; and Virginia. Rock Creek Park administers Battery Kemble, Fort Bayard, Fort Reno, Fort DeRussy, Fort Stevens, Fort Slocum, Fort Totten, and Fort Bunker Hill.

Open to Public: Daily from dawn to dusk.

Admission Fees: Free.

Visitor Services: Call about ranger-led tours and special ceremonies.

Directions: Fort Stevens is located at 13th and Quackenbos sts., NW, in Washington, DC.

For More Information

To receive the brochure "Fort Circle Parks," contact the Rock Creek Nature Center at ☎ **202/426-6829.** See also entries in this *Guide* for Fort Foote in Fort Washington, Maryland, and Fort Ward in Alexandria, Virginia.

FREDERICK DOUGLASS (1818–95)

Frederick Douglass National Historic Site, Washington, DC. (Photograph courtesy of The Civil War Trust.)

"*Human government is for the protection of rights, and when human government destroys human rights it ceases to be a government and becomes a foul and blasting conspiracy. If you look over your list of rights, you do not find among them any right to make a slave of your brother.*"

—*Frederick Douglass*

Frederick Douglass spent his early years in a home broken beyond most people's comprehension. His mother, a slave, was forced to leave him as an infant, and he

continues

never knew the identity of his white father. He lived in poverty with grandparents and cousins. Beyond that, Douglass was a slave—listed on an inventory along with mules and bushels of wheat, and subject to being sold on a whim.

But adversity did not break the spirit of young Douglass; he possessed an intellectual curiosity undeterred by his circumstances. At age 8, he was sent to Baltimore as a house servant where he became fascinated by the "mystery of reading" and decided that education was "the pathway from slavery to freedom." Because it was illegal to educate slaves, Douglass learned to read and write by trading bread for reading lessons and tracing over words in discarded spelling books until his handwriting was smooth and graceful. By age 13, he was reading articles about the "abolition of slavery" to other slaves. When he escaped to freedom at age 20, Douglass eagerly shared his hard-earned wisdom.

Douglass' lifetime triumphs were many: abolitionist, women's rights activist, author, owner/editor of an antislavery newspaper, fluent speaker of many languages, Minister to Haiti, and the most respected African American orator of the 19th century. In his closing years at Cedar Hill, he was deemed the "Sage of Anacostia," an accolade that celebrated the intellectual spirit within him that never grew old.

Credit: National Park Service

---

3 **Site:** FREDERICK DOUGLASS NATIONAL HISTORIC SITE, 1411 W St., SE, Washington, DC 20020, ☎ 202/426-5961

Description: Frederick Douglass, the nation's leading black spokesman during the 19th century, lived at this home from 1877 to 1895. Douglass was U.S. minister to Haiti in 1889.

Open to Public: *Summer:* Daily 9am–5pm. *Winter:* Daily 9am–4pm.

Admission Fees: Admission to the Visitor Center is free; advance notice is suggested. *Tours of the home:* Adults $3, seniors $1.50, children under 6 free. Call DESTINET at ☎ 800/365-2267 for advance tickets. Tickets may be purchased on-site if space is available. Approved school groups admitted free—call DESTINET at ☎ 800/401-4775 for reservations.

Visitor Services: Visitors center, museum.

Regularly Scheduled Events: *Feb 14:* Wreath laying on Douglass' birthday.

Directions: From downtown: cross the 11th St. (Anacostia) Bridge to Martin Luther King (MLK) Ave. and turn left on W St. The home is on top of the hill at 14th and W sts., SE. From I-295 north or south: take Pennsylvania Ave. east exit. Proceed east on Pennsylvania Ave. 2 blocks to Minnesota Ave. Turn right on to Minnesota to Good Hope Rd. Turn right on Good Hope Rd., proceed one-half block, turn left on 14th St., and turn left on W.

4 **Site:** LINCOLN MEMORIAL, 23rd St., NW, Washington, DC 20242, ☎ 202/485-9880

Description: This classical structure contains Daniel Chester French's monument sculpture of the 16th president of the United States. Lincoln's Gettysburg Address and Second Inaugural Address are carved on the marble walls.

Open to Public: Daily 8am–midnight. Closed Christmas.

Admission Fees: Free.

Visitor Services: Handicapped access.

Directions: The memorial is located at the western end of the Mall, in downtown Washington between Constitution and Independence aves. at 23rd St., NW. Because of limited parking, visitors are strongly encouraged to use METRO. The Smithsonian METRO stop on the Mall is approximately 10 blocks from the Lincoln Memorial. The National Park Service's Tourmobile stops at all monuments.

---

5 **Site:** NATIONAL MUSEUM OF HEALTH AND MEDICINE. Mailing address: 6825 16th St., NW, Washington, DC. 20306-6000, ☎ 202/782-2200

Description: At the time of the Civil War, before the X-ray was discovered and the germ theory of disease had taken hold, most physicians had never seen a gunshot wound and didn't know how to treat one. Amputation was the most common treatment for serious leg or arm injury, and more soldiers died of disease than from enemy bullets. The National Museum of Health and Medicine was established in response. The organizers of the Army Medical Museum, founded in 1862, hoped to centralize information gained through the experiences of Union doctors on the battlefield and share it with medical practitioners through exhibitions and publications. The Army doctors here performed the autopsies on President Lincoln and John Wilkes Booth. Today, the museum continues to address contemporary health concerns, but the newly expanded exhibit on Civil War medicine continues to be a featured attraction. The display includes icons such as the lead bullet that took Abraham Lincoln's life.

Open to Public: Daily 10am–5:30pm. Closed Christmas.

Admission Fees: Free.

Visitor Services: Rest rooms, telephones, group tours, wheelchair accessible, ASL interpreters available with advance notice, dining facilities nearby.

Directions: Located 5 miles north of the White House between 16th St. and Georgia Ave., NW, in Building 54 on the Walter Reed Army Medical Center Campus. From downtown: take 16th St., NW, beyond Carter Baron Amphitheatre and the junction of Military Rd. At the first gate after Aspen St., turn right onto the medical center campus. At the circle, turn right onto 14th St. Proceed 1 block to stop sign. Museum is on the left. From I-495: take exit 31-B/Georgia Ave.-Silver Spring. Follow Georgia Ave. south beyond the junction with East-West Hwy. (Rte. 410), Alaska Ave. and Fern St., to Elder St., NW. Turn right onto the medical center campus. Turn right at the stop sign and follow winding road past the hospital/garage complexes to the horseshoe-shaped drive at the museum's entrance.

---

6 **Site:** UNITED STATES COLORED TROOPS "SPIRIT OF FREEDOM" MEMORIAL, 10th and U sts., NW, Washington, DC 20009, ☎ 202/667-2667

Description: This national monument is the "first" national memorial to the 208,480 colored soldiers and their 7,000 white officers who fought in the American Civil War from 1862 to 1865. The monument features sculptor Ed Hamilton's "Spirit of Freedom" memorial. The names of the soldiers are engraved on plaques, placed on curved walls behind the sculpture. The Memorial Theme Park is by Devrouax & Purnell architects, and designed by Ed Dunson.

Open to Public: Opens July 15, 1998. Daily 24 hours. Group tours by appointment: 9am–5pm.

Admission Fees: Free.

Visitor Services: None; a visitors center is planned for the future.

Regularly Scheduled Events: *May:* Memorial Day ceremony; *Nov:* Veterans Day ceremony.

Directions: Located at the U St./Cardozo METRO station on the green line, at the intersection of U St. and Vermont Ave., NW.

---

7 **Site:** ULYSSES S. GRANT MONUMENT, U.S. Capitol Grounds West, Washington, DC.

Description: The Grant Memorial is one of the most important sculptural groups in Washington. It consists of a central equestrian statue of Grant with two sculptured groups of military figures situated at either end of a large marble platform.

Open to Public: Daily 24 hours.

Admission Fees: Free.

Visitor Services: None.

Directions: Located at Union Square at the east end of the Mall, directly below the west grounds of the Capitol. Because of limited parking, visitors are strongly encouraged to use METRO. Use Smithsonian, South Capitol, or Union Station METRO stops. The Smithsonian METRO stop on the Mall is approximately 10 blocks from the Grant Monument. The National Park Service's Tourmobile stops at all monuments.

WEST VIRGINIA

HE SLAVERY QUESTION, which between 1830 and 1860 tore at the fabric of the nation, left the Commonwealth of Virginia equally divided. Perhaps the most incendiary of events connected with the slavery issue took place on what is now West Virginian soil, with the seizure of the federal arsenal at Harpers Ferry in 1859 by the fiery abolitionist John Brown. His plan for arming the slaves of northern Virginia and inciting a general uprising, together with the secrecy with which his plan was carried out, threw the South into a panic.

In the wake of Fort Sumter and President Lincoln's call for volunteers, sentiment in the Virginia Convention shifted. Many delegates who had opposed secession now opposed the president's intention to use coercive federal powers against a state just as vigorously. When the questions of Virginia's position came to a vote, the majority cast their ballots to join the newly formed Confederate States of America. However, of the 47 delegates from western Virginia, more than two-thirds voted against leaving the Union.

The future of the newly proposed state depended on control of western Virginia by the Union. From the outset of the war, both the Union and Confederate governments endeavored to hold West Virginia because of its valuable salt resources, its productive farms, and the strategic section of the Baltimore and Ohio Railroad that traversed the eastern and northern sections of the state. Moreover, both sides were well aware of the psychological advantages in controlling West Virginia.

Most of the decisive fighting in West Virginia took place before the end of 1861. In the eastern Panhandle, positions sometimes changed hands with bewildering rapidity. Military action there revolved around efforts to gain or retain control of valuable segments of the Baltimore and Ohio Railroad. In the campaigns in the Shenandoah Valley, West Virginia's distinguished Confederate General Thomas Jonathan "Stonewall" Jackson played a vital part. Farther south, the Confederates took the initiative and pushed Union troops out of Fayetteville and Charleston. Other than some daring Confederate raids in central West Virginia, there were few important battles in the state after 1862. With the engagements at White Sulphur Springs, or Rocky Gap, and Droop Mountain in the autumn of 1863, the Confederates had been forced out of most of West Virginia.

During the early years of the Civil War, the statehood issue continued to be debated. The restored Government of Virginia eventually approved the separation, and Congress passed the West Virginia statehood bill. Although he had misgivings, President Lincoln issued a proclamation under which West Virginia entered the Union on June 20, 1863, as the 35th state.

by Jeffrey Harpold, West Virginia Division of Tourism

West Virginia

1 Camp Allegheny
2 Rich Mountain Battlefield Civil War Site
3 Bulltown Historic Area
4 Cheat Summit Fort
5 Grafton National Cemetery
6 Harpers Ferry National Historical Park
7 Droop Mountain Battlefield State Park
8 Lewisburg National Register
   Historic District/Visitor Center
9 Belle Boyd House/Civil War Museum
   of the Lower Shenandoah Valley
10 Philippi Covered Bridge
11 Philippi Historic District

12 Shepherdstown Historic District
13 Carnifex Ferry Battlefield State Park
14 Jackson's Mill Historic Area
15 West Virginia Independence Hall

For West Virginia Tourism information call 800/CALL-WVA.

Bartow

1 **Site:** CAMP ALLEGHENY. Mailing address: 200 Sycamore St., Elkins, WV 26241,
☎ 304/636-1800

Description: Established by Confederate forces in the summer of 1861 to control the Staunton-Parkersburg Turnpike, this camp, at 4,400 feet above sea level, was one of the highest of the Civil War. Although Confederate Gen. Edward Johnson's troops won the battle against Union forces under the command of Gen. R. H. Milroy, the loss of men due to the harsh winter climate and the logistical nightmare of keeping the camp supplied contributed to the decision to abandon it in April 1862.

Open to Public: Daily from dawn to dusk.

Admission Fees: Free.

Visitor Services: Interpretive signs.

Directions: From I-81 at Staunton: take U.S. 250 west to just beyond the Virginia/West Virginia line, turn left at County Rd. 3, take a right at the T, and go 2 more miles. *Note:* Road is sometimes closed because of snow; call ☎ 304/636-1800 for road information.

Beverly

2 | **Site:** RICH MOUNTAIN BATTLEFIELD CIVIL WAR SITE, P.O. Box 227, Beverly, WV 26253, ☎ 800/422-3304 or 304/637-RICH (7424)

Description: Rich Mountain Battlefield Civil War Site includes the battle site, Confederate Camp Garnett, and connecting section of the old Staunton-Parkersburg Turnpike. On July 11, 1861, Union troops under Gen. George B. McClellan routed Confederates holding the pass over Rich Mountain. This victory led to General McClellan's appointment to command the Army of the Potomac. It also gave the Union control of northwestern Virginia, allowing the formation of the state of West Virginia two years later.

Open to Public: Daily from dawn to dusk.

Admission Fees: Free.

Visitor Services: Trails. *Note:* Visitor information, a display, and a gift shop are located in Beverly.

Regularly Scheduled Events: *Semiannually, 1999, 2001,* Reenactment/living history.

Directions: From I-79: take exit 99 at Weston, take U.S. Rte. 33 east to Elkins, and then U.S. Rte. 219/250 south to Beverly. Turn west in Beverly onto Rich Mountain Rd. and follow road 5 miles up the mountain to battlefield. Camp Garnett is 1.5 miles farther. *Note:* Road is sometimes closed because of snow. Call either of the numbers listed above to check local weather information.

Burnsville

3 | **Site:** BULLTOWN HISTORIC AREA, c/o Burnsville Lake, Corps of Engineers, HC 10, Box 24, Burnsville, WV 26335, ☎ 304/452-8170 (number for visitors center, May–Sept) or 304/853-2371 (office)

Description: The Battle of Bulltown occurred at the site of fortifications on a knoll overlooking a key covered bridge that once crossed the Little Kanawha River along the Weston-Gauley Turnpike. The highway was the artery for transportation in Central West Virginia connecting the northern and southern portions of the state. Had Confederate Commander "Mudwall" Jackson's (Stonewall's cousin) assault on Bulltown been successful, he would have cut communications between troops in northern West Virginia and the Kanawha Valley, creating an opportunity to march on

Wheeling, the center of Union support in West Virginia.

At the site are fortifications dug to protect the fort, the burial site of seven unknown Confederate soldiers, intact sections of the Turnpike, and the Cunningham House. The Cunningham House housed supporters of the Confederacy at the time of the Civil War. Today, it serves as the center for Historic Bulltown Village, which dates from before the Civil War and includes farm buildings, two relocated log homes, and the log St. Michael's Church.

Open to Public: *Interpretive center:* May–Sept: 10am–6pm.

Admission Fees: Free.

Visitor Services: Camping, trails, interpretive center, information, rest rooms, handicapped access. (Some trails are paved; unpaved trails may require someone to assist visitors in wheelchairs.) Seasonal tours of battlefield and historic village, or by appointment.

Directions: From I-79: exit at Flatwoods, WV, or Roanoke, WV; follow signs for Bulltown, Burnsville Lake (approximately 10 miles from Flatwoods and 20 miles from the Roanoke exit on U.S. 19 and State Rte. 4).

Durbin

4 **Site:** CHEAT SUMMIT FORT. Mailing address: 200 Sycamore St., Elkins, WV 26241, ☎ 304/636-1800

Description: Gen. George B. McClellan ordered this pit and parapet fort to be built in 1861 under the command of Gen. R. H. Milroy to secure the Staunton-Parkersburg Turnpike and protect the Baltimore and Ohio Railroad. The Confederate failure to take the fort in September 1861 was central in the failure of Robert E. Lee's western Virginia campaign.

Open to Public: Daily from dawn to dusk.

Admission Fees: Free.

Visitor Services: Brochure, interpretive signs, viewing platform, trails.

Regularly Scheduled Events: *Apr or early May:* Semiannual living history and reenactment.

Directions: From I-79 near Weston, WV: take U.S. 33 east to Elkins; then take U.S. 250 south to just before Cheat Bridge. Turn right at the sign, right again at the T, and go about 1 mile to the top. *Note:* Road is sometimes closed because of snow; call ☎ **304/636-1800** for road information.

Grafton

5 **Site:** GRAFTON NATIONAL CEMETERY, 431 Walnut St., Grafton, WV 26354, ☎ 304/265-2044

Description: Grafton was established in 1867 by Congressional legislation to offer a final resting place for the men who died during the Civil War. Burials were removed from other cemeteries to make Grafton the final resting place for 2,133 soldiers, including 664 unknown soldiers. Notably, Grafton contains the grave of the Civil War's first land engagement casualty, Pvt. T. Bailey Brown.

Open to Public: Daily from dawn to dusk.

Admission Fees: Free.

Visitor Services: Information, rest rooms.

Regularly Scheduled Events: *May:* Memorial Day parade and service—yearly since 1879; *Nov:* Veterans Day service.

Directions: From I-79: take Rte. 250 for approximately 10 miles; then take Rte. 50 into Grafton.

Harpers Ferry

6 **Site:** HARPERS FERRY NATIONAL HISTORICAL PARK, P.O. Box 65, Harpers Ferry, WV 25425, ☎ 304/535-6223

Description: Harpers Ferry, the site of abolitionist John Brown's 1859 raid on the First Federal Arsenal, changed hands eight times during the war. It became the base of operations for Union invasions into the Shenandoah Valley. Stonewall Jackson achieved his most brilliant victory here in September 1862, when he captured 12,500 Union soldiers.

Open to Public: Daily 8am–5pm.

Admission Fees: Bicycles, motorcycles, and walk-ins $3. Cars $5.

Visitor Services: Trails, museum, gift shop, information, rest rooms, handicapped access.

Regularly Scheduled Events: *Last Sat in June:* Freedom's Birth—An American Experience, with fireworks; *Second Saturday in Sept:* Civil War living history weekend; *Second full weekend in Oct:* Election Day, 1860; *First weekend in Dec:* Keeping Christmas.

Directions: From Washington: take I-270 north to I-70 to west Rte. 340. From Gettysburg: take MD Rte. 15 south to west Rte. 340. From Shenandoah Valley: take I-81 north to WV 51 east. From Baltimore: take I-70 west to Rte. 340 west.

View of Harpers Ferry National Historical Park from Maryland Heights. (Photograph courtesy of Harpers Ferry National Historical Park.)

Hillsboro

7 **Site:** DROOP MOUNTAIN BATTLEFIELD STATE PARK, HC 64, P.O. Box 189, Hillsboro, WV 24946, ☎ 304/653-4254

Description: Droop Mountain Battlefield is the site of one of West Virginia's largest

and last important Civil War battles. The battle was fought on November 6, 1863, between the Union army of Gen. William Averell and the Confederate army of Gen. John Echols. Echols's army was pushed south into Virginia and never regained control of southeastern West Virginia.

Open to Public: Daily 6am–10pm.

Admission Fees: Free.

Visitor Services: Trails, museum, information, rest rooms.

Directions: Take I-64 to Lewisburg, WV; travel north on U.S. Rte. 219 for 27 miles.

Lewisburg

8 **Site:** LEWISBURG NATIONAL REGISTER HISTORIC DISTRICT/VISITORS CENTER, 105 Church St., Lewisburg, WV 24901, ☎ 800/833-2068 or 304/645-1000

Description: Lewisburg was the site of a Civil War battle on May 23, 1862, when Union forces attempted to sever railroad communications between Virginia and Tennessee. There is a Confederate cemetery in town, a library used as a hospital with Confederate graffiti on the walls, a church with a cannonball hole, another church that served as a Confederate morgue, and a monument to the Confederate dead.

Open to Public: *Visitors Center:* Mon–Sat 9am–5pm. *Museum:* Mon–Sat 10am–4pm.

Admission Fees: $3 for the North House.

Visitor Services: Lodging, gas, food, museum, gift shop, information, rest rooms.

Directions: From I-64: take exit 169, travel south on U.S. 219 for 1.5 miles, turn right on U.S. 60 (Washington St.), proceed 2 blocks, and turn left onto Church St.

Martinsburg

9 **Site:** BELLE BOYD HOUSE/CIVIL WAR MUSEUM OF THE LOWER SHENANDOAH VALLEY, 126 East Race St., Martinsburg, WV 25401, ☎ 304/267-4713

Description: Belle Boyd, West Virginia's best-known Civil War spy, lived in this house. Belle endorsed the Confederate cause, even shooting a Yankee soldier. She supplied information to Stonewall Jackson about enemy activities and was imprisoned twice. Also on-site is the Civil War Museum of the Lower Shenandoah Valley and the Berkeley County Museum. The archive division offers facilities to research the local Berkeley, Jefferson, and Morgan areas.

Open to Public: Mon–Sat 10am–4pm.

Admission Fees: Free.

Visitor Services: Gift shop, information, rest rooms, handicapped access.

Regularly Scheduled Events: *Third weekend in May:* Belle Boyd's Birthday; *Three weekends following Thanksgiving:* Christmas open house.

Directions: The Belle Boyd House is located in Martinsburg, WV at 126 E. Race

St. Martinsburg is immediately east of I-81 and is reached via West Virginia exits 12, 13, and 16. U.S. Rte. 11 and State Routes 9 and 45 run through Martinsburg on Queen St. Queen St. is Martinsburg's main street and divides the cross streets. From Queen St., proceed east on Race St. and go 1 block to the Belle Boyd House at 126.

BELLE BOYD

Isabelle "Belle" Boyd was one of the Confederacy's most famous spies. She grew up in Martinsburg, Virginia (now West Virginia), in a family with strong Southern ties. During the Civil War, her father was a soldier in the Stonewall Brigade, and at least three other members of her family were convicted of being Confederate spies. On July 4, 1861, she shot and killed a Union soldier who was accosting her mother in her home. According to her autobiography, "In Camp and Prison," Boyd also passed military information to Gen. Stonewall Jackson a number of times during his 1862 Valley Campaign and in particular at the battle of Front Royal on May 23, 1862.

According to the story, Boyd was visiting her aunt in Front Royal when her aunt's house was seized by Union soldiers. Boyd eavesdropped on the soldiers as they planned their next move. She then crossed the battle lines, just before the battle began, in order to get the information to Jackson. She was fired upon by Union troops, but arrived safely with valuable information about troop strength, disposition, and intentions.

Boyd was well known to the Union army and the press, who dubbed her "La Belle Rebelle," "the Siren of the Shenandoah," and the "Secesh Cleopatra."

Boyd was arrested six or seven times and imprisoned in Washington, D.C. No model inmate, Boyd waved Confederate flags from her window, sang "Dixie," and devised a unique way of communicating with the outside world. Her contact would throw a rubber ball into her cell, and Boyd would sew messages inside the ball and toss it back through the bars in the window.

Credit: Berkeley County Historical Society

Philippi

10 Site: PHILIPPI COVERED BRIDGE, 124 North Main St., Philippi, WV 26416, ☎ 304/457-1225

Description: The bridge witnessed the first land battle of the Civil War on June 3, 1861. During this battle, Union troops took command of the bridge and used it as a barracks.

Open to Public: Daily from dawn to dusk.

Admission Fees: Free.

Visitor Services: Lodging, gas, camping, trails, gift shop, information, rest rooms, handicapped access.

Directions: From I-79: take exit 115, follow Rte. 20 south to Rte. 57 east, and take U.S. Rte. 119 north to Philippi (22 miles from exit 115).

---

11 **Site:** PHILIPPI HISTORIC DISTRICT, 124 North Main St., Philippi, WV 26416, ☎ 304/457-1225

Description: The City of Philippi was the site of the first land battle of the Civil War on June 3, 1861. It was also the site of the first amputation of the Civil War on James Hanger. Philippi is home to many historic sites, as well as a historical museum containing Civil War–era artifacts.

Open to Public: Daily from dawn to dusk.

Admission Fees: Free.

Visitor Services: Lodging, gas, camping, trails, food, museum, gift shop, information, rest rooms, handicapped access.

Regularly Scheduled Events: *First weekend of June:* Blue and Gray Reunion (including reenactment of the Battle of Philippi).

Directions: From I-79: take exit 115, follow Rte. 20 south to Rte. 57 east, and take U.S. Rte. 119 north to Philippi (22 miles from exit 115).

Shepherdstown

12 **Site:** SHEPHERDSTOWN HISTORIC DISTRICT, Shepherd College, Shepherdstown, WV 25443, ☎ 304/876-2786

Description: In the wake of the battle of Antietam, the town became one vast Confederate hospital with public and private buildings in town serving as military hospitals for the wounded. On September 20, 1862, the last significant battle of the Maryland campaign occurred at Boteler's Ford, about a mile down the Potomac River from Shepherdstown. Elmwood Cemetery, on the outskirts of town, has a Confederate section with the remains of Confederate soldiers, most of whom were casualties of the 1862 Maryland Campaign. Henry Kyd Douglas, a staff officer of Stonewall Jackson, is buried here.

Open to Public: Daily from dawn to dusk.

Admission Fees: Free.

Visitor Services: Lodging, gas, food, gift shops, information.

Directions: From I-81 south: take exit 16E, take Rte. 9 east to Rte. 45 east, and proceed 8 miles to Shepherdstown. From I-81 north: take exit 12, take Rte. 45 east to Rte. 9 east, proceed 7 miles to Kerneysville, go left on Rte. 480 (at Kerneysville), and proceed 4 miles to Shepherdstown.

Summersville

13 **Site:** CARNIFEX FERRY BATTLEFIELD STATE PARK, Rte. 2, P.O. Box 435,
Summersville, WV 26651, ☎ 304/872-0825

Description: This state park is the site of a Civil War battle on September 10, 1861. This Union victory halted any further attempt to take the Kanawha Valley.

Open to Public: *Park:* Daily from dawn to dusk. *Museum:* Memorial Day weekend–Labor Day weekend: Sat, Sun, and holidays 10am–5pm.

Admission Fees: Free.

Visitor Services: Trails, museum, information, rest rooms, picnic facilities.

Regularly Scheduled Events: *Sept:* Battle reenactment during Civil War Weekend.

Directions: Located off Rte. 129 approximately 5 miles west of U.S. Rte. 19 near Summersville. U.S. Rte. 19 is a north-south connection between I-77 and I-79.

Weston

14 **Site:** JACKSON'S MILL HISTORIC AREA, P.O. Box 670, Weston, WV 26452,
☎ 304/269-5100

Description: The Jackson's Mill Museum is the midpoint of a historic area representing the life of Gen. Thomas "Stonewall" Jackson. Greatly influenced by his Uncle Cummins, who raised him after the death of his parents, young Tom developed much of his character by building and working in this mill.

Open to Public: Tues–Sun 10am–5pm. Nov–Apr closed.

Admission Fees: Adults $3, children $2, groups (25 or more) $2/person.

Visitor Services: Trails, museum, gift shop, information, rest rooms, handicapped access.

Regularly Scheduled Events: *June and Aug:* West Virginia Saturday Nights; *Labor Day Weekend:* Stonewall Jackson Arts & Crafts Jubilee; call for other events.

Directions: From I-79: take exit 99 and turn west on U.S. Rte. 33 toward Weston. Go approximately 4 miles to the third stoplight; turn right on U.S. Rte. 19 north. Go approximately 5 miles to Jackson's Mill Rd. on the left; turn left on Jackson's Mill Rd. Proceed approximately 2.5 miles to Jackson's Mill on the right.

Wheeling

15 **Site:** WEST VIRGINIA INDEPENDENCE HALL, 1528 Market St., Wheeling, WV 26003,
☎ 304/238-1300

Description: Journey back in time to 1862 when Wheeling was in Virginia, a state ripped apart by the Civil War. The state of West Virginia was born in this building, now a National Historic Landmark, during that conflict. The museum focuses on the creation of the state, with changing exhibits on West Virginia's culture and history.

Open to Public: Daily 10am–4pm. Closed on state holidays and Sun in Jan–Feb.

Admission Fees: Free. Guided group tours $2/person (reservation required).

Visitor Services: Museum, interpretive film, audio tour, rest rooms, handicapped access.

Directions: Located between I-70 and I-470 in downtown Wheeling. From I-70: proceed south on Main St. to 16th St.; turn left and go 1 block to Market St. The building is across Market St. on the left; proceed through the light and turn left into the parking lot behind the building.

Index

GET THE DIRT ON THE CIVIL WAR.

Nearly 130 years after the last shot was fired, the final battle of the
Civil War is just beginning. Today, dozens of historic battlefields are
endangered and completely unprotected by federal, state or local laws. Join
in our plot to save them. For ever $25 you send, we'll preserve one acre of
historic and threatened battlefield in your name, a loved one's or ancestor's
and send you an honorary deed of ownership. Call or mail the coupon. And
help keep America's history from becoming just a memory.

THE CIVIL WAR TRUST™

Enriching Our Future By Preserving Our Past.

1-800-CW-TRUST

HERE'S THE SCOOP.

I wish to have ____ acre(s) of endangered battlefield preserved in the following name(s):

_____

I am enclosing $25 for each acre. Please mail ____ honorary deed(s) of ownership to:

Name _____	Payment enclosed:
Address _____	Check Money Order VISA MasterCard AmericanExpress
City _____	Card # _____
State _____	Exp. Date _____
Zip _____	Signature: _____
Phone _____	Contributions are tax deductible to the extent allowed by law.

Mail to: The Civil War Trust, 2101 Wilson Blvd, Ste. 1120, Arlington, VA 22201. Or call 1-800-CW-TRUST.

THE HISTORY CHANNEL®
WHERE THE PAST COMES ALIVE™

is a proud sponsor of

The Civil War Trust's
Official Guide
To The Civil War Discovery Trail

The History Channel has entered
the exciting world of travel
with our newly formed
travel-related business
History Channel Traveler.™

Visit our **History Channel Traveler** website at
www.HistoryTravel.com

Get around Mississippi easier than Grant did.

For your free Mississippi *Travel Planner*,
call 1-800-WARMEST (927-6378).

The South's Warmest Welcome
MISSISSIPPI

Some people live for the moment. Others live for the past.

West Virginia

West Virginia is just a short drive from your home,
but you'll feel like you've traveled to another time when
you visit Harper's Ferry, Stonewall Jackson's boyhood
home, museums and more. To make your next vacation
a truly historic one, call us for more information.

1·800·CALL·WVA